The Family, Creditors, and Insolvency

The Family, Creditors, and Insolvency

by

Gareth Miller

LL.M., Ph.D., Solicitor
Emeritus Professor of Law
The Norwich Law School
University of East Anglia

OXFORD
UNIVERSITY PRESS

OXFORD

UNIVERSITY PRESS

Great Clarendon Street, Oxford OX2 6DP

Oxford University Press is a department of the University of Oxford.
It furthers the University's objective of excellence in research, scholarship,
and education by publishing worldwide in

Oxford New York

Auckland Bangkok Buenos Aires Cape Town Chennai
Dar es Salaam Delhi Hong Kong Istanbul Karachi Kolkata
Kuala Lumpur Madrid Melbourne Mexico City Mumbai Nairobi
São Paulo Shanghai Taipei Tokyo Toronto

Oxford is a registered trade mark of Oxford University Press
in the UK and in certain other countries

Published in the United States
by Oxford University Press Inc., New York

British Library Cataloguing in Publication Data

Data available

Library of Congress Cataloging-in-Publication Data
Miller, J. Gareth
The family, creditors, and insolvency / by Gareth Miller.
    p. cm.
Includes index.
    ISBN 0–19–926935–1 (alk. paper)
    1. Debtor and creditor—England. 2. Family—Economic aspects—
England. I. Title
    KD2166.M55 2004
    346. 4207'7—dc22

                                                            2004021964

1 3 5 7 9 10 8 6 4 2

Typeset by Newgen Imaging Systems (P) Ltd., Chennai, India
Printed in Great Britain
on acid-free paper by
Biddles Ltd., King's Lynn

Preface

The ability of members of a family to continue to live in the family home and to maintain their standard of living may be seriously affected by the claims of creditors whether or not there is a breakdown in the relationship between the spouses or cohabitants. In these situations family law and family lawyers have to take into account the impact of those aspects of law dealing with debt recovery and insolvency. Those acting for creditors have to take into account the effect of claims of members of the debtor's family. This book seeks to examine the law that is likely to be relevant in these situations.

I have endeavoured to state the position on the basis of materials available to me on 1 April 2004. This also happens to be the date when many of the provisions of the Enterprise Act 2002 relating to personal insolvency came into force. These make important changes in the law of bankruptcy which reflect an increased emphasis on the rehabilitation of a bankrupt so enabling him or her to make a fresh start. The increased incidence of insolvency in the last decade or so has provoked more discussion about the objectives of bankruptcy in England and Wales and I have included references to some overseas literature for those who may be interested in different perspectives. What seems to be in little doubt is that, in the light of increased borrowing, especially by consumers, the problems arising from debt, whether they lead to re-possession of the family home or bankruptcy, are likely to increase rather than decrease. Financial problems, whether arising from consumer spending or business failure, which provided the impetus for recent changes, are likely to involve not only the debtor but also his or her family.

I am grateful to the editor and publishers of *Tolley's Insolvency Law and Practice* for permission to draw on material from the following articles written by me for that journal:

'The Effect of Insolvency on Financial Provision and Property Adjustment on Divorce' [1994] 10(3) IL & P 66;
'Applications by a Trustee in Bankruptcy for Sale of the Family Home' [1999] 15(6) IL & P 176;
'Income Payments Orders' [2002] 18(2) IL & P 43.

Tolley have also agreed to my drawing on material from the third edition of my book on *Family Property and Financial Provision*. I am grateful to Jordan

Publishing Ltd for permission to draw on material from the following articles written by me:

'The Effect of Insolvency on Applications for Financial Provision' (1998) 10 C & FLQ 29;
'Bankruptcy as a Means of Enforcement in Family Proceedings' [2002] 22 Family Law 21.

I am grateful to Sweet & Maxwell Ltd for permission to draw on material from the following articles written by me:

'Transactions Defrauding Creditors' [1998] Conv. 362;
'Financial Provision and Insolvency' [1999] PCB 381.

I would also like to record my thanks to my wife for her support and encouragement throughout the writing of this book.

Gareth Miller
Norwich Law School
University of East Anglia
June 2004

Contents—Summary

Contents

Table of Cases

Table of Statutes

Table of Secondary Legislation

Table of European Legislation

Abbreviations

CCR   County Court Rules
CPR   Civil Procedure Rules
IA   Insolvency Act 1986
IVA   individual voluntary arrangement
RSC   Rules of the Supreme Court

1

INTRODUCTION
THE CONFLICTING CLAIMS OF
CREDITORS AND THE FAMILY

The ability of a family to continue to live in the family home and to maintain their standard of living may be seriously affected by the claims of their creditors. This may happen even though there is no dispute between the spouses or cohabitants, though in practice financial problems will often accompany a breakdown of the relationship. If their relationship does break down then the conflict is likely to become three sided. In these situations family law and family lawyers have to take into account the impact of those aspects of law dealing with debt recovery and insolvency.

Even if the relationship of a married or unmarried couple has not broken down, it may become necessary for a practitioner, whether advising the debtor and his family or the creditor, to consider the extent of the protection afforded to the family in proceedings for the enforcement of payment. A secured creditor is likely to look to the property over which it has a charge for payment of the amount secured. However, it may be faced by a claim by the debtor's spouse or cohabitant or other family member who joined in to provide the security that the mortgage is not binding on him or her because of some misrepresentation, undue influence or other vitiating conduct. Chapter 3 looks at the circumstances in which such a defence may be successful, the consequences when it is successful, and the steps that a creditor needs to take to prevent it being successful. Chapter 4 considers the enforcement of mortgages which are binding on the mortgagors and the extent to which the law has intervened to protect occupation of the home by the borrower and his family. Even if a mortgage is not fully effective against every mortgagor, or if an unsecured creditor has obtained a charging order against the interest of one joint owner of the home, the creditor may seek an order for sale under the Trusts of Land and Appointment of Trustees Act 1996 and such applications are considered in Chapter 5.

The claims of creditors may become such that an individual is effectively insolvent. This may lead to his or her bankruptcy which will have a profound impact not only on the debtor personally, but also on members of his or her family. The basic principles of bankruptcy, its effect on the property and income of the bankrupt, and the restrictions to which he or she becomes subject are considered in Chapter 6 in the light of charges made by the Enterprise Act 2002. Bankruptcy is not, however, the inevitable consequence of insolvency and the debtor may enter into a voluntary arrangement to obtain some relief from his or her creditors without suffering the disadvantages of bankruptcy, while creditors may not always consider it worthwhile to force a debtor into bankruptcy if there is little to gain. The alternatives to bankruptcy are considered in Chapter 7.

If the debtor's marriage breaks down then the law relating to bankruptcy or individual voluntary arrangements in particular may come into conflict with the powers of the divorce court under the Matrimonial Causes Act 1973 to make orders for financial provision and property adjustment. If bankruptcy occurs before applications for financial relief have been determined, the exercise of powers by the divorce court will be seriously affected. The problems which then arise are considered in Chapter 8. Orders already made may come in for challenge as may other transfers of property by the debtor to his or her spouse or other members of his or her family. The circumstances in which such orders and transfers may be set aside or modified for the benefit of the creditors are considered in Chapter 9. Even if such orders are complete and their validity unchallenged their enforcement may be problematic especially in the case of orders for periodical payments and lump sum payments in the event of the bankruptcy of the former spouse who is liable to pay. Chapter 10 examines these problems together with the possible use of bankruptcy as a weapon for the enforcement of orders against that spouse.

Finally, if the family home or other property has to be sold to satisfy the claims of the creditors of one of its co-owners it becomes important not only to be clear as to their precise beneficial interests in the proceeds of sale, but also to ensure that the burden of debts does not also fall on the debtor's co-owner. It is beyond the scope of this book to examine the principles of resulting, implied and constructive trusts and proprietary estoppel upon which reliance may be placed in establishing a beneficial interest in property such as the family home which may have been vested in the name of only one of the spouses or cohabitants. However, even when the beneficial interests are, or have been, clearly established, it may become important to determine how the burden of debts should be borne between the co-owners. Chapter 11 looks at equitable accounting and the equity of exoneration which may have an important role to play in this situation.

2

THE CLAIMS OF CREDITORS

2.1 INTRODUCTION

2.1.1 Is it a secured or an unsecured debt?

It is important to distinguish between debts which are secured and those which are not. A secured creditor will be able to resort to the property over which he or she has a charge to recover the amount due to him or her and will thus also gain priority over unsecured creditors in bankruptcy. If the proceeds of sale of the mortgaged property are insufficient to discharge the debt, then the mortgagee may prove for the shortfall as a general creditor. If there is a surplus then this must be paid to the debtor's trustee in bankruptcy for the benefit of his or her general creditors. The problems which may arise in relation to the validity of mortgages are considered in Chapter 3 and the remedies available to a mortgagee whose mortgage is valid are considered in Chapter 4. The remedies available to unsecured creditors are considered later in this chapter and an unsecured creditor may become a secured creditor by obtaining a charging order in respect of specific property of the debtor.

2.1.2 Whose debt is it?

In the context of family breakdown it is likely to become important to determine precisely who is liable in respect of a particular debt. A debt may be the sole responsibility of the husband or the wife or it may be a joint debt. The fact that a debt is the legal responsibility of one spouse alone does not necessarily mean that the other spouse will not be affected by action taken by the creditor if the debt relates to some item or service upon which the family as a whole relies. If the spouse responsible for such a debt has left the home then it becomes especially important for the spouse and family remaining in the home to reach an agreement with the creditor concerned where the debt relates to the property, essential services to the property, or items essential for the household. Although responsibility for a debt may appear to be joint this may not be so. Thus a husband may be solely liable for debt incurred by the use of a credit card even though the wife has a card in her own name if the account is in the husband's name.

2.1.3 Joint liability

If both spouses are responsible for a debt then it may be important to determine whether liability is joint or joint and several. If liability is joint then the creditor must pursue all the debtors together, whereas if liability is joint and several then the creditor may sue the debtors individually or jointly for the whole amount of the debt. Generally there will be a right of contribution between a husband and wife who are jointly and severally liable, so that if a creditor recovers the whole debt from one spouse then that spouse is entitled to a contribution from the other spouse, though that may turn out to be of limited practical value.[1] This may result in one spouse having to discharge a debt largely incurred for the benefit of the other spouse. In *Royal Bank of Scotland plc v Fielding*,[2] it was held that joint bank account holders will be jointly and severally liable for any overdraft incurred on the account consequent on borrowing by one joint account holder without reference to the other. The Court of Appeal said that it was of no concern to a bank how a husband and wife chose to operate their joint account unless there was some limitation imposed by the account holders themselves, of which the bank was on notice. As a result the wife was liable to the bank for the husband's borrowing on the joint account even though she had not known or authorized his borrowing.

There must generally be some express wording in the agreement giving rise to the debt providing for joint and several liability for it will rarely be implied. In *AIG Group (UK) plc v Martin*,[3] where two partners had entered into a joint mortgage in which they were described together in a standard clause as 'the mortgagor', the House of Lords held that the partners were jointly and severally liable and one partner was liable to repay not only sums advanced by the bank to him, whether jointly or solely, but also the sums that had been advanced solely to the other partner.

---

[1] *Deering v Earl of Winchelsea* (1787) 2 Bos & P 270 and County Courts Act 1984, s 48.
[2] [2004] EWCA Civ 64.   [3] [2002] 1 All ER 353.

2.2 THE RELEVANCE OF DEBTS ON APPLICATIONS FOR ANCILLARY RELIEF

2.2.1 Taking debts into account

A court exercising its powers to order financial provision and property adjustment under the Matrimonial Causes Act 1973 will need to take into account the debts, secured or unsecured, of both parties. Under s 25(2)(a) the court is required to have regard to the 'income earning capacity, property and other financial resources' of each of the parties to the marriage. In considering the capital assets of the parties it is the net value of the assets that the court must take into account. Thus in relation to the value of the matrimonial home account must be taken of any mortgages affecting the property and also the possible charge in respect of legal aid costs. The costs of the sale of any property and any capital gains tax that may become payable must also be taken into account as well as other debts specifically charged on the property.

Section 25(2)(b) requires the court to have regard to the 'financial needs, obligations and responsibilities which each of the parties has or is likely to have in the foreseeable future'. The obligations and responsibilities of the parties may include not only debts incurred before the breakdown of the marriage, but also debts incurred thereafter as part of the process of re-adjustment to their separation. The latter in particular may need to be balanced against the competing claims of the debtor's family. In *Delaney v Delaney*,[4] the husband had given up the tenancy of a one bedroom flat, which was unsuitable for access by the children and, with the woman he hoped to marry, purchased a property on a basis which involved an increased financial commitment. The Court of Appeal did not find this unreasonable even though it left him with insufficient resources to maintain fully his former wife and children. Ward LJ said that 'there is a life after divorce' and the husband was entitled to order his life in such a way as would 'hold in reasonable balance the responsibilities to his existing family which he carries into his new life, as well as his proper aspirations for that new future'.[5] In assessing the needs of the parties it is open to the court to distinguish between 'hard' debts and 'soft' debts. Thus in *M v B (Ancillary Proceedings: Lump Sum)*,[6] Thorpe LJ thought that there was force in the criticism that the judge had failed to give sufficient weight in considering the wife's list of liabilities to the distinction between hard debts, such as a debt owed to a bank, and soft debts, such as borrowings from members of her family.

In dealing with applications for financial provision under the Matrimonial Causes Act 1973, the court does not have power to exercise a form of bankruptcy

---

[4] [1990] 2 FLR 457. See also *Stockford v Stockford* (1982) 3 FLR 58 in relation to a new mortgage.   [5] [1990] 2 FLR 457, 461.
[6] [1998] 1 FLR 53, 60.

jurisdiction. Thus, in the absence of consent, there is no power to order that one half of the net proceeds of sale of a former matrimonial home should be applied to discharge the debts of the husband not connected with an interest in that property, with any surplus to be paid to the wife.[7]

2.2.2 The possibility of future bankruptcy

In *Mullard v Mullard*,[8] the Court of Appeal took the view that a court exercising its powers under the 1973 Act should not be deterred from making an order for the transfer of property in favour of the wife by the possibility that the transfer might subsequently be set aside if the husband became bankrupt. The court made an order for the transfer of the husband's interest in the former matrimonial home to the wife despite the very substantial debts which had been incurred by the husband in improving the house. Balcombe LJ went on to say that: 'Being realistic, the likelihood of the husband's creditors taking proceedings to set it aside is one which I could contemplate with some equanimity. If they do so be it.'[9] In view of this possibility, however, the order for periodical payments in favour of the wife was not dismissed, but reduced to a nominal amount.[10]

2.3 THE CONSUMER CREDIT ACT 1974

2.3.1 Scope

An agreement for the provision of credit to an individual may be a 'regulated agreement' under the Consumer Credit Act 1974 and, if so, will benefit from a number of provisions designed to protect the borrower. These include provisions relating to the licensing of persons carrying on consumer credit business, provisions prescribing the information to be made available to the debtor, and formalities required when agreements are concluded or terminated.[11] Two provisions will be considered in the following paragraphs namely those relating to the granting of time for the making of payments and those relating to extortionate bargains.

An agreement will be a regulated agreement if the amount of credit provided does not exceed the prescribed amount, which is currently £25,000, and is not an exempt agreement.[12]

There is an extensive definition of exempt agreements in s 16 of the Consumer Credit Act 1974 supplemented by orders made by the Secretary of State under

---

[7] *Mullard v Mullard* (1982) 3 FLR 330; *Burton v Burton* [1986] 2 FLR 419.

[8] (1982) 3 FLR 330.   [9] ibid 334.

[10] See also *Harman v Glencross* [1986] Fam 81, 97 and 199, *per* Balcombe LJ.

[11] See *Director General of Fair Trading v First National Bank plc* [2001] UKHL 52. The effect of the European Convention on Human Rights was considered in *Wilson v Secretary of State for Trade and Industry* [2003] UKHL 40.

[12] Section 8. 'Credit' includes a cash loan, and any other form of financial accommodation: s 9.

powers conferred by the Act. The result is that a loan by a bank or building society will be exempt even though the amount of the loan does not exceed £25,000 provided that it comes within one of several specified exemptions in the Consumer Credit (Exempt Agreements) Order 1989.[13] These include a loan to enable the borrower to buy land or provide a dwelling on land and which is secured by a mortgage on land. A loan for alterations to a dwelling will also be exempt when the creditor has also provided or re-financed credit which was used to buy the land or buildings on the security of a mortgage on them.

2.3.2 Time orders

The court may make a 'time order' under s 129 if it appears to be just to do so:

(a) on an application for an enforcement order; or
(b) on an application made by a debtor or hirer under this provision after service on him of—
  (i) a default notice, or
  (ii) a notice under section 76(1) or 98(1);[14] or
(c) in an action brought by a creditor or owner to enforce a regulated agreement or any security, or recover possession of any goods or land to which a regulated agreement relates.

A time order must provide one or both of the following, as the court considers just:[15]

(a) the payment by the debtor or hirer or surety of any sum owed under a regulated agreement or a security by such instalments, payable at such times, as the court, having regard to the means of the debtor or hirer and any surety considers reasonable;

(b) the remedying by the debtor or hirer of any breach of a regulated agreement (other than the non-payment of money) within such period as the court may specify.

In such a time order the court may include such provision as it considers just for amending any agreement or security in consequence of a term of the order.[16]

The scope of these provisions was considered by the Court of Appeal in *Southern & District Finance plc v Barnes, J & J Securities v Ewart* and *Equity Home Loans v Lewis*[17] which were heard together. Leggatt LJ said that:

When a time order is applied for, or a possession order sought of land to which a regulated agreement applies, the court must first consider whether it is just to make

---

[13] SI 1989/869 as amended.

[14] Section 76(1) is concerned with the right of a creditor to enforce certain terms of a regulated agreement such as demanding earlier payment of any sum. Section 98 is concerned with the duty of a creditor to give notice of termination in non-default cases.   [15] Section 129(2).

[16] Section 136.   [17] (1995) 27 HLR 691, 698.

a time order. That will involve consideration of all the circumstances of the case, and of the position of the creditor as well as the debtor.

In *First National Bank plc v Syed*,[18] Dillon LJ had said that consideration of what is just does not exclude consideration of the creditor's position. In that case he did not think it just in the circumstances, including the fairly long history of default, to require the plaintiff to accept the instalments the defendants could afford when those would be too little to keep down the accruing interest on the defendant's account.

In *Southern & District Finance plc v Barnes*,[19] Leggatt LJ went on to say that:

When a time order is made, it should normally be made for a stipulated period on account of temporary financial difficulty. If, despite the giving of time, the debtor is unlikely to be able to resume repayment of the total indebtedness by at least the amount of the contractual instalments, no time order should be made. In such circumstances it will be more equitable to allow the regulated agreement to be enforced.

In that case the question arose as to the meaning of the phrase 'any sum owed' within the scope of a time order. The Court of Appeal held that the judge at first instance had been wrong in finding that the 'sum owed' for this purpose could relate only to the unpaid instalments under the agreement. Leggatt LJ said:

When a time order is made relating to the non-payment of money:

(a) The "sum owed" means every sum which is due and owing under the agreement, but where possession proceedings have been brought by the creditor that will normally comprise the total indebtedness; and

(b) The court must consider what instalments would be reasonable both as to amount and timing, having regard to the debtor's means.

It is also now established that if the court makes a time order it has power to reduce the rate of interest if it is 'in consequence of a term' of the order, even though no application has been made to reopen the agreement as an extortionate credit bargain.[20] Leggatt LJ said:

The court may include in a time order any amendment of the agreement, which it considers just to both parties, and which is a consequence of a term of the order. If the rate of interest is amended, it is relevant that smaller instalments will result both in a liability to pay interest on accumulated arrears and, on the other hand, in an extended period of repayment. But to some extent the high rate of interest usually payable under regulated agreements already takes account of the risk that difficulties in repayment may occur.

He pointed out that if a time order is made when the sum owed is the whole of the outstanding balance under the loan, then 'there will inevitably be consequences for the term of the loan or for the rate of interest or both'.

---

[18] [1991] 2 All ER 250, 256.   [19] (1995) 27 HLR 691, 698.   [20] ibid 698.

Finally Leggatt LJ said that '[i]f justice requires the making of a time order, the court should suspend any possession order that it also makes, so long as the terms of the time order are complied with'.

2.3.3 Extortionate credit bargains

If the court finds a credit bargain extortionate it may reopen the credit agreement so as to do justice between the parties.[21] A credit agreement for this purpose means any agreement (other than an exempt agreement) between an individual ('the debtor') and any other person ('the creditor') by which the creditor provides the debtor with credit of any amount. A credit bargain for this purpose means the credit agreement where no transaction other than the credit agreement is to be taken into account in computing the total charge for credit. Where one or more other transactions are to be taken into account in computing the total charge for credit, then it means the credit agreement and those other transactions.[22]

A credit agreement may, if the court thinks just, be reopened on the ground that the credit bargain is extortionate, on an application to the appropriate court for that specific purpose by the debtor or by any surety.[23] It may also be reopened at the instance of the debtor or a surety in any proceedings to which the debtor and creditor are parties, for the enforcement of the agreement, any security relating to it, or any linked transaction, or in other proceedings in any court where the amount paid or payable under the credit agreement is relevant.[24]

In reopening the agreement, the court may, for the purpose of relieving the debtor or a surety from payment of any sum in excess of that fairly due and reasonable, by order:

(a) direct accounts to be taken;
(b) set aside the whole or part of any obligation imposed on the debtor or surety by the credit bargain or any related agreement;
(c) require the creditor to repay the whole or part of any sum paid under the credit bargain or any related agreement by the debtor or a surety, whether paid to the creditor of any other person;
(d) direct the return to the surety of any property provided for the purposes of the security; or
(e) alter the terms of the credit agreement or any security instrument.

---

[21] Consumer Credit Act 1974, ss 137 and 139. No application can be made under s 139 by the trustee of a bankrupt's estate or by an undischarged bankrupt. A trustee in bankruptcy may however, make an application in respect of an extortionate credit transaction under s 343 of the Insolvency Act 1986. See ch 9, para 9.2.3.   [22] Consumer Credit Act 1974, s 137(1)(2).
[23] For the appropriate court see s 139(5) which provides that an action may brought only in the county court in the case of (a) a regulated agreement, or (b) an agreement (not being a regulated agreement) under which the creditor provides the debtor with fixed sum credit or running account credit.   [24] Consumer Credit Act 1974, s 139(1).

The court may make any such order notwithstanding that its effect is to place a burden on the creditor in respect of an advantage unfairly enjoyed by another person who is a party to a linked transaction.[25] It must not, however, alter the effect of any judgment.[26]

A credit agreement is extortionate if it (a) requires the debtor or a relative of his to make payments (whether unconditionally, or on certain contingencies) which are grossly exorbitant, or (b) otherwise grossly contravenes ordinary principles of fair dealing.[27] In determining whether a credit bargain is extortionate, regard must be had to such evidence as is adduced concerning the following matters:[28]

(a) the interest rates prevailing at the time it was made;

(b) the age, experience, business capacity, and state of health of the debtor and the degree to which, at the time of making the credit bargain, he was under financial pressure, and the nature of that pressure;

(c) the degree of risk accepted by the creditor, having regard to the value of any security provided; the creditor's relationship to the debtor and whether or not a colourable cash price was quoted for any goods or services included in the credit bargain.

In relation to a linked transaction the factors to which the court must have regard include the question of how far the transaction was reasonably required for the protection of debtor or creditor, or was in the interest of the debtor.[29]

All these matters must be considered as at the date when the credit bargain is made and at no other time. Thus where under the terms of the agreement the lender may vary the rate of interest, subsequent rates of interest are irrelevant to the question whether the credit bargain is extortionate. However, where the agreement so provides there is an implied term that the lender will not set rates of interest dishonestly, for an improper purpose, capriciously or arbitrarily, or unreasonably, ie in a way that no reasonable lender, acting reasonably, would do.[30] In *Paragon Finance plc v Nash*,[31] Dyson LJ said: 'If greater protection is to be accorded to borrowers, that is a matter for Parliament.'

In *Wills v Woods*,[32] Sir John Donaldson MR acknowledged that the Consumer Credit Act 1974 'gives and is intended to give the court the widest possible control over credit bargains which, for a variety of reasons, might be considered "extortionate".' However, he emphasized that 'the word is "extortionate", not "unwise".' He thought that the jurisdiction seemed 'to contemplate at least a substantial imbalance in bargaining power of which one party has taken

---

[25] Consumer Credit Act 1974, s 139(3).   [26] ibid s 139(4).   [27] ibid s 138(1).
[28] ibid s 138(2)(3)(4).   [29] ibid s 138(5).
[30] *Per* Dyson LJ in *Paragon Finance plc v Nash* [2002] EWCA Civ 1466, [2002] 1 WLR 685, paras [63]–[66].   [31] [2002] EWCA Civ 1466, para [83].
[32] [1984] CCLR 7.

advantage'. In *Davies v Direct Loans Ltd*, Edward Nugee QC sitting as a deputy High Court judge said in relation to the second listed factor:[33]

Nearly every purchaser who borrows money in order to complete his purchase is under some degree of financial pressure. It is only if the lender takes advantage of the pressure that this factor is in my judgment relevant in considering whether the loan is extortionate.

However, he had earlier pointed out that 'the test is not whether the creditor has acted in a morally reprehensible manner, but whether one or other of the conditions of section 138(1) is fulfilled'. Although 'it may be thought that if either condition is fulfilled there is likely to be something morally reprehensible about the creditor's conduct, the starting and ending point in determining whether a credit bargain is extortionate must be the words of section 138(1)'.[34] While this is so, the terms of the credit bargain must be viewed in the context of the circumstances of the particular case. Terms which might appear to be unobjectionable in the case of a borrower with business experience who is not under great pressure may be viewed differently in the case of a borrower in a weak position where the creditor has taken advantage of the situation. In practice it seems that the courts have not readily found credit bargains to be extortionate.[35] In the recent case of *Broadwick Financial Services Ltd v Spencer*[36] the Court of Appeal emphasized that the test of 'extortionate' was a high one which would be satisfied only if payments were grossly exorbitant, or the bargain otherwise grossly contravened ordinary principles of fair dealing or both.

2.4 UNFAIR TERMS IN CONSUMER CONTRACTS

The provisions of a mortgage agreement may be subject to a test of fairness under the Unfair Terms in Consumer Contracts Regulations 1999.[37] These regulations apply to unfair terms in contracts between a seller or a supplier and a consumer.[38] A contractual term which has not been individually negotiated will be regarded as unfair if, contrary to the requirement of good faith, it causes a significant imbalance in the parties' rights and obligations under the contract, to the detriment of the consumer. The regulations may therefore apply to the standard terms on which a loan is made.[39] A term which is found to be unfair is

---

[33] [1986] 1 WLR 823, 832. Improper pressure may be alleged against a third party as in *Coldunell Ltd v Gallon* [1986] QB 1184.   [34] [1986] 1 WLR 823, 831.

[35] See *Ketley Ltd v Scott* [1980] CCLR 37. This is so even though s 171(7) of the 1974 Act provides that if a debtor alleges that a credit bargain is extortionate it is for the creditor to prove the contrary.

[36] [2002] EWCA Civ 35, [2002] 1 All ER (Comm) 446.

[37] SI 1999/2083 replacing SI 1994/3159. The regulations implement Council Dir (EC) 93/13 [1993] OJ L95/29.   [38] Reg 4.

[39] Reg 5. A term is to be regarded as not having been individually negotiated where it has been drafted in advance and the consumer has therefore not been able to influence the substance of the term.

not binding on the consumer.[40] Generally the unfairness of a term is assessed taking into account the nature of the goods or services for which the contract was concluded and by referring, at the time of conclusion of the contract, to all the circumstances attending the conclusion of the contract and to all the other terms of the contract or of another contract on which it is dependent. However, no assessment of the fairness of a term is to be made if it either (a) defines the main subject matter of the contract, or (b) concerns the adequacy of the price or remuneration, as against the goods or services sold or supplied provided it is in plain, intelligible language.[41]

The potential of the regulations for providing relief for a borrower under a standard form of mortgage agreement seems limited. In *Director General of Fair Trading v First National Bank plc*,[42] the court was concerned with a common-form loan agreement used by the bank which contained a term providing that, in the event of default by the borrower in making his repayments, interest would continue to be payable at the contractual rate until any judgment obtained by the bank was discharged. The House of Lords held that the term in issue was not a core term so that its fairness could be assessed. However, it went on to find that the term was not unfair. Lord Bingham said that in judging the fairness of the term it was necessary to consider the position of typical parties when the contract is made.[43] He continued:

The essential bargain is that the bank will make funds available to the borrower which the borrower will repay, over a period, with interest. Neither party could suppose that the bank would willingly forgo any part of its principal or interest. If the bank thought that outcome at all likely, it would not lend. If there were any room for doubt about the borrower's obligation to repay the principal in full with interest, that obligation is very clearly and unambiguously expressed in the conditions of the contract. There is nothing unbalanced or detrimental to the consumer in that obligation; the absence of such a term would unbalance the contract to the detriment of the lender.

He pointed out that a secured lender who does not obtain a money judgment, but instead proceeds for possession and sale under the mortgage may obtain interest at the contract rate provided for in the mortgage down to the date when he is actually repaid, and in his opinion there is nothing unbalanced or detrimental to the consumer in that result either.[44]

A borrower who finds himself in difficulties regarding repayment of a loan should look to the possibility of a time order under s 129 of the Consumer Credit Act 1974. The problem, as noted by the House of Lords, is that in practice borrowers are not aware of the effect of s 129 or indeed s 136 regarding extortionate credit bargains and their attention is not drawn to them in the

---

[40] Reg 8.　　[41] Reg 6.

[42] [2001] UKHL 52, [2002] 1 AC 481. The regulations in issue were in fact the regulations made in 1994 which were superseded by the 1999 Regulations. They are very much to the same effect and must be construed to give effect in the United Kingdom to Council Dir (EC) 93/13.

[43] ibid para [20].　　[44] ibid para [21].

prescribed forms so that 'judgments will routinely be entered in the county court without the court considering whether to exercise its powers under the sections.'[45]

2.5 ENFORCEMENT

2.5.1 The choice of method of enforcement

There are a number of possible methods of enforcement to which a creditor who has obtained judgment against a spouse or cohabitant may resort to enforce payment. Such methods of enforcement may also be used by a spouse or cohabitant seeking to enforce payment of a sum due from the other spouse or cohabitant. The choice or method will, of course, depend upon the circumstances of the case and in particular upon the financial position of the person liable to make payment. Essentially the choice lies between seeking payment from the income or capital of the debtor. The debtor's income may be reached by an attachment of earnings order.[46] His or her goods may be seized under a writ or warrant of execution and debts owing to him or her may be intercepted by third party debt orders. Where the debtor has a capital asset that can be charged, then a creditor may seek a charging order followed by an order for sale. The more important of these methods are considered briefly in the following paragraphs of this chapter. If the debtor is or appears to be insolvent then a creditor may petition for bankruptcy. This is considered more fully in Chapter 6 and in Chapter 10 in relation to matrimonial debts. Bankruptcy will provide a debtor with protection from action taken by his creditors to enforce payment of the sums due to them, but at the price of surrendering his capital assets for the benefit of his creditors. There are alternative methods whereby a debtor can obtain such relief without being made bankrupt and these are considered in Chapter 7.

2.5.2 Attachment of earnings orders

An attachment of earnings order is directed to the debtor's employer and instructs him to make periodical deductions from the debtor's earnings and pay them to the collecting officer of the court, as specified in the order.[47] The order must specify the normal deduction rate and the protected earnings rate. The normal deduction rate is the rate, expressed as a periodical sum, at which the court thinks it reasonable for the debtor's earnings to be applied to meeting his

---

[45] ibid, *per* Lord Bingham at para [23]. For ss 129 and 136, see para 2.3 above.

[46] Income from property may be reached by the appointment of a receiver by way of equitable execution. See CPR Sch 1, RSC Ord 51 in relation to the High Court. In relation to the county court, see CCR Ord 32.   [47] Attachment of Earnings Act 1971, s 6(1).

liability for the debt. The protected earnings rate is the rate, expressed as a periodical sum, below which having regard to the debtor's resources and needs, the court thinks it reasonable that the earnings actually paid to him should not be reduced.[48]

A county court may make an attachment of earnings order to secure the payment of a judgment debt other than a debt of less than £5 or such other sum as may be prescribed by county court rules or payments under an administration order.[49] A judgment obtained in the High Court can be transferred to a county court so that an attachment of earnings order may be obtained.

2.5.3 Seizure of goods

A creditor may obtain an order for the seizure of the debtor's goods by the appropriate official. The goods will then be sold and the proceeds applied in discharge of the amount due to the creditor concerned. In the High Court proceedings are commenced by a writ of *fieri facias* and execution of the order is the responsibility of the sheriff. In the county court the enforcement of a warrant of execution is the responsibility of the bailiff. In the execution of any writ of execution issued from the High Court or any warrant of execution from a county court, against the goods of any person, the relevant officer may seize any goods of that person except the following:[50]

(a) such tools, books, vehicles, and other items or equipment as are necessary to that person for use personally by him in his employment, business or vocation;

(b) such clothing, bedding, furniture, household equipment, and provisions as are necessary for satisfying the basic domestic needs of that person and his family.

The County Courts Act 1984 provides that if at any time it appears to the satisfaction of the court that any party to any proceedings is unable from any cause to pay any sum recovered against him or any instalment of such sum, the court may, in its discretion, stay any execution issued in the proceedings for such time and on such terms as the court thinks fit, and so from time to time until it appears that the cause of inability has ceased.[51]

2.5.4 Third party debt orders (formerly Garnishee Proceedings)

A third party debt order requires a third party to pay sums due to the debtor to the latter's creditor who has obtained the order and not to the debtor to whom

---

[48] Attachment of Earnings Act 1971, s 6(5).

[49] ibid s 1(2). See CPR Sch 1, CCR Ord 27 for the procedure for making an application. Administration orders are considered in ch 7.

[50] Supreme Court Act 1981, s 138(3A) as inserted by the Courts and Legal Services Act 1990, s 15(2), County Courts Act 1984, s 89 as amended by the Courts and Legal Services Act 1990, s 15(2).

[51] Section 88.

it was formerly due.[52] The first stage is to obtain an interim order which is made on an ex parte application without a hearing. The second stage is the hearing on notice at which the order will be made final unless there are grounds for objection. If it is made final it can be enforced against the third party as an order to pay money.[53]

The debt owed by the third party debtor must be owed to the debtor alone and not to the debtor and another jointly. Thus in *Hirschon v Evans*,[54] it was held that a garnishee order, as it was then called, could not be made against a bank in relation to a joint bank account in the names of a husband and wife in respect of a debt owed by the husband alone.

A former wife may be able to obtain a third party debt order to secure payment of amounts due to her from her former husband under maintenance orders. Thus in *Cohen v Cohen*,[55] the former wife, who was owed arrears of maintenance, was able to obtain what was then a garnishee order in respect of the proceeds of sale of the former matrimonial home in the husband's sole name and held in the client account of the purchaser's solicitors.

2.6 CHARGING ORDERS

2.6.1 The scope of the Charging Orders Act 1979

The Charging Orders Act 1979 enables an unsecured creditor who has obtained a judgment or order of the High Court or a county court requiring payment of a sum of money to him by the debtor to apply to the court for a charging order. This is an order imposing on such property of the debtor as may be specified in the order a charge for securing the payment of any money due or to become due under the judgment or order.[56] The effect of a charging order is, therefore, to make the judgment creditor a secured creditor. A charge imposed by a charging order has the like effect and is enforceable in the same courts and in the same manner as an equitable charge created by the debtor by writing under his hand.[57] An order affecting land such as a charging order is void against a purchaser for value of the land unless it is registered.[58]

---

[52] In 2002, the number of applications for such orders increased by 33% to 5,499: Judicial Statistics Annual Report 2002.   [53] CPR, r 72.

[54] [1938] 2 KB 801.   [55] (1983) 4 FLR 451.

[56] Section 1(1). In 2002, the number of applications for charging orders increased by nearly 38% to 30,309: Judicial Statistics Annual Report 2002.   [57] Section 3(4).

[58] Land Charges Act 1972, s 6(1)(4), as amended by the Supreme Court Act 1981, s 152(1), Sch 5 and County Courts Act 1984, s 148(1), Sch 2, para 8, and Land Registration Act 2002, ss 29(1) and 87.

2.6.2 Property over which a charging order may be made

A charge may be imposed by a charging order on any interest held by the debtor beneficially (a) in land, certain kinds of securities specified in s 2(2), or funds in court or, (b) under any trust.[59] Thus, by virtue of (b) a charge may now be imposed on the beneficial interest of a joint owner under a trust of land.[60] A charge may also be made against any interest held by a person as trustee if the interest is in such an asset and the whole beneficial interest under the trust is held by the debtor unencumbered and for his own benefit, or, where there are two or more debtors all of whom are liable to the creditor for the same debt and they together hold the whole beneficial interest under the trust unencumbered and for their own benefit. Thus where co-owners are liable to the creditor for the same debt a charging order may be imposed on the legal estate held by them as trustees for their own benefit.

It is essential that the applicant can show that the debtor has a beneficial interest under a trust. In *Field v Field*,[61] Wilson J held that it was clear that the husband had no beneficial interest under the trusts of a pension scheme. He had entitlements at certain times to require the trustees to deploy their assets for his benefit by the purchase of an annuity and he had a right to elect to receive a lump sum. However, the entitlements did not given him a beneficial interest under the trusts and no charging order was therefore possible. The debtor's wife therefore failed in her attempt to enforce against her husband's personal pension, payment of the amount remaining due under a lump sum order. He also pointed out that a clause in the deed governing the pension expressly provided that no annuity or lump sum benefit payable under the scheme was capable of being charged. The court could have overridden that provision for the purpose of making financial provision orders,[62] but that stage had passed.

2.6.3 Procedure

Where the order to be enforced is a maintenance order of the High Court then an application may be made to the High Court or a county court. Where the judgment or order to be enforced is a judgment or order of the High Court exceeding the county court limit, an application for a charging order may be made to the High Court or a county court. In any other case application may be made to a county court.[63] The procedure is now governed by the Civil Procedure Rules.[64]

---

[59] Section 2(1).

[60] See *National Westminster Bank Ltd v Stockman* [1981] 1 WLR 67 in relation to the trust for sale replaced by the trust of land.   [61] [2003] 1 FLR 376.

[62] See Pensions Act 1995, s 166(4).

[63] Section 1(2) as amended by the Administration of Justice Act 1982, Sch. 3, Pt. II, paras 2, 3(b). The 'county court limit' means the county court limit for the time being specified in an Order in Council under s 145 of the County Courts Act 1984.

[64] Replacing RSC Ord 50 and CCR Ord 31.

In the first instance an application, which need not be served on the judgment debtor, will be for an interim charging order (formerly a charging order nisi). The application must be supported by a statement of truth (an affidavit) which:

(a) identifies the judgment or order to be enforced and states the amount unpaid at the date of the application;
(b) states the name of the judgment debtor and of any creditor of his whom the applicant can identify;
(c) gives full particulars of the subject matter of the intended charge; and
(d) verifies that the interest to be charged is owned beneficially by the judgment debtor.

An interim charging order will require the debtor to show cause, specifying the time and place for further consideration of the matter, and imposing the charge in any event until that time.

When the matter is subsequently considered the court must either make a final order (formerly a charging order absolute) with or without modifications, or discharge it. The order may be made either absolutely or subject to conditions as to notifying the debtor or as to the time when the charge is to become enforceable, or as to other matters.[65]

In deciding whether to make a charging order the court must consider all the circumstances of the case and, in particular, any evidence before it as to (a) the personal circumstances of the debtor, and, (b) whether any creditor of the debtor would be likely to be unduly prejudiced by making the order.[66]

2.6.4 Enforcement

A judgment creditor who has obtained a final charging order will need to take further steps to enforce the order. Application may be made for a receiver to be appointed to collect any income from the property charged or for an order for sale of the property. This application will be made under the Civil Procedure Rules, r 73(10) if the judgment debtor owns the entire beneficial interest in the property subject to the charge. If the judgment debtor owns only part of the beneficial interest in the property, and the charging order has been obtained only against that interest, then it will be necessary for the judgment creditor to apply to the court for an order for sale under s 14 of the Trusts of Land and Appointment of Trustees Act 1996.[67]

2.6.5 The position of the judgment debtor's spouse

It will be apparent that there are two stages at which the interests of the judgment debtor's spouse may fall to be considered. The first is the making of

---

[65] Section 3(1). [66] Section 1(5). [67] Replacing Law of Property Act 1925, s 30.

a final charging order and the second is when the judgment creditor, having obtained the final order, seeks to enforce that order by an application for sale.

At the first stage the interest of the judgment debtor's wife is one of the circumstances of the case to be taken into account whether she is a co-owner of the property or merely entitled to a right of occupation. However, although the creditor is not entitled to a charging order as of right, he is normally justified in expecting that an order will be made against the debtor's interest.[68] An important factor is whether or not the wife has already filed a petition for divorce and made an application for ancillary relief which may include an application for a transfer of property order affecting the matrimonial home which is the subject of the application for a charge. The question then arises as to whether the matter should be transferred to the family court to be determined alongside the wife's application for financial relief. In *Harman v Glencross*,[69] Balcombe LJ set out how he thought the court should deal with the problem.

First, he said that '[w]here a judgment creditor has obtained a charging order *nisi* on the husband's share in the matrimonial home and his application to have that order made absolute is heard before the wife has started divorce proceedings, there is, of course, no other court to which the application for the charging order absolute can be transferred, the wife having no competing claim to the husband's share'. In these circumstances he thought it was difficult to see why the court should refuse to make the charging order absolute leaving the wife to seek protection for her occupation of the home when the judgment creditor took steps to seek an order for sale under s 30 of the Law of Property Act 1925 which then applied.

Secondly, he said that '[w]here a charging order *nisi* has been made after the wife's petition, then on the application for a charging order absolute the court should consider whether the circumstances are such that it is proper to make the charging order absolute even before the wife's application for ancillary relief has been heard by the Family Division'. Balcombe LJ considered that there would be cases (such as *Llewellyn v Llewellyn* unreported but heard immediately after *Harman v Glencross* and referred to in the report) where the figures are such that, even if the charging order is made absolute and then the charge is realized by a sale of the house, the resultant proceeds of sale (including any balance of the husband's share after the judgment debt has been paid) will clearly be sufficient to provide adequate alternative accommodation for the wife and children.

Thirdly, '[u]nless it appears to the court hearing the application for the charging order absolute that the circumstances are so clear that it is proper to make the order there and then, the usual practice should be to transfer the application to the Family Division so that it may come on with the wife's

---

[68] *Roberts Petroleum Ltd v Bernard Kenny Ltd* [1983] 2 AC 192 and *First National Securities Ltd v Hegarty* [1985] QB 850, 867.   [69] [1986] Fam 81, 99–100.

application for ancillary relief and one court can then be in a position to consider all the circumstances of the case'.

Fourthly, he said that '[o]nce the charging order absolute has been made, it would normally require some special circumstance, e.g. where . . . the wife had no proper opportunity to put the case before the court, for the charging order to be set aside under section 3(5) of the 1979 Act and thereby deprive the judgment creditor of his vested right'. This was the case in *Harman v Glencross* itself where the creditor had obtained a charging order absolute on the husband's interest in the matrimonial home without serving the application on the wife or giving her notice of it. The wife had already petitioned for divorce and commenced proceedings for ancillary relief. In *Austin-Fell v Austin-Fell*[70] the creditor had already obtained a charging order against the husband's half share of the matrimonial home before the wife petitioned for divorce and sought a discharge of the charging order. The application for discharge and the application for ancillary relief in divorce proceedings were heard at the same time in the Family Division.

In *Harman v Glencross*,[71] Fox LJ emphasized that the purpose of a transfer to the Family Division of an application for a charging order (or for the discharge of such an order) is simply to ensure that the court is fully appraised of the circumstances of the case so far as the debtor and his family are concerned. It is not to be treated as if it were a wife's application under the matrimonial jurisdiction for the disposition of the husband's property for the benefit of the wife and children. Balcombe LJ said that when considering the circumstances, the court should bear in mind the statement of Sir Denys Buckley in *First National Securities Ltd v Hegerty*[72] that a judgment creditor is justified in expecting that a charging order over the husband's beneficial interest in the matrimonial home will be made in his favour.[73]

The court should first consider whether the value of the equity in the home is sufficient to enable the charging order to be made absolute (or to stand) and be realized at once even though that may result in the wife and children being housed at a lower standard than they might reasonably have expected had only the husband's interests been taken into account against them. Failing that, the court should make only such an order as may be necessary to protect the wife's right of occupation (with the children where appropriate) bearing in mind that the court is holding the balance, not between the wife and the husband, but between the wife and the judgment creditor. If the judgment creditor asks, even in the alternative to his claim to an immediate order, for a *Mesher* type of order,[74] then exceptional circumstances should be required before the court should make an order for the outright transfer of the husband's share in the house to the wife, thereby leaving nothing on which the judgment creditor's charging order can bite, even in the future.[75] In *Harman v Glencross*, such an

---

[70] [1989] 2 FLR 497.   [71] [1986] Fam 81, 105.   [72] [1985] QB 850.
[73] [1986] Fam 81, 99.   [74] See *Mesher v Mesher* [1980] 1 All ER 126.
[75] *Austin-Fell v Austin-Fell* [1989] 2 FLR 497, 505, *per* Waite J.

order had been made by Ewbank J at first instance and the Court of Appeal had refused to interfere with his exercise of his discretion though clearly regarding it as an exceptional case. This was emphasized by Waite J in the subsequent case of *Austin-Fell v Austin-Fell*[76] where again a balance had to be struck between the family security claimed by the wife and children in matrimonial proceedings and the commercial security claimed by the husband's business creditor in charging order proceedings. However, Waite J noted two significant differences between the case before him and *Harman v Glencross*.

First, the judgment debt in *Harman v Glencross* represented a very much higher proportion, when measured against the total value of the beneficial interest in the property, than in the case before him. The equity in the property in the former case was £22,400 so that a charge on the husband's half interest for the debt of £13,000 would have exhausted that interest entirely. In *Austin-Fell*, the equity was worth £60,000 and the judgment debt was £10,000. Secondly, in *Harman v Glencross*, the judgment creditor adopted an 'all or nothing' approach to the enforcement of his security seeking only an immediate charge. He did not ask for the alternative option of postponement to be considered and, although Fox LJ indicated that postponement was the solution he would personally have favoured, the Court of Appeal did not criticize the decision of Ewbank J to treat that option as not being open to the court in that case because it had not been requested by the judgment creditor. This was not the case in *Austin-Fell*.

In the latter case an immediate sale and payment of the judgment creditor would leave insufficient to give the wife any prospect of being re-housed in the area of the present home in accommodation suitable to herself and the girls. 'It would be unfairly harsh to the wife and unduly favourable to the judgment creditor to force her at this stage to move to another area, or to a different part of the country altogether in search of cheaper housing and to leave behind her mother, her pupils and the school which have become familiar to the girls, all for the sake of ensuring immediate payment of the bank's debt.'[77] The necessity of paying off the bank's debt in ten years' time with the interest that had accumulated in the meantime, might no doubt be expected to involve the wife in a degree of hardship, just as the necessity of waiting ten years for its money might be expected to involve a degree of hardship for the bank. Nevertheless, a postponed enforcement order represented the fairest balance between the competing claims of wife and creditor.

Harman v Glencross was also distinguished in *Worsick v Worsick*[78] where the house was in the sole name of the husband and there was no way of postponing the charges. It was a question of upholding the charges or discharging them. Balcombe LJ said:

In so far as there is a competition between outside creditors and a wife, where the outside creditors cannot be asked to wait for their money, but the issue is whether or not they

---

[76] [1989] 2 FLR 497.   [77] ibid 505, *per* Waite J.   [78] CA, 7 May 1991.

should lose their charging order altogether, I find difficulty in seeing on what basis the court would be justified in saying that the banks, certainly on the figures here, should lose their charging orders altogether. They may be postponed, but that is not possible here.

If the court makes a final charging order without any condition protecting the wife's interests then she will be left to oppose any application for an order for sale by the judgment creditor. Such an application will be made under s 14 of the Trusts of Land and Appointment of Trustees Act 1996 and is considered in Chapter 5.

3

THE ENFORCEABILITY OF A MORTGAGE

3.1 INTRODUCTION—THE PROBLEMS

A mortgagee will have taken steps to ensure that the mortgage is valid and effective against the mortgagor before the amount secured is advanced. If the legal estate is vested in joint names of husband and wife or cohabitants then the mortgage will almost certainly have been executed by both co-owners as joint mortgagors. The mortgagee will also have sought to ensure that there are no valid claims from persons other than the mortgagor or mortgagors which might affect the enforceability of its security. If the legal estate is vested in the name of one person alone then generally the mortgagee will have obtained from any person who may have, or claim to have, a right to occupy the property by virtue of a beneficial interest in the property or otherwise, a signed form consenting to such interest being postponed to the interest of the mortgagee. Such consents are also likely to be obtained from other persons, such as parents, who might assert a claim to a beneficial interest. Indeed this is often done even where the legal estate in the property is in the joint names of mortgagors so that equitable interests would be overreached on a sale of the property.[1]

If a person claiming a beneficial interest is in occupation of the mortgaged property, the title to which is vested solely in another, then the effect of that occupation in relation to registered land is to give that person an overriding interest.[2] In relation to unregistered land, occupation is relevant in giving notice to a mortgagee that the occupier may have rights in or over the property so that further inquiry is necessary to ascertain the extent of such rights, if any.[3] Apart from matters capable of registration under the Land Charges Act which have not been registered, if a mortgagee fails to make such inspections and inquiries as ought reasonably to be made he will be deemed to have notice of those rights and it is not open to him to say that if he had made a further inspection he would still not have found the claimant in occupation.[4]

In practical terms if a mortgage advance is being made to fund the initial purchase of residential property, it is very unlikely that a person who is not a mortgagor will have priority over the mortgage advance in respect of an equitable beneficial interest which he or she claims on the basis of occupation of the property. This is because the mortgage will generally be completed before the mortgagor and any spouse or cohabitant enters into occupation. It is true that in the case of registered land, completion of a transfer, in the traditional sense of the exchange of the transfer for the purchase price, must be followed by the making of an appropriate entry on the register—registration. There is inevitably an interval of time between completion and registration. In *Abbey National Building Society v Cann*,[5] the House of Lords held that, while the relevant date for determining the existence of overriding interests which will affect the estate transferred or created is the date of registration, the relevant date for determining whether a claimant to a right is in actual occupation for the purposes of s 70(1)(g) of the Land Registration Act 1925 (now para 2 of Sch 3 to the Land Registration Act 2002) is the date of completion. Accordingly a claimant who enters into occupation of the property after completion, but before registration of a transfer or mortgage, will not have an overriding interest on the basis of that occupation.

A greater threat is posed to a mortgagee when money is advanced on the security of property acquired by the mortgagor or mortgagors at an earlier date.

---

[1] See para 3.10 below.

[2] Land Registration Act 2002, Sch 3, para 2 (formerly Land Registration Act 1925, s 70(1)(g)); *Williams & Glyn's Bank v Boland* [1981] AC 487, 504. This does not apply to an interest of a person of whom inquiry was made before the disposition and who failed to disclose the right when he could reasonably have been expected to do so.   [3] *Hunt v Luck* [1902] 1 Ch 428.

[4] *Kingsnorth Finance Co Ltd v Tizard* [1986] 1 WLR 783, 794.

[5] [1991] AC 56. See now Land Registration Act 2002, s 29(2).

In such circumstances the mortgage is likely to be a re-mortgage of the property with the proceeds being used to pay off an existing mortgage. A mortgagor may choose to re-mortgage the property with the object of obtaining a more favourable rate of interest on a loan of the same amount as the redeemed mortgage, but difficulties have more commonly arisen where the new mortgage is for a larger capital sum which is used partly to redeem the existing mortgage, but also for other purposes possibly unknown to his or her spouse or cohabitant. In the case of joint mortgagors one of them may have forged the signature of the other to a new mortgage, and surplus funds, after redeeming the old mortgage, may be dissipated on other purposes of the wrongdoer without the knowledge of the other mortgagor. A joint mortgagor may argue that a mortgage is not binding on him or her because he or she was induced to enter into the mortgage by the misrepresentation or undue influence of the other joint mortgagor. As a result, for a variety of reasons, a new mortgagee may find itself without an effective mortgage against one joint owner or claimant to a beneficial interest in the property. Indeed in some cases it may find that the mortgage is completely ineffective as where the sole owner of the property has been induced to mortgage it for the benefit of another.

This chapter will consider, first, the circumstances in which a mortgagor may not be bound by a mortgage as a result of invalidating conduct on the part of the mortgagee or invalidating conduct on the part of a co-mortgagor by which the mortgagee is affected. Consideration will then be given to the circumstances in which a mortgagor will be regarded as having consented to a new mortgage—subordination. Where a mortgage is completely ineffective then a lender may be able to take advantage of the doctrine of subrogation and step into the shoes of the mortgagee whose mortgage has been redeemed. It will then have the remedies available to a mortgagee which are considered in Chapter 4. If the mortgage is effective against only one of two joint mortgagors then it will be necessary for the mortgagee to seek an order for possession as a creditor under s 14 of the Trusts of Land and Appointment of Trustees Act 1996 which is considered in Chapter 5. Finally it must be borne in mind that if one mortgagor is entitled to have a mortgage set aside on the basis of invalidating conduct by the other mortgagor which affects the mortgagee, then if the mortgagors' marriage is terminated by divorce it is essential that proceedings to set aside the mortgage are conducted consistently with an application for property adjustment under the Matrimonial Causes Act 1973.

3.2 VITIATING FACTORS

3.2.1 Misrepresentation

Misrepresentation may relate to such matters as the amount of the secured debt, the time during which the charge would remain in force or some other material matter.[6] Thus in *Barclays Bank plc v O'Brien*,[7] the husband had mis-represented to his wife that liability under the mortgage was limited to £60,000 and would last for only three weeks.

If a misrepresentation is to lead to an equitable or legal remedy it must have led to a false impression about some material matters being held by the victim. In *Royal Bank of Scotland plc v Etridge (No 2)*,[8] Mrs Etridge had no impression at all as to the nature of the documents she was signing. No false impression had been planted on her by Mr Etridge. Mr Etridge's silence did not lead her to form, or to continue to hold, any false impression. She did not bother to read the documents that were placed before her for signature, and no one explained them to her. This meant that, although she did not know what she was signing, she was not persuaded to sign by any misrepresentation.[9] Moreover, even if there has been a misrepresentation to her, it must have led her to sign the relevant documents. Thus, in *Etridge* the judge had found as a fact that if the nature and content of the documents had been explained to Mrs Etridge, she would still have signed. Accordingly, 'if there had been any misrepresentation as to the nature and content of the documents, it had no relative causative effect'.[10]

In *Royal Bank of Scotland plc v Etridge (No 2)*,[11] Lord Nicholls issued a cautionary note when he said that 'when a husband is forecasting the future of his business, and expressing his hopes or fears, a degree of hyperbole may be only natural. Courts should not too readily treat such exaggerations as misstatements'.

3.2.2 Duress

Originally the principle of duress was 'narrow in its scope, restricted to the more blatant forms of physical coercion, such as personal violence' that might be used to persuade a person to enter into a transaction.[12] The principle has developed so as to include 'overt acts of improper pressure or coercion such an unlawful threats' so that there is 'much overlap' between duress and undue influence. Although the exact scope of duress may be open to debate, it remains a relatively narrow concept likely to be of limited use except in extreme cases.

3.2.3 Undue influence

3.2.3.1 *Meaning*
A transaction will be regarded as having been procured by the exercise of undue influence of one person over another whenever the consent of the latter 'ought

---

[6] Lord Scott in *Etridge* [2001] UKHL 44, para [140], [2002] 2 AC 773.
[7] [1994] 1 AC 180.   [8] [2001] UKHL 44.
[9] See also *Mortgage Agency Services Number Two Ltd v Chater* [2003] EWCA Civ 490.
[10] [2001] UKHL 44, para [223], *per* Lord Scott.   [11] ibid para [32].
[12] ibid *per* Lord Nicholls, para [6].

not fairly to be treated as the expression of [that] person's free will'. It 'arises out of a relationship between two persons where one has acquired over another a measure of influence, or ascendancy, of which the ascendant person then takes unfair advantage'. Such influence provides scope for misuse without any specific overt acts of persuasion. The relationship between the two persons may be such that 'without more, one of them is disposed to agree to a course of action proposed by the other'.

The situation in which this will typically occur is 'where one person places trust in another to look after his affairs and interests, and the latter betrays this trust by preferring his own interests'. This may be distinguished from overt acts of improper pressure or coercion such as unlawful threats which would amount to duress although Lord Nicholls acknowledged that there may be some overlap.[13] In *Etridge*, Lord Nicholls also added a cautionary note when he said that statements or conduct by a husband should not be regarded as undue influence if they do not exceed what may be expected of a reasonable husband in the circumstances.[14]

3.2.3.2 *The classes of undue influence*

Cases of undue influence have traditionally been divided into two classes.[15] The first class is commonly referred to as 'actual undue influence' and comprises cases in which the court will uphold a plea of undue influence only if it is satisfied that such influence has been affirmatively proved on the evidence (class 1). The second class comprises cases commonly referred to as cases of 'presumed undue influence' in which the relationship between the parties will lead the court to 'presume undue influence' unless evidence is adduced proving the contrary (class 2).

Where a person alleges that he or she entered into a transaction as a result of actual undue influence exerted by another, it is for the person making the allegation to prove it affirmatively. It does 'not depend upon some pre-existing relationship between two parties though it is most commonly associated with and derives from such a relationship'.[16] In contrast presumed undue influence 'necessarily involves some legally recognised relationship between the two parties'.[17] The reference to a 'presumption' of undue influence has proved confusing and it is perhaps preferable to refer to class 2 undue influence as 'relational' undue influence and to refer to class 1 undue influence as 'non-relational'.[18]

---

[13] ibid *per* Lord Nicholls, paras [7], [8], and [9].   [14] ibid para [32].

[15] ibid *per* Lord Scott, paras [151]–[152] referring to summary of Slade LJ in *BCCI v Aboody* [1990] 1 QB 923, 953 and *Allcard v Skinner* (1887) 36 Ch D 145.

[16] *Per* Lord Hobhouse in *Etridge (No 2)*, para [103].   [17] ibid.

[18] See Birks and Chin, 'On the Nature of Undue Influence' in Beatson and Friedmann (eds), *Good Faith in Contract* (OUP, 1995), Ch 3.

In *Barclays Bank plc v O'Brien*,[19] Lord Browne-Wilkinson adopted the classification of undue influence made in the Court of Appeal in *Bank of Credit and Commerce International SA v Aboody*,[20] which not only distinguished between class 1 and class 2 undue influence, but identified two ways in which the confidential relationship necessary for class 2 could be established.

Class 2A cases comprise certain relationships which as a matter of law raise the presumption that one party had influence over the other. Such relationships are limited in number. In *Royal Bank of Scotland plc v Etridge (No 2)*, Lord Nicholls said a 'sternly protective attitude' had been adopted by the law in relation to certain relationships 'in which one party acquires influence over another who is vulnerable and dependent'. He gave as examples the relationships between parent and child, guardian and ward, trustee and beneficiary, solicitor and client, and medical advisor and patient. In these cases it will be sufficient for the complainant to prove the existence of the type of relationship and it is not necessary for him or her to prove that he or she 'actually reposed trust and confidence in the other party'.[21] In other words in these cases the law presumes that one party had influence over the other. Lord Hobhouse stressed that 'there is no presumption properly so-called that the confidence has been abused. It is a matter of evidence.' He said:[22]

It is a fallacy to argue from the terminology normally used, "presumed undue influence", to the position, not of presuming that one party reposed trust and confidence in the other, but of *presuming* that an abuse of that relationship has occurred; factual inference, yes, once the issue has been properly raised, but not a *presumption*.

Even if there is no relationship falling within class 2A, the complainant may establish the de facto existence of a relationship under which he or she generally reposed trust and confidence in another so as to raise a presumption of undue influence within class 2B. In *Etridge* the House of Lords was critical of class 2B. Lord Hobhouse said that 'the so-called class 2B presumption should not be adopted'. It is not a useful forensic tool.[23] Lord Scott said that class 2A is useful in identifying particular relationships where the presumption arises, but doubted the utility of the class 2B classification. He continued:[24]

The presumption in class 2B cases, however, is doing no more than recognising that evidence of the relationship between the dominant and subservient parties, coupled with whatever other evidence is for the time being available, may be sufficient to justify a finding of undue influence on the balance of probabilities. The onus shifts to the defendant. Unless the defendant introduces evidence to counteract the inference of undue influence that the complainant's evidence justifies, the complainant will succeed. In my opinion the presumption of undue influence in Class 2B cases has the same function in undue influence cases as res ipsa loquitur has in negligence cases. It recognises an evidential state of affairs in which the onus has shifted.

---

[19] [1994] 1 AC 180, 189.   [20] [1990] 1 QB 923, 953.   [21] [2001] UKHL 44, para [18].
[22] ibid para [104].   [23] ibid para [107].   [24] ibid para [161].

Lord Nicholls, delivering the principal judgment,[25] thought the usage of the label 'presumed undue influence' 'can be a little confusing'. He emphasized that the use of the term 'presumption' in this context is 'descriptive of a shift in the evidential onus on a question of fact'.[26] There are two prerequisities.[27]

First, it must be shown 'that the complainant reposed trust and confidence in the other party, or the other party acquired ascendancy over the complainant'. Secondly, it must be shown 'that the transaction is not readily explicable by the relationship of the parties'.

The second prerequisite is a necessary limitation on the width of the first prerequisite.[28] Where a gift of a small amount is made to a person standing in a confidential relationship to the donor, some proof of the exercise of the influence of the donee must be given. The mere existence of the influence is not enough. Where the gift is 'so large as not to be reasonably accounted for on the ground of friendship, relationship, charity, or other ordinary motives on which ordinary men act, the burden is upon the donee to support the gift'.[29]

Lord Nicholls noted that in *National Westminster Bank plc v Morgan*[30] Lord Scarman had attached the label 'manifest disadvantage' to this second ingredient necessary to raise the presumption and that this had been causing difficulty. It might be apt enough when applied to straightforward transactions such as a substantial gift or a sale at an undervalue, but experience had shown that the expression could give rise to misunderstanding. The label was being understood and applied in a way which did not accord with the meaning intended by Lord Scarman its originator. The label should be discarded.[31]

3.2.3.3 *Husband and wife*
It is now well established that the relationship of husband and wife is not one which gives rise to a presumption of undue influence within class 2A. However, in *Barclays Bank plc v O'Brien*,[32] Lord Browne-Wilkinson said that a wife could bring herself within class 2B and raise a presumption of undue influence if she proved that she generally reposed trust and confidence in her husband in relation to their financial affairs. In *Royal Bank of Scotland plc v Etridge (No 2)*,[33] Lord Nicholls said that the reason there is no class 2A presumption in the case of a husband and wife is that 'there is nothing unusual or strange in

---

[25] ibid para [17]. Lord Bingham (para [4]) said that while the opinions of Lord Nicholls and Lord Scott show some difference of expression and approach he did not himself discern any significant difference of legal principle applicable to the cases before them and he agreed with both opinions. If such differences existed, it was 'plain that the opinion of Lord Nicholls commands the unqualified support of all members of the House'. [26] Para [16].
[27] ibid para [21]. [28] ibid para [24].
[29] ibid para [22] quoting from the judgment of Lindley LJ in *Allcard v Skinner* (1887) 36 Ch D 145, 185. [30] [1985] AC 686, 703–7.
[31] [2001] UKHL 44, paras [26]–[29]. [32] [1994] 1 AC 180, 189–90.
[33] [2001] UKHL 44, para [19].

a wife, from motives of affection or for other reasons, conferring substantial financial benefits on her husband'. However, he went on to say that:

Although there is no presumption, the court will nevertheless note, as a matter of fact, the opportunities for abuse which flow from a wife's confidence in her husband. The court will take this into account with all the other evidence in the case. Where there is evidence that a husband has taken unfair advantage of his influence over his wife, or her confidence in him, "it is not difficult for the wife to establish her title to relief". (See *Re Lloyds Bank Ltd, Bomze v Bomze* [1931] 1 Ch 289 at 302 per Maugham J)

Later he said:[34]

I do not think that, *in the ordinary course*, a guarantee of the character I have mentioned is to be regarded as a transaction which, failing proof to the contrary, is explicable only on the basis that it has been procured by the exercise of undue influence by the husband. Wives frequently enter into such transactions. There are good and sufficient reasons why they are willing to do so, despite the risks involved for them and their families. They may be enthusiastic. They may not. They may be less optimistic than their husbands about the prospects of the husbands' businesses. They may be anxious, perhaps exceedingly so. But this is a far cry from saying that such transactions as a class are to be regarded as prima facie evidence of the exercise of undue influence by husbands.

He emphasized the phrase 'in the ordinary course', and acknowledged that there will be cases where a wife's signature of a guarantee or a charge of her share in the matrimonial home does call for explanation.

Lord Scott too was unable to accept the proposition that 'if a wife, who generally reposes trust and confidence in her husband, agrees to become surety to support his debts or his business enterprises a presumption of undue influence arises'. A relationship of trust and confidence between a wife and a husband was not something special but rather the norm. In the situation where the financial and business decisions of the family were primarily taken by the husband, he would not expect evidence to be necessary to establish the existence of trust and confidence between them but to demonstrate its absence. Indeed he went further and said that even where experience had led the wife to doubt the wisdom of her husband's financial and business decisions he would not regard her willingness to support those decisions with her own assets as an indication that the husband had exerted undue influence over her.[35] He went on to emphasize that: 'In the surety wife cases it should, in my opinion be recognised that undue influence, though a possible explanation for the wife's agreement to become surety, is a relatively unlikely one.'[36]

He noted that *O'Brien* was a misrepresentation case and that, although undue influence had been alleged, the pressure which the husband had brought to bear to persuade his reluctant wife to sign was not regarded by the judge or the Court of Appeal as constituting undue influence. The wife's will had not been overborne by her husband's pressure.

---

[34] [2001] UKHL 44, paras [30]–[31].   [35] ibid para [159].   [36] ibid para [162].

If therefore a wife is able to show that she reposed trust and confidence in her husband in relation to their financial affairs and that the transaction into which she has entered is not readily explicable by their relationship, a presumption of undue influence will arise in the sense that there is a shift in the evidential burden of proof and it will be for the husband to produce evidence to rebut the inference of undue influence. However, in the light of the passages quoted from the *Etridge* case the initial hurdle facing a surety wife may not be easy to surmount.

3.2.4 Unconscionability

The equitable jurisdiction to set aside a transaction on the ground of uncon-scionability is long established though not often exercised in recent times. The earlier authorities were reviewed in *Fry v Lane*[37] where Kay J said that

...where a purchase is made from a poor and ignorant man at a considerable under-value, the vendor having no independent advice, a Court of equity will set aside the transaction.... The circumstances of poverty and ignorance of the vendor and the absence of independent advice throw upon the purchaser, when the transaction is impeached, the onus of proving, in Lord Selborne's words, that the purchase was "fair, just, and reasonable".[38]

In the more recent case *Portman Building Society v Dusangh*,[39] Ward LJ in answering the question 'What are the hallmarks of unconscionability?' turned to *Multiservice Bookbinding Ltd v Marden*[40] where Browne-Wilkinson J said:

In my judgment a bargain cannot be unfair and unconscionable unless one of the parties to it has imposed the objectionable terms in a morally reprehensible manner, that is to say, in a way which affects his conscience.

Ward LJ also said:[41]

It may be that the absence of legal advice is not so much an essential freestanding requirement, but rather a powerful factor confirming the suspicion of nefarious dealing which the presence of advice would serve to dispel.

It has been acknowledged that there are similarities between unconscion-ability and undue influence as grounds for setting transactions aside.[42] Indeed it has been suggested that they should be merged.[43] However, others would

---

[37] (1889) 40 Ch D 312, 322. In *Cresswell v Potter* [1978] 1 WLR 255, 257 Megarry J sought to modernize the language by suggesting that 'poor' could be replaced by a 'member of the lower income group' and 'ignorant' by 'less highly educated'.

[38] *Per* Lord Selborne in *Aylesford v Morris* (1873) LR 8 Ch App 483, 491. For more modern formulation in the family context see Megarry J in *Cresswell v Potter* [1978] 1 WLR 255, 257.

[39] CA, 19 April 2000.

[40] [1979] Ch 84, 110. He referred also to the analysis of Sir Peter Millett QC sitting as a deputy judge at first instance in *Alec Lobb (Garages) Ltd v Total Oil (Great Britain) Ltd* [1983] 1 WLR 87, 94. [41] CA, 19 April 2000.

[42] See Millett LJ in *Credit Lyonnais Bank Nederland NV v Burch* [1997] 1 All ER 144, 153.

[43] See the arguments in Capper, 'Undue Influence and Unconscionability' (1998) 114 LQR 479.

preserve the distinction which does appear to still exist. The focus in uncon-scionability is on the conduct of the stronger party to a transaction in exploiting the weakness of the other.[44] One party, usually the defendant has acted in a way which is morally reprehensible. In contrast undue influence focuses on the weakness of the consent of one party 'owing to an excessive dependence on the other'.[45] In practical terms, in the context of mortgages, unconscionability has been overshadowed by undue influence in recent times and the burden of establishing unconscionability seems a very heavy one to discharge.

It was most recently considered by the Court of Appeal in *Portman Building Society v Dusangh*[46] where a 72-year-old man of Indian origin who was illiterate and with a poor understanding of spoken English had entered into a mortgage of his home in order to raise money for his son who was acquiring a business. At first instance the judge had found that there was no undue influence or misrepres-entation on the part of the son. The Court of Appeal had to consider whether the mortgage should be set aside as an unconscionable bargain. Ward LJ said there was 'nothing, absolutely nothing, which came close to morally reprehensible conduct or impropriety'.[47] The son had in no way taken unconscientious advantage of the father's illiteracy, his lack of business acumen, or his paternal generosity in coming to the assistance of his son in purchasing a business.

In *Credit Lyonnais Bank Nederland NV v Burch*,[48] Miss Burch was a junior employee of the company which was the principal debtor. She had entered into an all-monies charge on her home making herself responsible for all the company's debts. She risked personal bankruptcy and the loss of her home for an increase in the overdraft facility of a company in which she had no direct financial interest. She succeeded in establishing undue influence on the part of the owner of the company and she did not seek to have the mortgage set aside as a harsh and unconscionable bargain. However, Nourse LJ thought that it might well have been arguable that she 'could directly against the bank, have had the legal charge set aside as an unconscionable bargain',[49] and Millett LJ thought the transaction was one which 'shocks the conscience of the court'.[50]

3.3 AVOIDING LIABILITY ON THE BASIS OF CONDUCT ON THE PART OF THE MORTGAGEE

3.3.1 Undue influence and other vitiating factors

It may be that a mortgagee or other creditor has exercised undue influence directly on the mortgagor or guarantor. The question has usually arisen in

---

[44] Described as 'defendant-sided' by Birks and Chin in 'On the Nature of Undue Influence' in Beatson and Friedmann (eds), *Good Faith in Contract Law* (OUP, 1995), 58.

[45] See ibid where it is described as 'plaintiff-sided'.

[46] CA, 19 April 2000, [2000] Lloyd's Rep Banking 197.   [47] ibid.

[48] [1997] 1 All ER 144.   [49] ibid 151.   [50] ibid 152.

relation to mortgages or guarantees obtained by banks, though it is now well established that the relationship between banker and customer is not one which ordinarily gives rise to a presumption of undue influence.[51] In the ordinary course of banking business a banker can explain the nature of the proposed transaction without laying himself open to a charge of undue influence. However, where the bank goes further and advises on more general matters germane to the wisdom of the transaction, it may 'cross the line' into an area in which there is a conflict of interest between the bank and the customer to whom advice is being given and thus give rise to a presumption of undue influence.[52] This was found to be the case in *Lloyds Bank Ltd v Bundy*[53] where an elderly farmer charged his farm as security for his son's indebtedness to the bank. This case may be regarded as exceptional in some respects, and the wider statements of Lord Denning MR in relation to undue influence being based on inequality of bargaining power were not approved by the House of Lords in *National Westminster Bank plc v Morgan*.[54] However, in that case Lord Scarman said that in considering the nature of the relationship necessary to give rise to the presumption of undue influence in the context of a banking transaction, Sir Eric Sachs in the Court of Appeal in *Lloyds Bank Ltd v Bundy* 'got it absolutely right'.[55] In *National Westminster Bank plc v Morgan*, the House of Lords held that a bank manager who had visited the wife in her home to seek her signature to a joint mortgage by her husband and herself to the bank had not 'crossed the line' so as to impose a duty on the bank to ensure that she had independent advice.

An allegation of unconscionability made against the mortgagee in *Portman Building Society v Dusangh*[56] was unsuccessful. Ward LJ said that 'for the lending by the building society to be unconscionable' it had to be 'against the conscience of the lender'. It must have acted with no conscience, with no moral sense that it was doing wrong. He concluded: 'The family wanted to raise money: the building society was prepared to lend it. One shakes ones head, but with sadness and with incredulity at the folly of it all, alas not with moral outrage. I am afraid the moral conscience of the court has not been shocked.'

3.3.2 Negligence

It seems that there is no duty on a bank or other mortgagee to explain the legal effect of a mortgage or guarantee to a customer or non-customer entering into such a transaction,[57] though obligations may arise under the principles established in *Royal Bank of Scotland plc v Etridge (No 2)*[58] which are considered in paragraph 3.4 below. In *Etridge*, Lord Nicholls noted that the practice of banks

---

[51] See Lord Scarman in *National Westminster Bank plc v Morgan* [1985] AC 686, 707.
[52] ibid 708–9.   [53] [1975] QB 326.   [54] [1985] AC 686.   [55] ibid 708.
[56] CA, 19 April 2000, [2000] Lloyd's Rep Banking 197.
[57] *Barclays Bank plc v Khaira* [1992] 1 WLR 623 disagreeing with dicta of Kerr LJ in *Cornish v Midland Bank plc* [1985] 3 All ER 513, 522–3.   [58] [2001] UKHL 44.

seemed to be not to have a private meeting with a wife about to enter into a joint mortgage to the bank or themselves take any other steps to bring home to the wife the risk she was running. He said that banks 'consider they would stand to lose more than they would gain by holding a private meeting with the wife' and they are, 'apparently, unwilling to assume the responsibility of advising the wife at such a meeting'. Instead they require a wife to seek legal advice.[59]

However, if a bank does explain to a person entering into a mortgage or guarantee the legal effect of the document he or she is being asked to sign, then the bank may be liable in damages to such a person if it negligently misstates the effect of the mortgage. Thus in *Cornish v Midland Bank plc*,[60] it was found that the bank's employees had failed to make clear to the wife that the mortgage was worded so as to secure any future borrowings that the bank might allow the husband. The statement that the mortgage was 'just like a building society mortgage' was misleading for a wife who believed she was merely securing a temporary loan of up to £2,000 for renovation of the house which was vested in joint names. The mortgage was not set aside as there was no undue influence by or on behalf of the bank, but the wife recovered damages from the bank for the financial loss flowing from the negligent advice. In *Perry v Midland Bank plc*,[61] it was held that the bank manager had failed to explain adequately to a wife the effect of a charge and in particular did not make it clear to her that the charge attached to her beneficial interest in the property as well as to that of the husband. Again the mortgage was not set aside as the husband had not acted as the agent of the bank and the bank had no notice of undue influence by him. Although the wife was thus entitled to damages the order for possession was upheld, notwithstanding that Fox LJ thought that the bank might be reluctant to enforce the order against the wife and daughter in view of the effect this would have on the damages recoverable

3.4 WHEN WILL THE MORTGAGEE BE AFFECTED BY THE UNDUE INFLUENCE OR MISREPRESENTATION OF THE HUSBAND?[62]

Where one spouse (usually the wife) has entered into an obligation to stand surety for the debt of the other spouse as a result of the undue influence, misrepresentation, or other invalidating conduct of the latter, then the creditor will generally be wholly ignorant of that fact. The creditor will be affected by the conduct of the principal debtor and hence be unable to enforce the surety obligation in two situations.

---

[59] [2001] UKHL 44, para [51].   [60] [1985] 3 All ER 513.   [61] [1987] Fin LR 236.

[62] In many of the cases, including *O'Brien and Etridge*, the mortgagee has in fact been a bank and this description will be retained where appropriate though the same general principles apply in relation to other mortgagees.

3.4.1 Agency

First, if the principal debtor was acting as agent for the creditor in obtaining the signature of the other spouse, then the creditor will be fixed with the wrong-doing of its own agent and the surety contract can be set aside as against the creditor. Although there may be cases where, without artificiality, it can properly be held that the husband was acting as the agent of the creditor in procuring the wife to stand as surety, such cases will be of very rare occurrence.[63] The mere fact that the mortgagee left it to the principal debtor to procure the surety's agreement to enter into the mortgage is 'no basis for an inference of agency'.[64]

3.4.2 Notice

The creditor will be bound by the actions of the principal debtor if it had actual or constructive notice of the undue influence or misrepresentation giving rise to the surety's right to have the transaction set aside. In *O'Brien*, Lord Browne-Wilkinson indicated that knowledge indicating the risk of class 2B undue influence or misrepresentation is sufficient to put a creditor on inquiry and so give the creditor constructive notice. He said:[65]

Therefore, in my judgment, a creditor is put on inquiry when a wife offers to stand surety for her husband's debt by the combination of two factors: (a) the transaction is on its face not to the financial advantage of the wife; and (b) there is a substantial risk in transactions of that kind that, in procuring the wife to act as a surety, the husband has committed a legal or equitable wrong that entitles the wife to set aside the transaction.

Accordingly, 'unless the creditor who is put on inquiry takes reasonable steps to satisfy himself that the wife's agreement to stand surety has been properly obtained, the creditor will have constructive notice of the wife's rights'.

In *Etridge*, Lord Nicholls said:[66] 'In my view, this passage, read in context, is to be taken to mean, quite simply, that a bank is put on inquiry whenever a wife offers to stand surety for her husband's debts.' He did not read (a) and (b) as factual conditions which must be proved in each case before a bank is put on inquiry. He did not understand Lord Browne-Wilkinson to have been saying that, in husband and wife cases, whether the bank is out on inquiry depends on its state of knowledge of the parties' marriage, or of the degree of trust and confidence the particular wife places in her husband in relation to her financial affairs. That would leave banks in a state of considerable uncertainty in a situation where it is important they should know clearly where they stand. The test should be simple and clear and easy to apply in a wide range of

---

[63] *Barclays Bank plc v O'Brien* [1994] 1 AC 180, 193–5.
[64] *Barclays Bank plc v O'Brien* [1992] 4 All ER 983, 1009, *per* Scott LJ, CA.
[65] [1994] 1 AC 180, 196.   [66] [2001] UKHL 44, para [44].

circumstances. He read (a) and (b) as Lord Browne-Wilkinson's broad explanation of the reason why a creditor is put on inquiry when a wife offers to stand surety for her husband's debts. These are the two factors which, taken together, constitute the underlying rationale.[67]

In relation to the type of transactions where a creditor is put on inquiry Lord Nicholls distinguished three situations.[68] First, the case where a wife becomes a surety for her husband's debts is, in this context, a straightforward case. The bank is put on inquiry. Secondly, on the other side of the line is the case where the money is being advanced, or has been advanced, to the husband and wife jointly. In such a case the bank is not put on inquiry unless the bank is aware that the loan is being made for the husband's purposes, as distinct from their joint purposes.[69] Thirdly, is the less clear cut case where the wife becomes surety for the debts of a company whose shares are held by her and her husband. The wife's shareholding may be nominal, or she may have a minority shareholding or an equal shareholding, with her husband. In his view in such cases the bank is put on inquiry, even when the wife is a director or secretary of the company. 'Such cases cannot be equated with joint loans. The shareholding interests, and the identity of the directors, are not a reliable guide to the identity of the persons who actually have the conduct of the company's business.'

Nevertheless, the identification of the true nature of a particular transaction may not be straightforward and this question was considered further by the Court of Appeal in *Mortgage Agency Services Number Two Ltd v Chater*.[70] In that case the Court of Appeal was satisfied that a mother had reposed trust and confidence in her son and that she had been induced to enter into a joint mortgage with him by his undue influence. The more difficult question was whether the mortgagee had been put on inquiry. The mother and son lived in a property which was transferred into their joint names by the mother and then jointly mortgaged to secure an advance used partly to pay off an existing mortgage, but principally to provide money for the son's business purposes. Scott Baker LJ said that the court detected 'a possible distinction between a transaction explicable only on the basis that undue influence had been exercised to procure it (Lord Scarman)[71] and one which called for an explanation, which if not given would enable the court to infer that it could only have been pro-cured by undue influence (Lord Nicholls)'.[72] Insofar as Lord Scarman had suggested a higher test, the court preferred the reformulated test given by Lord Nicholls in *Etridge*.[73]

---

[67] [2001] UKHL 44, para [46].   [68] ibid paras [48]–[49]
[69] *CIB Mortgages plc v Pitt* [1994] 1 AC 200.
[70] [2003] EWCA Civ 490, [2004] 1 P & CR 4.
[71] *In National Westminster Bank plc v Morgan* [1985] AC 686, 703–7.
[72] [2003] EWCA Civ 490, para [30].
[73] Scott Baker LJ referred specifically to para [14] of the judgment of Lord Nicholls in *Etridge* though this section of the judgment was dealing with the burden of proof and presumptions in relation to undue influence.

Scott Baker LJ said that the mortgagee was not a detective and it did not matter what an alert underwriter might have inferred as a possibility. There was nothing to tell the mortgagee that what lay behind the transaction was a commercial loan to the son and there was no obligation to ask questions, although it was not entitled to shut its eyes to the obvious.[74] There was no reason why it should not have taken the application as one for a joint loan for the improvement of their joint living circumstances. He said:[75]

There was nothing to put a prudent lender on inquiry that this might in reality be a commercial loan and that undue influence might possibly underlie the transaction. What mattered was that the transaction could perfectly reasonably be accounted for by the ordinary motives of mother and son. As Lord Nicholls said, where a joint loan (there to husband and wife) is made, a bank is not put on inquiry unless the bank is aware that the loan is being made for the husband's purposes rather than for their joint purposes. Here the bank was not aware that the loan was being made for the son's business purposes rather than the mother and son's joint purposes.

3.4.3 Application to other relationships

In *Etridge*,[76] Lord Nicholls made clear that the position is the same if a husband stands surety for his wife's debts and also in the case of unmarried couples, whether heterosexual or homosexual, where the bank is aware of the relationship. Cohabitation is not essential as the Court of Appeal had rightly decided in *Massey v Midland Bank plc*.[77] Later he emphasized that 'the law does not regard sexual relationships as standing in some special category of their own so far as undue influence is concerned. Sexual relationships are no more than one type of relationship in which an individual may acquire influence over another individual'. The *O'Brien* decision could not 'sensibly be regarded as confined to sexual relationships, although these are likely to be its main field of application at present. What is appropriate for sexual relationships ought, in principle, to be appropriate also for other relationships where trust and confidence are likely to exist'.[78]

The courts had already recognized this in cases such as *Credit Lyonnais Bank Nederland NV v Burch*[79] where the same principle was applied to the relationship of employer and employee and a junior employee in a company had provided security to the bank for the company's overdraft. The bank knew facts from which the existence of a relationship of trust and confidence between the employee and the owner of the company, could be inferred.

In view of this wider application of the *O'Brien* principle it was necessary to consider the circumstances which will put the mortgagee on inquiry.

---

[74] [2003] EWCA Civ 490, para [63].   [75] ibid para [67].
[76] [2001] UKHL 44, para [47].   [77] [1995] 1 All ER 929, 933.
[78] [2001] UKHL 44, para [82].
[79] [1997] 1 All ER 144. See also *Avon Finance Co Ltd v Bridger* [1985] 2 All ER 281 (parents and son).

Lord Nicholls acknowledged that the reality of life is that the relationships in which undue influence can be exercised are infinitely various and cannot be exhaustively listed or defined. There was 'no rational cut-off point, with certain relationships being susceptible to the *O'Brien* principle and others not'. The only practical way forward was to regard mortgagees as being 'put on inquiry' in every case in which the 'relationship between the surety and debtor is non-commercial'.[80] In such a situation if the mortgagee does not take reasonable steps to bring home to the surety the risks she is running, then the mortgagee will be deemed to have notice of any claim the surety may have that the transaction was procured by undue influence or misrepresentation on the part of the debtor.

In *First National Bank plc v Achampong*,[81] the Court of Appeal held that the fact that the undue influence came not from the principal debtor, but from the claimant's husband who was one of her co-guarantors, 'did not the less put the bank on inquiry'.

3.5 THE OBLIGATIONS OF A MORTGAGEE WHEN PUT ON INQUIRY

3.5.1 The objective

Before considering the steps which a mortgagee should take, it is important to bear in mind what such steps are designed to achieve. In *Etridge*,[82] Lord Nicholls emphasized that such steps are not concerned to discover whether the surety wife has been subjected to undue influence or misrepresentation. They are concerned to minimize the risk that she has been subjected to undue influence or misrepresentation. He said:[83]

The furthest a bank can be expected to go is to take reasonable steps to satisfy itself that the wife has had brought home to her, in a meaningful way, the practical implications of the proposed transaction. This does not wholly eliminate the risk of undue influence or misrepresentation. But it does mean that a wife enters into a transaction with her eyes open so far as the basic elements of the transaction are concerned.

Lord Scott explained that 'the bank does not have to take steps to satisfy itself that there is no undue influence. It must take steps to satisfy itself that the wife understands the nature and effect of the transaction.'[84] Accordingly, the purpose of the steps 'in the ordinary surety wife case, would be to satisfy the bank that the wife understood the nature and effect of the transaction she was entering into'.[85]

---

80 [2001] UKHL 44, para [87].   81 [2003] EWCA Civ 487, para [23].
82 [2001] UKHL 44, para [41].   83 ibid para [54].
84 ibid paras [163]–[164].   85 ibid para [165].

3.5.2 The required steps

3.5.2.1 *Pre-Etridge transactions*

In the *O'Brien case* Lord Browne-Wilkinson[86] said that a bank could reason-ably be expected to take steps to bring home to the wife the risk she was running by standing as surety and to advise her to take independent advice. In *Etridge*,[87] Lord Nicholls said that that test is applicable to past transactions which included all cases then before the House. Later he said:[88]

> In respect of past transactions, the bank will ordinarily be regarded as having discharged its obligations if a solicitor who was acting for the wife in the transaction gave the bank confirmation to the effect that he had brought home to the wife the risks she was running by standing as surety.

In such cases the failure of the solicitor properly or sufficiently to advise his client, a failure not known to the bank and not inconsistent with the con-firmation given by the solicitor to the bank, would not put the bank under any additional obligation.[89] However, as Lord Scott pointed out in the subsequent case of *National Westminster Bank plc v Amin*[90] it is essential to establish that the solicitor was in fact acting for the surety/mortgagor and not for the bank which was not clear in that case. Even if the solicitor was acting for the surety/mortgagor this will not necessarily mean that the bank will succeed. In *Etridge*, Lord Nicholls had referred not to what would be an inevitable conclusion, but to what would 'ordinarily' be the conclusion. In *Amin*, there were features which raised the question whether something more might not be required of the bank before it could claim to be free of constructive notice of undue influence or other impropriety on the part of the debtor son. Thus it was alleged that the bank was aware of the fact that Mr and Mrs Amin could not speak English and might therefore be especially vulnerable to exploitation. The letter from the bank to the solicitors merely asked them to attend to 'the formalities' and the solicitor's letter to the bank simply stated that he had explained the terms and conditions but said nothing about their apparent understanding of the explanation. While such understanding could be assumed once an explanation had been given such an assumption might not be safe in the circumstances of the case. In *Amin*, the case was remitted to the County Court for trial to resolve the issues of fact.

In *First National Bank plc v Achampong*,[91] Blackburne J in the Court of Appeal said that 'the House of Lords in *Etridge (No 2)* has now made clear that

---

[86] [1994] 1 AC 180, 196–7.   [87] [2001] UKHL 44, para [50].   [88] ibid para [80].

[89] *Per* Lord Scott in *National Westminster Bank plc v Amin* [2002] UKHL 9, para [21].

[90] ibid para [22].

[91] [2003] EWCA Civ 487, para [35]. He noted that previous authority had not been explicit in this respect. Indeed in some earlier cases such as *Bank of Baroda v Rayarel* [1995] 2 FLR 376 it would appear that the mere fact that the bank knew that the wife had a solicitor may have sufficed to afford it protection.

the fact alone that the bank knows that a solicitor is acting is not sufficient'. The bank 'must have proper grounds for thinking that the solicitor has advised her on the risks she runs from entering into the transaction whether or not, in fact, the solicitor has properly discharged his duty to her'.[92]

3.5.2.2 *Post-Etridge transactions*

For the future, Lord Nicholls said, a bank would satisfy the requirement of bringing home to the wife the risk she is running by standing as surety 'if it insists that the wife attend a private meeting with a representative of the bank at which she is told of the extent of her liability as surety, warned of the risk she is running and urged to take independent legal advice. In exceptional cases the bank, to be safe, has to insist that the wife is separately advised'.[93] However, he noted that the practice of banks had been not to have a private meeting with the wife, but to require the wife to seek independent advice and to seek 'written confirmation from a solicitor that he has explained the nature and effect of the documents to the wife'.[94] Many of the difficulties which had arisen in the cases before the court stemmed from serious deficiencies, or alleged deficiencies, in the quality of the legal advice given to the wives. Lord Nicholls did not think that Lord Browne-Wilkinson in *O'Brien* had stated that banks should be obliged to hold a private meeting with the surety, and he did not consider that they ought to be compelled to take this course.[95] It was not unreasonable for banks to prefer that the task should be undertaken by an independent legal advisor. 'Ordinarily it will be reasonable that a bank should be able to rely upon confirmation from a solicitor, acting for the wife, that he has advised the wife appropriately.' The position will be otherwise 'if the bank knows that the solicitor has not duly advised the wife or . . . if the bank knows facts from which it ought to have realised that the wife has not received the appropriate advice. In such circumstances the bank will proceed at its own risk'.[96]

3.6 SOLICITOR'S ADVICE

The extent of the responsibilities of a solicitor who is advising the wife will be determined in the first place by the terms, express or implied, of his retainer. The solicitor will need to explain to the wife the purpose of his involvement, and that if the wife subsequently suggests that her will was overborne by her husband, or that she did not properly understand the implications of the transaction, the mortgagee will rely upon his involvement to rebut that suggestion.[97]

---

[92] [2003] EWCA Civ 487, para [33]. See also *Lloyds TSB Bank v Holdgate* [2002] EWCA 1543, para [23] where Mance LJ stressed the necessity for the solicitor to be involved in an advisory role and not merely an 'execution only' role.   [93] [2001] UKHL 44, para [50].
[94] ibid para [51].   [95] ibid para [55].   [96] ibid paras [56]–[57].
[97] ibid para [64], *per* Lord Nicholls.

The solicitor will also need to obtain confirmation from the wife that she wishes him to act for her in giving her the necessary advice 'on the legal and practical implications of the proposed transaction'. On receiving instructions to that effect the advice required from the solicitor will depend upon the circumstances of the case. Lord Nicholls set out the core minimum of the matters which such advice should typically cover.[98]

First the solicitor 'will need to explain the nature of the documents and the practical consequences these will have for the wife if she signs them'. The solicitor should point out that if her husband's business does not prosper she could lose her home which may be her only substantial asset, as well as the family's home. She could end up being made bankrupt. In the words of Lord Scott, the solicitor should 'explain to the wife, on a worst case footing, the steps the bank might take to enforce its security'.[99]

Secondly, the solicitor 'will need to point out the seriousness of the risks involved'. This will involve telling her the purpose of the proposed new facility and the amount and principal terms of the new facility making it clear if the bank might increase the amount of the facility, or change its terms, or grant a new facility, without reference to her. It is important that she is informed of the amount of her liability under her guarantee. The solicitor should discuss with the wife her financial means, including her understanding of the value of the property being charged and whether she or her husband have any other assets out of which repayment could be made if the husband's business should fail. These matters are relevant to a consideration of the risk involved in the mortgage. Lord Scott suggested that the solicitor should 'make sure the wife understands the extent of the liabilities that may come to be secured under the security' and also 'explain the likely duration of the security'. He should also 'ascertain whether the wife is aware of any existing indebtedness that will, if she grants the security, be secured under it'.[100]

Thirdly, the solicitor 'will need to state clearly that the wife has a choice. The decision is hers and hers alone. Explanation of the choice facing the wife will call for some discussion of the present financial position, including the amount of the husband's present indebtedness, and the amount of his current overdraft facility'.

Fourthly, the solicitor 'should check whether the wife wishes to proceed. She should be asked whether she is content that the solicitor should write to the bank confirming he has explained to her the nature of the documents and the practical implications they may have for her, or whether, for instance, she would prefer him to negotiate with the bank on the terms of the transaction'. Thus it might be appropriate to negotiate 'the sequence in which the various securities will be called upon or a specific or lower limit to her liabilities'. No confirmation should be given to the bank by the solicitor without the wife's authority.

---

[98] ibid para [65].   [99] ibid para [169].   [100] ibid.

Lord Nicholls had earlier emphasized that it was not for the solicitor to veto the transaction by declining to confirm to the bank that he has explained the documents to the wife and the risks she is taking upon herself. A solicitor who concludes that a transaction is not in the wife's best interests will give the wife reasoned advice to that effect. However, 'at the end of the day the decision on whether to proceed is the decision of the client, not the solicitor. A wife is not to be precluded from entering into a financially unwise transaction if, for her own reasons, she wishes to do so'. Although that was the general rule he acknowledged that there might be exceptional circumstances in which 'it is glaringly obvious that the wife is being grievously wronged' and in such a case the solicitor should decline to act further.[101]

3.7 INDEPENDENT ADVICE

It is not essential that the solicitor advising the wife should act for her alone in relation to the mortgage transaction. The solicitor advising the wife may also be acting for her husband in relation to the transaction or for the bank. Lord Nicholls considered the arguments in favour of the need for the solicitor to act for the wife alone, and the arguments for the view that he may also act for the husband or the bank.[102] He concluded that overall the latter were more weighty than the former and that the advantages of employing a solicitor acting solely for the wife did not justify the additional expense this would involve for the husband. He emphasized that when a solicitor accepts instructions to advise a surety wife he 'assumes responsibilities directly to her, both at law and professionally'. He is acting for the wife alone and is concerned only with her interests and must consider whether there is any conflict of duty or interest involved.[103]

Lord Scott considered that in acting for the bank the solicitor's role is essentially administrative in seeing that the security document is validly executed and, if necessary, registered, and obtaining documents of title for the bank. Since he has no consultative role vis-à-vis the bank, Lord Scott did not consider that his duties to the bank prejudice his suitability to advise the wife.[104] The position where the solicitor is also acting for the husband presented a little more difficulty for it was the existence of the risk of undue influence or misrepresentation on the husband's part that made it necessary for the bank to be satisfied that the wife had been appropriately advised. However, in the ordinary case a mortgagee is entitled to rely on the professional competence and propriety of the solicitor to provide appropriate advice to the wife even though he is

---

[101] [2001] UKHL 44, paras [61]–[62]. It is, of course important that the solicitor has sufficient information upon which to base his advice. See para 3.8.3. below.

[102] ibid paras [72] and [73] respectively.

[103] ibid para [74].   [104] ibid para [173].

also acting for the husband. A mortgagee should only insist on the wife being given advice by a solicitor who is not also acting for the husband if it knows of some reason for suspecting undue influence or other improper conduct on the part of the husband.[105]

3.8 THE POSITION OF THE MORTGAGEE

3.8.1 Steps to be taken by the mortgagee

The steps which a mortgagee should take to protect itself when it is put on inquiry were considered in paragraph 3.5.2 above. In relation to pre-*Etridge* and post-*Etridge* transactions a crucial feature is the confirmation to be obtained from a solicitor acting for the wife or other surety that he has given the wife or other surety appropriate advice. In relation to post-*Etridge* transactions, Lord Nicholls set out in more detail the obligations of a bank and these seem equally applicable to other mortgagees.

3.8.2 Confirmation of independent advice

If a mortgagee is to take free from notice of any impropriety on the part of the principal debtor/husband it will need to obtain confirmation in writing from the solicitor acting for the wife that he has given her appropriate advice. The mortgagee should also check directly with the wife the name of the solicitor she wishes to act for her. Accordingly a mortgagee 'should communicate directly with the wife informing her that for its own protection it will require written confirmation from a solicitor, acting for her, to the effect that the solicitor has fully explained to her the nature of the documents and the practical implications they will have for her'. She should also be informed of the purpose of this requirement and be asked to nominate a solicitor 'to advise her, separately from her husband, and act for her in giving the necessary confirmation' to the mortgagee. It should be made clear to her that the solicitor may be the same solicitor as is acting for her husband in the transaction, but she should be asked whether she would prefer that a different solicitor should act for her in providing the mortgagee with the necessary confirmation. It is essential that the mortgagee receives an appropriate response directly from the wife before proceeding further.[106]

Since the solicitor is acting for the wife, he is not accountable to the mortgagee for his advice and the mortgagee is not to be imputed with knowledge of what passed between the solicitor and the wife. If the advice given by the wife's

---

[105] ibid para [174] referring to Lord Browne-Wilkinson in *O'Brien* [1994] 1 AC 180, 197.
[106] [2001] UKHL 44, para [79], *per* Lord Nicholls.

solicitor to her is deficient then ordinarily this is a matter between the wife and her solicitor. The mortgagee is entitled to assume that the solicitor has advised the wife properly unless it knows that this is not so, or if it knows of facts from which it ought to have realized that this is not so.[107] Obviously if the solicitor fails to provide the appropriate confirmation then, in the absence of other evidence, the mortgagee will not have reasonable grounds for being satisfied that the wife's agreement has been properly obtained. If it proceeds with the transaction then its legal rights will be subject to any equity existing in favour of the wife.[108]

3.8.3 Provision of information

If the mortgagee, through its representatives, is not prepared to explain the implications of the transaction, then it must provide the solicitor who is to advise the wife with the financial information which is needed for this purpose. This is especially relevant if the mortgagee is a bank which is likely to have a better picture of the husband's financial affairs than the solicitor. It should, therefore, 'become routine practice for banks, if relying on confirmation from a solicitor for their protection, to send to the solicitor the necessary financial information'. What is necessary will, of course, depend on the circumstances of the case, but will normally include the purpose for which 'the proposed new facility has been requested, the current amount of the husband's indebtedness, the amount of his current overdraft facility, and the amount and terms of any new facility'.[109] The solicitor should also be provided with a copy of any written application for the facility made by the husband. The bank will need the consent of the husband to the provision of this information and if he is not prepared to give his consent then 'the transaction will not be able to proceed.'

3.8.4 Knowledge of invalidating conduct

If the mortgagee believes or suspects that that the husband has misled his wife or that the wife is not entering into the transaction of her own free will, it must inform the wife's solicitor of the facts giving rise to its belief or suspicion. These are likely to be exceptional cases.[110]

3.8.5 Written confirmation

In every case the mortgagee should obtain from the wife's solicitor a written confirmation that the appropriate advice has been given to the wife.

---

[107] [2001] UKHL 44, *per* Lord Nicholls, para [78].   [108] See Lord Hobhouse, para [122].
[109] ibid *per* Lord Nicholls, para [79].   [110] ibid.

3.9 THE EFFECT WHEN THE MORTGAGEE IS BOUND BY THE PRINCIPAL DEBTOR'S CONDUCT

Where a wife or other family surety succeeds in showing that the mortgagee is affected by invalidating conduct on the part of the mortgagor, the surety will be entitled in equity to have the mortgage transaction set aside so far as it concerns her. The fact that, even in the absence of invalidating conduct on the part of the principal debtor, the surety would have been prepared to join in a mortgage for a lesser sum, will not prevent the mortgage being set aside in its entirety as against the surety.[111] This was established in *TSB Bank plc v Camfield*,[112] where a wife was persuaded by her husband to charge her beneficial interest in the matrimonial home as security for loan facilities to her husband for his business purposes. The husband had falsely represented to his wife that the maximum liability to be secured by the charge was £15,000. She was willing to execute the charge on that basis. The bank had constructive notice of the husband's misrepresentation and the wife was held to be entitled to have the charge set aside as against her. The bank invited the court to substitute a charge for £15,000 on the ground this would sufficiently meet the equity of the case since the wife had been willing to execute the charge to that extent. The court refused to do so, either by setting the charge aside in part, or by imposing terms on the relief sought.

The Court of Appeal took the view that the question of partial enforcement of a charge against a wife who establishes undue influence or misrepresentation had not been determined by the House of Lords in *Barclays Bank plc v O'Brien*[113] although the facts were similar.[114] The husband had misrepresented to his wife that liability was limited to £60,000 and would last for only three weeks. A possession order had been made suspended on terms that the £60,000 was paid to the bank with liability for the balance being stood over. The £60,000 was eventually paid so the question of partial enforcement did not arise for decision and Mrs O'Brien was held to be entitled to have the legal charge set aside as against the bank.

Although the court is not entitled to impose terms on the surety's rescission of a mortgage, it is a well established principle that a person who elects to rescind a transaction must restore or give allowance for benefits received under that transaction. Under the principle of *restitutio in integrum* (or counter-restitution)

---

[111] This situation is, of course, more likely to arise where the surety has joined in the mortgage as a result of a misrepresentation on the part of the principal debtor rather than as a result of undue influence on his part.

[112] [1995] 1 FLR 751. Followed in *Bank Melli Iran v Samadi-Rad* [1995] 2 FLR 367. See also the earlier case *Allied Irish Bank plc v Byrne* [1995] 2 FLR 325.   [113] [1994] 1 AC 180.

[114] [1995] 1 FLR 751, *per* Nourse LJ at 433 and 436, *per* Roch LJ at 438.

the parties must be restored to their pre-transaction position.[115] Thus where a wife has been induced by the undue influence of her husband to enter into a mortgage to secure a loan not only for the husband's business purposes, but which is also used partly for improvements to the family home, she will be required to give an allowance for the benefit she has received.[116] In *Dunbar v Nadeem*,[117] the Court of Appeal made it clear that had the wife succeeded in establishing undue influence on the part of her husband, the benefit which the wife would have been required to restore would have been not merely half the amount of the loan, but the interest in the equity of redemption in the property acquired with the aid of the loan.

However, the benefit to her must be a direct financial benefit and it is not enough that she received the sum advanced merely 'as part of the conduit pipe through which' the sum went to the husband's business.[118] Similarly any indirect benefit which a wife may receive from the success of the husband's business supported by the loan should not give rise to any requirement of counter-restitution.[119]

Although, subject to the requirements of counter-restitution, the setting aside of a mortgage for undue influence or misrepresentation is an 'all or nothing' process, there may be cases where the parts affected by undue influence or misrepresentation may be severed from those that are not so affected, thereby enabling the latter to be enforced. In *Barclays Bank plc v Caplan*,[120] Mr Jonathan Sumption QC sitting as a deputy judge of the Chancery Division said that neither *Allied Irish Bank plc v Byrne* nor *TSB Bank plc v Camfield* was authority for the proposition that setting aside must be an '"all or nothing" process" even in a case where the objectionable features of the document can readily be severed from the rest without rewriting it'.[121] Applying the common law principles this would require that (i) the unenforceable features are capable of being removed by the excision of words, without the necessity of adding to or modifying the wording of what remains, and (ii) the removal does not alter the character of the instrument or the balance of rights and obligations contained in it. Thus where the original mortgage agreement was not affected by undue influence but a subsequent agreement for further advances was so affected, then the latter could be severed and only the original agreement enforced since the sums guaranteed in each case were not interdependent. He acknowledged that such cases would be rare.

---

[115] *Erlanger v New Sombrero Phosphate Co* (1878) 3 App Cas 1218. It seems that if *restitutio in integrum* is impossible monetary compensation may be given. See in a different context *Mahoney v Purnell* [1997] 1 FLR 612.   [116] See *Midland Bank plc v Greene* [1995] 2 FLR 827.

[117] [1998] 2 FLR 457.

[118] *Per* Ferris J in *Allied Irish Bank plc v Byrne* [1995] 2 FLR 325, 355.

[119] See the reasoning to the contrary in *Bank Melli Iran v Samadi Rad* (1994) 26 HLR 612 at first instance. This decision was reversed on appeal ([1995] 1 FLR 751) following *TSB Bank plc v Camfield*.   [120] [1998] 1 FLR 532.

[121] ibid 546.

3.10 SUBORDINATION—THE EFFECT OF AGREEING TO POSTPONEMENT

3.10.1 Express consent

It was noted in the introduction to this chapter that it is common for mortgagees to obtain the written consent of persons in occupation of the property being mortgaged to the subordination of their rights of occupancy to the rights and powers of the mortgagee. In *Woolwich Building Society v Dickman*,[122] the Court of Appeal held that, if appropriately drafted, and in the absence of any finding of undue influence or misrepresentation, such a consent can be effective to cover rights of occupancy arising under a tenancy as well as occupancy rights derived from a licence or beneficial interest. The fact that the mortgagees had been under a misapprehension as to the nature of the occupation did not deprive the consent of legal effect, though in the particular circumstances it was not effective to subordinate to the rights of the mortgagee the rights arising under a protected tenancy in existence at the date of the mortgage.

3.10.2 Imputed consent

Even though there is no express consent on the part of an occupier of mortgaged property to subordinate his or her rights to those of the mortgagee, such consent may in certain circumstances be imputed. In *Bristol & West Building Society v Henning*,[123] the Court of Appeal held that in the absence of any express declaration of trust or agreement relating to the beneficial interest in the property the occupier's right depended on the imputed intention of the parties. Since the female cohabitant knew of and supported the obtaining of a mortgage advance towards the purchase price of the property, it was 'impossible' to impute to the parties any intention other than that she had authorized the man to raise the mortgage advance from the building society and that her rights were to be subject to the rights of the building society as mortgagee.

This decision was applied and extended by the Court of Appeal in *Equity and Law Home Loans Ltd v Prestidge*.[124] It was held that where an occupying cohabitant was aware of a mortgage advance at the time of the purchase of a property so that she was deemed to have consented to it, then consent to a re-mortgage of the property should be imputed to her notwithstanding her lack of knowledge of it, but only up to the amount of the original loan. Thus the new mortgage had priority only to the extent of the original loan. Mustill LJ said

---

[122] [1996] 3 All ER 204. There is a suggestion by Waite LJ at 211 that in the case of registered land such consents 'could have no effect upon the mandatory rights they enjoyed under s 70(1)(g) [of the Land Registration Act 1925] unless a provision to that effect was "expressed on the register"'.

[123] [1985] 1 WLR 778. This was applied in relation to registered land in *Paddington Building Society v Mendelsohn* (1985) 59 P & CR 224. [124] [1992] 1 WLR 137.

that any other answer would be absurd. It would mean that if the man had in good faith and with the knowledge of the woman transferred the mortgage to another building society in order to obtain, for example, a more favourable rate of interest, the woman would receive a windfall. She would no longer be subject to an encumbrance which she had intended should be created as a result of a transaction 'which could not do her any harm and of which she was entirely ignorant'.[125] Later he said:[126]

The new mortgage was made against a background of a consent by [the woman] to the creation of an encumbrance so that the transaction could proceed. This imputed consent must, in common sense, apply to the creation of a new encumbrance in replacement of the old, whether [the woman] knew about it or not, provided that it did not change [the woman's] position for the worse.

There is some overlap between subordination on the basis of imputed consent and subrogation which is considered in the next section.

3.11 SUBROGATION

If money advanced to the owner of property is used by him to discharge an earlier mortgage on the property, then the person advancing the money may be entitled to a charge over the property by way of subrogation. The person advancing the new loan will then acquire security for the loan with the priority of the discharged mortgage,[127] but only to the extent to which the new loan has in fact discharged that mortgage. Thus where the discharged mortgage secured a smaller sum than the new loan, the person advancing the new loan will be subrogated only to the extent of the amount secured by the discharged mortgage.[128] The new lender will not, of course, need to rely on subrogation when it advances the money in return for a new charge on the property. However, subrogation will be important when it does not obtain such a charge or where a charge is not fully effective. Thus a new charge may have been effectively signed by only one of two joint owners because, for example, one joint owner forged the signature of the other joint owner.[129] A person entitled to subrogation stands in the shoes of the secured creditor whose mortgage has been redeemed. In *Esso Petroleum Co Ltd v Hall Russell & Co Ltd*[130] Lord Jauncey said:

What is, however, absolutely clear from the authorities is that the rights and remedies to which the indemnifier is subrogated are those which were vested in the person to whom payment has been made, no more and no less...

---

[125] [1992] 1 WLR 143.   [126] ibid 144.

[127] See *Butler v Rice* [1910] 2 Ch 277; *Ghana Commercial Bank v Chandiram* [1960] AC 745.

[128] See *Eagle Star Insurance v Karasiewicz* [2002] EWCA Civ 940.

[129] See *Western Trust & Saving Ltd v Rock* (CA, 26 February 1993).

[130] [1989] AC 643, 672.

Thus the person entitled to subrogation will be entitled not only to capital, but also to interest and indeed compound interest if the original mortgagee was so entitled.[131]

Subrogation may arise even though the debtor may know nothing whatever about the transaction which has caused a third party to become subrogated to the rights of his original creditor.[132] It may also extend to what has been called 'sub-subrogation' as shown in *Castle Phillips Finance v Piddington*.[133] In that case there were three successive mortgage transactions, only one of which was effective as against the wife, who owned the mortgaged property which was the matrimonial home. The first was a mortgage to Lloyds Bank to secure her husband's loan account and overdraft which had been effective. Subsequently the husband decided to change from Lloyds to Barclays. He told the wife that she would be charging the house to secure a loan for roof repairs to the house, but she in fact executed an all monies charge and the husband borrowed an additional £8,000 and Barclays paid off the husband's debts on the Lloyds accounts. Later, the husband and an accomplice raised money from the plaintiff money lenders by forging documents purporting to bind both the husband and wife to a joint borrowing with the wife's property as security. The wife knew nothing of this arrangement, and the moneylenders' advance discharged the debts to Barclays including the balances on the account for the roofing repairs and the account to pay off the Lloyds loans. Barclays was entitled to the Lloyds' security by subrogation when Barclays discharged the debt to Lloyds, thinking it was to obtain an effective security for its own money. When the plaintiff discharged the debt to Barclays thinking it was obtaining an effective security for its own money, it became entitled to the same security as Barclays did. Accordingly, by subrogation the plaintiff became entitled to the same security as that held by Barclays, that is to say the Lloyds' charge.[134]

In recent cases it has been held that subrogation is a remedy to prevent unjust enrichment and it would be a mistake to regard it as turning entirely upon the question of intention, whether common or unilateral. In *Banque Financiere de la Cite v Parc (Battersea) Ltd*[135] Lord Hoffman said that it should be recognized

---

[131] See *Western Trust & Saving Ltd v Rock,* above, where Peter Gibson LJ said that prima facie the new mortgagee succeeds to the whole security, and that means to all the rights relating to capital and interest. However, he said there might be special circumstances which made it inequitable for the new mortgagee to take the same rate of interest as that to which the original mortgagee was entitled if, for example, the contractual rate of the new loan was less that the interest rate payable under the original mortgage as in *Chetwynd v Allen* [1899] 1 Ch 353 where the lower rate was held to be applicable. [132] *Brocklesby v Temperance Permanent Building Society* [1895] AC 173.
[133] [1995] 1 FLR 783, 792.
[134] See Peter Gibson LJ at 792. See also *UCB Group Ltd v Hedworth* [2003] EWCA Civ 1717 where UCB was held to be entitled to be subrogated to the lien to which an earlier mortgagee, whose mortgage was ineffective, had become entitled on financing part of the purchase price of various properties.
[135] [1999] 1 AC 221, 234. See also *Boscawen v Bajwa* (1995) 70 P & CR 391 where funds provided by a building society to finance a purchase of property were transferred via the purchaser's solicitors

that it is a restitutionary remedy and that the appropriate questions are therefore:

(1) whether the defendant would be enriched at the plaintiff's expense;
(2) whether such enrichment would be unjust; and
(3) whether there are nevertheless reasons of policy for denying a remedy.[136]

This does not mean that questions of intention may not be highly relevant to the question of whether or not enrichment has been unjust. Thus as against a borrower, subrogation to security will not be available where the transaction was intended merely to create an unsecured loan.[137] Lord Hoffman said that he did not express a view on the question of where the burden of proof lies in these matters though he noted cases where it had been held that if a plaintiff's money was used to discharge a secured liability, he was presumed to intend that the mortgage should be kept alive for his own benefit. However, he said that:

if it is recognised that the use of the plaintiff's money to pay off a secured debt and the intentions of the parties about whether or not the plaintiff should have security are only materials upon which a court may decide that the defendant's enrichment would be unjust, it could be argued that on general principles it is for the plaintiff to make out a case of unjust enrichment.[138]

The right of a mortgagee to subrogation may be upheld even though the effect is to circumvent the protection which a joint beneficial owner who is not bound by the mortgage has vis-à-vis the mortgagee if the beneficial owner would otherwise be unjustly enriched at the expense of the mortgagee. In *Eagle Star Insurance v Karasiewicz*,[139] a wife who was joint beneficial owner of property with her husband was found to be not bound by a mortgage to Eagle Star and as she was in occupation of the property at the time of the mortgage she had an overriding interest. However, the Court of Appeal held that Eagle Star was entitled to be subrogated to the rights of an earlier mortgage of the property which had been discharged out of the advance from Eagle Star. The earlier mortgage had been binding on the wife, and as she had not at the time of the mortgage been in occupation of the property, she did not have an overriding interest binding on the original mortgagee. Arden LJ said that if subrogation were denied then the wife would be enriched at Eagle Star's expense and such enrichment would be unjust as she would receive a windfall if she obtained her share free from the original charge to which Eagle Star was subrogated.

---

to the vendor's solicitors who used them to discharge the vendor's mortgage on the property. The purchase and hence the legal charge which the building society had intended to secure the loan was never completed. It was held that the building society was subrogated to the rights of the vendor's discharged mortgage.

[136] In *Orakpo v Manson Investments Ltd* [1978] AC 95, it was considered that it would be contrary to the terms and policy of the Moneylenders Acts to allow restitution.

[137] See *Paul v Speirway Ltd* [1976] Ch 220.   [138] [1999] 1 AC 221, 234.

[139] [2002] EWCA Civ 940.

Thus subrogation was applied even though this enabled the protection given to the wife's overriding interest against the new mortgagee to be circumvented.

3.12 FORGED SIGNATURE

Where one co-owner has forged the signature of the other co-owner on a mortgage of the property vested in their joint names the mortgage will be ineffective against the latter.[140] It will however, be effective against the interest of the former.[141] If the co-owners held the beneficial interest in the property as joint tenants then it is generally thought that the mortgage will effect a severance of that joint tenancy and the co-owners will become tenants in common of the beneficial interest.[142] If the mortgagee wishes to enforce the security by effecting a sale of the property it will be necessary to make an application for an order for sale under the Trusts of Land and Appointment of Trustees Act 1996[143] considered in Chapter 5, rather than proceed to exercise the remedies of a mortgagee considered in Chapter 4.

It should also be noted that, although the mortgage as such may be ineffective against the co-owner whose signature has been forged, if the proceeds of the mortgage advance were used to discharge an earlier mortgage then the mortgagee may be subrogated to the rights of the mortgagee under the earlier discharged mortgage.[144]

3.13 RELATIONSHIP WITH PROCEEDINGS FOR ANCILLARY RELIEF

Where a failure to maintain mortgage repayments coincides with the breakdown of the mortgagors' marriage it is essential to bear in mind the interrelation between proceedings under the Matrimonial Causes Act 1973 seeking a property adjustment order and proceedings in which it is alleged that a charge on the property is ineffective on the basis of undue influence or other vitiating factor. The remedies must be pursued consistently. In *First National Bank plc v Walker*,[145] the wife pursued ancillary relief proceedings in which a property adjustment order was made requiring her husband to transfer his interest in the jointly owned former matrimonial home to her. This was on the footing that

---

[140] *The Mortgage Corporation v Shaire* [2000] 2 FCR 222. See also *Ahmed v Kendrick* (1988) 56 P & CR 120 which concerned a forged signature on a transfer.

[141] See Law of Property Act 1925, s 63.

[142] See however the discussion by Nield, 'To Sever or not to Sever: The Effect of a Mortgage by One Joint Tenant' [2001] Conv 462.

[143] See *Bank of Ireland Home Mortgages Ltd v Bell* [2001] 2 FLR 809.

[144] See *The Mortgage Corporation v Shaire* [2000] 2 FCR 222.   [145] [2001] 1 FLR 505.

the mortgage of that property in favour of the bank was valid.[146] She also attempted to defend proceedings for possession of the property brought by the bank on the basis that the mortgage was voidable because she had executed the mortgage as a result of the undue influence of her husband. The Court of Appeal held that it was not acceptable for her to pursue a claim for ancillary relief on the footing that the charge was valid and to defend a claim for possession on the footing that it was voidable. Sir Andrew Morritt V–C said:[147]

In my view it is plain that a claim against the bank to set aside the charge and the loan which it secures for the undue influence of one joint and several debtor over the other is secondary to and parasitic on the existence of such a claim by one such debtor against the other. Notice alone does not give rise to a cause of action against the bank. It enables the cause of action and the claim for relief against the other debtor to be made effective against the secured creditor who has obtained an interest in the relevant property.

He therefore rejected the submission for the wife that the rights against the husband and her rights against the bank were different in nature and in no way inter-dependent. On the contrary, her rights against the bank were dependent on the existence of her rights against her husband. Thus since the wife had in effect acknowledged that as between her and her husband the mortgage was not voidable at her instance, she could not then allege it was voidable as against the bank.

Chadwick LJ pointed out that if the wife had pursued the possession proceedings to a successful conclusion the result would be that her former husband would lose the right to contribution and indemnity against her and out of any proceeds of the realization of the property which, at the time of the order, both he and the court were entitled to expect existed and would be preserved.[148]

---

[146] Sir Andrew Morritt V–C (paras [51]–[53]) pointed out that the conveyance of the husband's interest to the wife included a clause specifically acknowledging the existence and validity of the mortgage. If the conveyance had been silent about incumbrances then it would have taken effect subject to such of them as were valid and enforceable.   [147] ibid paras [35]–[36].

[148] ibid para [76].

4

ENFORCING THE SECURITY

4.1 ACTION BY A MORTGAGEE ON DEFAULT BY A MORTGAGOR

In the event of default by a borrower, the mortgagee has a number of possible remedies. The mortgagee could seek foreclosure of the mortgage, ie an order terminating the borrower's right to redeem the mortgage, but resort to this remedy is now very rare. The mortgagee also has power to appoint a receiver, but this will normally only be appropriate where the subject matter of the mortgage is let and there is income from tenants.[1] The most likely remedy to which a mortgagee will resort is that of sale of the mortgaged property so that the amount due under the mortgage can be recovered from the proceeds of sale. If there is a balance due after satisfaction of the mortgagee's claim and expenses then the borrower will be entitled to this. If there is a shortfall then the mortgagee can pursue a personal claim against the borrower for the shortfall. In practice a mortgagee will usually seek an order for possession of the mortgaged property as a preliminary to the exercise of the power to sell the property so that the property can be sold with vacant possession. Sale of the property while it is still occupied by the borrower is likely to be very

---

[1] Law of Property Act 1925, s 101.

difficult and entry into possession without a court order may, if violence is used or threatened, amount to a criminal offence. It is therefore appropriate to start by considering the circumstances in which a mortgagee can obtain an order for possession before considering the exercise of the power of sale and the right to maintain a personal action for any shortfall after the exercise of that right.

4.2 POSSESSION

4.2.1 The right

Although an order for possession of a mortgaged property may be viewed as a remedy, the mortgagee has a right to possession which is fundamental to the mortgage relationship. In much quoted words Harman J pointed out in *Four-Maids Ltd v Dudley Marshall (Properties) Ltd*[2] that the right to take possession can be exercised 'before the ink is dry on the mortgage'. It is not of course anticipated that the mortgagee will seek possession unless and until the mortgagor is in default under the terms of the mortgage. Indeed the mortgage deed will often contain a provision to this effect. A right of possession in favour of the mortgagor may be implied in certain circumstances, but this will not often be done.[3] However, if a mortgage provides that the mortgagee has a right to possession when default is made, this will be construed as conferring on the mortgagor a right to possession until default.[4]

When the mortgagee's right to possession is not subject to any such express or implied restriction, or is no longer subject to any such restriction because of the mortgagor's default, the court formerly had no jurisdiction to decline to make an order for possession or to adjourn the hearing, whether on terms of keeping up payments or paying arrears, if the mortgagee could not be persuaded to agree to this course. The sole exception to this was that the application might be adjourned for a short time to afford to the mortgagor a chance of paying off the mortgagee in full or otherwise satisfying him, but this was not permissible if there was no reasonable prospect of this occurring.[5]

---

[2] [1957] Ch 317, 320.

[3] In *Esso Petroleum Co Ltd v Alstonbridge Properties Ltd* [1975] 1 WLR 1474, 1484, Walton J accepted 'that the court will be ready to find an implied term in an instalment mortgage that the mortgagor is to be entitled to remain in possession against the mortgagee until he makes default in payment of one of the instalments. But there must be something upon which to hang such a conclusion in the mortgage other than the mere fact that it is an instalment mortgage'. See also *Western Bank Ltd v Schindler* [1977] Ch 1, where the Court of Appeal refused to imply such a term.

[4] See *Birmingham Citizens Permanent Building Society v Caunt* [1962] Ch 883.

[5] ibid, *per Russell J 912. See Cheltenham & Gloucester Building Society v Norgan* [1996] 1 All ER 449, 451.

4.2.2 Statutory intervention

The rigour of the position at common law was mitigated by s 36 of the Administration of Justice Act 1970. This provides:

(1) Where the mortgagee under a mortgage of land which consists of or includes a dwelling-house brings an action in which he claims possession of the mortgaged property, not being an action for foreclosure in which a claim for possession of the mortgaged property is also made, the court may exercise any of the powers conferred on it by subsection (2) below if it appears to the court that in the event of its exercising the power the mortgagor is likely to be able within a reasonable period to pay any sums due under the mortgage or to remedy a default consisting of a breach of any other obligation arising under or by virtue of the mortgage.

(2) The court—
    (a) may adjourn the proceedings, or
    (b) on giving judgment, or making an order, for delivery of possession of the mortgaged property, or at any time before the execution of such judgment or order, may—
        (i) stay or suspend execution of the judgment or order, or
        (ii) postpone the date for delivery of possession, for such period or periods as the court thinks reasonable.

These powers can be exercised only if it appears to the court that in the event of their exercise the mortgagor is likely to be able within a reasonable period to pay any sums due under the mortgage or to remedy any other default. In *Halifax Building Society v Clark*,[6] it was held that the condition would be satisfied only if there was a prospect of all the sums due under the mortgage being paid within a reasonable period, so that if the principal sum secured by the mortgage had become due on default, it was the amount necessary to redeem the mortgage which had to be considered and not merely the arrears. In that case there was no such prospect.[7] The effect of this restrictive interpretation was alleviated by s 8 of the Administration of Justice Act 1973. This provides:

(1) Where by a mortgage of land which consists of or includes a dwelling-house or by any agreement between the mortgagee under such a mortgage and the mortgagor, the mortgagor is entitled or is to be permitted to pay the principal sum secured by instalments or otherwise to defer payment of it in whole or in part, but provision is also made for earlier payment in the event of any default by the mortgagor or of a demand by the mortgagee or otherwise, then for the purposes

---

[6] [1973] Ch 307.
[7] In *First Middlesbrough Trading and Mortgage Co Ltd v Cunningham* (1974) 28 P & CR 69, the Court of Appeal accepted the argument that the entire original mortgage term was the reasonable period for the purposes of s 36.

of s 36 of the Administration of Justice Act 1970 ... a court may treat as due under the mortgage on account of the principal sum secured and of interest on it only such amounts as the mortgagor would have expected to be required to pay if there had been no such provision for earlier payment.

(2) A court shall not exercise by virtue of subsection (1) above the powers conferred by s 36 of the Administration of Justice Act 1970 unless it appears to the court not only that the mortgagor is likely to be able within a reasonable period to pay any amounts regarded (in accordance with subsection (1) above) as due on account of the principal sum secured, together with the interest on those amounts, but also that he is likely to be able by the end of that period to pay any further amounts that he would have expected to be required to pay by then on account of that sum and of interest on it if there had been no such provision as is referred to in subsection (1) above for earlier payment.

Thus under s 8(1) the court may treat as due under the mortgage in respect of principal and interest only such sums as the mortgagor would have expected to be required to pay if there had been no provision for earlier payment, ie only such instalments as are due to date. However, under s 8(2) the court in exercising its discretion under s 36 must have in mind not only the unpaid instalments already due, but also the instalments that will fall due during the 'reasonable period' that is contemplated in s 36(1).

4.2.3 Conditions for application of the sections

The combined effect of the statutory provisions is that the following conditions must therefore be satisfied before the court can exercise its powers under ss 36 and 8:

(1) The subject matter of the mortgage must be 'land which consists of or includes a dwelling-house'.

(2) There must be a provision whereby the mortgagor is entitled or permitted to pay the principal sum by instalments or otherwise to defer payment thereof with a provision for earlier payment in the event of any default by the mortgagor or of a demand by the mortgagee or otherwise. Such provisions must be in the mortgage or in the agreement between the parties.

(3) It must appear to the court that in the event of it exercising the power the mortgagor is likely to be able within a reasonable period to pay any sums due under the mortgage or to remedy a default consisting of a breach of any other obligation arising under or by virtue of the mortgage.

4.2.4 The subject matter of the mortgage must be 'land which consists of or includes a dwelling-house'

The statutory powers only apply if the subject matter of the mortgage is 'land which consists of or includes a dwelling-house'. A 'dwelling-house' 'includes any building or part thereof which is used as a dwelling'.[8] Moreover, 'the fact that part of the premises comprised in a dwelling-house is used as a shop or office or for business, trade or professional purposes shall not prevent the dwelling-house from being a dwelling-house for the purposes of this Part of the Act'.[9] In *Royal Bank of Scotland v Miller*,[10] where the mortgaged property consisted of a night club with a flat above, the Court of Appeal held that if the flat was occupied as a dwelling at the relevant time then s 36 applied. Moreover, it did not matter whether that flat was occupied by the mortgagor or by the manageress of the club even though the mortgage contained a provision prohibiting the mortgagor from parting with possession or sharing possession or occupation of the property. If the property had been occupied by the manageress then this would be a breach of a condition of the mortgage and would amount to default within s 36(1). However, such default would not prevent the property from being a dwelling-house as defined in s 39(1) though it would be relevant in the exercise of the powers given by s 36(2) which may only be exercised if it appears to the court that the mortgagor is likely to be able to remedy the default within a reasonable period.

In *Royal Bank of Scotland v Miller*, Dyson LJ said that 'the time at which the land is required to consist of or include a dwelling-house so as to attract the benefits of the subsection is the time when the mortgagee brings an action in which he claims possession of the mortgaged property.'[11] It was not necessary for the application of the section that the mortgaged property consisted of or included a dwelling-house at the time when the mortgage was granted. As a matter of construction this was the most natural interpretation of the subsection which is couched in the present tense. This interpretation was supported by the purpose of the subsection which is to afford protection to the mortgagors of dwelling-houses from the full rigours of the law as explained in *Birmingham Citizens Permanent Building Society v Caunt*. He said:[12]

In essence the statutory purpose was to afford a degree of protection to a limited class of individuals who were at risk of losing dwelling houses because of default of their obligations under mortgages.

It therefore does not matter that the loan was not advanced in order to acquire domestic property if it included such accommodation at the time when proceedings were commenced.

4.2.5 There must be a provision whereby the mortgagor is entitled or permitted to pay the principal sum by instalments or otherwise to defer payment thereof

The traditional building society mortgage where the loan is repayable by regular instalments, each including an element of principal in addition to the interest

---

[8] Administration of Justice Act 1970, s 39(1).   [9] ibid s 39(2).
[10] [2001] EWCA Civ 344.   [11] ibid para [25].   [12] ibid para [22].

due, clearly falls within the section. The section also applies to an endowment mortgage, under which payment of the principal sum secured is postponed until a date in the future when an insurance policy matures to provide the sum necessary to discharge that principal sum. In *Royal Bank of Scotland v Grimes*,[13] Sir John Arnold P, in the Court of Appeal, said that the court could give 'to the conception of "deferred payment" a definition which includes any case in which there is a stated period before the end of which payment does not require to be made which extends into a defined future'. In *Centrax Trustees Ltd v Ross*,[14] Goulding J held that the section applied to a mortgage which provided for repayment on a date six months after the date of the mortgage because it was apparent from other provisions in the mortgage, in particular the provision for payment of interest, that the mortgagor would be entitled to defer payment of the principal indefinitely beyond the fixed date so long as interest was paid.

On the other hand, in *Habib Bank Ltd v Tailor*,[15] the section was held to be inapplicable to a charge securing an ordinary banking overdraft whereby payment of the principal sum was not due from the borrower until a demand for payment was made. Accordingly, until that time there was no due date from which deferment of payment could be made. Moreover, the charge did not provide for the mortgagor to defer payments of the principal after demand had been made and there was no provision in the charge for payment to be made earlier than the date of demand in the event of default. An order for possession was upheld.[16]

The relationship between the decisions in *Habib* and *Grimes* was recently considered by the Court of Appeal in *Royal Bank of Scotland v Miller*[17] where the mortgage was granted to secure the mortgagor's obligations to the mortgagee bank. At the time the mortgagor had two accounts with the bank, a loan account and a business account. The loan account was in respect of a loan made at the time of the mortgage for the purposes of refurbishing a night club. It was to be repayable from the maturity proceeds of personal equity plans in ten years' time. The Court of Appeal rejected an argument that there was no entitlement to defer within s 8 because the obligation was to repay the loan in ten years' time and there was no deferment of that obligation. Counsel for the bank relied on the statement of Oliver LJ in *Habib* that deferment involved 'the deferment of payment after it has become due'.[18] However, it was pointed out by Dyson LJ that *Habib* had been considered most carefully by the Court of Appeal in *Grimes* and that *Grimes,* which was impossible to distinguish from the case before him, should be followed.[19]

Nevertheless, there must be an 'agreement' to defer payments and 'although it would be appropriate to give that word a wide rather than a narrow meaning,

---

[13] [1985] QB 1179, 1189.   [14] [1979] 2 All ER 952.   [15] [1982] 1 WLR 1218.
[16] See Tromans, 'Mortgages: Possession by Default' [1984] Conv 91.
[17] [2001] EWCA Civ 344, para [25].   [18] [1982] 1 WLR 1218, 1225.
[19] [2001] EWCA Civ 344, paras [41]–[43].

it cannot extend to an arrangement which is not contractually or otherwise legally enforceable'.[20] Where payment is not due until demand and there is no provision for earlier payment, s 8 will not apply simply because the mortgagor is granted an indulgence by the mortgagee. Thus in *Rees Investments Ltd v Groves*[21] where the mortgagee had the right simply to call in the loan and seek possession, the mortgagors failed to comply with the generous terms for payment allowed by the mortgagees. Neuberger J said that it would not only be unfair on the mortgagees if their indulgence conferred rights under s 8 that would not otherwise exist, but it would discourage banks from offering customers such indulgences and thus work to the detriment of borrowers.

4.2.6 It must appear to the court that in the event of it exercising the power, the mortgagor is likely to be able within a reasonable period to pay any sums due under the mortgage or to remedy a default consisting of a breach of any other obligation arising under or by virtue of the mortgage

4.2.6.1 *The sums due under the mortgage*

As noted above s 8 of the Administration of Justice Act 1982 supplemented this part of s 36. First, the court may treat as due under a mortgage only such amounts of principal and interest as the mortgagor would have expected to be required to pay if there had been no provision for earlier payment on default.[22] Secondly, however, the court must not exercise its discretionary powers under s 36 on this basis unless it appears that the mortgagor is likely within a reasonable period to pay not only the sums so treated as due, but also that he is likely to be able by the end of that period to pay any further amounts that he would have expected to be required to pay by then on account of principal and interest if there had been no provision for earlier payment on default.[23] In *First National Bank plc v Syed*,[24] Dillon LJ said:

It cannot be proper, with a view ostensibly to clearing the arrears within a reasonable period, to make an order for payments which the defendants cannot afford and have no foreseeable prospects of being able to afford within a reasonable time. Equally it cannot be proper, under these sections, to make an order for payments which the defendants can afford if those will not be enough to pay off the arrears within a reasonable period and also cover the current instalments.

4.2.6.2 *The absence of default*

The implication would seem to be that if there are no arrears or the arrears have been cleared then s 36 does not apply and the court has no power to suspend an order for possession in the absence of any other breach of obligation under the

---

[20] *Per* Neuberger J in *Rees Investments Ltd v Groves* (Ch D, 27 June 2001). The court expressly did not go into the question of any estoppel that might arise. [21] ibid.
[22] Section 8(1).
[23] Section 8(2). See *Abbey National Mortgages plc v Bernard* (1995) 71 P & CR 257, 262, *per* Peter Gibson LJ. [24] [1991] 2 All ER 250, 255.

mortgage. This question was considered in *Western Bank Ltd v Schindler*[25] where the terms of the mortgage as drafted were unusual. Under the terms of the legal charge dated 4 January 1973 the mortgagor was under no obligation to pay any interest until the contractual date for repayment of the principal sum which was 4 January 1983 when interest would be payable on the principal sum from the date of the legal charge. The mortgagor allowed a life policy taken as collateral security to lapse, but there had been no default under the mortgage and there was no sum due. The mortgagee sought possession of the mortgaged property and the Court of Appeal had to consider the applicability of s 36. Buckley and Scarman LJJ held that s 36 was applicable. Buckley LJ said:[26]

> If sub-s. (1) is read literally, the conditional clause introduced by the words "if it appears to the court" (which I shall refer to as the "conditional clause") appears to restrict the operation of the section to cases in which some sum is due or some default has taken place and remains unremedied when the application comes before the court. This, however, seems to me to lead to a ridiculous result.

A defaulting mortgagor would be in a better position than one not in default. Parliament could not have intended such an irrational and unfair result and he sought an alternative construction. On the true construction of the section it applies to any case in which a mortgagee seeks possession, whether the mortgagor be in arrears or otherwise in default under the mortgage or not, but, where the mortgagor is in arrears or in default, the discretion is limited by the conditional clause. On the facts the judge had correctly exercised the discretion which he had to make an order for possession having regard to all the circumstances. In particular he was fully entitled to take into account that as a result of the failure of the collateral security provided by the policy charge, the debt was almost certainly inadequately secured. Goff LJ, dissenting, took the view that s 36 does not apply where there is no default. The anomalies and absurdities said to flow from the literal construction might be more apparent than real because of the equitable liability to account on the footing of wilful default. Where there has been no default or any default has been remedied, the mortgagee will not ordinarily be in a position to exercise any power of sale and, therefore, will generally not wish to obtain possession.[27] The order for possession was upheld by all three members of the Court of Appeal and it was therefore unnecessary to decide what would have been the appropriate period of postponement.[28]

4.2.7 The exercise of the discretionary powers

The circumstances in which the court can exercise its discretionary powers under s 36 to adjourn proceedings, stay or suspend execution of a judgment or

---

[25] [1977] Ch 1.   [26] ibid 12.   [27] ibid 26.
[28] Buckley LJ had a preference for the full length of the mortgage and this is supported by *Cheltenham & Gloucester Building Society v Norgan* [1996] 1 All ER 449.

order, or postpone the date for delivery of possession, are therefore limited. Any such adjournment, stay, suspension or postponement under s 36 may be made subject to such conditions with regard to payment by the mortgagor of any sums secured by the mortgage or the remedying of any default as the court thinks fit.[29]

Deferment of an order for possession is likely to be sought with a view to the mortgagor remaining in possession indefinitely on the basis of clearing the arrears or otherwise remedying any default under the mortgage. It may alternatively be sought so as to enable the mortgagor to sell the property.

4.2.8 Postponing an order for possession to enable arrears to be cleared

The court may defer the delivery of possession 'for such period or periods as the court thinks reasonable'. The statutory provisions do not give any guidance as to what should be regarded as a 'reasonable period' for the purpose of clearing the arrears. Although there were early indications that the period of the mortgage should be regarded as a reasonable period,[30] in practice a much shorter period was allowed for payments to be brought up to date.[31] However, in *Cheltenham & Gloucester Building Society v Norgan,* the Court of Appeal adopted 'the full term of the mortgage as the starting point for calculating a "reasonable period" for payment of arrears'.[32] Although he would not go quite so far as to say that it should be an 'assumption' Waite LJ said:[33]

... the logic and spirit of the legislation require, especially in cases where the parties are proceeding under arrangements such as those reflected in the CML statement, that the court should take as its starting point the full term of the mortgage and pose at the outset the question: would it be possible for the mortgagor to maintain payment-off of the arrears by instalments over that period?

Not only would such an approach be consistent with the policy declared by the Council of Mortgage Lenders,[34] but it would avoid the disadvantages which both lender and borrower are liable to suffer, especially in the matter of costs,

---

[29] Subsection (3) The court may from time to time vary or revoke any conditions imposed: subs (4).
[30] See *First Middlesbrough Trading and Mortgage Co Ltd v Cunningham* (1974) 28 P & CR 69, CA.
[31] See Supreme Court Practice (1995) Vol 1, para 88/5/9.
[32] [1996] 1 All ER 449, 459, *per* Waite LJ.   [33] ibid 458.
[34] Evans LJ (462) said that the Council of Mortgage Lenders statement showed that mortgage lenders have a number of options available to them when payments are in arrears. They include even extending the term of the loan as well as deferring payments of interest and capitalising the interest payments which are in arrears. He also referred to clause 10 which read:

'Possession 10. Lenders seek to take possession only as a last resort. They are in business to help people to buy homes, not to take homes away from them. ...'

Given those statements of policy it could not be said that it was not appropriate to take account of the whole of the remaining part of the original term when assessing a 'reasonable period' for the payment of arrears. In determining a 'reasonable period' the statement of the Council of Mortgage Lenders became 'directly relevant' (461).

if frequent attendance before the court is necessary as a result of multiple applications under s 36. Moreover, by taking the period most favourable to the borrower, if his or her hopes of repayment prove to be ill-founded and the new instalments initially ordered as a condition of suspension are not maintained, but themselves fall into arrears, the mortgagee can be heard with justice to say that the mortgagor has had his chance. The powers of the court under s 36, although in theory capable of being exercised again and again, 'should not be employed repeatedly to compel a lending institution which has already suffered interruption of the regular flow of interest to which it was entitled under the express terms of the mortgage, to accept assurances of future payment from a borrower in whom it has lost confidence'.[35]

Evans LJ provided a helpful summary of the judgments as a guide in future cases. He said that the following considerations are likely to be relevant:[36]

(a) How much can the borrower reasonably afford to pay, both now and in the future?
(b) If the borrower has a temporary difficulty in meeting his obligations, how long is the difficulty likely to last?
(c) What was the reason for the arrears which have accumulated?
(d) How much remains of the original term?
(e) What are the relevant contractual terms, and what type of mortgage is it, ie when is the principal due to be repaid?
(f) Is it a case where the court should exercise its power to disregard accelerated payment provisions (s 8 of the 1973 Act)?
(g) Is it reasonable to expect the lender, in the circumstances of the particular case, to recoup the arrears of interest
  (1) over the whole of the original term, or
  (2) within a shorter period, or even
  (3) within a longer period, ie by extending the repayment period?
  Is it reasonable to expect the lender to capitalize the interest, or not?
(h) Are there any reasons affecting the security which should influence the length of the period for payment?

'In the light of the answers to the above, the court can proceed to exercise its overall discretion, taking account also of any further factors which may arise in the particular case.'

Waite LJ acknowledged that the approach adopted by the court would 'be liable to demand a more detailed analysis of present figures and future projections than it may have been customary for the courts to undertake'. In particular, 'there is likely to be a greater need to require of mortgagors that they should furnish the court with a detailed "budget", of the kind that' had been provided in that case. It may also be necessary to provide detailed evidence,

---

[35] [1996] 1 All ER 449, 459–60, *per* Waite LJ.   [36] ibid 463.

if necessary by experts, 'to see if and when the lender's security will become liable to be put at risk as a result of imposing postponement of payments in arrear'.[37]

Problems in relation to mortgage payments often coincide with matrimonial difficulties so it may also be appropriate for the court to consider the impact or potential impact which orders for financial provision may have on the ability to pay sums due under the mortgage of the matrimonial home. It will also be relevant to take into account assistance that may be available by way of income support when the court is determining whether the mortgagor is likely, within a reasonable period, to pay the sums due under the mortgage.

4.2.9 Assistance by way of income support

A person entitled to income support may receive assistance with the payment of interest due under a loan, whether secured or unsecured, taken out to buy the property or an interest in the property normally occupied as a home by the claimant.[38] Assistance is also available in respect of interest on a loan taken out for repairs and improvements to the home. Where only part of the loan has been used for a qualifying purpose assistance will only be given for a proportionate part of the interest.[39] A spouse or cohabitant of a mortgagor may obtain assistance where the mortgagor is failing to make payments of interest due under the mortgage. No assistance is available in respect of instalments of capital or premiums payable in respect of an endowment policy assigned to the mortgagee.

The fact that a mortgagor is receiving such assistance with interest payments will be relevant when the court is determining whether he is likely, within a 'reasonable period', to be able to pay the sums due under the mortgage. However, there are restrictions on the amount of interest in respect of which assistance can be given.[40] First, assistance is only available in relation to interest on eligible loans to the extent that they do not in the aggregate exceed a certain figure which is currently £100,000.[41] Secondly, interest will be payable only at the standard Department of Social Security rate of interest applicable at the time and will not be met immediately on a claim for income support being made.[42]

---

[37] [1996] 1 All ER 449, 459.

[38] See Income Support (General Regulations) 1987 (SI 1987/1967), Sch 3 as substituted by Social Security (Income Support and Claims and Payments) Amendment Regulations 1995 (1995/1613), reg 2 and Sch 1.

[39] As occurred, e.g. in *Cheltenham & Gloucester Building Society v Grant* (1994) 26 HLR 703.

[40] See *Town & Country Building Society v Julien* (1991) 24 HLR 312 where the mortgagor failed to show that he was likely to be able to pay the sums due under a mortgage securing a loan of £630,000. It had been determined that he was entitled to income support only on the basis of the cost of suitable alternative accommodation at £110,000 and not on the full amount of the mortgage.

[41] SI 1987/1967, Sch 3, para 11 as substituted by SI 1995/1613.

[42] SI 1987/1967, Sch, 3 para 12 as substituted by SI 1995/1613 as amended by Income Support (General) (Standard Interest Rate Amendment)(No 2) Regulations 2004 (SI 2004/440). This is now 5.33%.

A distinction is drawn between 'existing' housing costs and 'new' housing costs. Mortgage interest will come within 'existing' housing costs if the mortgage agreement was entered into before 2 October 1995. Mortgage interest will come within 'new' housing costs if entered into on or after that date except that in limited circumstances a re-mortgage of the same property on or after that date will be regarded as 'existing' housing costs. In the case of 'existing' housing costs, no assistance will be given in relation to mortgage interest for the first eight weeks. After that period assistance will be given for 50 percent of the eligible mortgage interest for the next eighteen weeks and assistance at 100 percent will be given only after twenty-six weeks. In the case of 'new' housing costs no assistance will be given for mortgage interest for the first thirty-nine weeks after which assistance will be given in respect of 100 percent of the eligible mortgage interest.[43] The amount of mortgage interest eligible for relief may also be restricted where the property occupied as the home is larger than is required by the mortgagor and his family having regard to suitable alternative accommodation.[44]

4.2.10 Postponing an order for possession to enable the mortgagor to sell the property

A mortgagor who has no prospect of discharging arrears due under a mortgage by instalments may propose to repay all sums due under the mortgage by a sale of the mortgaged property. A postponement to enable the mortgagor to effect such a sale is permissible and may be desirable as a sale by a mortgagor in possession is likely to realise more than a sale by a mortgagee. In *Royal Trust Co v Markham*, Sir John Pennycuick said:[45]

A mortgagor may well be in a position, by selling his property, to discharge all sums due under the mortgage and produce a surplus for himself. If he has a purchaser immediately in view, still more if he has signed a contract for sale, then the condition seems to me to be plainly satisfied, and I cannot see any reason in principle why that method of satisfying the condition should be treated as repugnant to the scheme of the section. On the contrary, it might be a personal hardship to a mortgagor if he were to be ousted from possession during the short period before the completion of a contemplated sale. Again, it might be a great financial hardship to him if the sale went off, since that might seriously affect the balance that would come to him in respect of the equity of redemption.

It seems that a lengthy postponement for the purpose of effecting a sale was not envisaged and it was clearly established that postponement must be for a defined period.[46]

---

[43] SI 1987/1967, Sch 3 as substituted by SI 1995/1613.
[44] SI 1987/1967, Sch 3 as substituted by SI 1995/1613, para 13 dealing with 'Excessive Housing Costs'. See *Town & Country Building Society v Julien* (1991) 24 HLR 312 mentioned above.
[45] [1975] 1 WLR 1416, 1422.   [46] ibid 1421–2.

In determining a reasonable period for postponement of an order for possession for this purpose the starting point will not be the remaining term of the mortgage.[47] It will be for the court to determine what is a reasonable period of postponement in the circumstances of the case. In particular the court will be concerned first with the prospects for the sale of the mortgaged property and the length of the period necessary to effect a sale. In *Target Home Loans Ltd v Clothier*,[48] Nolan LJ, after concluding that there was no way in which the mortgagor was going to meet his mortgage commitments except by a sale, said:

> That leads to the question: is there a prospect of an early sale? If so is it better in the interests of all concerned for that to be effected by [the mortgagors] or by the mortgage company? If the view is that the prospects of an early sale for the mortgagees as well as for [the mortgagors] are best served by deferring an order for possession, then it seems to me that that is a solid reason for making such an order *but the deferment should be short*.

It is also relevant that there has already been considerable delay in realizing a sale of the property. In *Target Home Loans Ltd v Clothier*, as a result of the order of the court below, the mortgagor had already had the benefit of three and a half months in which to sell part of the mortgaged property. The Court of Appeal made an order for possession in three months' time and Nolan LJ said that in his view, in the light of the circumstances of the case, there should be no further deferment.

Although generally in the case of the sale of mortgaged property an adjournment or suspension will be allowed only if a sale will take place within a short period of time, there is no absolute rule to this effect. In *National & Provincial Building Society v Lloyd*,[49] Neill LJ said that if there is clear evidence that the completion of the sale of a property, perhaps by piecemeal disposal, could take place in six or nine months or even a year, there is no reason why a court could not come to the conclusion in the exercise of its discretion under the two sections that the mortgagor was likely to be able within a reasonable period to pay any sums due under the mortgage.[50] The question of a 'reasonable period' would be a question for the court in the individual case. In that case, however, the Court of Appeal concluded that there was insufficient evidence about the sale of the remaining property comprised in the mortgage to justify the conclusion that the mortgagor was likely within a reasonable period to pay the sums due under the mortgage.

The court will also need to be assured that the mortgaged property provides adequate security for the debt. Since the sale of the mortgaged property will remove the mortgagee's security it is essential that the proceeds of sale will be sufficient to clear not only the arrears but also the principal sum secured and

---

[47] See Auld LJ in *Bristol & West Building Society v Ellis* (1996) 29 HLR 282, 286–7.

[48] [1994] 1 All ER 439, 447. Italics added.   [49] [1996] 1 All ER 630, 638.

[50] In *Bristol & West Building Society v Ellis* (1996) 29 HLR 282, 287, Auld LJ said that whilst a period of one year might be a likely maximum in many cases he did not read the words of Neill LJ as establishing it as a rule of law or as a matter of general guidance.

interest accruing until sale.[51] In *National & Provincial Building Society v Lloyd*,[52] where the loan agreement had allowed for partial redemption of the mortgage if the mortgagor sought to dispose of part of the mortgaged property, the court was not satisfied on the available evidence regarding the possible sale of remaining parts of the mortgaged property that the mortgagor would within a reasonable period be able to discharge the sums due under the mortgage.

Even if the power to suspend execution under s 36 cannot be exercised because it is unlikely that the borrower can repay the arrears within a reasonable period the court had a residual jurisdiction, but a strictly limited one, to postpone the giving of possession for a short period in order to enable the property to be sold by the mortgagor.[53] In *Cheltenham & Gloucester plc v Booker*,[54] the Court of Appeal held that there was, in theory at least, a similar jurisdiction to defer the giving of possession for a short time in order to enable the property to be sold by the mortgagee. Millett LJ said that there was no reason in principle why the court should accede to a mortgagee's insistence that immediate possession prior to the sale should be given to him if the court was satisfied:

(a) that possession will not be required by the mortgagee pending completion of the sale but only by the purchasers on completion;
(b) that the presence of the mortgagor pending completion will enhance, or at least not depress, the sale price;
(c) that the mortgagor will co-operate in the sale by showing prospective purchasers around the property and so forth; and
(d) that he will give possession to the purchaser on completion.

However, he emphasized that while the jurisdiction existed, experience showed that those conditions were seldom likely to be satisfied. It should be sparingly and cautiously exercised for there is an inherent illogicality in entrusting conduct of the sale to the mortgagee and yet leaving the mortgagor in possession pending completion unless the mortgagee has agreed to this course. Those conditions were not satisfied in that case.

A stay or suspension to enable a mortgagor in possession to sell part only of the mortgaged property may be appropriate if the proceeds will be sufficient to discharge the mortgage debt.[55]

---

[51] [1996] 1 All ER 630, 635 and 639, *per* Neill LJ. See also Browne LJ in *Royal Trust Co of Canada v Markham* [1975] 1 WLR 1416, 1423. [52] ibid 639–40.

[53] *Per* Millett L.J. in *Cheltenham & Gloucester plc v Booker* (1996) 73 P & CR 412, 415 referring to Russell J in *Birmingham Citizens Permanent Building Society v Caunt* [1962] 1 Ch 883, 912 and Sir John Pennycuick V-C in *Royal Trust Co of Canada v Markham* [1975] 1 WLR 1416, 1420.

[54] (1996) 73 P & CR 412, 415–16.

[55] See Hart J in *Barclays Bank plc v Alcorn* [2002] EWHC 498 (Ch) although in that case it was not appropriate. See also *National & Provincial Building Society v Lloyd*, mentioned above, where a piecemeal disposal of the mortgaged property was envisaged.

4.2.11 Postponing possession when the mortgagor has a cross-claim

In proceedings for possession a mortgagee's right to possession will not be defeated by a cross-claim of the mortgagor in the absence of some contractual or statutory provision to the contrary.[56] This follows from the established rule that a mortgagee is entitled to possession at any time after the mortgage is executed except in so far as his rights are limited by contract or statute.[57] In *National Westminster Bank plc v Skelton*[58] Slade LJ said that the 'principle is applicable both where the cross-claim is a mere counterclaim and where there is a cross-claim for unliquidated damages which, if established, would give rise to a right by way of equitable set-off'. In the case of a counter-claim it makes no difference that the claim is liquidated and in excess of the mortgage arrears. Slade LJ left open the case where a mortgagor establishes that he has a claim to a quantified sum by way of equitable set-off. He said: 'Possibly such a claim might have the effect of actually discharging the mortgage debt.'[59] The principle is the same even where the mortgagor is only a guarantor and not the principal debtor.[60]

However, in the case of a mortgage of a dwelling-house it may be appropriate to grant a stay under s 36 pending trial of a cross-claim to a set-off if the existence and prospects of success of the claim could, 'in all the circumstances, be regarded as enabling the sums due to be paid within a reasonable time'.[61] In *Ashley Guarantee plc v Zacaria*,[62] the defendant mortgagors had charged a dwelling-house as security for money due from a trading company. Their defence to a claim for possession was that the company had cross-claims against the mortgagee which gave it an equitable right of set-off for an unliquidated sum exceeding the amount due and that they had a counter-claim for rectification of the legal charge so as to limit their liability to £50,000 being considerably less

---

[56] *Mobil Oil Co Ltd v Rawlinson* (1981) 43 P & CR 221; *Ashley Guarantee plc v Zacaria* [1993] 1 WLR 62; *National Westminster Bank plc v Skelton (Note)* [1993] 1 WLR 72; *Midland Bank plc v McGrath* [1996] EGCS 61, CA. In *Skelton* (77) Slade LJ stressed that the claim was simply for possession and not payment. 'Protection by contract will only be afforded by clear terms either expressly formulated or to be implied' *per* Anthony Lincoln J in *Skelton* (82). In *Zacaria*, Ralph Gibson LJ thought that possibly, in a particular case an implied term could be held to have arisen which would exclude the immediate right to possession, but it was 'obvious' that there were difficulties against such an implication in most ordinary cases and no such term was alleged in that case (70–1).

[57] See Ralph Gibson LJ in *Ashley Guarantee plc v Zacaria* [1993] 1 WLR 62, 70. He noted that in *National Westminster Bank plc v Skelton* [1993] 1 WLR 72, 77 Slade LJ had stressed that the court was concerned with a claim for possession and not payment.   [58] [1993] 1 WLR 72, 78.

[59] In *Ashley Guarantee plc v Zacaria* [1993] 1 WLR 62, 66, Nourse LJ said that was not a question that arose for decision. The mortgagors had not established that the aggregate value of the cross claims came anywhere near the amount of the principal debtor's indebtedness to the mortgagee. The principal debtor was therefore in default under the mortgage.

[60] See *Ashley Guarantee plc v Zacaria* [1993] 1 WLR 62.

[61] *Per* Ralph Gibson LJ in *Ashley Guarantee plc v Zacaria* [1993] 1 WLR 62, 71.

[62] [1993] 1 WLR 62.

than the sum due. The Court of Appeal held that these cross-claims did not prevent an order for possession being made, but Woolf LJ thought that the judge to whom the case was remitted to consider the effect of s 36 might well regard the claim for rectification which had not been adjudicated upon 'as being a matter of materiality'.[63] In the earlier case of *Citibank Trust Ltd v Ayivor*[64] a counter-claim for damages on the basis that the mortgagee had misled the mortgagors into supposing that the property was free from damp and rot did not prevent an order for possession being made. In relation to s 36, Mervyn Davies J said that he did not feel able to say that the existence of the counter-claim meant that the defendants were likely 'to be able within a reasonable period' to pay off the arrears. He said: 'Even if I assume that the defendants' prospects of success on the counterclaim are good that does not justify me in concluding that the defendants are likely soon to reduce the arrears by paying over any damages they may recover.'[65]

4.2.12 Evidence

Whether the mortgagor is 'likely' to be able within a reasonable period to pay any sums due under the mortgage is a question of fact to be determined by the judge on the evidence before him. If there is no such evidence as was the case in *Royal Trust Co of Canada v Markham*, then the court cannot exercise its powers under s 36.[66] Moreover, as noted above the approach adopted by the Court of Appeal in *Cheltenham & Gloucester Building Society v Norgan* means that more detailed information about the mortgagor's financial position will be necessary.[67] However, it is not always necessary for the mortgagor to provide such information by affidavit or on oath. In *Cheltenham & Gloucester Building Society v Grant*, Nourse LJ said that it was not the function of the Court of Appeal 'to lay down rigid rules as to how busy district and county court judges should satisfy themselves of what they have to be satisfied for the purposes of sections 36 and 8'.[68] Clearly, it would sometimes be prudent for the mortgagor to put in an affidavit before the hearing. If the material placed before the court by the mortgagor is challenged by the mortgagee, the proper course is for the mortgagee to put the mortgagor to proof and, if need be, to seek an adjournment so that the defendant's evidence can be tested in cross-examination.[69] In that case no point on the absence of sworn evidence by the mortgagor had been taken by the mortgagee either before the district judge or before the judge on appeal from her decision and the Court of Appeal refused to interfere with judge's exercise of discretion.

Where a postponement of possession is sought to enable the mortgaged property to be sold, the importance of ensuring that the mortgaged property

---

[63] [1993] 1 WLR 71, *per* Woolf LJ.   [64] [1987] 1 WLR 1157, 1164.   [65] ibid 1164.
[66] [1975] 1 WLR 1416, 1422.   [67] See para 4.2.8 above.
[68] (1994) 26 HLR 703, 707.   [69] ibid 709, *per* Wall J.

will continue to provide adequate security means that the court should approach estate agents' estimates of sale prices with 'reserve'.[70] If there is disagreement or uncertainty about the valuation of the mortgaged property then an independent valuation may be desirable.

4.2.13 The powers of the court

The court is given a variety of powers to allow a mortgagor a reasonable period to pay the sums due under the mortgage or remedy any other default. Thus apart from the power to adjourn proceedings, under s 36(2)(b) the court may on giving judgment, or making an order, for delivery of possession of the mortgaged property, or at any time before the execution of such judgment or order, (i) stay or suspend execution of the judgment or order, or (ii) postpone the date for delivery of possession, for such period or periods as the court thinks reasonable. While these powers will cease once a warrant for possession has been executed,[71] it is not clear whether they will cease on commencement of the process of execution.

Where the court makes an order for possession, but postpones the date for delivery of possession or stays or suspends such an order, the postponement must be for a definite period. There is no power to make an indefinite suspension.[72] The court must be satisfied that the mortgagor is likely to be able by the end of the period of suspension to pay the amount that he would have expected to be required to pay during that period. Unless a definite period is fixed it will be impossible for the court to form any view on this point.[73]

Where the mortgagor seeks time to sell off part only of the mortgaged property in order to satisfy the mortgage debt, any stay or suspension will relate to the whole property. Section 36 does not enable the court to grant a stay or suspension in relation to part only of the property so as to allow the mortgagor to remain in possession of the remainder.[74]

---

[70] *Per* Auld LJ in *Bristol & West Building Society v Ellis* (1996) 29 HLR 282, 288 referring to Nolan LJ in *Target Home Loans Ltd v Clothier* [1994] 1 All ER 439, 445.

[71] *National Provincial Building Society v Ahmed* [1995] 38 EG 138, CA; *Cheltenham & Gloucester Building Society v Obi* (1996) 28 HLR 22, CA. Unless the order itself is set aside or the warrant had been obtained by fraud or there had been an abuse of process or oppression in its execution. See *Hammersmith & Fulham LBC v Hill* [1994] 2 EGLR 51 and *Leicester City Council v Aldwinckle* (1991) 24 HLR 40.

[72] *Royal Trust Co of Canada v Markham* [1975] 1 WLR 1416, 1421–2.

[73] ibid 1423, *per* Browne LJ. However, in *Western Bank Ltd v Schindler* [1976] 2 All ER 393, 400 in relation to a case where there was no sum due or other subsisting default, Buckley LJ 'did not dissent from the view that the court could, if it thought it reasonable to do so, grant an adjournment, suspension or postponement for an indefinite period . . . with liberty to apply'.

[74] See Hart J in *Barclays Bank plc v Alcorn* [2002] EWHC 498 (Ch). In that case there was the added complication that the mortgagors had given up possession of part of the property and sought a stay in relation to the remainder while the property was sold by one of the mortgagors. See McMurtry [2002] Conv 594.

Where there are two mortgagors it is not in general right for the court to make an order requiring one of the mortgagors to leave within a period during which the other mortgagor is in possession and entitled to be in possession. This is particularly so where the mortgagors are husband and wife and share the home as such.[75]

Any adjournment, stay, suspension or postponement under s 36 may be made subject to such conditions with regard to payment by the mortgagor of any sums secured by the mortgage or the remedying of any default as the court thinks fit.[76] The court may from time to time vary or revoke any such condition.[77] Where an order for possession is suspended on condition that arrears are paid as provided in the order, this is not strictly an order for payment of the arrears. The mortgagee may also seek judgment for sums due under the mortgage. In that case the money judgment should generally be suspended on the same terms as, and in line with, the suspension of the possession order.[78]

4.2.14 Possession without a court order

A mortgagee, or a person acting on his behalf, who obtains, or seeks to obtain, possession of mortgaged property without first obtaining a court order will be guilty of a criminal offence if he uses or threatens violence in order to secure entry knowing that there is someone present on the premises at the time who is opposed to the entry which the violence is intended to secure.[79] However, no offence will be committed if the property is unoccupied and the mortgagee takes possession without a court order. Moreover, if the mortgagee is able to obtain possession in this way without a court order then the mortgagor will not have the benefit of the protection afforded by s 36. This conclusion was reached in *Ropaigealach v Barclays Bank plc*[80] where the Court of Appeal rejected the submission that a court order was necessary in every instance. Chadwick LJ said:[81]

I find it impossible to be satisfied that Parliament must have intended, when enacting section 36 of the Act of 1970, that the mortgagee's common law right to take possession by virtue of his estate should only be exercisable with the assistance of the court.

---

[75] *Albany Home Loans Ltd v Massey* (1997) 73 P & CR 509, 513, *per* Schiemann LJ. In that case the mortgagees proffered an undertaking not to enforce the order against the husband until an order for possession was made against the wife and became enforceable or she vacated voluntarily. On this basis the order for possession against the husband was upheld. In the absence of such an undertaking an adjournment would have been appropriate. [76] Section 36(3).
[77] Section 36(4).   [78] See further para 4.4 below.
[79] Criminal Law Act 1977, s 6(1). The fact that a person has any interest in or right to possession or occupation of any premises will not for this purpose constitute lawful authority for the use or threat of violence by him or anyone else for the purpose of securing his entry onto those premises (subs (2)).
[80] [1998] EWCA Civ 1960. It seems that the mortgagors were not living at the property which was 'undergoing repair or refurbishment' and for that purpose was empty. The Court of Appeal approached the question of the applicability of s 36 on the basis that the mortgagee had gone into possession though that question of fact had not been resolved.   [81] ibid para [41].

This conclusion was reached with reluctance in view of its restriction on the applicability of s 36.[82] It also had implications if a mortgagee chose to exercise the power of sale without first obtaining possession.[83]

4.3 SALE

4.3.1 The power of sale

Although a mortgagee will generally seek an order of the court for possession of the mortgaged property as a preliminary to a sale, no court order is necessary in order to carry out the actual sale. Where the mortgage is made by deed, the mortgagee has an implied statutory power, when the mortgage money has become due, to sell, or to concur with any other person in selling, the mortgaged property to the like extent as if they had been conferred by the mortgage deed.[84] In practice the mortgage deed will usually have conferred on the mortgagee an express power of sale to supersede the statutory power. It is also usual for the mortgage deed to provide that for the purposes of s 101 the mortgage money is to become due after a fixed period, which is often six months. Section 103 provides that a mortgagee must not exercise the power of sale conferred by s 101 unless and until:

(i) Notice requiring payment of the mortgage money has been served on the mortgagor or one of two or more mortgagors, and default has been made in payment of the mortgage money, or of part thereof, for three months after such service; or

(ii) Some interest under the mortgage is in arrear and unpaid for two months after becoming due; or

(iii) There has been a breach of some provision contained in the mortgage deed or in this Act, or in an enactment replaced by this Act, and on the part of the mortgagor, or of some person concurring in making the mortgage, to be observed or performed, other than and besides a covenant for payment of the mortgage money or interest thereon.

A purchaser from the mortgagee must ensure that the mortgagee's power of sale under s 101 has arisen, but is not under any obligation to investigate whether the sale is authorized under s 103.[85] After the property has been conveyed by the mortgagee to the purchaser, s 104(2) provides that the latter is protected against any irregularity. Thus while a mortgagor can seek to prevent an unauthorized

---

[82] *Per* Clarke LJ. Henry LJ said: 'This anomaly and this problem are not identified for the first time in the present case.' They had been the subject of academic comment in the past and were considered by the Law Commission in the Working Paper PWP No 99 and the Report, Law Com No 271.   [83] See further para 4.3.2 below.

[84] Law of Property Act 1925, s 101.   [85] ibid s 104(2).

sale before it has been completed, once there has been a conveyance of the mortgaged property to the purchaser the mortgagor must look to the mortgagee for compensation for any loss suffered as a result of an unauthorized sale. However, a purchaser will not be protected if he or she was aware of any facts showing that the power of sale had not become exercisable or there was some impropriety in the sale.[86]

A mortgagee exercising the statutory power of sale has power, by deed, to convey the property sold, for such estate and interest therein as it is by the Law of Property Act authorized to sell or convey or may be the subject of the mortgage, freed from all estates, interests, and rights to which the mortgage has priority, but subject to all estates, interests, and rights which have priority to the mortgage.[87] If there is more than one mortgage affecting the property then each mortgagee has the power of sale, though, of course. a sale will be subject to any prior mortgage.

4.3.2 Sale without an order for possession

Although a mortgagee will usually seek an order for possession prior to effecting a sale with vacant possession, it is possible, though not very likely, for the mortgagee to exercise the power of sale even though it has not (or could not) obtain an order for possession. In this event the protection afforded by s 36 of the Administration of Justice Act would be rendered ineffective as it applies only to orders for possession.[88] In *National Provincial Building Society v Ahmed*,[89] the Court of Appeal confirmed that the mortgagor's equity of redemption is extinguished by the exchange of contracts of sale of the mortgaged property by the mortgagee to a purchaser. In that case there had been an order for possession which had been executed and there was therefore no longer any power under s 36. However, Millett LJ said that

if the order for possession had not been executed so that the court still retained jurisdiction to suspend it, *and the mortgagor or his tenants were in possession at the date of the contract for sale so that the purchaser had notice of the mortgagor's rights, the mortgagee* would be unable to rely upon the contract to defeat the mortgagor's application.[90]

That was not the position in that case. Nevertheless, in *Ropaigealach v Barclays Bank plc*,[91] where the mortgagee had been able to obtain possession without

---

[86] Crossman J in *Waring v London and Manchester Assurance Co. Ltd* [1935] Ch 311, 318. In relation to registered land see also Land Registration Act 2002, s 52.

[87] Law of Property Act 1925, s 104(1).

[88] This view was taken by the Law Commission in Law Com. Working Paper No 99, Land Mortgages, 3.69 where it was said that since 'such a sale terminates the mortgagor's interest in the property, the purchaser presumably would have no difficulty in obtaining a possession order against the mortgagor after completion'. See also Haley, 'Mortgage Default: Possession, Relief and Judicial Discretion' (1997) 17 JLS 483, 489.   [89] [1995] 38 EG 138.

[90] ibid 140. Italics added.   [91] [1998] EWCA Civ 1960.

a court order, Clarke LJ said that while the view of Millett LJ expressed in the italicized words was undoubtedly desirable, it was not easy to see how it worked if the effect of the contract for sale is to extinguish the mortgagor's equity of redemption.[92] The question did not fall for determination in that case so that doubt continues to exist.

4.4 MONEY JUDGMENT

4.4.1 The right to obtain a money judgment

A mortgagee is entitled to exercise all his remedies concurrently so that when the court makes an order for possession then he is also entitled in principle to a judgment for the sum of money due and payable under the terms of the mortgage. He cannot, in respect of the money claim be in a worse position than if he had lent unsecured.[93] If default on an instalment mortgage has resulted in the whole advance becoming immediately repayable, then that is the amount for which he is entitled to judgment. A money judgment may be important if the proceeds of sale of the property following repossession are insufficient to clear the mortgage debt in full. In such circumstances 'the mortgagee will be able to proceed against the borrower without delay and without the need for coming back before the court'.[94]

However, where the court has made an order for possession suspended under s 36(2) of the Administration of Justice Act 1970, the money judgment should also normally be suspended for so long as the possession order is suspended. The court has power under s 71(2) of the County Courts Act 1984 to suspend or stay any judgment for such time and on such terms as the court thinks fit, if it appears to the satisfaction of the court that a party to any proceedings is unable from any cause to pay any sum recovered against him or any instalment of such a sum.[95] The discretion under s 71(2) should be exercised consistently with the exercise of the discretion under s 36 of the 1970 Act and s 8 of the 1973 Act. 'In the normal way, therefore, the money judgment would be suspended for so long as the possession order is suspended. In adopting that course, the Judge would not be contravening or frustrating the legislative purpose enshrined in section 8.'[96]

---

[92] Counsel for the borrower submitted that in the case of a sale the court would have the same power to prevent the purchaser from actually taking possession as it has to prevent the mortgagee himself from taking possession because by s 39(1) of the 1970 Act 'mortgagee' includes 'any person deriving title under the original...mortgagee'.

[93] *Per* Hoffman LJ in *Cheltenham & Gloucester Building Society v Grattidge* (1993) 25 HLR 454, 457–8.   [94] ibid 457, *per* Hoffman LJ.

[95] A similar discretion in relation to execution is conferred by s 88.

[96] *Per* Lloyd LJ in *Cheltenham & Gloucester Building Society v Grattidge* (1993) 25 HLR 454, 457–8. The decision in *Grattidge* was followed in *Cheltenham & Gloucester Building Society v Johnson* (1996) 73 P & CR 293. See also Nourse LJ in *Cheltenham & Gloucester Building Society v Grant* (1994) 26 HLR 703, 708.

In *Cheltenham & Gloucester Building Society v Grattidge*, Hoffman LJ emphasized that the two statutory discretions are separate and there might well be cases in which it would be proper to exercise them differently. It was not necessary for the purposes of that case to speculate on what such cases might be.[97]

4.4.2 Limitation on recovery of shortfall

When a sale by a mortgagee who has obtained possession of the mortgaged property fails to produce a sum that is sufficient to discharge the mortgage debt, it may not be worthwhile for the mortgagee to take action to recover the shortfall immediately. It may be necessary to wait until the mortgagor's financial position improves, but in the meantime the shortfall is likely to increase significantly in view of the interest which will continue to accrue on the outstanding debt.[98] Moreover the mortgagee's rights of action may become barred under the Limitation Act 1980.

The right to sue for the mortgage debt will have arisen on the date specified in the mortgage deed. This will commonly be when there has been default by the mortgagor in the payment of a specified number of instalments. In *Bristol & West plc v Bartlett*,[99] the Court of Appeal held that in other than exceptional cases (which the court could not then envisage) claims for a mortgage debt will be governed by s 20 of the 1980 Act even though the mortgagee has exercised its power of sale before issuing proceedings. This means that the mortgagee has twelve years from the accrual of the cause of action to sue for the principal of the debt,[100] but only six years to sue for interest.[101]

4.4.3 Appropriation to interest or capital

Since different limitation periods apply to capital on the one hand and interest on the other hand, it is important to establish whether sums received by the

---

[97] (1993) 25 HLR 454, 457–8.

[98] This may be either interest due under the terms of the mortgage deed or statutory interest accruing on the debt.

[99] [2002] EWCA Civ 1181. This was one of three conjoined appeals. See Longmore LJ at para [14] rejecting the argument that once the power of sale has been exercised by the mortgagee the express covenant to pay ceased to be effective and is replaced by an implied covenant to pay.

[100] Subs (1). Accordingly, s 5 of the 1980 Act which provides that an action founded on a simple contract may not be brought after six years from the accrual of the cause of action does not apply. Section 8(1) which applies to actions 'upon a speciality' also lays down a period of twelve years and the Court of Appeal in *Bartlett* said it did not matter whether s 8(1) or s 20(1) applied but they considered that s 20 applied, because the specific limitation provisions relating to mortgages take precedence over the general provisions relating to specialities. In the later case of *Scottish Equitable plc v Thompson* [2003] EWCA Civ 225, it was not an academic question since it was acknowledged by the lender that as there was no covenant to repay in the mortgage it could not bring an action on a specialty. The Court of Appeal followed *Bartlett* and held that s 20 applied.   [101] Subs (5).

mortgagee are to be appropriated to capital or to interest. It is well established that when a debtor makes a payment to his creditor he may appropriate the money to capital or interest as he chooses and the creditor must apply it accordingly. If the debtor does not make any appropriation at the time of the payment then the right of appropriation passes to the creditor.[102] A creditor may appropriate a payment to interest even though the claim for interest has become statute-barred.[103] In the absence of any appropriation then payments will be appropriated to interest before capital unless a contrary intention appears. Where sums are received by the mortgagee directly from a third party the mortgagor will have no opportunity to appropriate. This occurred in *West Bromwich Building Society v Crammer*[104] where the mortgagee received not only the proceeds of sale of the property but also damages as a result of a claim against surveyors for negligence. Neuberger J held that in such circumstances the mortgagee had a right to appropriate these sums to interest in the first place.

4.4.4 Money judgments and bankruptcy

If the mortgagee obtains a money judgment then in the event of default on the part of the mortgagor he may be made bankrupt. The trustee in bankruptcy may seek an order for the sale of the property under s 14 of the Trusts of Land and Appointment of Trustees Act 1996. In view of the degree of protection afforded to a mortgagor under s 36 of the Administration of Justice Act 1970 there may be cases where the mortgagee will prefer to seek possession through the mortgagor's bankruptcy. This is considered further in Chapter 5.[105]

4.5 SALE OF MORTGAGED PROPERTY ON THE APPLICATION OF THE MORTGAGOR

Circumstances may arise in which the mortgagor may wish the mortgaged property to be sold even though the mortgagee does not yet wish to do so. In such circumstances the mortgagor may apply for an order for sale under s 91 of the Law of Property Act 1925. This provides:

(1) Any person entitled to redeem mortgaged property may have a judgment or order for sale instead of for redemption in an action brought by him either for redemption alone, or for sale alone, or for sale or redemption in the alternative.

---

[102] See Lord Macnaghten in *The Mecca* [1897] AC 286, 293.

[103] This was conceded in *West Bromwich Building Society v Crammer* [2002] EWHC 2618 (Ch), para [19]. See in relation to debts generally *Stepney Corporation v Osofsky* [1937] 3 All ER 289; *Mills v Fowkes* (1839) 5 Bing N C 465.　　　　　　　　[104] [2002] EWHC 2618 (Ch), paras [31]–[33].

[105] Para 5.9.

(2) In any action, whether for foreclosure, or for redemption, or for sale, or for the raising and payment in any manner of mortgage money, the court, on the request of the mortgagee, or of any person interested either in the mortgage money or in the right of redemption, and, notwithstanding that—

(a) any other person dissents; or

(b) the mortgagee or any person so interested does not appear in the action;

and without allowing any time for redemption or for payment of any mortgage money, may direct a sale of the mortgaged property, on such terms as it thinks fit, including the deposit in court of a reasonable sum fixed by the court to meet the expenses of sale and to secure performance of the terms.

Until the decision of the Court of Appeal in *Palk v Mortgage Services Funding plc*,[106] it was the practice of the Chancery Court only to entertain an application for sale by the mortgagor if the proceeds of sale were expected to be sufficient to discharge the entirety of the mortgage debt. In that case the Court of Appeal held that the court has power under s 91(2) to make an order of sale on the application of a mortgagor, notwithstanding that the proceeds of sale will be insufficient to discharge the mortgage debt, ie where there is a negative equity. However, the limits of that decision have been made clear in the subsequent decision of the Court of Appeal in *Cheltenham & Gloucester plc v Krausz*.[107]

In *Palk v Mortgage Services Funding plc*, the mortgagee had refused consent to a sale of the mortgaged property negotiated by the mortgagors and obtained an order for possession with a view to letting the property and postponing sale until a higher price could be obtained. However, it was established that the rental under the proposed letting would fall significantly short of the interest that the mortgagor would save if the property was sold. On the evidence before the court the likelihood of Mrs Palk suffering increased loss if the mortgagee's plan proceeded was so high as to make the plan oppressive to her. Her liability would be open-ended and in view of the shortfall between the likely rental and the interest continuing to fall due, her liability would increase indefinitely. The risk of increased loss to her under her repayment obligation far outweighed the prospect of any gain the company might make from its proposed realization scheme for the house. The one was unacceptably disproportionate to the other. The only prospect of recouping the shortfall lay in the hope that there would be a substantial rise in house prices generally. It was not a case where sale was being postponed for a reason specific to the mortgaged property, for example, pending the outcome of an application for planning permission for development. Finally, the Vice-Chancellor pointed out that a sale at the direction of the court would not preclude the mortgagee from buying the property and thus obtaining the opportunity of waiting to see what happened to house prices.

---

[106] [1993] Ch 330.   [107] [1997] 1 All ER 21.

Accordingly, notwithstanding the fact that the proceeds of sale would not be sufficient to discharge the mortgage debt it was appropriate to order a sale under s 91(2).

In *Cheltenham & Gloucester plc v Krausz*, the circumstances in which the mortgagor sought an order for sale were quite different. A possession order had been made in 1991 on the application of the mortgagees and on four occasions warrants for possession were issued. An accommodation was reached on each occasion, but the defendants breached the terms of each accommodation. A fifth warrant was issued in 1995 by which time the mortgagor had obtained a valuation of the property at £65,000 and an offer to purchase the property at that price from a charitable trust which assisted borrowers facing dispossession. The mortgagees considered the property to be worth more and refused to agree to the sale. The mortgagors applied for a suspension of the warrant for possession and indicated their intention of applying for an order for sale under s 91(2). The Court of Appeal unanimously allowed the appeal of the mortgagees from the stay of the warrant for possession granted by the county court judge pending determination of the application under s 91(2). The judge had no jurisdiction to suspend a warrant for possession in order for a mortgagor to make an application for sale under s 91(2).

The distinction between *Palk* and *Krausz* was explained by Millett LJ as follows:[108]

Palk v Mortgage Services Funding plc ... was a case in which the mortgagee had no wish to realise its security in the foreseeable future, whether by sale or foreclosure. It established that in such a case the mortgagor might obtain an order for sale even though the proceeds of sale would be insufficient to discharge the mortgage debt. It does not support the making of such an order where the mortgagee is taking active steps to obtain possession and enforce its security by sale. Still less does it support the giving of the conduct of the sale to the mortgagor in a case where there is negative equity, so that it is the mortgagee who is likely to have the greater incentive to obtain the best price and the quickest sale.

In *Palk*, the issue was simply whether or not the property should be sold. In *Krausz*, the issue was in effect who should have conduct of the sale—the mortgagee or the mortgagor.

4.6 THE CONSUMER CREDIT ACT 1974

Although most mortgages affecting residential property are likely to be outside the scope of the Consumer Credit Act 1974, a mortgagor may be able to take advantage of the provisions of the Act which were considered in Chapter 2.

---

[108] ibid 30–1.

4.7 UNFAIR TERMS IN CONSUMER CONTRACTS

The possibility that the provisions of a mortgage agreement may be subject to a test of fairness under the Unfair Terms in Consumer Contracts Regulations was considered in Chapter 2.[109]

4.8 THE EUROPEAN CONVENTION ON HUMAN RIGHTS

The European Convention on Human Rights, which was incorporated into English law by the Human Rights, Act 1998, provides in Article 8 that:

(1) Everyone has the right to respect for his private and family life, his home and his correspondence.

(2) There shall be no interference by a public authority with the exercise of this right except such as is in accordance with the law and is necessary in a democratic society in the interests of national security, public safety or the economic well-being of the country, for the prevention of disorder or crime, for the protection of health or morals, or for the protection of the rights and freedoms of others.

The possible impact of Article 8 on proceedings for possession by a mortgagee had been considered by the Commission in *Wood v UK*.[110] In that case, the Commission rejected the claim of a mortgagor that repossession of the mortgaged property after she had fallen into arrears in her mortgage payments constituted a breach of her right under Article 8 to respect for her home. The Commission said that the re-possession 'was in accordance with the terms of the loan and the domestic law and was necessary for the protection of the rights and freedom of others, namely the lender'.[111] In *Harrow LBC v Qazi*,[112] Lord Scott said that there was

no suggestion that this decision was reached by weighing up the applicant's interest in retaining her home against the mortgagee's interest in enforcing its security. The Commission's conclusion makes it clear, in my opinion, that a mortgagor cannot invoke Art 8 in order to diminish the contractual and proprietary rights of the mortgagee under the mortgage. Article 8 is simply not applicable.

---

[109] Para 2.4.   [110] (1997) 24 EHRR CD 69.   [111] ibid 70–1.

[112] [2003] UKHL 43, para [135]. This concerned possession proceedings brought by a local authority as landlord.

5

ORDERS FOR SALE

5.1 INTRODUCTION—SEEKING AN ORDER FOR SALE

There are a number of circumstances in which a creditor may seek an order for sale of the family home of the debtor. When a person is in financial difficulties a secured creditor such as a mortgagee of the family home will usually resort to his remedies as a mortgagee and seek an order for possession of the mortgaged property with a view to a sale. This was considered in Chapter 4. If the mortgagor becomes bankrupt then the mortgagee will usually choose to rely on his security, but if there is a significant equity in the property, then the mortgagor's trustee in bankruptcy may seek an order for the sale of the property with the mortgage being discharged out of the proceeds of sale and the balance becoming available for unsecured creditors. This chapter will consider the circumstances in which a sale will be ordered of the family home on the application of a trustee in bankruptcy and the limited protection afforded to the bankrupt's family both where the home was vested in the bankrupt's name alone and where the home was vested in the joint names of the spouses.

A creditor may find that it is entitled to a charge over only part of the beneficial interest in the property. This may be because one spouse forged the signature of the other spouse, or persuaded the other spouse to sign the mortgage over the jointly owned property by undue influence or misrepresentation which affects the creditor. In these circumstances a creditor who wishes to obtain the sale of the property will have to seek an order for sale under the Trusts of Land and Appointment of Trustees Act 1996.

A further possibility is that a creditor who was originally an unsecured creditor may obtain a charging order in respect of the debtor's interest in the family home under the Charging Orders Act 1979 which was considered in Chapter 2.[1] This too may extend to only part of the beneficial interest in the home unless the debtor is sole beneficial owner. Again the creditor will need to enforce its charge by seeking an order for sale.

It is also necessary to consider the situation in which a mortgagee chooses to sue the mortgagor on his personal covenant to pay the amount due with a view to forcing him into bankruptcy in the event of default, so that an order for sale will be sought by the mortgagor's trustee in bankruptcy.[2]

5.2 HOME OWNED SOLELY BY THE DEBTOR

5.2.1 Matrimonial home rights

Where the matrimonial home is in the sole ownership of a debtor spouse, then apart from statute, the other spouse has no rights of occupation which can bind a creditor. A wife's right to remain in occupation of a matrimonial home vested solely in her husband's name was held to be purely personal and not binding on his trustee in bankruptcy or other successors in title.[3]

The Matrimonial Homes Act 1967[4] conferred on a spouse in whom the legal estate was not vested (the 'non-entitled spouse') statutory rights of occupation and provided a means whereby such rights could be protected against third parties by registration. However, even though protected by registration in the appropriate manner, such statutory rights of occupation were void against the trustee in bankruptcy of the 'entitled spouse' or the trustee under a conveyance or assignment of his or her property for the benefit of his or her creditors generally.[5] The position was reversed by the Insolvency Act 1985, the relevant provisions of which are now contained in the Insolvency Act 1986.[6]

The relevant provisions of the Matrimonial Homes Act 1983 have now been replaced by provisions in Pt IV of the Family Law Act 1996. Under the 1996 Act a non-entitled spouse is entitled to 'matrimonial home rights' which are in the same terms as the statutory rights of occupation which they replace.

---

[1] Para 2.5 above. [2] See para 5.9 below.
[3] *National Provincial Bank Ltd v Ainsworth* [1965] AC 1175.
[4] Subsequently the Matrimonial Homes Act 1983. [5] Section 2(7).
[6] Section 336(2) as amended by Family Law Act 1996, Sch 8, para 57.

The 'matrimonial home rights' conferred on a spouse who is not entitled to occupy the home by virtue of any estate, interest or contract are:[7]

(a) if in occupation, a right not to be evicted or excluded from the dwelling-house or any part of it by the other spouse except with the leave of the court given by an order under section 33;

(b) if not in occupation, a right with the leave of the court so given to enter into and occupy the dwelling-house.

This does not apply to a dwelling-house which has at no time been, and which was at no time intended by the spouses to be, a matrimonial home of theirs.[8] A spouse's matrimonial home rights continue:

(a) only so long as the marriage subsists, except to the extent that an order under section 33(5) otherwise provides; and

(b) only so long as the other spouse is entitled to occupy the dwelling-house by virtue of an estate, interest or contract, except where provision is made by section 31 for those rights to be a charge on an estate or interest in the dwelling-house.[9]

Nothing occurring in the initial period of bankruptcy, that is, the period beginning with the day of the presentation of the petition for the bankruptcy order and ending with the vesting of the bankrupt's estate in a trustee, is to be taken as having given rise to any matrimonial home rights in relation to a dwelling-house comprised in the bankrupt's estate.[10]

5.2.2 Orders for possession

Since the matrimonial home rights of the non-entitled spouse constitute a charge on the property which will bind the trustee in bankruptcy of the entitled spouse if duly protected, it will then be necessary for the trustee in bankruptcy to apply to the court for an order under s 33 of the 1996 Act if he wishes to obtain possession free from the matrimonial home rights.[11] The orders which the court may make under s 33 include an order restricting or terminating the matrimonial home rights.[12] Such an application must be made to the court having jurisdiction in relation to the bankruptcy. The court may make such order under s 33(1) as it thinks just and reasonable having regard to:

(a) the interests of the bankrupt's creditors,

(b) the conduct of the spouse or former spouse, so far as contributing to the bankruptcy,

(c) the needs and financial resources of the spouse or former spouse,

---

[7] Family Law Act 1996, s 30(2).　　[8] ibid s 30(7).　　[9] ibid s 30(8).
[10] IA 1986, s 336(1) as amended by Family Law Act 1996, Sch 8, para 57.
[11] ibid s 336(2) as amended.　　[12] Section 33(3).

(d) the needs of any children,[13] and

(e) all the circumstances of the case other than the needs of the bankrupt.[14]

Where such an application is made after the end of the period of one year beginning with the first vesting of the bankrupt's estate in a trustee, the court must assume, unless the circumstances of the case are exceptional, that the interests of the bankrupt's creditors outweigh all other circumstances.[15]

It will be seen that the wording here is similar to that applicable to cases where the bankrupt's spouse has a beneficial interest in the home and detailed consideration will be given there to the interpretation of the term 'exceptional circumstances'.[16] However, at this point it is appropriate to note *Re Bremner*[17] where the bankrupt's spouse had no beneficial interest in the matrimonial home. The bankrupt was aged 79 and in very bad health and he had recently been diagnosed as having inoperable cancer. His life expectancy was reckoned in months, probably no more than six months. His wife was aged 74 and his only carer. Mr Jonathan Sumption QC, sitting as a High Court judge, accepted that the wife had:

an independent interest in remaining in the property, arising not only from her occupation over many years but from the fact that she is caring for her terminally ill husband.[18]

This need was a need of hers which was distinct from that of her husband, albeit that it arose out of the same factual background. It was an interest which the court should recognize.

Under a provision introduced by the Enterprise Act 2002, an application for an order for the sale or possession of a property must be dismissed if the value of the bankrupt's interest in the property is below a prescribed figure.[19]

Generally therefore the protection afforded to the spouse of a bankrupt is very limited and cannot be longer than one year from the beginning of the bankruptcy unless there are exceptional circumstances. However, it may be argued that this is not compliant with Article 8 of the European Convention on Human Rights and Fundamental Freedoms which provides that everyone has the right to respect for his private and family life, his home, and his correspondence. The Court of Appeal has granted permission for an appeal in which this point was raised in relation to s 335A which applies similar criteria in relation to applications for sale of property which is jointly owned.[20]

---

[13] See *Harris v Habanec* (CA, 25 April 1997) where leave to appeal was granted on the basis that matters relating to the bankrupt's son had not been specifically addressed.

[14] IA 1986, s 336(4) as amended.   [15] IA 1986, s 336(5) as amended.

[16] Para 5.5.2 below.   [17] [1999] 1 FLR 912.   [18] ibid 919.

[19] IA 1986, s 313A introduced by the Enterprise Act 2002, s 261(3). See para 8.7 below.

[20] *Jackson v Bell* [2001] EWCA Civ 387, [2001] Fam Law 879. See para 5.8 below.

5.2.3 A bankrupt caring for children

In some cases the bankrupt may have no spouse or no spouse entitled or willing to occupy the family home, but is responsible for the upbringing of children. Section 337 of the Insolvency Act 1986 is designed to provide limited protection to occupation of the home in this situation. It applies where:

(i) a person who is entitled to occupy a dwelling-house by virtue of a beneficial estate or interest is adjudged bankrupt; and

(ii) any persons under the age of 18 with whom that person had at some time occupied that dwelling-house had their home with that person at the time when the bankruptcy petition was presented and at the commencement of the bankruptcy.[21]

If these conditions are satisfied, then whether or not the bankrupt's spouse (if any) has matrimonial home rights under the Family Law Act 1996, the bankrupt is given rights of occupation as against the trustee of his estate.[22] These are the same as the matrimonial home rights conferred on a non-entitled spouse by the Family Law Act 1996.[23] They have effect as if they were rights under the 1996 Act and an application for leave to enter and occupy is to be treated as an application for an order under s 33 of that Act. These rights of occupation constitute a charge on so much of the bankrupt's estate or interest in the dwelling-house as vests in the trustee, having the like priority as an equitable interest created immediately before the commencement of the bankruptcy. The 1996 Act has effect, with necessary modifications, as if the charge on the estate or interest of the trustee were a charge under that Act on the estate or interest of a spouse.[24]

The effect, therefore, is that in order to obtain possession of the home it will be necessary for the trustee to apply for an order under s 33 of the 1996 Act. The application must be made to the court having jurisdiction in relation to the bankruptcy.[25] On such an application the court must make such order as it thinks just and reasonable having regard to:[26]

(a) the interests of the creditors;

(b) the bankrupt's financial resources;

(c) the needs of the children; and

(d) all the circumstances of the case other than the needs of the bankrupt.

Where such an application is made after the end of the period of one year beginning with the first vesting under the Insolvency Act of the bankrupt's estate in a trustee, the court must assume, unless the circumstances of the case

---

[21] IA 1986, s 337(1).   [22] IA 1986, s 337(2).   [23] Pt IV, s 30(2). See para 5.2.1 above.
[24] IA 1986, s 337(2) and (3) as amended by the Family Law Act 1996, Sch 8, para 58.
[25] IA 1986, s 337(4).   [26] IA 1986, s 337(5).

are exceptional, that the interests of the bankrupt's creditors outweigh all other considerations.[27]

5.2.4 'Unmarried' debtors

Where the debtor is not married then his or her cohabitant will not have the benefit of matrimonial home rights. Where a creditor obtains a charging order in respect of property which is solely owned by the debtor then any cohabitant or children of the debtor will have little or no defence against an application by the creditor for an order for sale. The Trusts of Land and Appointment of Trustees Act 1996 will not apply as there will be no trust for land as there would be if the home were jointly owned. Accordingly s 15 of that Act which specifies matters to be taken into account by the court in determining whether or not to order a sale on an application under s 14 of that Act will not apply.[28] This apparent lacuna was noted in *Pickering v Wells*[29] where a creditor had obtained a charging order over property owned solely by the debtor who lived there with her three children. Mr D Oliver QC sitting as a High Court judge noted that the case did not fall within either ss 14 and 15 of the 1996 Act on the one hand, or s 335A of the Insolvency Act 1986 dealing with applications by trustees in bankruptcy on the other. He had to consider whether the welfare and needs of those in occupation could be taken into account under RSC Ord 88, r 5A(2)(f). He concluded that the proper interpretation of that provision is that the underlying purpose is to ensure that the court has notice, for the purposes of exercising the discretion whether or not to enforce a charging order, of all competing proprietary interests in the property so that it can take account of the proprietary interests of third parties. It did not extend to considerations of the welfare or needs of those in occupation of the property.[30]

5.3 HOME OWNED JOINTLY BY THE DEBTOR AND HIS SPOUSE OR THIRD PARTY

5.3.1 The court's power to order a sale

Where a husband and wife are jointly entitled to the beneficial interest in the matrimonial home, the non-bankrupt spouse will generally be entitled to receive the appropriate share of the proceeds of sale if the home is sold at the insistence of the trustee in bankruptcy. However, apart from the disruption involved in having to move home, the non-bankrupt spouse's share may, by itself, be

---

[27] IA 1986, s 337(6).   [28] These provision are considered in para 5.3 below.

[29] [2002] 2 FLR 798.

[30] He also considered that the position was not affected by Art 8 of the European Convention on Human Rights: ibid 800.

insufficient to purchase alternative accommodation. The non-bankrupt spouse may not therefore be prepared to concur in a sale and in that event the trustee in bankruptcy may apply to the court for an order for sale. The same situation may arise in relation to an unmarried couple when one of the cohabitants becomes bankrupt.

Where the family home was vested in the joint names of a husband and wife or any other co-owners, then up until January 1997 the legal estate would have been held on trust for sale for themselves as beneficial owners as joint tenants or tenants in common. An application for sale by one co-owner, or by a creditor or trustee in bankruptcy would have been made under s 30 of the Law of Property Act 1925. The trust for sale was abolished and replaced by the trust of land by the Trusts of Land and Appointment of Trustees Act 1996 with effect from 1 January 1997. As from that date an application for an order for sale by one co-owner or by a creditor or trustee in bankruptcy of one or both the co-owners must be made under s 14 of the Trusts of Land and Appointment of Trustees Act 1996. This provides:

(1) Any person who is a trustee or has an interest in property subject to a trust of land may make an application for an order under this section.
(2) On an application for an order under this section the court may make any such order—
  (a) relating to the exercise by the trustees of any of their functions (including an order relieving them of any obligation to obtain the consent of, or to consult, any person in connection with the exercise of any of their functions), or
  (b) declaring the nature or extent of a person's interest in property subject to the trust,
  as the court thinks fit.

Thus in addition to a co-owner, subsection (1) covers a creditor. As the bankrupt's beneficial interest in the home will have vested in the trustee in bankruptcy the trustee will clearly have an interest in the property for this purpose. By virtue of subsection 2(a) the court may make an order for sale of the property.

5.3.2 Factors to be taken into account

Before 1997 it had become established that, while the court had a discretion whether or not to order a sale, the interests of creditors were likely to prevail.[31] The voice of the other spouse would only prevail in exceptional circumstances. It was also established that the same approach should be adopted by the court in considering an application for an order for sale by a trustee in bankruptcy and by a creditor with a charge over the interest of one co-owner.[32]

---

[31] *Re Citro (A Bankrupt)* [1991] Ch 142, 157, *per* Nourse LJ.
[32] *Lloyds Bank plc v Byrne* (1991) 23 HLR 472.

The matters to which the court is to have regard in determining an application for an order under s 14 of the Trusts of Land and Appointment of Trustees Act 1996 are set out in s 15 of the Act. Section 15(1) provides that they include:

(a) the intentions of the person or persons (if any) who created the trusts,
(b) the purposes for which the property subject to the trust is held,
(c) the welfare of any minor who occupies or might reasonably be expected to occupy any land subject to the trust as his home, and
(d) the interests of any secured creditor of any beneficiary.

Under s 15(3) the matters to which the court is to have regard also include the circumstances and wishes of any beneficiaries of full age and entitled to an interest in possession in property subject to the trust or (in the case of dispute) of the majority (according to the value of their combined interests). However, s 15 does not apply where an application is made by a trustee in bankruptcy.[33] The position on such applications is governed by s 335A of the Insolvency Act 1986.[34] A different approach is, therefore, now appropriate in relation to an application by a creditor and an application by a trustee in bankruptcy.[35]

5.4 APPLICATIONS BY CREDITORS

5.4.1 The approach of the courts

In relation to an application for an order for sale by a creditor chargee it seems that the court has greater flexibility under s 15 than it previously enjoyed. In *The Mortgage Corporation v Shaire*,[36] Neuberger J analysed the effect of the 1996 Act on the previous law and concluded that s 15 had 'changed the law' and that as 'a result of s 15 the court has greater flexibility than heretofore, as to how it exercises its jurisdiction on an application for an order for sale'.[37] In *Bank of Ireland Home Mortgages Ltd v Bell*,[38] Peter Gibson LJ said:

The 1996 Act, by requiring the court to have regard to the particular matters specified in s 15, appears to me to have given scope for some change in the court's practice.

The extent of this 'greater flexibility' is not yet clear on the basis of the decisions to date.

Certainly in *The Mortgage Corporation v Shaire*, it could be argued that the greater flexibility provided by s 15 was an important factor in encouraging a practical solution. In that case the property concerned had been transferred into

---

[33] Section 15(4).

[34] Inserted by Trusts of Land and Appointment of Trustees Act 1996, Sch 3, para 23.

[35] See Neuberger J in *The Mortgage Corporation v Shaire* [2000] 2 FCR 222, 238.

[36] [2000] FCR 222, 237 et seq.   [37] ibid 239.

[38] [2001] BPIR 429, 436, para [31]. See also the analysis of the effect of the 1996 Act by Neuberger J in *The Mortgage Corporation v Shaire* [2000] 2 FCR 222, 237 et seq.

the joint names of Mrs Shaire and her cohabitant, a Mr Fox, following Mrs Shaire's divorce. They had mortgaged the property to the Chase Manhattan Bank ('Chase'). After Mr Fox's subsequent death it was discovered that he had forged Mrs Shaire's signature on two further charges on the property one of which was to The Mortgage Corporation ('TMC'). Neuberger J concluded that Mrs Shaire was entitled to a 75 per cent share in the beneficial interest in the property and Mr Fox was entitled to a 25 per cent share. Although Mrs Shaire was not bound by the charge in favour of TMC, since part of the amount advanced had been used to redeem the Chase mortgage, TMC was subrogated to the Chase mortgage in relation to her 75 per cent share in the property.[39] Since Mr Fox's estate was insolvent TMC was in effect the owner of Mr Fox's 25 per cent share. Neuberger J went through the statutory factors in s 15 and then stood back to look at the position of both parties. If Mrs Shaire and her son had to leave the home it would be a real and significant hardship, but not an enormous one since she would have a substantial sum that she could put towards a smaller home. For TMC to be locked into a quarter of the equity in a property would be a significant disadvantage unless they had a proper return and proper protection so far as insurance and repair was concerned.

A practical solution was to agree a valuation of the property and convert the 25 per cent interest of TMC into a loan with Mrs Shaire as sole owner paying interest on that loan to TMC as well as on the amount of the Chase loan to which TMC had been subrogated. However, if this course involved a liability which Mrs Shaire could not meet or if TMC satisfied the court that this was a liability she could not meet, it would not be right to refuse an order for sale.

In *Bank of Ireland Home Mortgages Ltd v Bell*, the position was that Mr and Mrs Bell held the property concerned on trust for themselves with the bank as an equitable chargee having an interest in the property.[40] The matters referred to in paragraphs (a) and (b) of s 15(1) were no longer operative following the departure of Mr Bell from the property. Their son, although a minor, was not far short of 18 so that his interest should receive only a very slight consideration under paragraph (c). Mrs Bell's poor health was a matter to which the judge could properly have regard, but it would provide a reason from postponing sale rather than refusing sale as the judge had done. On the other hand, Peter Gibson LJ went on to say that 'a powerful consideration is and ought to be whether the creditor is receiving proper recompense for being kept out of his money, repayment of which is overdue'.[41] It was plain that by refusing sale the judge had condemned the bank to go on waiting for its money with no prospect of recovery from Mr and Mrs Bell. The debt was increasing all the time and

---

[39] For the effect of subrogation, see ch 3, para 3.11.

[40] In possession proceedings the judge had ordered rectification of the charges register to delete the charge in favour of the creditor on the basis that Mrs Bell had not signed the mortgage. He declared that the creditor was entitled to an equitable charge over the property.

[41] He referred to *Mortgage Corporation plc v Shaire*.

already exceeding what could be realized on a sale. That seemed to him to be very unfair to the bank and an order for sale was appropriate.[42] Despite the scope for change provided by s 15 he said: 'Nevertheless, a powerful consideration is and ought to be whether the creditor is receiving proper recompense for being kept out of his money, repayment of which is overdue.'[43]

This was again an important consideration in *First National Bank plc v Achampong*[44] where Mr and Mrs Achampong had mortgaged the property which was their home to secure a loan to Mrs Achampong's cousin for business purposes. It was found that the mortgage was ineffective against Mrs Achampong because her participation had been procured by the undue influence of her husband. In relation to the mortgagee's application under s 14, the Court of Appeal made an order for sale. Blackburne J giving the main judgment said:[45]

Prominent among the considerations which lead to that conclusion is that, unless an order for sale is made, the bank will be kept waiting indefinitely for any payment out of what is, for all practical purposes, its own share of the property.

The interests of the secured creditor were therefore the dominating factor in *Bell* and *Achampong* and probably also in *Shaire* as a sale would be ordered if the compromise solution was unacceptable or unworkable. However, it is instructive to look at the assessment made of the factors mentioned in paragraphs (a), (b), and (c). In *Shaire*, Neuberger J said that there was no evidence as to the intention of Mrs Shaire and Mr Fox as to what was to happen to the house if Mr Fox died.[46] In relation to (b) it was difficult to say for what purpose the house was held. For Mrs Shaire it could said that the purpose was to provide a home for herself and her son, but for TMC it was partly as security and partly a beneficial interest. In *Bell*, the court was left to assume that the intention of the parties had been that the property should be their matrimonial home, but Peter Gibson LJ said that 'that purpose ceased to be operative' once Mr Bell had left and the parties subsequently had been divorced.[47] Similarly, in *Achampong*, Blackburne J said that, insofar as the intention of the Achampongs was to provide themselves with a matrimonial home, and insofar as that was the purpose for which the property was held on trust, that consideration was now spent as Mr Achampong had left and there had been no contact between the spouses for some years. The marriage was effectively at an end. The position of one co-owner left in occupation of the jointly owned property is going to be difficult in relation to paragraphs (a) and (b) on the basis that the property was acquired as a joint home. It may be possible to show that the property was

---

[42] See also *First National Bank plc v Achampong* [2003] EWCA Civ 487.

[43] [2001] BPIR 429, para [31].   [44] [2003] EWCA Civ 487.   [45] ibid para [65]

[46] Neuberger J added that Mr Fox changed the basis on which he held his interest when, albeit unknown to Mrs Shaire, he charged his interest for sums to assist in his business, referring to Evans-Lombe J in *Bankers Trust Co v Namdar* (Ch D, 18 July 1995).

[47] [2001] BPIR 429, 435, para [27].

intended to provide a home for them both while they lived and for the survivor on the death of one co-owner, though in *Shaire* there was no evidence of this. It is hardly likely that the parties will have intended the property to continue to be the home of one of them after breakdown of the relationship. It remains to be seen what weight will be attached to the welfare of any minor who occupies or might reasonably be expected to occupy the property as his home. In *Shaire* there was no minor child and in *Bell* the son was not far short of 18 and therefore should only have been given a very slight consideration. In *Achampong* the children had long grown up, though one was suffering from a mental disability and remained in the home. The factors specified in s 15(1) are not exclusive. Mrs Bell's ill health was regarded as relevant, but Neuberger J considered that this would a reason for postponing sale rather than refusing sale. Mrs Shaire had a majority share in the beneficial interest in the property and though she obviously wished to continue to live in the property this was not decisive when weighed against the interest of TMC not merely as minority beneficial owner but as creditor.

It may be concluded from these cases that when the court came to weigh the various factors, those favouring a sale as requested by the creditor outweighed the factors pointing to a refusal or any long term postponement unless some compromise was possible as suggested in *Shaire*. The task of tilting the balance in favour of the occupier will not be easy, but it must have been the intention that the balance would be tilted more in favour of the debtor's co-owner and family than is the case on an application for an order for sale by a trustee in bankruptcy where exceptional circumstances must be shown to avoid an order for sale.

5.4.2 Implementation of an order for sale

Even if an order for sale is made the court must consider when it is to take effect. This aspect was not determined in any of the three cases considered above, but some guidance may be obtained from the earlier case of *Barclays Bank v Hendricks*[48] where Laddie J said:

It seems to me that the period before the innocent spouse has to give up possession should be such as to allow sufficient time to facilitate the departure from the property without adding unnecessarily to the distress and dislocation which will, in any event, be suffered by the innocent spouse and the children. However, any such period should be as short as possible in the circumstances and any period more than a few weeks should be avoided if it is likely to cause significant hardship to the chargee.

In that case the original order would have required Mrs Hendricks and her children to vacate the property within a few weeks which would be in the middle of the children's school term. While no time for a move would, from the

---

[48] [1996] 1 FLR 258, 264.

children's perspective, be perfect, it seemed to Laddie J that it might be possible to lessen the distress to them, and consequently to Mrs Hendricks, if she was required to vacate by a date which would enable the family to move over the school holidays and thus avoid the trauma of moving in the middle of the school term.

5.5 APPLICATIONS BY A TRUSTEE IN BANKRUPTCY[49]

5.5.1 The relevant factors

An application for an order for sale under s 14 of the 1996 Act by a trustee in bankruptcy of one co-owner must be made to the court having jurisdiction in relation to the bankruptcy.[50] On such an application the court must make such order as it thinks just and reasonable having regard to the matters set out in s 335A(2) of the Insolvency Act 1986 and not s 15(1) and (3) of the 1996 Act. These matters are as follows:

(a) the interests of the bankrupt's creditors;
(b) where the application is made in respect of land which includes a dwelling house which is or has been the home of the bankrupt or the bankrupt's spouse or former spouse—
    (i)   the conduct of the spouse or former spouse, so far as contributing to the bankruptcy,
    (ii) the needs and financial resources of the spouse or former spouse, and
    (iii) the needs of any children; and
(c) all the circumstances of the case other than the needs of the bankrupt.

Where an application is made in relation to the home of an unmarried couple, then paragraph (b) does not apply as it is limited to a dwelling-house which is or has been the home of the bankrupt's spouse or former spouse. In such a case therefore the court must have regard only to '(a) the interests of the bankrupt's creditors' and '(c) all the circumstances of the case other than the needs of the bankrupt'.

If the application is made after the end of the period of one year from the date of the first vesting of the bankrupt's estate in a trustee, the court must assume, unless the circumstances of the case are exceptional, that the interests of the bankrupt's creditors outweigh all other considerations.[51]

Where the property in which the bankrupt has an interest is a dwelling-house which at the date of the bankruptcy was the sole or principal residence of the bankrupt, his spouse or former spouse, then the court must dismiss the

---

[49] See Miller, 'Applications by a Trustee in Bankruptcy for Sale of the Family Home' (1999) 15 (6) IL & P 176.   [50] IA 1986, s 335A(1).
[51] IA 1986, s 335A(3).

application for sale if the value of the bankrupt's interest is below a prescribed amount.[52] The provision dealing with 'low value homes' introduced by the Enterprise Act 2002 is considered further in paragraph 5.7 below, but it should be noted that it is the value of the bankrupt's interest which must be below the prescribed value and not the value of the property in which that interest subsists.

5.5.2 Exceptional circumstances

The effect of s 335A(3) is therefore that, at least after the expiration of the period of one year from the vesting of the estate in the trustee in bankruptcy, there is an assumption that the interests of the creditors will outweigh all other considerations unless there are exceptional circumstances. Thus in the case of both married and unmarried couples an order for sale on the application of a trustee in bankruptcy is likely to be refused only if there are 'exceptional circumstances'. However, although the 'presence of exceptional circumstances is a necessary condition to displace the assumption that the interests of the creditors outweigh all other considerations ... the presence of the exceptional circumstances does not debar the court from making an order for sale'.[53]

In *Claughton v Charalambous*,[54] Jonathan Parker J rejected the invitation to lay down guidelines for the future assistance of trustees in bankruptcy as to what may or may not constitute 'exceptional' or 'special' circumstances. He said that:

it would be entirely inappropriate for this court to attempt to lay down what circumstances may be regarded as exceptional in any particular case when Parliament itself has not chosen to do so.

The court is being asked, in effect, to make a value judgment and must look at all the circumstances and conclude whether or not they are exceptional. That process, in his view, left very little scope for interference by an appellate court. In more recent cases exceptional circumstances have been successfully established, with the state of health of the bankrupt's spouse being an important factor.

5.5.3 The bankrupt's family—the 'normal' and the 'exceptional'

Although s 335A requires the court to take into account the needs and financial resources of the bankrupt's spouse or former spouse and the needs of any children, it is clear that the disruption caused by having to leave the family

---

[52] IA 1986, s 313A inserted by the Enterprise Act 2002, s 261(3) with effect from 1 April 2004. The prescribed value is £1,000: Insolvency Proceedings (Monetary Limits)(Amendment) Rules 2004 (SI 2004/547), para 2.

[53] *Per* Lawrence Collins QC in *Harrington v Bennett* [2000] BPIR 630, 633 referring to *Re Raval* [1998] 2 FLR 718.   [54] [1999] 1 FLR 740, 744.

home will not generally be regarded as exceptional. In *Re Citro*,[55] Nourse LJ said that:

... it is not uncommon for a wife with young children to be faced with eviction in circumstances where the realisation of her beneficial interest will not produce enough to buy a comparable home in the same neighbourhood, or indeed elsewhere. And, if she has to move elsewhere, there may be problems over schooling and so forth. Such circumstances, while engendering a natural sympathy in all who hear them, cannot be described as exceptional. *They are the melancholy consequences of debt and improvidence with which every civilised society has been familiar.*

5.5.4 Special needs and ill health

On the other hand, in *Re Bailey*[56] it had been recognized by Walton J that if a home had been specially adapted to suit the needs of a handicapped child, the circumstances would be 'so special that undoubtedly this court would hesitate long before making an immediate order for sale'. In *Re Densham*,[57] a postponement was sought on the basis of the nervous illness which all the troubles had brought upon the wife, as well as the possible harmful effects of a sale on the children. It was clear that what was being sought was an indefinite adjournment to soften the blow of losing the home, and a postponement was rejected. However, it seems that the court might have been more sympathetic if the object had been 'to achieve some particular remedial purpose, such as to enable a course of treatment to be completed ... '[58]

This was in fact the basis of a finding of exceptional circumstances in the more recent case of *Judd v Brown*.[59] Harman J said that the circumstances were wholly different from any he had seen in the previous authorities other than *Re Mott*,[60] where the hardship that would be suffered by an elderly lady, the mother of the bankrupt, by her being forced to leave her home of forty years standing, appears to have been the main factor supporting a finding of exceptional circumstances. In *Judd v Brown*, the wife of one of the bankrupt brothers involved had recently been diagnosed as suffering from cancer and had undergone extensive surgery. She was undergoing chemotherapy and it was essential to avoid all stress. The treatment was expected to continue for some further five or six months. Harman J said that the wife's:

... illness for which everyone must feel deep sympathy, plainly creates difficulties of a very different character from such difficulties as obtaining substitute accommodation or arranging for children's schooling which are foreseeable and long-term conditions. This event must have been sudden, unforeseeable, of very recent occurrence, of gravity and is directly affected by the orders now sought. Although cancer in various forms attacks many people yet I think that as a matter of normal language people would say that

---

[55] [1991] Ch 142, 157. Italics added.   [56] [1977] 1 WLR 278, 284.
[57] [1975] 1 WLR 1519.   [58] ibid 1531.   [59] [1998] 2 FLR 360.
[60] Noted in Current Law [1987] CLY 212.

a sudden and serious attack was an exceptional circumstance in any individual's life. When recovery from the attack is directly related to the orders sought it is, in my judgment, what is properly to be described as an exceptional reason for refusing the orders. If the occurrence of life-threatening illness is not an exceptional event I find it difficult to know what such an event can be. In this case the oncologist's view of the importance of security to his patient's possible recovery seems to me to reinforce the relevance of [the wife's] illness. Further, the fact that a comparatively short time will enable matters to be resolved, it is to be hoped by a happy outcome, differentiates this particular case on its facts from a case of some person who suffers a long-term illness of indeterminate duration.[61]

An appeal against the refusal to order possession of the family home, the home of the other brother, together with other property, was not proceeded with so far as the two homes were concerned.[62]

In *Re Raval*,[63] it was argued for the trustee that *Judd v Brown* was authority for the proposition that in cases of illness it is only where the medical need is sudden and short term rather than long term and of indeterminate duration, that the circumstances can be said to be exceptional. However, Blackburne J said:[64]

I can well envisage circumstances, for example, a person who suffers from terminal cancer but whose life expectancy simply cannot be judged, and whose illness therefore could properly be described as long term and of indeterminate duration, which it would be proper to describe as exceptional and where no order for possession should be made.

In that case the bankrupt's wife had, for many years suffered from paranoid schizophrenia and in 1991 she had been admitted to hospital under s 3 of the Mental Health Act 1983 for some two years, and following this she had been a day hospital patient for two years or so. Since then she had been receiving monthly home visits by a community psychiatric nurse. The medical evidence indicated that her mental state had become and remained stable although she remained vulnerable to 'adverse life events' which could cause a relapse in her condition. A move to a new home carried such a risk though it was not the move itself, but the condition she might move to and access to social support that she might have afterwards, that constituted the risk factor. There was no appeal against the finding of the registrar that the circumstances were exceptional, but questions were raised regarding the period of suspension of the order for possession. Blackburne J held that the registrar had been correct to conclude that the circumstances of the case were indeed exceptional. The uncontroverted evidence was that a move to accommodation which was too small to serve the family's needs having regard to the ages of the children for whom the Ravals continued to have day-to-day responsibility, or which, because of its location,

---

[61] [1998] 2 FLR 360, 364.

[62] The decision of the Court of Appeal making orders for possession in relation to the property other than the matrimonial homes is reported at [1999] 1 FLR 1191.

[63] [1998] 2 FLR 718, 724.   [64] ibid 725.

deprived Mrs Raval of her current support network both from family and from neighbours, could trigger a relapse.

In *Claughton v Charalambous*,[65] the wife was aged approximately 60 and, according to medical evidence, she was in very poor health in that she suffered from renal failure and chronic osteoarthritis so that she could walk only with great difficulty with the aid of a Zimmer frame, and furthermore needed a wheelchair. It was also established that the property in which she lived was fitted with a chair-lift. In consequence, if she were to have to move it would either have to be to a ground floor property, or possibly a nursing home, or, again, to a property fitted with a chair-lift. The judge found that her medical condition, coupled with her life expectancy and the way she lived, were exceptional circumstances.

It seems doubtful whether the health of the bankrupt could by itself form the basis of a finding of exceptional circumstances since s 335A(2) requires to have regard to 'all the circumstances of the case *other than the needs of the bankrupt'*. However, the position may be otherwise in relation to its effect on the bankrupt's spouse as appears from *Re Bremner*[66] which was considered in paragraph 5.2.2 above as the bankrupt's spouse had no beneficial interest in the home and it was therefore an application for an order under the Family Law Act 1996.

5.5.5 Conduct and contributions of the spouse

If the bankrupt's spouse has been guilty of reckless expenditure and obviously knowingly benefited from the bankrupt's financial mismanagement, then this is likely to be taken into account under paragraph (b) as a factor militating against postponement. Where, on the other hand, the bankrupt's wife has contributed the whole or a substantial part of the purchase price of the home which has been vested in the joint names of the spouses, the wife will not be able to go behind the express declaration of beneficial interests.[67] However, it would seem fair to take this into account in determining the timing of a sale especially where the wife may have struggled to maintain the home in the face of the bankrupt's irresponsible behaviour. Nevertheless, in *Re Gorman*[68] this did not carry much weight. In that case the wife had provided £2,000 of the purchase price of £5,800 and costs. The balance had been provided by a mortgage advance, but Vinelott J said that it was immaterial that she had paid all the mortgage instalments—that was a matter to be dealt with on taking an account following sale. In *Harrington v Bennett*,[69] the judge said that the fact that the bankrupt's spouse had kept up the mortgage payments, did not make the circumstances exceptional even though half of those payments enured to the benefit of the bankrupt's estate.

---

[65] [1999] 1 FLR 740.   [66] [1999] 1 FLR 912.
[67] See *Boydell v Gillespie* (1971) 216 EG 1505 and *Re Gorman* [1990] 1 All ER 717.
[68] ibid.   [69] [2000] BPIR 630, 635.

5.5.6 Prospective claims and expectations of the spouse

The fact that the husband's interest in the property might be transferred to the wife as a result of an order in divorce proceedings between them is unlikely to provide much assistance to the wife in her efforts to seek postponement of a sale. Once a husband has been adjudicated bankrupt and his share has vested in his trustee in bankruptcy then no order for the transfer of that property can be made under the Matrimonial Causes Act 1973.[70]

Where no transfer of property order has been obtained in divorce proceedings before commencement of the husband's bankruptcy, the wife may have a claim for damages against her solicitors in negligence. In *Re Gorman*,[71] Vinelott J had delayed the operation of an order for sale for six months in the light of evidence that the bankrupt's wife had prima facie a strong claim in negligence against her former solicitors for their failure to apply for a property adjustment order when she obtained the decree nisi of divorce. If that claim was successful then she would probably have been in a position to purchase the trustee's share in the property. The trustee was given liberty to apply should the proceedings against the former solicitors not be pursued with due despatch or should they be abandoned.

In contrast in *Trustee of the Estate of Bowe v Bowe*,[72] Jonathan Parker J refused to defer an order for sale pending the pursuit by the bankrupt's wife of a claim in negligence against her former solicitors in relation to their conduct of applications for financial provision and property adjustment in the divorce proceedings. The wife believed that the building society had agreed to the transfer of property to her, but Jonathan Parker J accepted that *Re Gorman* was distinguishable. In the case before him no action was on foot, whereas in *Re Gorman* the writ had been issued some eighteen months before the hearing before the judge. Moreover, there was only the faintest suggestion of the possibility of a claim, whereas in *Re Gorman* the judge took the view that the claim was prima facie a strong one. Even if a transfer had been made it would be open to attack or possibly be voidable pursuant to the provisions of the Insolvency Act 1986. He said: 'In my judgment, therefore, this case is a mile away from the facts of *Re Gorman* and I therefore derive no assistance from the way in which Vinelott J approached the problem which faced him in that case.'[73]

5.5.7 The interests of the bankrupt's creditors

The interests of the bankrupt's creditors will generally involve the realization of the home at the earliest possible date. The impact of delay may be particularly serious for a small business creditor whereas different considerations may

---

[70] See ch 8.   [71] [1990] 1 All ER 717, [1990] 1 WLR 616.   [72] [1998] 2 FLR 439.

[73] ibid 449. See also the assessment of the wife's claim on an application for leave to appeal in *Jackson v Bell* [2001] EWCA Civ 387, paras [11] and [27].

apply, for example, to a bank.[74] In *Re Bailey,*[75] it was said that it was relevant to consider what the creditors may have to pay by way of interest for any borrowing they themselves have to make to fill the gap until they are paid. In *Re Gorman,*[76] Vinelott J was concerned with the fact that the creditors had already been kept out of their money for very many years during a period of high interest rates and, regretfully, inflation, and could look to nothing except the proceeds of sale of the property to pay a dividend on their debts.

A significant consideration is the extent to which the proceeds of the home will be sufficient to cover the claims of the creditors for capital and interest at the end of the period of postponement. In *Re Citro,*[77] Nourse LJ regarded *Re Holliday*[78] as exceptional because it was highly unlikely that postponement of payment of the debts would cause any great hardship to any of the creditors. The debts, together with statutory interest for the period of postponement, were amply covered by the husband's share in the matrimonial home. In *Re Citro*, Nourse LJ regarded this as the special feature of the case which helped the wife's voice to prevail. It was detrimental to the creditors to be kept out of a commercial rate of interest and the use of the money for five years, but if the principal was safe it was understandable that that detriment was not treated as being decisive, even in inflationary times. He thought it was probably exceptional for creditors to receive 100p in the £ plus statutory interest in full, and the passage of years before they did so did not make it less exceptional. In *Re Raval,*[79] Blackburne J said that in this respect *Re Holliday* was wholly different from the case before him. Even if the estate in *Re Raval* was currently solvent any lengthy postponement in the realization of the estate's half-share of the property might prejudice the interests of his two creditors who had been kept waiting since 1989. Accordingly, a postponement is less likely to be granted where it will result in the creditors receiving a smaller proportion of their claim for capital and interest.

In some cases it will be clear from the outset that the creditors will receive nothing from the proceeds of the home. In the *Trustee of the Estate of Bowe v Bowe,*[80] Jonathan Parker J held that the bankrupt's creditors have an interest in an order for sale being made, notwithstanding that the entirety of the bankrupt's share in the net proceeds of the property may be swallowed up in defraying the expenses of the bankruptcy. If that be the case then the interests of the creditors under s 336(5) will prevail over the other factors listed in that subsection. There are two reasons why the bankrupt's creditors have an interest in an order for sale in these circumstances. First, if there be after-acquired property, or the possibility of after-acquired property coming to light, then the discharging of the expenses of the bankruptcy, which inevitably will take priority to the preferential or other provable debts, is in the interests of the

---

[74] See *Re Holliday* [1981] Ch 405.   [75] [1977] 1 WLR 278, 282.
[76] [1990] 1 All ER 717, 728.   [77] [1991] 1 Ch 142, 157.   [78] [1980] Ch 405.
[79] [1998] 2 FLR 718, 726–7.   [80] [1998] 2 FLR 439, 446.

creditors, who may find themselves in receipt of a distribution following the realization of any such after-acquired property. Secondly, even if there is no question of after-acquired property to be brought into account, it remains in the interests of the bankrupt's creditors that the expenses of the bankruptcy, including the remuneration of the trustee (who the creditors themselves have appointed and who has carried out his statutory duties effectively as their representative in the context of a bankruptcy process devised for their benefit) should be discharged so far as possible out of the assets of the bankrupt. He said:[81]

> In short, in my judgment, no relevant distinction can be drawn for the purposes of construing s 336(5), between the expenses of the bankruptcy and provable debts. Far from being an affront to common sense this conclusion seems to me to reflect the reality of the situation.

Moreover, the fact that the entirety of the proceeds of sale would be swallowed up in paying the expenses of the bankruptcy was not an exceptional circumstance for the purposes of subsection (5).[82] However, this does not mean that it is not a factor that can be taken into account by the court. In *Claughton v Charalambous*,[83] Jonathan Parker J rejected the suggestion that the judge had fallen into error by noting and taking into account the fact that the creditors would not receive any dividend. He said: 'He was not attributing no weight to their interests, merely assessing what weight it would be right to attach to them'.

5.5.8 Balancing the interests of secured and unsecured creditors

Where the amount due to a secured creditor will exhaust the proceeds of sale, a sale may be refused if the unsecured creditors or the bankrupt's wife are likely to be prejudiced. A trustee in bankruptcy should not allow his position to be used for the sole benefit of a creditor who does not surrender his security.[84] In *Re Ng*,[85] there was evidence of an arrangement between the trustee in bankruptcy and the building society to which the home was charged, under which the trustee was to take proceedings for possession. The prospects of success of the society on an application as chargee of the bankrupt's beneficial interest and of the trustee on the application under s 30 were the same.[86] Lightman J could discover no explanation for the arrangement, but could only infer that the reason was to save the society any unwelcome publicity involved in taking proceedings for the eviction of mortgagors and a sale over the heads of the mortgagors of the matrimonial home. He said that '[t]hrough the medium of

---

[81] ibid.   [82] See also *Harrington v Bennett* [2000] BPIR 630, 634.

[83] [1999] 1 FLR 740, 746.

[84] *Per* Robert Walker LJ in *Judd v Brown* [1999] 1 FLR 1191, 1198.   [85] [1998] 2 FLR 386.

[86] However, if the society, as mortgagee, had brought proceedings for possession, such proceedings would not have been likely to succeed since the wife was, with funds from social security, paying the interest as it accrued due.

the arrangement, the society has sought to achieve its goal of a sale whilst shrouding from the public gaze its participation in the exercise'.[87] Criticizing the procedure adopted, Lightman J said:[88]

A trustee in bankruptcy is not vested with the powers and privileges of his office so as to enable himself to accept engagement as a hired gun. His duty is to exercise his powers and privileges for the benefit of the creditors for whom he is appointed a trustee.

If he had thought that there was any real possibility that the wife would be placed in any disadvantage by the course adopted he would have dismissed the application. However, it was conceded that on any application for an order for sale by the society, the society would succeed and that accordingly the adoption of the present procedure in its place had occasioned no prejudice. The need for the mortgagee to institute new proceedings would, of course, also have increased the costs.

In *Judd v Brown*,[89] Harman J appeared to have regarded the trustee as having allowed himself to be made a catspaw for one separate creditor, namely a bank which was the secured creditor. In the Court of Appeal Robert Walker LJ thought that, in contrast to the position in *Re Ng*, there was no evidence indicating that the bank was in any way exploiting the position or powers of the trustee. He said:[90]

In the absence of sufficient evidence to the contrary the judge should, it seems to me, have assumed that the trustee in bankruptcy was the best person to assess what course was in the interests of the creditors (and in particular of the unsecured creditors), and should have addressed his attention to the issue posed in s 335A(3); that is, whether the circumstances were truly exceptional or whether the interests of the two sets of creditors...must outweigh all other considerations.

The comments of Lightman J in *Re Ng* were quoted with approval by Robert Walker LJ in the subsequent case *Trustee in bankruptcy of Bukhari v Bukhari*.[91]

5.5.9. A bankrupt's own petition

In *Re Holliday*,[92] the Court of Appeal also referred to the fact that the husband had been made bankrupt on his own petition, and that 'none of the creditors thought fit themselves to present a bankruptcy petition' and it was 'quite impossible to know whether any one of them would have done so if the debtor had not himself presented such a petition'. In *Re Lowrie*,[93] Walton J referred to the fact that in *Re Holliday* 'the petition in bankruptcy had been presented by the husband himself as a tactical move, and quite clearly as a tactical move, to avoid a transfer of property order in favour of his wife, or ex-wife, at a time

---

[87] [1998] 2 FLR 387.   [88] ibid 388.   [89] ibid 360, 390.
[90] [1999] 1 FLR 1191, 1199.   [91] [1999] BPIR 157, 160.
[92] [1981] Ch 405, 425, *per* Sir David Cairns.   [93] [1981] 3 All ER 353, 355.

when no creditors whatsoever were pressing' and it appeared that he might be in a position to pay his debts out of income over a period of time. However, that was only one factor and would not by itself have been sufficient to justify postponement. In *Re Citro*,[94] Nourse LJ said that

I would not myself have regarded it as an exceptional circumstance that the husband had presented his own petition even "as a tactical move". That was not something of the creditors choosing and could not fairly be held against them.

5.5.10 When should an order for sale take effect?

Even when a court determines that there are no exceptional circumstances justifying postponement of the operation of an order for sale, it still has to decide precisely when the innocent spouse must leave the home. Indeed in *Re Citro*, where the court determined that there were no exceptional circumstances, a moratorium of six months was granted by the court, though unfortunately the reasoning of the court is not reported. Some assistance may be found in the judgment of Laddie J in *Barclays Bank plc v Hendricks*[95] dealing with an application by a chargee of the matrimonial home whom he considered to be in the same position in this respect as a trustee in bankruptcy at the time.

When the court determines that there are exceptional circumstances, any period of suspension of an order for sale will reflect the strength and nature of the exceptional circumstances. A balance has to be struck between the interests of the bankrupt's spouse and her family which have been found to be exceptional, and the interests of the creditors. Where the exceptional circumstances are related to the spouse's illness, the period of suspension is likely to be related to the expected period of that illness or to what is deemed necessary for suitable alternative accommodation to be obtained. Thus in *Re Raval*,[96] Blackburne J concluded that the order should have provided for a period of suspension of one year:

This should have been sufficient to enable steps to be taken to ensure that suitable alternative accommodation, which may well have to be provided by the local authority, can be found which would be adequate in size for Mrs Raval's needs and which will be located in an area where she can continue to enjoy the social support network which, coupled with the monthly visits she receives from the community psychiatric nurse and with the medication she receives, form a very important element in maintaining her mental stability.

In fact the period allowed was a little over one year. There was nothing to suggest that she would not continue to suffer from paranoid schizophrenia for the foreseeable future, and there was nothing intrinsic about the property such as, for example, adaptations to suit her needs. It was unlikely that the local

---

[94] [1991] 1 Ch 142, 157.   [95] [1996] 1 FLR 258, 264 considered at para 5.4.2. above.
[96] [1998] 2 FLR 718, 726.

authority could earmark suitable alternative accommodation for her use in advance of an order for possession being made, and possibly even before the issue of a writ of possession. Mrs Raval's share of the proceeds of sale would be at least £40,000 and the bankrupt would have at least £200 per month available to apply towards acquiring suitable alternative accommodation.

An indefinite suspension will be rare, but may be preferred to a fixed term of suspension even when the expected period of need is short. In *Judd v Brown*[97] the property occupied by Josephine Brown (the wife suffering from cancer) was one of several properties in respect of which an order was sought and no order for possession was made. Harman J said that viewing that property alone, he would have refused to make an order for possession of the property. The effect of making an order for possession and sale but suspending it for say eight months to allow Mrs Brown's treatment to run its course and for its result to be perceived, would be likely to have the effect of imposing considerable immediate stress upon her. That would be directly harmful to her prospects of recovery. He declined 'to suspend a sword, not of Damocles but one which descends inevitably and perceptibly month by month, over Josephine's possession of her home'. Even where the exceptional circumstances are not necessarily short term an indefinite suspension may be considered justified as in *Claughton v Charamboulous*, where not only was the wife's health regarded as exceptional, but the interests of the creditors would not be prejudiced by such an order.[98]

5.5.11 The balancing exercise

Although in exercising its discretion the court is engaged in balancing the factors involved, where more than one year has elapsed since the first vesting of the estate in the trustee, the presumption is that the interests of the creditors will outweigh all other considerations. At this stage the scales are therefore already weighted in favour of the creditors. The scales can be tipped in favour of the bankrupt's family by a combination of circumstances affecting the family and circumstances weakening the interests of the creditors. The intention was that the court should regard the period of one year as the normal maximum breathing space to be allowed to the members of the family under normal circumstances, to enable them to adjust to their changed circumstances and either to seek alternative accommodation or arrange the buying out of the bankrupt's estate.[99] The policy embodied in the legislation is clear—that only

---

[97] [1998] 2 FLR 360, 366.

[98] In *Re Mott* [1987] CLY 212 the order made by Hoffman J was that a sale of the property should be postponed until after the death of the bankrupt's mother who was then aged 70. In *Judd v Brown* [1998] 2 FLR 360, 365, Harman J said that 'That was a wholly indeterminate period which might end in one year or in 10 years. It was a period dependent on an event which must certainly terminate the human concerns of the mother of the bankrupt.'

[99] See HC Vol 83, Col 547 where it was said that: 'The court may, of course, allow only a shorter period, or no period at all, if circumstances warrant it.'

limited protection is to be afforded to a bankrupt's family in relation to their occupation of the family home even though it is part owned by the bankrupt's spouse. In these circumstances the scope for the exercise of discretion has been limited, and it had seemed that *Re Holliday* would remain the only reported case where the bankrupt's spouse had succeeded in showing exceptional circumstances. The cluster of recent cases has shown that the hurdle is not an impossible one, though even if it is surmounted, the period of postponement will not necessarily be a long one. Hardship, even extreme or exceptional hardship, will not necessarily be enough for they also show that it must be balanced against hardship and disadvantage that might be suffered by the creditors.[100]

5.6 PROVISIONS APPLICABLE WHEN A SALE IS POSTPONED

5.6.1 Questions arising on postponement

The provisions of ss 336 and 337 mean that the rights of occupation of the bankrupt's spouse or former spouse, or indeed, of the bankrupt himself, may outweigh for a time the interests of the bankrupt's creditors in relation to the family home. The trustee may therefore be unable sell the property. Even in the absence of any order of the court postponing the sale of the property, the trustee may be unable in practical terms to dispose of the property because there is a negative equity. Postponement of the sale of a property comprised in the estate raises questions in relation to the release of the trustee on completing the administration of the estate, the effect of payments required to be made by a bankrupt as a condition of being allowed to continue to occupy the property and as to the benefit of any subsequent increase in the value of that property. The specific provisions dealing with these questions are considered in the following paragraphs.

5.6.2 Charge on the dwelling-house

Section 313 of the Insolvency Act 1986 provides that where any property consisting of an interest in a dwelling-house which is occupied by the bankrupt, or by the bankrupt's spouse or former spouse, is comprised in the bankrupt's estate, and the trustee is for any reason unable for the time being to realize that property, the trustee may apply to the court for an order imposing a charge on the property for the benefit of the bankrupt's estate. If the court imposes such

---

[100] *In Claughton v Charalambous* [1999] 1 FLR 740, 744, Jonathan Parker J said that 'the test to be applied . . . is not one of extreme hardship, a test which Hoffman J appears to have applied in the case of *Re Mott (A Bankrupt)*, but exceptional circumstances'.

a charge on any property the benefit of that charge is comprised in the bankrupt's estate. Such an order made in respect of property vested in the trustee must provide in accordance with the rules, for the property to cease to be comprised in the bankrupt's estate and to vest in the bankrupt, subject to the charge and any prior charge.[101] Certain supplemental provisions of the Charging Orders Act 1979 are applied to orders under section 313.[102]

The court must dismiss the application if the value of the bankrupt's interest in the dwelling-house is below a prescribed amount which is at present £1,000.[103] In determining the value of the bankrupt's interest for this purpose, the court must disregard that part of the value of the property in which the bankrupt's interest subsists which is equal to the value of (a) any loans secured by mortgage or other charge against the property, (b) any other third party interest, and (c) the reasonable costs of sale.[104]

In its original form the charge was enforceable *up to the value from time to time of the property secured*, for the payment of any amount which was payable otherwise than to the bankrupt out of the bankrupt's estate and of interest on that amount at the prescribed rate. The effect was that any increase in the value of the property after the date of the order accrued to the bankrupt's estate. As a result of an amendment made by the Enterprise Act 2002 the charge is now enforceable only up to the *'charged value from time to time'*.[105] The 'charged value' means the amount specified in the charging order as the value of the bankrupt's interest in the property at the date of the order plus interest on that amount from the date of the charging order at the prescribed rate.[106] This means that the benefit of any increase in the value of the property after the date of the order will accrue to the bankrupt and not to his estate. The value of the bankrupt's interest in the property at the date of the charging order will therefore be an important matter to be determined at that date.[107]

The importance of a charge (or an application for a charge) under s 313 is in relation to the release of the trustee in bankruptcy. Where it appears to a trustee that the administration of the bankrupt's estate is for practical purposes complete, he will need to summon a final general meeting of the bankrupt's creditors with a view to obtaining his release.[108] Generally, a trustee must not summon such a meeting where he has been unable to realize property comprised

---

[101] IA 1986, s 313(3).   [102] IA 1986, s 313(4).

[103] IA 1986, s 313A inserted by the Enterprise Act 2002, s 261(3) with effect from 1 April 2004. See further para 5.7 below.

[104] IA 1986, s 313(2B) and the Insolvency Proceedings (Monetary Limits) (Amendment) Rules 2004 (SI 2004/547), para 3, inserting para 5 into the Insolvency Proceedings (Monetary Limits) Order 1986 (SI 1986/1996).

[105] IA 1986, s 313(2) as amended by the Enterprise Act 2002, s 261(2).

[106] IA 1986, s 313(2A).

[107] A charged value may not be varied by an order under s 3(5) of the Charging Orders Act 1979.

[108] IA 1986, s 331. This does not apply if the trustee is the Official Receiver.

in the estate consisting of an interest in a dwelling-house which is occupied by the bankrupt or by the bankrupt's spouse or former spouse. However, a trustee will be able to call a meeting and obtain his release if the court has made an order under s 313 or has declined to make an order on the trustee's application under s 313.[109]

5.6.3 Payments

Where any premises comprised in the bankrupt's estate are occupied by him (whether by virtue of s 337 or otherwise) on condition that he makes payments towards satisfying any liability arising under the mortgage of the premises or otherwise towards the outgoings of the premises, the bankrupt does not, by virtue of those payments, acquire any interest in the premises.[110] This preserves the existing position.

5.6.4 Bankrupt's home ceasing to form part of the estate

A trustee in bankruptcy may have taken no action to realize the interest of the bankrupt in a dwelling-house, because it represented only a negative equity. Although a considerable time may have elapsed during which the bankrupt will have obtained his automatic discharge, the property has remained vested in the trustee as part of the bankrupt's estate.[111] If the trustee subsequently finds that the property has increased substantially in value he may consider it worthwhile to seek an order for sale much to the surprise of the former bankrupt and his family who have remained in occupation and may have been maintaining mortgage payments in respect of the property. The Enterprise Act 2002 introduced a provision designed to limit the time during which a trustee will be able to seek an order for sale.

This provision is now contained in s 283A of the Insolvency Act 1986 and applies where property comprised in the bankrupt's estate consists of an interest in a dwelling-house which at the date of the bankruptcy was the sole or principal residence of (a) the bankrupt, (b) the bankrupt's spouse, or (c) a former spouse of the bankrupt.[112] At the end of the period of three years beginning

---

[109] IA 1986, s 332.   [110] IA 1986, s 338.

[111] If the bankrupt's spouse reaches agreement with the trustee for the transfer to her of the bankrupt's interest in the property for a nominal sum, it is essential that the agreement is properly finalised. See *Boorer v Boorer* [2002] BPIR 21 where it was held that the trustee in bankruptcy was perfectly entitled to require payment for the transfer of the bankrupt's share in the matrimonial home to the bankrupt's wife when he discovered that there was equity in the property although he had earlier agreed to treat the home as having a negative equity and indicated that he was prepared to transfer that interest to her for a nominal sum. The mere fact that earlier a transfer document had been prepared did not raise an estoppel or evidence a binding agreement.

[112] IA 1986, s 283A(1) inserted by the Enterprise Act 2002, s 261.

with the date of the bankruptcy the interest in that dwelling-house will cease to be comprised in the bankrupt's estate, and vest in the bankrupt without conveyance, assignment, or transfer.[113] However, this will not apply if during that period of three years:[114]

(a) the trustee realizes the interest concerned;
(b) the trustee applies for an order for sale in respect of the dwelling-house,
(c) the trustee applies for an order for possession of the dwelling-house,
(d) the trustee applies for an order under s 313 imposing a charge on that interest, or
(e) the trustee and the bankrupt agree that the bankrupt shall incur a specified liability to his estate (with or without the addition of interest from the date of the agreement) in consideration of which the interest concerned shall cease to form part of the estate.

Where the trustee makes an application of a kind mentioned in (b), (c), or (d) above during the three year period and it is dismissed, then, unless the court orders otherwise the interest to which the application relates will on the dismissal of the application (a) cease to be comprised in the bankrupt's estate, and (b) vest in the bankrupt (without conveyance, assignment or transfer).[115]

It should be noted that the court may substitute for the period of three years a longer period (a) in prescribed circumstances, and (b) in such other circumstances as the court thinks appropriate.[116] The rules may make provision for s 283A to have effect with the substitution of a shorter period for the period of three years in specified circumstances (which may be described by reference to action to be taken by a trustee in bankruptcy).[117]

The rules may also, in particular, make provision requiring or enabling the trustee of a bankrupt's estate to give notice that s 283A applies or does not apply, and about the effect of such a notice. They may also require the trustee of a bankrupt's estate to make an application to the Chief Land Registrar where this is necessary for example, to reflect the re-vesting of the interest in the bankrupt.[118]

Where an individual has been adjudged bankrupt on a petition presented before s 283A came into force on 1 April 2004, there are similar provisions under which an interest in a dwelling-house will re-vest in him after a transitional

---

[113] IA 1986, s 283A(2). If the bankrupt does not inform the trustee or the official receiver of his interest in a property before the end of the period of three months beginning with the date of the bankruptcy, the period of three years will not begin with the date of the bankruptcy, but will begin with the date on which the trustee or official receiver becomes aware of the bankrupt's interest: subs (5). [114] IA 1986, s 283A(3).
[115] IA 1986, s 283A(4). [116] IA 1986, s 283A(6). [117] IA 1986, s 283A(7).
[118] IA 1986, s 283A(8). See subs (9) for further possible provisions.

period of three years from that date unless the trustee takes one of the specified steps to prevent this happening.[119]

5.7 LOW VALUE HOMES

The Enterprise Act 2002 introduced a provision designed to protect the interest of a bankrupt in property if the trustee applies for an order for sale of the property, for an order for possession or for an order imposing a charge on the property under s 313 provided the interest is of low value. This provision applies to property comprised in the bankrupt's estate consisting of an interest in a dwelling-house which at the date of the bankruptcy was the sole or principal residence of (i) the bankrupt, (ii) the bankrupt's spouse, or (iii) the former spouse of the bankrupt. If the value of the bankrupt's interest is below a pre-scribed amount then the court must dismiss the trustee's application.[120] In determining the value of the bankrupt's interest for this purpose, the court must disregard that part of the value of the property in which the bankrupt's interest subsists which is equal to the value of (a) any loans secured by mortgage or other charge against the property, (b) any other third party interest, and (c) the reasonable costs of sale.[121] It must be emphasized that it is the value of the bankrupt's interest which must be below the prescribed value and not the value of the property in which that interest subsists.

5.8 THE EUROPEAN CONVENTION ON HUMAN RIGHTS

Under Article 8 it is provided that everyone has a right to respect for his private and family life, his home and his correspondence. Paragraph 2 provides that:

There shall be no interference by a public authority with the exercise of this right except such as is in accordance with the law and is necessary in a democratic society in the interests of ... the rights and freedoms of others.

In *Jackson v Bell*,[122] Sir Andrew Morritt V-C said:

The right and freedoms of others plainly encompass the rights of the creditors of the bankrupt, and there is, therefore, a balance to be struck between the rights and interests of the bankrupt's family, on the one hand, and his creditors on the other. It seems to me

---

[119] Enterprise Act 2002, s 261(7)–(10).

[120] IA 1986, s 313A inserted by s 261(3) of the Enterprise Act 2002. The prescribed figure is £1,000: Insolvency Proceedings (Monetary Limits)(Amendment) Order 2004 (SI 2004/547).

[121] Insolvency Proceedings (Monetary Limits)(Amendment) Rules 2004 (SI 2004/547), para 3, inserting para 5 into the Insolvency Proceedings (Monetary Limits) Order 1986 (SI 1986/1996).

[122] [2001] EWCA Civ 387, para [24].

there is an important point here for the consideration of the Court of Appeal as to quite how that balance is struck and how, where the property sought to be sold is a dwelling house and the former matrimonial home, how the words "exceptional circumstances" are to be construed and in any given case applied.

Permission to appeal was granted but unfortunately the case does not seem to have proceeded further.

5.9 BANKRUPTCY AND MORTGAGE ACTIONS

Although a mortgagee of the family home will generally rely on his remedies as a mortgagee which were considered in Chapter 4 and seek possession of the mortgaged property with a view to a sale, it is also entitled to sue the mortgagor on the personal covenant. If the mortgagee obtains a money judgment then in the event of default the mortgagor may be made bankrupt and the trustee in bankruptcy may seek an order for the sale of the property. The protection afforded to the mortgagor and his family under s 335A of the Insolvency Act 1986 is more limited than that afforded to the mortgagor under the Administration of Justice Act 1970. Such a course of action has the disadvantage that the mortgagee will have to surrender its security and obviously this will only be attractive if the claims of other creditors are not such as to make it likely that the proceeds of sale of the property will not be sufficient to discharge all the debts in full. In practice such a course of action is most likely to be chosen when a mortgagee has failed to obtain an order for possession because the mortgage is found not to bind one of the mortgagors, because the mortgagee is affected by constructive notice of undue influence or misrepresentation on the part of the other mortgagor whom it is sought to make bankrupt.

This was the case in *Alliance & Leicester plc v Slayford*[123] where the mortgagee had commenced proceedings for possession of mortgaged property against a mortgagor husband. His wife was successful in arguing that she had a small beneficial interest in the property and that the form of consent to the mortgage which she had signed had been obtained as a result of her husband's undue influence without appropriate advice. Following the refusal of the court to make an order for possession against her, the building society obtained leave to amend the pleadings to claim a money judgment. This course of action was strongly criticized by the county court judge, but allowed by the Court of Appeal which held, in the first place, that the mortgagee was not precluded from bringing subsequent proceedings for a money judgment because it had not

---

[123] [2001] 1 All ER (Comm) 1. See also *Zandfarid v Bank of Credit and Commerce International SA* [1996] 1 WLR 1420.

sought and obtained such a judgment in the possession proceedings as originally constituted.[124] Secondly, there was:

no abuse of process in a mortgagee, who has been met with a successful *O'Brien* type defence taken by the wife of the mortgagor, merely choosing to pursue his remedies against the mortgagor by suing on the personal covenant with a view as an unsecured creditor to bankrupting him, even though this may lead to an application by the trustee in bankruptcy for the sale of the property in which the wife has an equitable interest.[125]

---

[124] The mortgagee was not subject to res judicata or to the rule in *Henderson v Henderson* (1843) Hare 100 which prevents a plaintiff raising in later proceedings a claim or cause of action which he could and should have raised in an earlier action which was taken to judgment. See *UCB Bank plc v Chandler* (2000) 79 P & CR 270, 273, and *Securum Finance Ltd v Ashton* [2001] Ch 291.

[125] ibid *per* Peter Gibson LJ at para [28].

6

BANKRUPTCY

6.1 INSOLVENCY AND BANKRUPTCY

6.1.1 Insolvency and bankruptcy

In everyday language insolvency and bankruptcy may be used as inter-changeable terms, but there is an important distinction to be drawn. Insolvency refers to a state of affairs in which an individual debtor is unable to discharge his financial obligations. This may be said to exist when his liabilities exceed his assets or when he is unable to discharge his obligations when they become due. Bankruptcy, on the other hand, is a legal status imposed by an order of the court. Insolvency will not necessarily lead to bankruptcy and there are other ways of dealing with the problems associated with that state of affairs.[1]

An individual may find himself in a state of insolvency and hence likely to be adjudicated bankrupt for a number of reasons of which business failure has in the past been the most important. The increased availability of credit for consumer items has undoubtedly led to an increase in bankruptcy in the recent decade and in 1999 the number of consumer bankruptcies reached 50 per cent

---

[1] See ch 7.

and in 2000 53 per cent.[2] However, it is concern about business bankruptcies and their effect on enterprise which has proved the impetus for recent proposals for reform culminating in the Enterprise Act 2002.

6.1.2 The nature and objectives of bankruptcy

The essence of bankruptcy is that the debtor's assets are vested in his trustee in bankruptcy to be realized for the benefit of creditors who will receive their appropriate share of the proceeds according to the statutory provisions designed to ensure fairness between all the creditors. Thus bankruptcy may be seen primarily as a means of realizing the assets of an insolvent debtor for the benefit of his creditors.[3] However, at the same time it is a means of relieving and protecting that individual from further demands by creditors for generally no action can be taken against the bankrupt during the period of bankruptcy outside the bankruptcy process. Life for the bankrupt—and his family—must go on, and he must have the means to support himself and his family—which is also in the interests of society in general. A balance must therefore be struck between the demand to satisfy his creditors and the need for the bankrupt and his family to maintain a reasonable standard of living. Indeed there is life beyond bankruptcy and one of its aims is to enable the insolvent to rehabilitate himself.[4] On discharge from bankruptcy the bankrupt, having been released from his debts can make a fresh start. There are exceptions to these general principles which will be considered in the course of this chapter.

Rehabilitation has been given another dimension in recent proposals for reform by the desire 'to encourage entrepreneurship and responsible risk taking, which will contribute to the creation of wealth and employment.'[5] In April 2000, The Insolvency Service published a consultation paper entitled 'Bankruptcy—A Fresh Start' proposing changes to the law relating to personal insolvency involving a move away from the 'one-size-fits-all' approach that was characteristic of the existing bankruptcy system so as to reduce the impact of financial failure on individuals and encourage a second chance.[6] The issue of a bankrupt's discharge 'should be separated from the question of his conduct and

---

[2] See 'Insolvency—A Second Chance' (Cm 5234), para 1.46. 'We appear to be moving towards the models present in the United States, Canada and Australia where consumer bankruptcies form a very significant majority of cases' (para 1.47).

[3] Contrast the position in the US. Thus Jackson said: 'Bankruptcy, at first glance, may be thought of as a procedure geared principally towards relieving an overburdened debtor from "oppressive" debt.' ('Bankruptcy, Non-Bankruptcy Entitlements, and the Creditors' Bargain' (1982) 91 Yale LJ 857.) This was not Jackson's own view of bankruptcy, which he saw primarily as a creditor's bargain.

[4] Report of the Review Committee on 'Insolvency Law and Practice' (The Cork Committee, 1982) (Cmnd 8558). See also *R v Lord Chancellor, ex p Lightfoot* [1999] 4 All ER 583.

[5] 'Insolvency—A Second Chance' (Cm 5234), para 1.1.

[6] This theme was evident too in the joint DTI/DfEE White Paper, 'Opportunity For All In a World of Change' (2001).

the need, where that conduct had been reprehensible, to protect the public and the commercial community from that bankrupt's irresponsibility in the future'.[7] In 2001, the DTI published a White Paper entitled 'Insolvency—A Second Chance' putting forward detailed proposals which would 'streamline the process and reduce the stigma for the vast majority of individuals, and encourage those who have failed, through no fault of their own, to try again'.[8] It emphasized the view that it 'is in the nature of risk-taking that, on occasions, there will be failure'. However, 'in a society which is genuinely enterprising the cost of failure must not be set so high that it acts as a deterrent to economic activity'.[9] The culmination was the Enterprise Act 2002 the relevant parts of which came into force on 1 April 2004. The effect is to liberalize the bankruptcy system for the majority of bankrupts while protecting society in general and the commercial community in particular from the minority found to be culpable, through a regime of Bankruptcy Restrictions Orders.

6.2 WHO MAY BE MADE BANKRUPT

A petition for a bankruptcy order to be made against an individual can be presented only if he (a) is domiciled in England and Wales, (b) is personally present in England and Wales on the day on which the petition is presented, or (c) at any time in the period of three years ending with that day he has been ordinarily resident, or has had a place of residence in England and Wales, or has carried on business in England and Wales.[10]

6.3 PETITIONS FOR A BANKRUPTCY ORDER

6.3.1 Entitlement to present

A petition for a bankruptcy order to be made against an individual may be presented to the court by a creditor or jointly by more than one creditor or by the individual himself.[11] A petition may also be presented by the supervisor of a voluntary arrangement approved under the Insolvency Act or by any person bound by such an arrangement, other than the debtor himself.[12] Once presented, a bankruptcy petition must not be withdrawn without leave of the court.[13]

---

[7] 'Bankruptcy—A Fresh Start,' para 7.3.   [8] (Cm 5234), para 1.1.
[9] ibid para 1.24.   [10] Insolvency Act 1986 ('IA 1986'), s 265(1).
[11] IA 1986, s 264(1). See further subs (1)(ba) and (bb) in relation to Council Reg (EC) 1346/2000 [2000] OJ L160/1.
[12] For the conditions that must be satisfied in this case, see IA 1986, s 276.
[13] IA 1986, s 266(2) and Insolvency Rules 1986, r 6.32

6.3.2 Creditor's petition

A creditor may present a petition in respect of a debt or debts only if, at the time the petition is presented, certain conditions are satisfied.[14] First the amount of the debt (or the aggregate amount of the debts) must be equal to or exceed the bankruptcy level. At present this is £750, but it may be increased by statutory instrument. Secondly, the debt, or each of the debts, must be for a liquidated sum payable to the petitioning creditor (or to one or more of the petitioning creditors) either immediately or at some certain future time, and must be unsecured.[15] Thirdly, the debt, or each debt, must be one which the debtor appears to be unable to pay, or, in the case of a debt which is not immediately payable, appears to have no reasonable prospect of being able to pay. Fourthly, there must be no outstanding application to set aside a statutory demand served under s 268 in respect of any of the debts.

There are only two ways in which it can be shown that a debtor appears to be unable to pay a debt which is immediately payable, namely (i) a failure to comply within three weeks with a statutory demand served on the debtor by the petitioning creditor, and (ii) a failure to satisfy execution or other process issued in respect of a judgment debt or court order in favour of the petitioning creditor.[16] A debtor can be shown to have no reasonable prospect of being able to pay a debt not immediately payable only on the basis of a failure to comply within three weeks with a statutory demand in the prescribed form requiring him to establish to the satisfaction of the creditor that there is a reasonable prospect that the debtor will be able to pay the debt when it falls due.[17] A petition based wholly or partly in respect of a debt which is the subject of a statutory demand may be presented before the end of the three week period if there is a serious possibility that the debtor's property, or the value of any of his property, will be significantly diminished during that period.[18]

6.3.3 The statutory demand

A creditor seeking to initiate the bankruptcy process can establish the inability of a debtor to pay a debt by serving on the debtor a statutory demand requiring

---

[14] IA 1986, s 267(2).

[15] A petition may be presented on the basis of a secured debt if either (a) the petition contains a statement that the creditor is willing, in the event of a bankruptcy order being made, to give up his security for the benefit of the bankrupt's creditors, or (b) the petition is expressed not to be made in respect of the secured part of the debt and states the estimated value at the date of the petition of the security for the secured part of the debt (s 269(1)). In the latter event the secured and unsecured parts of the debt are to be treated as separate debts for this purpose (s 269(2)).

[16] IA 1986, s 268(1). See *Re a Debtor (No 340 of 1992)* [1996] 2 All ER 211, CA.

[17] IA 1986, s 268(2).

[18] IA 1986, s 270. See however, s 271(2) which provides that in that event a bankruptcy order may not be made until the three week period has elapsed.

the debtor to pay the debt or compound it to the creditor's satisfaction or, if it is not immediately payable, to show that there is a reasonable prospect that he will be able to pay the debt when it falls due. The form and content of a statutory demand are set out in the Insolvency Rules.[19] It must specify whether it is made in respect of an existing debt or a debt not immediately payable, and if founded on a judgment or order, it must give details of the judgment or order. If the creditor holds any security in respect of the debt, the demand must specify the full amount of the debt, the nature of the security, and the value which the creditor puts upon it at the date of the demand. The amount of which payment is claimed by the demand must be the full amount of the debt, less the amount specified as the value of the security.[20] It must include an explanation to the debtor of the purpose of the demand and the fact that, if the debtor does not comply with the demand, bankruptcy proceedings may be commenced against him. It must specify the time within which the demand must be complied with, if that consequence is to be avoided, and the methods of compliance open to the debtor. It must also inform the debtor of his right to apply to the court for the statutory demand to be set aside.

The debtor may, within the period of eighteen days from the date of the service on him of the demand apply to the appropriate court for an order setting the statutory demand aside. Subject to any order of the court, the time limited for compliance with the statutory demand ceases to run as from the date on which the application is filed in the court.[21] On receipt of the application the court, may, if satisfied that no sufficient cause is shown for it, dismiss it without giving notice to the creditor. The time limited for compliance with the demand then begins to run again. If the application is not so dismissed, the court must fix a venue for it to be heard and give notice to the debtor, creditor and other persons concerned. On the hearing of the application, the court must consider the evidence available and may either summarily determine the application or adjourn it giving such directions as it thinks appropriate.[22]

The court may grant the application if:

(a) the debtor appears to have a counter-claim, set-off, or cross demand which equals or exceeds the amount of the debt or debts specified in the statutory demand; or

(b) the debt is disputed on grounds which appear to the court to be substantial; or

(c) it appears that the creditor holds some security in respect of the debt claimed by the demand, and either the creditor has failed to comply with the requirements of r 6.1(5) with regard to that security set out above, or the court

---

[19] Insolvency Rules 1986, rr 6.1 and 6.2. Service is dealt with in r 6.3.
[20] ibid r 6.1(5).   [21] ibid r 6.4.   [22] ibid r 6.5.

is satisfied that the value of the security equals or exceeds the full amount of the debt; or

(d) the court is satisfied on other grounds, that the demand ought to be set aside.

The last paragraph confers a broad discretion on the court to set aside a statutory demand, but it is clear from a number of decisions that the existence of one or more defects in a statutory demand will not necessarily justify setting it aside if the debtor has suffered no injustice. In *Re a Debtor (No 1 of 1987 ex p Lancaster)*,[23] Nicholls LJ said:

The court will exercise its discretion on whether or not to set aside a statutory demand having regard to all the circumstances. That must require the court to have regard to all the circumstances as they are at the time of the hearing before the court. There may be cases where the terms of the statutory demand are so confusing or misleading that, having regard to all the circumstances, justice requires that the demand should not be allowed to stand. There will be other cases where, despite such defects in the contents of the statutory demand, those defects have not prejudiced and will not prejudice the debtor in any way, and to set aside the demand in such a case would serve no useful purpose.

Thus if the debtor was wholly unable to pay the debt the only practical consequence of setting aside a statutory demand would be that the creditor would serve a revised statutory demand which would inevitably not be complied with but which would have increased the costs. In that case the statutory demand had overstated the amount of the debt but the Court of Appeal held it to be inappropriate to set it aside Nicholls LJ said that '... the mere overstatement of the amount of the debt in a statutory demand is not, by itself and without more, a ground for setting aside a statutory demand'.[24]

If the court dismisses the application, it must make an order authorizing the creditor to present a bankruptcy petition either forthwith, or on or after a date specified in the order.[25] The debtor may appeal against the decision of the court under s 375(2) of the Insolvency Act 1986.

6.3.4 Proceedings on a creditor's petition—the hearing of the petition

Generally a bankruptcy petition will not be heard unless at least fourteen days have elapsed since it was served on the debtor.[26] If the debtor wishes to oppose the petition he must, at least seven days before the date of the hearing, file a notice stating the grounds on which he opposes the making of a bankruptcy order. A copy of the notice must be served on the petitioning creditor.[27] He must

---

[23] [1989] 1 WLR 271, 279.
[24] ibid 279. See also *Re a Debtor (No 51 of 1991)* [1992] 1 WLR 1294.
[25] Insolvency Rules 1986, r 6.5(6).
[26] ibid r 6.18(1). A petition may be heard earlier in special circumstances. See r 6.18(2).
[27] ibid r 6.21.

also be given notice by any other creditor who intends to appear at the hearing of the petition.[28] It is essential that the petitioning creditor appears at the hearing,[29] but the court may proceed in the absence of the debtor.

The court must not make a bankruptcy order on a creditor's petition unless it is satisfied that the debt or one of the debts in respect of which the petition was presented is either:

(a) a debt which, having been payable at the date of the petition or having since become payable, has neither been paid nor secured or compounded for, or

(b) a debt which the debtor has no reasonable prospect of being able to pay when it falls due.[30]

Whether a debt has been paid is a question of fact. The prospects of payment of future debts is a matter of evidence. The securing or compounding of a debt is a matter of agreement between debtor and creditor. A composition with a creditor will normally involve accepting a partial payment whether by a lump sum or instalments.[31] In determining for this purpose what constitutes a reasonable prospect that the debtor will be able to pay a debt when it falls due, it is to be assumed that the prospect given by the facts and other matters known to the creditor at the time he entered into the transaction resulting in the debt was a reasonable prospect.[32] The effect of this is that it must be shown that at the time when the debt was incurred there was a reasonable prospect of it being paid, but that circumstances have changed since that date.

Even though one of these threshold conditions is satisfied, the court may nevertheless dismiss the petition if it is satisfied that the debtor is able to pay all his debts. In determining for this purpose whether the debtor is able to pay all his debts, the court must take into account his contingent and prospective liabilities.[33] It may also dismiss the petition if it is satisfied:

(a) that the debtor has made an offer to secure or compound for a debt in respect of which the petition is presented,

(b) that the acceptance of that offer would have required the dismissal of the petition, and

(c) that the offer has been unreasonably refused.

In *Re a debtor (No 32 of 1993)*,[34] Mr Timothy Lloyd QC sitting as a High Court Judge said that the test is whether a reasonable creditor, in the position of the petitioning creditor, and in the light of the actual history as disclosed to the court, would have accepted or refused the offer. However, there can be a range of reasonable positions on the part of hypothetical reasonable creditors. In order to conclude that the refusal was unreasonable the court has to be satisfied

---

[28] ibid r 6.23.   [29] See r 6.26 for the consequences if he does not appear.
[30] IA 1986, s 271(1).   [31] See *Re a Debtor (No 32 of 1993)* [1995] 1 All ER 628, 630–1.
[32] IA 1986, s 271(4).   [33] IA 1986, s 271(3).   [34] [1995] 1 All ER 628, 639–40.

that no reasonable hypothetical creditor would have refused the offer, and that the refusal of the offer was therefore beyond the range of possible reasonable actions in the context.

The judge considered the matters which a hypothetical reasonable creditor would take into account when deciding whether or not to accept an offer or rather to press for a bankruptcy order. He would be likely to regard past history of offers and payments and the prospects of limited or negligible recovery in bankruptcy as having substantial relevance. Such a hypothetical creditor might well also regard it as relevant that, whatever the eventual outcome of the bankruptcy in financial terms for the creditors, a bankruptcy order would at least result in a fuller investigation than could be achieved by inquiries on behalf of the creditor on an ad hoc basis. He would not necessarily simply regard the issue as one of comparing the economic outcome of two different propositions, nor that the risk of a nil return for the creditors from the bankruptcy would necessarily lead the creditor to favour a bird in the hand.[35] In that case it was held that although a different creditor might have accepted the debtor's offer for £15,000 to be paid by third parties in full settlement of the creditor's claim for some £33,638.86, it could not be said that no reasonable creditor would have refused the offer. Taking all the evidence into account, and accepting that the position should be considered only as between this actual creditor and the debtor, and without regard to the position of whatever other creditors there might be, the judge could not conclude that no reasonable creditor could have refused this offer.

The court has a general power, if it appears to it appropriate to do so on the grounds that there has been a contravention of the rules or for any other reason, to dismiss a bankruptcy petition or to stay proceedings on such a petition. Where it stays proceedings on a petition, it may do so on such terms and conditions as it thinks fit.[36]

If a petitioning creditor is unable or does not wish to pursue the petition, the court may substitute another creditor for him provided the substituted creditor would have been able to present a bankruptcy petition on the date the petition was presented.[37] Although a creditor who could not have presented a bankruptcy petition at the time when the petitioning creditor presented the petition cannot be substituted for the petitioning creditor, he can apply for a 'change of carriage order' which will enable him to take control of the proceedings.[38]

6.3.5 Debtor's petition

A debtor may present a petition only on the ground that he is unable to pay his debts.[39] Only debts, or such parts of debts currently payable, are to be

---

[35] [1995] 1 All ER 628, 639–40.   [36] IA 1986, s 266(3).

[37] Insolvency Rules 1986, r 6.30. Where a bankruptcy order is subsequently made then any payment which had been made to the original petitioning creditor will be a void disposition within s 284 of the IA 1986.   [38] Insolvency Rules 1986, r 6.31. *Re Purvis* [1997] 3 All ER 663.

[39] IA 1986, s 272(1).

considered in determining inability to pay for this purpose.[40] A statement of the debtor's affairs giving, inter alia, particulars of his assets and liabilities must accompany the petition.

In certain circumstances an individual voluntary arrangement may be more appropriate than bankruptcy and it is provided that on the hearing of a debtor's petition the court must not make a bankruptcy order if it appears to the court that certain conditions are satisfied.[41] These conditions are:

(a) that if a bankruptcy order were made the aggregate amount of the bankruptcy debts, so far as unsecured, would be less than the small bankruptcies level which is currently £40,000;[42]

(b) that if a bankruptcy order were made, the value of the bankrupt's estate would be equal to or more than the minimum amount which is currently £4,000;[43]

(c) that within the period of five years ending with the presentation of the petition the debtor has neither been adjudged bankrupt nor made a composition with his creditors in satisfaction of his debts or a scheme of arrangement of his affairs; and

(d) that it would be appropriate to appoint a person to prepare a report under s 274 as to the feasibility of a voluntary arrangement.

If these conditions are satisfied the court must appoint an insolvency practitioner to prepare a report. On considering the report the court may make an interim order for the purpose of facilitating the consideration and implementation of a proposal for a voluntary arrangement, or if it thinks it would be inappropriate to make such an order, it may then make a bankruptcy order.[44]

A significant proportion of bankruptcy petitions are presented by the debtors themselves. Thus in 2002 the number of petitions presented by debtors in the county court was 15,600 as compared with 7,082 petitions presented by creditors. In the High Court 907 petitions were presented by debtors and 9,248 petitions by creditors making a total of 16,507 debtors' petitions and 16,330 creditors' petitions.[45] In *R v Lord Chancellor, ex p Lightfoot*,[46] Simon Brown LJ noted the benefits of doing so, namely the immediate release of the debtor from importunate creditors, from the bailiff's knock on the door and in due course release from his debts at the end of the bankruptcy period. However, such petitions can only be presented on payment of a deposit (at present £250) as security against the fees which the official receiver will incur, once the order is

---

[40] *Re A Debtor (No 17 of 1966)* [1967] 1 All ER 668. Thus only instalments currently payable were relevant.   [41] IA 1986, s 273.

[42] Insolvency Proceedings (Monetary Limits) (Amendment) Order 2004, SI 2004/547. This came into force on 1 April 2004.   [43] SI 2004/547. This figure became effective on 1 April 2004.

[44] IA 1986, s 274(3).

[45] Judicial Statistics Annual Report (2002). The figures for petitions by debtors include petitions by the legal representatives of deceased debtors.   [46] [1999] 4 All ER 583, 585.

made, in examining the debtor's affairs and administering his assets. In that case Mrs Lightfoot was unable to pay this deposit, as are, it seems, large numbers of debtors. Nevertheless, the Court of Appeal held that the requirement of a deposit did not interfere with the right of access to the court and there was no infringement of Articles 6(1) or 14 of the Convention for the Protection of Human Rights and Fundamental Freedoms.

The advantage to be gained by a debtor from filing a petition does however, have the potential for abuse especially where the debtor faces claims for financial provision and property adjustment in matrimonial proceedings. In such circumstances an application for annulment by the debtor's spouse may be appropriate and this is considered later.[47]

6.4 CONDUCT OF THE BANKRUPTCY

On the making of a bankruptcy order the official receiver becomes the receiver and manager of the bankrupt's estate until the estate vests in the trustee in bankruptcy under s 306 on his appointment.[48] The function of the official receiver during this period is to protect the estate and the bankrupt is under a duty to:

(a) deliver possession of his estate to the official receiver, and
(b) deliver up to the official receiver all books, papers, and other records of which he has possession or control and which relate to his estate and affairs (including any which would be privileged from disclosure in any proceedings).[49]

Although the Act imposes a requirement upon the official receiver to investigate the conduct and affairs of each bankrupt (including his conduct and affairs before the making of the bankruptcy order) and make such report (if any) to the court as he thinks fit, this does not apply if he thinks such an investigation is unnecessary.[50]

Where a bankruptcy order is made in a case in which an insolvency practitioner's report has been submitted to the court under s 274 the court, if it thinks fit, may on making the bankruptcy order appoint the person who made the report as trustee.[51]

Where a bankruptcy order is made at a time when there is a supervisor of a voluntary arrangement approved in relation to the bankrupt, the court, if it thinks fit, may on making the bankruptcy order appoint the supervisor of the arrangement as trustee.[52]

---

[47] See para 6.10.4 below.   [48] IA 1986, s 287.   [49] IA 1986, s 291(1).
[50] IA 1986, s 289(1)(2) as substituted by Enterprise Act 2002, s 258.
[51] IA 1986, s 297(4). For individual voluntary arrangements see ch 7, para 7.6.
[52] IA 1986, s 297(5).

In other cases where a bankruptcy order has been made it is the duty of the official receiver, as soon as practicable in the period of twelve weeks beginning with the day on which the order was made, to decide whether to summon a general meeting of the bankrupt's creditors for the purpose of appointing a trustee of the bankrupt's estate.[53] If the official receiver decides not to summon such a meeting, he shall, before the end of the period of twelve weeks give notice of his decision to the court and to every creditor of the bankrupt who is known to the official receiver or is identified in the bankrupt's statement of affairs.[54] As from the giving of such a notice to the court, the official receiver is the trustee of the bankrupt's estate.[55] The official receiver is likely to base his decision on whether or not the bankrupt's estate is sufficient to justify the appointment of an insolvency practitioner. However, any creditor may request the official receiver to summon a meeting of creditors for the purpose of appointing the trustee, and if the request appears to be made with the concurrence of not less than one quarter, in value, of the bankrupt's creditors he must summon the requested meeting.[56] If the meeting fails to appoint a trustee the official receiver must decide whether to refer the question of appointment to the Secretary of State. If he decides not to refer the matter to the Secretary of State or if the latter declines to make an appointment, the official receiver must give notice of his decision or that of the Secretary of State to the court. As from the giving of such a notice the official receiver is the trustee of the bankrupt's estate.[57]

The function of a trustee in bankruptcy is to get in, realize and distribute the bankrupt's estate in accordance with the provisions of the Act. In the carrying out of that function and in the management of the bankrupt's estate the trustee is entitled, subject to those provisions, to use his own discretion.[58] The powers of the trustee are conferred by s 314 of the Act and set out in detail in Sch 5 to the Act.

6.5 VESTING OF THE BANKRUPT'S PROPERTY

6.5.1 General principle

The bankrupt's estate vests in the trustee immediately on his appointment taking effect or, in the case of the official receiver, on his becoming trustee. Such vesting is automatic without any conveyance, assignment, or transfer.[59] The bankrupt's estate comprises, in the first place, all property belonging to or vested in the bankrupt at the commencement of the

---

[53] IA 1986, s 293(1).   [54] IA 1986, s 293(2).   [55] IA 1986, s 293(3).
[56] IA 1986, s 294(1)(2).   [57] IA 1986, s 295.   [58] IA 1986, s 305(2).
[59] IA 1986, s 306(1) and (2). For the effect of a restraint order under the Proceeds of Crime Act 2002, see s 306A.

bankruptcy, with the exception of certain exempted property.[60] This may be augmented by

(a) 'after-acquired property'—property acquired by the bankrupt thereafter and before his discharge—if claimed by the trustee by notice in writing under s 307;
(b) the 'excess value of excluded property' if claimed by the trustee by notice in writing under s 308; and
(c) certain tenancies which may be claimed by the trustee under s 308A.[61]

6.5.2 The meaning of 'property'

Section 436 provides that, except in so far as the context otherwise requires, ' "property" includes money, goods, things in action, land and every description of property wherever situated and also obligations and every description of interest whether present or future or vested or contingent, arising out of, or incidental to, property...'. As Aldous LJ pointed out in *Ord v Upton*[62] this 'is not in truth a definition of the word "property". It only sets out what is included'. In *In re Celtic Extraction Ltd*,[63] Morritt LJ said that the 'word "property" is not a term of art but takes its meaning from its context'. In the context of bankruptcy, the policy of the legislation requires it to have a wide meaning for the benefit of creditors to counterbalance the release of the bankrupt from his debts. Indeed in *Bristol Airport plc v Powderill*,[64] Sir Nicholas Browne-Wilkinson V-C observed in relation to s 436 that: 'It is hard to think of a wider definition of property.' Nevertheless there are limits and some principles can be discerned in the cases.

6.5.3 An existing item

In *Re Campbell*,[65] Knox J said that as a matter of construction he was unable to accept that the word 'property' in this context was intended to describe anything other than an existing item of property. It was not susceptible of referring to something which had no present existence but might possibly come into existence on some uncertain event in the future. He distinguished between two situations. 'The first is when there is a contingent interest in property, for example, the right to receive £50,000 under a legacy contingently on attaining the age of x years when one is x-y years old.' If there is a trust fund, there is existing property in respect of which there is a contingent interest. That was quite different from the situation before him where there

---

[60] IA 1986, s 283(1) and (2).

[61] In addition, of course, property may be reclaimed by the trustee under, eg s 339 on the basis that it was disposed of in a transaction at an undervalue. See ch 9.

[62] [2000] Ch 352, 360.   [63] [2001] Ch 475, 483, para [26].   [64] [1990] Ch 744, 759.

[65] [1996] 2 All ER 537, 540.

was 'the possibility of achieving an interest in something which presently does not exist but may exist in the future'. At the date of the bankruptcy order in that case the bankrupt had only the prospect of receiving an award from the Criminal Injuries Compensation Board and Knox J held that this did not amount to an interest in property which vested automatically in the trustee in bankruptcy under s 306.[66] There was no right to enforce any form of award from the Board.

In contrast in *Patel v Jones*,[67] the legal right to a pension was vested in Mr Patel before he became bankrupt. He had a present legal right to compel payment of the pension and other benefits in future and on certain contingencies. That right was a 'chose in action' within the very wide description of 'property' in s 436 of the 1986 Act and vested in the trustee in bankruptcy. The fact that the pension did not become payable until after the bankruptcy was irrelevant to the existence of the property right. The fact that the occasion for the payment of pension benefits did not occur until Mr Patel was made redundant after the bankruptcy was irrelevant to the existence and vesting of the right.

In *Performing Right Society Ltd v Rowland*,[68] Robert Walker J had to consider whether the trustee in bankruptcy was entitled to distributions of royalties falling to be made by the Society after the commencement of the bankruptcy in respect of works written by the bankrupt before his bankruptcy. He held that the right to distributions from the Society in respect of works completed prior to a writer member's bankruptcy was not a mere expectancy or possibility, but a transmissible property right, not dependent on the performance of further obligations on the part of the writer member. The right vested in the trustee in bankruptcy on his appointment. Although membership as such was personal, the general scheme of the Society's articles and rules showed that the right to distributions could pass to others either by assignment or by operation of law.

The right to receive distributions from the Society in respect of post-bankruptcy works did not strictly arise, and the trustee did not seek to argue that such distributions from the society would be payable to the trustee in the absence of either a notice given by the trustee under s 307, or an income payments order under s 310 (which could not occur in that case because the bankrupt had been discharged). Robert Walker J expressed the view, obiter, that this was correct, since there cannot be present property rights (as opposed to contractual rights) in a song which has not yet been written, or in royalties and distributions which may become payable in future in respect of a musical work which, for the present, is simply non-existent. If it does come into existence it does so by virtue of the songwriter's own creative efforts, whether or not under a contract of employment.[69]

---

[66] Quaere as to whether it might be after acquired property within s 307.

[67] [2001] EWCA Civ 779. Following *Re Landau* [1998] Ch 223. See further the para 6.6 on Income Payments Orders.   [68] [1997] 3 All ER 336.

[69] ibid 348. See also *Bailey v Thurston & Co Ltd* [1903] 1 KB 137, 145–6.

6.5.4 Transferability

In *Dear v Reeves*, Mummery LJ said:[70]

The distinguishing feature of a right of property, in contrast to a purely personal right, is that it is transferable: it may be enforced by someone other than the particular person in whom the right was initially vested.

The Court of Appeal held that a right of pre-emption was property within s 436 and vested in the trustee in bankruptcy.[71] The right of pre-emption in that case was expressly assignable by clause (4) of the deed creating it. While it might be difficult to put a value on the right as the grantor might never decide to sell the property, it was not necessary for a right to have any present or immediate value for it to be 'property' within s 436. The relevant question was whether it was, in its legal nature, property. If it was, it only fell outside the bankrupt's estate by some specific exclusion. He referred to *de Rothschild v Bell*[72] where the Court of Appeal held that a continuation tenancy under Pt I of the Landlord and Tenant Act 1954 had clear incidents of a property nature, in particular because it retained from the contractual tenancy the character of assignability.

Transferability was also considered essential in *In re Celtic Extraction Ltd*[73] where the Court of Appeal considered the features which are likely to be found if a statutory exemption or licence is to be regarded as property within s 436. Thus in that case the requirement that the transferor and transferee should join in the application demonstrated the transferability of the waste management licence even though it took form of a surrender and re-grant by the Environment Agency.

6.5.5 Existing value

In *de Rothschild v Bell*,[74] Buxton LJ said that it did not matter that in practical terms the 'property' when held by a bankrupt might be of no value to the creditors. Even if it was necessary to consider the value of the right of continuation of a tenancy in the hands of the bankrupt, it was far from being so clear that such a tenancy would never have value in the hands of a trustee in bankruptcy as to disqualify the right from ever being a component of the bankrupt's estate. In *Patel v Jones*,[75] Mummery LJ said that the fact that the right to receive future payments under a pension scheme might have no immediate value did not prevent it being 'property' for this purpose.

---

[70] [2001] EWCA Civ 277, para [40].
[71] *Pritchard v Briggs* [1980] Ch 338 was distinguished on the basis that it was not an insolvency case, but concerned a question of competing priority between two registrations on the Land Charges Register.   [72] [2000] QB 33, 48–9, *per* Buxton LJ.
[73] [2001] Ch 475, 489, para [33].   [74] [2000] QB 33, 48–9.
[75] [2001] EWCA Civ 779, para [36].

On the other hand, despite their value, some assets may be excluded from the bankrupt's estate on the basis that they are peculiarly personal to him and his life as a human being. *In Haigh v Aitken*,[76] Rattee J held that this was the case in relation to the bankrupt's personal correspondence. This was so even though the correspondence might be worth a considerable sum if sold and made available to the media.

6.5.6 Rights of action

Property for the purposes of s 436 may include a chose in action, ie a right to property or payment of money which can be enforced by action. This will include the right to claim payment of a debt or damages for a tort or for breach of contract. The general principle is that all such rights of the bankrupt which can be exercised beneficially for the creditors pass to the trustee in bankruptcy and the right to recover damages may pass even though they are unliquidated.[77]

6.5.7 Personal rights of action excluded

However, this is subject to an important exception. A right of action does not pass to the trustee in bankruptcy where it is solely related to matters personal to the bankrupt, ie 'where the damages are to be estimated by reference to pain felt by the bankrupt in respect of his body, mind or character and without immediate reference to his rights of property'.[78] In *Heath v Tang*,[79] Hoffman LJ said that actions for defamation and assault are obvious examples, and actions for damages for pain and suffering arising from personal injuries will generally not vest in the trustee. Accordingly the bankruptcy does not affect the ability of the bankrupt to litigate such claims and if he is successful he may retain the sums recovered, for otherwise he might have no incentive to enforce his right. However, it seems that if damages from such a claim are invested, the investment can be claimed by the trustee.[80]

6.5.8 The distinction between 'personal' and 'proprietary' claims

The distinction between 'personal' and 'proprietary' claims will not always be easy. In *Davis v Trustee in Bankruptcy of Davis*,[81] the bankrupt alleged that as a result of medical negligence he had suffered a personality change which in turn had led him to engage in unwise business dealings resulting in his bankruptcy. Evans-Lombe J held that this was in the nature of a personal injury claim and

---

[76] [2003] 3 All ER 80.   [77] *Per* Erle J in *Beckham v Drake* (1849) 2 HL Cas 579, 603.

[78] ibid 604, *per* Erle J and *Wilson v United Counties Bank Ltd* [1920] AC 102

[79] [1993] 1 WLR 1421.

[80] See Sedley LJ in *Grady v Prison Service* [2003] EWCA Civ 527, paras [11] and [21] referring to *Re Wilson, ex p Vine* (1878) 8 Ch D 364.   [81] [1998] BPIR 572.

therefore did not vest in the trustee in bankruptcy.[82] However, the mere fact that money becomes payable to a bankrupt as a result of bodily injury will not necessarily prevent it vesting in his trustee in bankruptcy. In *Cork v Rawlins*,[83] sums became payable to the bankrupt under two policies of insurance when he became permanently disabled and entitled to permanent disablement benefit as a result of an accident which he suffered while working as a self-employed gardener before his bankruptcy. The Court of Appeal held that the right to the benefits under the policies vested in the trustee in bankruptcy as part of the bankrupt's estate. The essence of the claim arising under the policies was the right to bring an action for payment under a contract. The sums had become payable 'not because of the satisfaction of a test of pain and suffering but because of the contractual test of what Keene LJ rightly called "employ-ability" '.[84] The policy monies did not relate to or represent or compensate for loss or damage to the bankrupt personally, nor were they measured by such loss or damage. Had the right to payment been triggered by the bankrupt's death, there was no question but that the monies would have been taken by the trustee. Payment was 'merely triggered by the permanent disablement being proved, thereby advancing the date of payment of what would otherwise not have been payable until death occurred'.[85]

Chadwick LJ pointed out that the insurance policies had been taken out for the purpose of discharging the insured's liability to a particular creditor, namely a building society under a mortgage, but the loan from the building society had been discharged from other assets which would otherwise have come into the bankrupt's estate. There was therefore no hardship in requiring that the right to payment should fall into the estate for the benefit of the creditors.[86]

In *Grady v Prison Service*,[87] the Court of Appeal held that a claim for rein-statement or re-engagement consequent on an unfair dismissal, and indeed a significant element of the compensation which can be awarded in lieu of these, is not a thing in action of the kind which forms part of a bankrupt's estate, even though the eventual fund (if an award is made) may be.[88] It is a claim of a unique kind which offers the restoration to the claimant of something which only the claimant can do. To vest it in the trustee in bankruptcy would be of no appreciable benefit to the creditors except to the extent that it might produce a money settlement (which would represent not a concession but a liquidation of the bankrupt's claim to her job). The creditors would probably be better served if the bankrupt could get her job back or a similar job in its place, and that was something the trustee could not do in her stead. Thus earnings beyond those needed for subsistence from a job in which the bankrupt was reinstated could be

---

[82] This did not mean that the bankrupt would be able to retain the entirety of the damages himself. Evans-Lombe J thought that the trustee might be able 'to lay claim to at least part of the proceeds of any judgment as after-acquired property of the bankrupt' (575).
[83] [2001] EWCA Civ 197.   [84] ibid para [25].   [85] ibid.   [86] ibid para [41].
[87] [2003] EWCA Civ 527.   [88] In contrast to a claim for wrongful dismissal, see para [22].

reached as those from his continuing employment can under an income payments order considered below at paragraph 6.6.[89]

6.5.9 Hybrid claims

Where there is a hybrid claim, ie 'a single cause of action which is partly for personal injury or loss of reputation (to which creditors are not entitled) and partly for financial loss (to which they normally are),'[90] this will vest in the trustee in bankruptcy. This was held to be the case in *Ord v Upton*[91] where the bankrupt's claim for damages for personal injury caused by negligence included substantial claims for loss of past and future earnings. The trustee claimed to be entitled to the damages for financial loss up to the bankrupt's discharge from bankruptcy. Although the cause of action for negligence vested in the trustee he would have to account as constructive trustee for the right to recover damages for pain and suffering and other personal losses.[92] Aldous LJ said:[93]

The idea that the cause of action should vest in the bankrupt would not be acceptable and compulsory joinder of both could lead to difficulties when the claim for loss of earnings was small compared with the potential costs of the litigation. In such a case the trustee, if the cause of action vested in him, would have to consider carefully his duty to the bankrupt and would probably, if requested, assign the cause of action to him.

The approach to hybrid claims was considered further by the House of Lords in *Mulkerrins v PricewaterhouseCoopers*.[94] In that case, the plaintiff alleged that the defendants had failed to act with proper skill and care with the result that she had been made the subject of a bankruptcy order rather than an individual voluntary arrangement (IVA). Her claim was clearly a hybrid one seeking damages for loss of reputation and future loss of earnings and particularly for the loss of her business which had not been the cause of her insolvency. However, it was an unusual claim as the bankruptcy itself was the cause of action and the district judge held that such a claim could not vest in the trustee under s 306.[95] This decision, from which there had been no appeal proved decisive. Whether it was right or wrong it bound the parties to the decision, namely the bankrupt and her trustee and through him her creditors. The defendants were not bound by it, but could not ignore it as they were not prejudiced by it. They would not have been prejudiced if it had vested in the trustee and a fortiori they were not prejudiced by the fact that the right of action

---

[89] ibid, *per* Sedley LJ, para [25].

[90] *Per* Lord Millett in *Mulkerrins v PricewaterhouseCoopers* [2003] UKHL 41, para [6].

[91] [2000] Ch 352.

[92] In *Cork v Rawlins* [2001] EWCA Civ 197, Peter Gibson LJ said that this appeared to be a remedial constructive trust.   [93] [2000] Ch 352, 371.

[94] [2003] UKHL 41.

[95] She seemed to have considered that this was a matter of timing which made the cause of action after-acquired property.

remained vested in the bankrupt. That was sufficient to dispose of the case and the plaintiff's claim was to be taken to form no part of the bankrupt estate available to her creditors, and she was at liberty to pursue it in her own name and for her own benefit. The question whether the claim was one which should have been regarded as vesting in the trustee was left open as it had not been fully argued. However, Lord Millett said that it should not be assumed that the district judge had been wrong and it should not be taken to be concluded by the judgment of the Court of Appeal in the present case.[96] He said:[97]

Mrs Mulkerrins' claim is an unusual one, for she complains of PwC's failure to prevent the making of a bankruptcy order against her. She claims damages representing the difference between her financial position as a result of the bankruptcy order and the financial position she would have enjoyed if she had entered into an IVA instead. Treating this claim as being wholly or mainly a claim in respect of financial loss, and even assuming that (contrary to the view of the district judge) it was not after-acquired property, it would be very surprising if a claim of this character could be made available to the creditors. *They would be claiming damages for the making of the very bankruptcy order under which their claim arose.* The greater part of their claim would represent damages for the closure of the nursing home, even though it was a going concern when it supposedly vested in the Official Receiver and was closed down by him. The creditors have received the full value of the bankrupt estate. The damages which Mrs Mulkerrins claims represents the value of what she lost by the making of the bankruptcy order; but while this could have been available to the creditors under an IVA, it could never have been made available to them in a bankruptcy.

6.5.10 The importance of timing

In *Ord v Upton*,[98] Aldous LJ drew attention to some oddities. Thus if, at the time of the bankruptcy, the bankrupt had in his bank a sum which included money paid as damages for a libel, that sum would vest in his trustee because the right to the money formed part of his estate and therefore was available to pay off the bankrupt's creditors. In contrast, a cause of action personal to the bankrupt, such as a libel action, which was not settled before the end of the bankruptcy will remain vested in the bankrupt as will any damages awarded after discharge from bankruptcy. If a cause of action is not personal to the bankrupt, it vests in the trustee and therefore any damages awarded whether before or after the discharge will be available to discharge the bankrupt's liabilities. A right of action for breach of contract which has accrued to the bankrupt before the date of his adjudication will pass to the trustee.[99] A right to sue for breach of contract which occurs after the date of the bankrupt's

---

[96] The Court of Appeal assumed that the claim vested in the trustee because it was wholly or largely a claim for financial loss, without considering the particular nature of the claim.

[97] ibid para [17]. Italics added. [98] [2000] Ch 352, 360.

[99] *Beckham v Drake* (1849) 2 HLC 579, 9 ER 1213. Cf *Hill v Smith* (1844) 12 M & W 618.

adjudication will remain in the bankrupt if it relates to a claim which is 'personal' to the bankrupt.[100]

6.5.11 Exempt property

Exempt property which does not form part of the estate vesting in the trustee comprises:[101]

(a) such tools, books, vehicles and other items of equipment as are necessary to the bankrupt for use personally by him in his employment, business or vocation;

(b) such clothing, bedding, furniture, household equipment and provisions as are necessary for satisfying the basic domestic needs of the bankrupt and his family.

However, where it appears to the trustee that the realizable value of the whole or part of such property exceeds the cost of a reasonable replacement for that property or part of it, the trustee may give notice in writing claiming that property or, as the case may be, that part of it for the bankrupt's estate. The property then vests in the trustee who must apply funds in the estate to the purchase by or on behalf of the bankrupt of a reasonable replacement. This duty has priority over the obligation of the trustee to distribute the estate. Property is a reasonable replacement for other property if it is reasonably adequate for meeting the needs met by the other property.[102] Notice must be given within a period of forty-two days beginning with the day on which the property in question first came to the knowledge of the trustee.[103]

In *Re Rayatt*,[104] it was held that the trustee had a statutory duty to apply funds in the purchase of a replacement car and that obligation could not, as a matter of the law of set-off, be diminished or extinguished by the fact that the bankrupt owed money to the trustee. Mr Michael Hart QC sitting as a High Court judge said that the legislative purpose was fairly clear: 'The bankrupt is to keep his car if it is needed for his employment, but if a cheaper one would serve equally well, the trustee can claim the car and allow a cheaper one to be purchased. The excess value falls into the estate, but the bankrupt is not impeded in his employment.'[105]

In *Pike v Cork Gully*,[106] where the Court of Appeal was satisfied that a horse box came within s 282(2), but the dispute as to the cost of a replacement was a matter to be decided by the county court, Millett LJ said:[107]

Replacement in this context does not mean another asset of a similar value to that which has been seized, but a less expensive asset which it would be reasonable for the bankrupt to use for the purpose of his business.

---

[100] *Bailey v Thurston & Co Ltd* [1903] 1 KB 137.   [101] IA 1986, s 283(2).
[102] IA 1986, s 308. It will be noted that the word 'reasonableness' appears both in the definition and in the term defined.   [103] IA 1986, s 309(1).
[104] [1998] 2 FLR 264.   [105] ibid 275.   [106] [1997] BPIR 723.   [107] ibid 725.

6.5.12 After-acquired property

Property which has been acquired by, or has devolved upon, the bankrupt since the commencement of the bankruptcy no longer vests automatically in the trustee in bankruptcy, but may be claimed for the bankrupt's estate by the trustee by giving notice to the bankrupt.[108] Upon service of the notice on the bankrupt the property to which the notice relates is vested in the trustee as part of the bankrupt's estate. The trustee's title to that property relates back to the time at which the property was acquired by, or devolved upon, the bankrupt.[109] Such a notice must not be served after the end of the period of forty-two days beginning with the day on which the property in question first came to the knowledge of the trustee except with leave of the court.[110] Where at any time after the commencement of the bankruptcy any property is acquired by the bankrupt or any property devolves upon him, he must give the trustee notice of the property within the prescribed period, which is twenty-one days of becoming aware of the facts.[111] The bankrupt is prohibited from disposing of the property within the period of forty-two days beginning with the date of the notice without the consent in writing of the trustee to do so.[112]

Notice may not be given in relation to property acquired by or devolving on the bankrupt after his discharge unless an order of the court granting the discharge has imposed a condition that property acquired after discharge is to be available for the benefit of creditors.[113] Excluded property such as tools of the bankrupt's trade and household effects, property held by the bankrupt as trustee and property excluded form the bankrupt's estate by any other enactment also cannot be the subject matter of such a notice.[114] Property for this purpose does not include any property which, as part of the bankrupt's income, may be the subject of an income payments order under s 310.[115] The distinction between after-acquired property and income for this purpose is considered further in paragraph 6.6.4.5 below.

A trustee in bankruptcy is not, by virtue of serving a notice in respect of after-acquired property, entitled to any remedy against a person who acquires that property from the bankrupt in good faith, for value, and without notice of the bankruptcy. This applies whether the property is acquired from the bankrupt before or after service of the notice. Similar protection is afforded to a banker who enters into a transaction with the bankrupt in good faith and without notice of the bankruptcy.[116]

---

[108] IA 1986, s 307(1).   [109] IA 1986, s 307(3).   [110] IA 1986, s 309(1).

[111] IA 1986, s 333(2) and Insolvency Rules 1986, r 6.200(1). However, where the bankrupt carries on a business he is not required to notify the trustee of any property which he acquires in the ordinary course of the business but must furnish the trustee with a half-yearly report on his trading activities, showing the total of goods bought and sold and the profit or loss arising from the business: r 6.200(4)(5).   [112] Insolvency Rules 1986, r 6.200(2).

[113] IA 1986, s 307(2)(c), ie unless an order was made under s 280(2)(c).

[114] IA 1986, s 307(2)(a) and (b).   [115] IA 1986, s 307(5).   [116] IA 1986, s 307(4).

After-acquired property may include a loan lawfully obtained by the bankrupt.[117]

6.5.13 Tenancies

The general principle is that leasehold property vests in the trustee in bankruptcy in the same way as other property. However, certain tenancies are excluded from automatic vesting.[118] These tenancies will vest in the trustee only if he serves notice in writing on the bankrupt.[119] These are:

(a) a tenancy which is an assured tenancy or an assured agricultural occupancy, within the meaning of Pt I of the Housing Act 1988, and the terms of which inhibit an assignment as mentioned in s 127(5) of the Rent Act 1977; or

(b) a protected tenancy, within the meaning of the Rent Act 1977, in respect of which, by virtue of any provision of Pt IX of that Act, no premium can lawfully be required as a condition of assignment; or

(c) a tenancy of a dwelling-house by virtue of which the bankrupt is, within the meaning of the Rent (Agriculture) Act 1976, a protected occupier of the dwelling-house, and the terms of which inhibit an assignment as mentioned in s 127(5) of the Rent Act 1977;

(d) a secure tenancy, within the meaning of Pt IV of the Housing Act 1985, which is not capable of being assigned, except in the cases mentioned in s 91(3) of that Act.

A statutory tenancy is a purely personal right and is not property within s 436. A statutory tenancy will not therefore vest in the tenant's trustee in bankruptcy.[120] However, although the occupation of a statutory tenant and his family may be safe as against the trustee in bankruptcy, they may be vulnerable to an action by the landlord if the original tenancy agreement contained a proviso for re-entry on the tenant's bankruptcy. In *Cadogan Estates Ltd v McMahon*,[121] the House of Lords held that where a tenant became bankrupt after becoming a statutory tenant there was a breach or non-compliance of an obligation in the former protected tenancy.

In contrast a continuation tenancy under Pt I of the Landlord and Tenant Act 1954 is property which will vest in the trustee in bankruptcy. In *de Rothschild v Bell*,[122] Buxton LJ regarded such a tenancy 'as having clear incidents of a property nature, in particular because it retains from the contractual tenancy the character of assignability'.

---

[117] *Hardy v Buchler* [1997] BPIR 643.
[118] IA 1986, s 283(3A) inserted by the Housing Act 1988, s 117.
[119] IA 1986, s 308A inserted by the Housing Act 1988, s 117.
[120] *Sutton v Dorf* [1932] 2 KB 304. [121] [2001] 1 AC 378.
[122] [2000] QB 33. For a detailed discussion see Davey [2000] Insolvency Lawyer 46.

Where a tenancy vests in the trustee then he takes subject to any matrimonial home rights of the bankrupt's spouse.[123]

6.5.14 Disclaimer of onerous property

A trustee in bankruptcy may disclaim any onerous property comprised in the bankrupt's estate so as to avoid further liability in respect of the property which might diminish the estate.[124] A disclaimer is effected by the trustee giving 'notice of disclaimer' in prescribed form and filing it with the court. A copy of the notice must be served within seven days on all persons with interests in the property or whom he considers it appropriate to inform.[125] A trustee may give notice of disclaimer in respect of property even though he has taken possession of it and endeavoured to sell it or otherwise exercised rights of ownership in relation to it. Notice of disclaimer cannot be given in respect of any property if a person interested in the property has applied in writing to the trustee requiring him to decide whether he will disclaim or not, and notice of disclaimer has not been given within twenty-eight days beginning with the day on which the application was made.[126]

Onerous property for this purpose means any unprofitable contract and any other property comprised in the bankrupt's estate which is unsaleable or not readily saleable or is such that it may give rise to a liability to pay money or perform any other onerous act.[127] A notice of disclaimer cannot be given in respect of any property that has been claimed for the estate under s 307 (after-acquired property) or s 308 (personal property of bankrupt exceeding reasonable replacement value), except with the leave of the court.[128]

A disclaimer operates so as to determine, as from the date of the disclaimer, the rights, interests, and liabilities of the bankrupt and his estate in, or in respect of, the property disclaimed. It also discharges the trustee from all personal liability in respect of that property as from the commencement of his trusteeship. However, it does not, except so far as is necessary for the purpose of releasing the bankrupt, the bankrupt's estate and the trustee from any liability, affect the rights or liabilities of any other person.[129] Any person sustaining loss or damage in consequence of the operation of a disclaimer is deemed to be a creditor of the bankrupt to the extent of the loss or damage and accordingly may prove for the loss or damage as a bankruptcy debt.[130]

A disclaimer of a leasehold property does not take effect unless a copy of the disclaimer has been served on every person claiming under the bankrupt as underlessee or mortgagee and no application has been made to the court within fourteen days for a vesting order in respect of the property or, where such an

---

[123] IA 1986, s 336(2).   [124] IA 1986, s 315.
[125] Insolvency Rules 1986, rr 6.178, 6.179, and 6.180.   [126] IA 1986, s 316(1).
[127] IA 1986, s 315(2).   [128] IA 1986, s 315(4).   [129] IA 1986, s 315(3).
[130] IA 1986, s 315(5).

application has been made, the court directs that the disclaimer is to take effect.[131]

A disclaimer of any property in a dwelling-house does not take effect unless a copy of the disclaimer has been served on every person in occupation of, or claiming a right to occupy, the dwelling-house, and no application has been made to the court within fourteen days seeking a vesting order in respect of the property, or where such an application has been made, the court directs that the disclaimer is to take effect.[132]

An application for an order for the vesting or delivery of the disclaimed property may be made under s 320 of the 1986 Act. An application may be made by:

(a) any person who claims an interest in the disclaimed property,

(b) any person who is under any liability in respect of the disclaimed property, not being a liability discharged by the disclaimer, or

(c) where the disclaimed property is a dwelling-house, any person who at the time when the bankruptcy petition was presented was in occupation of, or entitled to occupy, the dwelling-house.

On such an application the court may make an order on such terms as it thinks fit for the vesting of the disclaimed property in, or for its delivery to, any person who claims an interest in it, or a person subject to a liability in respect of it. Where the disclaimed property is a dwelling-house, the property may be vested in any person who at the time when the bankruptcy petition was presented was in occupation of or entitled to occupy the dwelling house. An order vesting the property in any person need not be completed by any conveyance assignment or transfer.[133] Special provisions relate to the vesting of leasehold property.[134]

In making a vesting order on such terms as it thinks fit, the court can impose terms which limit the amount to be received by a mortgagee in whom the property is vested to the amount due under the mortgage. It may also provide for the destination of any surplus and this may include payment of the whole or part thereof to the trustee in bankruptcy for the benefit of the creditors. It is true that the trustee in bankruptcy, having disclaimed property under s 315 cannot then seek an order restoring the property to the bankrupt's estate by seeking a vesting order under s 320 in his own favour. However, in *Lee v Lee*,[135] Ferris J held that where a third party, such as a mortgagee, has applied for and obtained a vesting order and, after satisfying its claim, there is a surplus, the court may make a vesting order on terms which directly or indirectly benefit the bankrupt's estate. In that case he dismissed an appeal in respect of a vesting order made on terms that the mortgagee pay one half of the surplus to the trustee and the other half into a bank account pending the determination of a claim by the bankrupt's wife to a beneficial entitlement of one half.

---

[131] IA 1986, s 317(1).   [132] IA 1986, s 318.   [133] IA 1986, s 320(6).
[134] IA 1986, s 321.   [135] [1998] 1 FLR 1018, 1024–5.

6.6 THE BANKRUPT'S INCOME

6.6.1 Income payments orders[136]

The post-bankruptcy earnings of the bankrupt do not form part of the bankrupt's estate which vests automatically in the trustee. Before any part of the bankrupt's income can be made available to his creditors, an income payments order must be obtained from the court under s 310 of the Insolvency Act 1986. Under s 310 the court may make 'an income payments order' claiming for the bankrupt's estate so much of the income of the bankrupt as may be specified in the order.[137] An income payments order may be made only on an application instituted by the trustee before the discharge of the bankrupt.[138] The court must not make an order the effect of which would be to reduce the income of the bankrupt (when taken together with payments by way of guaranteed minimum pension and payments giving effect to the bankrupt's protected rights as a member of a pension scheme) 'below what appears to the court to be necessary for meeting the reasonable domestic needs of the bankrupt and his family'.[139] An income payments order must specify the period during which it is to have effect. The period specified may end after the discharge of the bankrupt, but cannot last for more than three years from the date on which the order was made.[140] Before the reduction in the period of bankruptcy from three years to one year by the Enterprise Act 2002, the general practice was to make orders which ran only up to the date of discharge even though there was power to extend its application beyond that date for a period of up to three years from the date of the order.[141] It seems clear that an earlier date for automatic discharge is not intended to indicate a shorter term for income payments orders and these are now more likely to continue after automatic discharge.[142]

Subject to the limitation on the length of the term, an income payments order may be varied on the application of the trustee or the bankrupt whether before or after discharge.[143]

---

[136] See Miller, 'Income Payments Orders' (2002) 18(2) IL & P 43.

[137] IA 1986, s 310 (1) as amended by the Enterprise Act 2002, s 259.

[138] IA 1986, s 310(1A) inserted by the Enterprise Act 2002, s 259.

[139] IA 1986, s 310(2). The words in brackets were inserted by the Pensions Act 1995, s 122, Sch 3, para 15. Where the court makes an income payments order it may, if it thinks fit, discharge or vary any attachment of earnings order that is for the time being in force to secure payments by the bankrupt (s 310(4)).   [140] IA 1986, s 310(6) as substituted by the Enterprise Act 2002, s 259(4).

[141] See 'Bankruptcy—A Fresh Start' a consultation paper issued by the Insolvency Service in 2000.

[142] Transitional provisions relating to income payments orders in existence at the commencement of the Enterprise Act 2002 are contained in Sch 19, para 7.

[143] IA 1986, s 310(6A) inserted by the Enterprise Act 2002, s 259.

6.6.2 Income payments agreements

The need to obtain a court order may now be avoided if the bankrupt enters into an income payments agreement under s 310A introduced by the Enterprise Act 2002.[144] This is a written agreement between the bankrupt and his trustee or between the bankrupt and the official receiver which provides that the bankrupt is to pay to the trustee or the official receiver an amount equal to a specified part or proportion of the bankrupt's income for a specified period. Alternatively it may provide that a third person is to pay to the trustee or the official receiver a specified proportion of money due to the bankrupt by way of income for a specified period.[145] A provision of an income payments agreement of either kind may be enforced as if it were a provision of an income payments order.[146] An income payments agreement must specify the period during which it is to have effect. The period may end after the discharge of the bankrupt, but cannot last for more than three years from the date on which the agreement was made.[147] Subject to that limitation an agreement may be varied either by written agreement between the parties, or by the court on an application made by the bankrupt, the trustee, or the official receiver. However, the court may not vary an agreement so as to include provision of a kind which could not be included in an income payments order. It must grant an application to vary an agreement if, and to the extent, that the court thinks variation is necessary to avoid the income of the bankrupt being reduced below what appears to be necessary for meeting the reasonable domestic needs of the bankrupt and his family as required by s 310(2).[148]

6.6.3 Effect of income payments orders and agreements

Sums received by the trustee under an income payments order or an income payments agreement form part of the bankrupt's estate.[149]

6.6.4 What is income within s 310?

6.6.4.1 *The general scope of s 310*

Under the previous legislation 'income' for the purposes of s 51 of the Bankruptcy Act 1914 came to be limited to income *eiusdem generis* with a salary,[150] but the Insolvency Act 1986 gives a wider definition.[151] Section 310(7) provides that for the purposes of s 310 'the income of the bankrupt comprises every payment in the nature of income which is from time to time made to him or to which he from time to time becomes entitled, including any payment in respect

---

[144] Enterprise Act 2002, s 260.   [145] IA 1986, s 310A (1).   [146] IA 1986, s 310A(2).
[147] IA 1986, s 310A(5).   [148] IA 1986, s 310A(6)(7).
[149] IA 1986, ss 310(5) and 310A(4).   [150] *Re Cohen* [1961] 1 Ch 246.
[151] See Evans-Lombe J in *Supperstone v Lloyd's Names* [1999] BPIR 832, 841.

of the carrying on of any business or in respect of any office or employment'. It also includes any payment under a pension scheme, but payments by way of guaranteed minimum pension and payments giving effect to the bankrupt's protected rights as a member of a pension scheme are excluded.[152]

While s 51 was also concerned with the income of a bankrupt, its role in the general scheme was different from that of s 310. Section 51 was not concerned with the vesting of the bankrupt's income which was achieved by the general vesting provisions of the legislation, but provided that the trustee in bankruptcy was only entitled to receive such income to the extent that an order of the court was obtained.[153] Under the scheme of the 1986 Act the position is different. Income received after the date of vesting does not automatically vest in the trustee, but only to the extent provided by an order under s 310. Therefore, the width of the definition of 'income' for the purposes of s 310 is crucial to enable the trustee to reach receipts that would not otherwise vest in him. Thus in *Re Landau*,[154] Ferris J said:

Indeed in its content and context section 310 itself provides for something equivalent to vesting in respect of a particular kind of property, i.e. income received under an income payments order obtained in accordance with the section.

However, despite the wide definition of income in s 310(7), the scope of s 310 is affected by two other statutory provisions already noted.

6.6.4.2 *Income derived from property vested in the trustee*
First, it is limited by s 306 which provides that property to which the bankrupt was entitled at the commencement of the bankruptcy vests automatically in the trustee. If the source of income can be regarded as having vested in the trustee as property under s 306, then s 310 is not needed to enable the trustee to reach it. In *Re Landau*, Ferris J rejected the view that s 310 also qualified the trustee's right to reach income already vested, ie operated in a manner similar to s 51.[155] The result is that, if the right to income has vested in the trustee as property, then the bankrupt will lose the right to the income entirely and thus the protection for him which s 310 embodies.

It seems clear that where property, such as land which produces a rental income, vested in the trustee at the commencement of the bankruptcy, then the rent will accrue to the trustee thereafter. It will not thereafter be income of the bankrupt and is not within s 310. The same applies to income from shares and securities vesting in the trustee. Difficulty has, however, arisen in relation to

---

[152] IA 1986, s 310(8). This is despite anything in ss 11 or 12 of the Welfare Reform and Pensions Act 1999 which prevent pension rights from vesting in the trustee in bankruptcy as part of the bankrupt's estate under s 306. See further the section on 'Pensions' in para 6.6.4.3 below. By s 310(9) 'guaranteed minimum pension' and 'protected rights' have the same meaning as in the Pension Schemes Act 1993. [153] See *Affleck v Hammond* [1912] 3 KB 162.
[154] [1998] Ch 223, 240. [155] ibid.

payments received, or to be received, by the bankrupt by way of pension and under certain contracts.

6.6.4.3 *Pensions*

The impact of bankruptcy on pensions has proved so controversial that special statutory provisions have been enacted in relation to petitions presented on or after 29 May 2000.[156] Nevertheless, some consideration of the cases in which the petition was presented before that date is appropriate because they examine the scope of s 310 and highlight the problems to which the section may give rise in relation to other income producing assets.

There was no doubt that payments from a pension scheme received by a bankrupt during the bankruptcy and constituting income were within s 310.[157] More controversial was the position in relation to sums payable under a pension scheme which have not fallen due for payment because the bankrupt has not retired prior to the bankruptcy and does not retire until after his discharge from bankruptcy. In *Re Landau*,[158] Ferris J was concerned with the annuity payable under a pension policy. The annuity did not become payable until after the bankrupt had been discharged under s 279, so that no income payments order was possible. However, he found that the bankrupt's bundle of contractual rights under the policy constituted a chose in action which fell within the definition of property in s 436 of the 1986 Act. As the property of the bankrupt at the commencement of the bankruptcy, it had vested automatically in the trustee under s 306. The fact that at the commencement of the bankruptcy nothing was immediately payable did not alter this in any way. Section 310 had no application to instalments of an annuity which had already vested in the trustee under s 306, since such instalments were not income paid to him, or to which he became entitled.

In *Jones v Patel*,[159] the court was concerned with the pension and lump sum payable under a statutory occupational pension scheme to the bankrupt following his redundancy. Mr Richard Engelhart QC, sitting as a High Court judge, said that by the time Mr Patel was made bankrupt he had acquired rights under the scheme albeit that no payment of pension would actually be made until his retirement or redundancy. He said that while *Re Landau* was concerned not with a pension payable under an occupational pension scheme but a personal pension, 'the underlying reasoning of Ferris J, if right, would be equally applicable to an occupational pension scheme'.[160] The Court of Appeal upheld the view that Mr Patel's rights under the pension scheme constituted a chose in action which was property within s 436 and so vested in the trustee even

---

[156] Welfare Reform and Pensions Act 1999.

[157] In *Kilvert v Flackett* [1998] 2 FLR 806 it was held that the lump sum payable on retirement was income for this purpose rather than after-acquired property.   [158] [1998] Ch 223.

[159] [1999] BPIR 509.   [160] ibid 512.

though nothing was immediately payable under it at the commencement of the bankruptcy.[161] This followed an unsuccessful attempt in *Dennison v Krasner* and *Lesser v Lawrence*[162] to persuade the Court of Appeal that such reasoning was wrong. Chadwick LJ said that s 310 was not intended to apply to income which the bankrupt received by virtue of some right to which he was entitled at the date of the bankruptcy order. In such a case the right, and the income received by virtue of that right, formed part of the bankrupt's estate under the provisions of s 283(1) of the 1986 Act. This will continue to be the position in relation to bankruptcies commenced before 29 May 2000. In relation to petitions presented on or after 29 May 2000, approved pension arrangements are excluded from a bankrupt's estate and will not vest in the trustee in bankruptcy.[163] The Act also contains provisions for rights under unapproved pension arrangements to be excluded from the bankrupt's estate by agreement or by an order of the court,[164] and for a trustee in bankruptcy to recover excessive contributions to a pension scheme in certain circumstances.[165] These provisions came into force on 6 April 2002.[166] Payments received by the bankrupt under a pension scheme may however be income which may be made subject to an income payments order or agreement.[167]

The consequences of the view taken in *Re Landau* and subsequent cases are twofold. First, 'income', the right to which has vested in the trustee, will not be subject to the protection afforded to the bankrupt by s 310 which is designed to ensure that he has sufficient to provide for his reasonable needs. Secondly, such 'income' will be paid to the trustee even after the bankrupt's discharge.

6.6.4.4 *Payment for services*
The approach of Ferris J in *Re Landau* was followed by Robert Walker J in *Performing Right Society Ltd v Rowland*[168] in determining entitlement to distributions of royalties on the bankruptcy of a member of the society. He held that the right to receive distributions in relation to works completed before a member's bankruptcy was a property right which vested in the member's trustee in bankruptcy under s 306. However, he considered that this did not apply in the case of distributions in respect of works completed subsequently although this question did not strictly arise for decision.[169]

---

[161] [2001] EWCA Civ 779. However, the trustee was not entitled to that part of the pension attributable to Mr Patel's post-bankruptcy service and contributions as he had made the contributions in the belief that he was enhancing his own pension rights.
[162] [2000] 2 All ER 239, 243.
[163] Welfare Reform and Pensions Act 1999, s 11 and SI 2000/1382.   [164] Section 12.
[165] Section 15. See ch 9.
[166] SI 2002/153. For a consideration of the changes and their effect see Greenstreet, 'Pensions and Bankruptcy: Recent Developments' (2001) 17 IL & P 43.
[167] See ss 310(7), (8), and (9) and 310A(4) considered above.   [168] [1997] 3 All ER 336.
[169] ibid 348, see further the consideration of this case at para 6.5.3, above.

There was, therefore, an essential distinction between performing rights in pre-bankruptcy works and in post-bankruptcy works. Where the bankrupt has completed his obligations under a contract and brought into existence a right to receive income prior to bankruptcy then that right will vest in the trustee. The position is the same as where the bankrupt had purchased an income producing asset prior to bankruptcy. On the other hand, where the bankrupt performs services after being made bankrupt, payment for those services will constitute income which can be reached by the trustee only under s 310. While the 1986 Act contains many significant departures from the earlier law, Robert Walker J considered that in relation to the very wide definition of 'property' in s 436, the well-known words of Cozens-Hardy LJ in *Bailey v Thurston & Co Ltd*[170] were still apposite:

It has been established for many years that, notwithstanding the generality of the language used in the Bankruptcy Acts, there are some contracts and some rights that do not vest in the trustee. For the present purpose it is sufficient to mention contracts for purely personal service. Such unexecuted contracts are not assignable by deed, and they are not, by virtue of the statute, vested in the trustee. If, however, at the date of the bankruptcy a sum of money is due in respect of services rendered under the contract, the trustee and not the bankrupt will take the money.

The crucial distinction therefore appears to be between contracts for services which have been performed and have thus given rise to a right to receive payments, and contracts for services which are yet to be performed and are thus unexecuted contracts. More generally it may be said that sums in the nature of income payable to the bankrupt will be reachable by the trustee only under s 310 unless they emanate from a contract which can be classified as property under s 436 which has vested in the trustee either on the commencement of the bankruptcy or as after acquired property. A contract will not be so regarded to the extent that it involves the performance of future services by the bankrupt.[171]

6.6.4.5 *Income which is not after-acquired property*

Secondly, the operation of s 310 is limited by s 307 which provides that after-acquired property vests in the trustee on notice. In principle any sum received after the commencement of the bankruptcy might be regarded as after-acquired property within s 307, but subsection (5) of that section provides: 'References in this section to property do not include any property which, as part of the bankrupt's income, may be the subject of an income payments order'. It therefore becomes necessary to consider what sums can be regarded as income for this purpose so as to be excluded from s 307. If so excluded they will fall within s 310.

---

[170] [1903] 1 KB 137, 145–6.

[171] The confusion which can arise is vividly illustrated by *Green v Satsangi* [1998] 1 BCLC 458 which Rimer J described as 'something of a tragedy of errors' (465).

In *Supperstone v Lloyd's Names Association Working Party*[172] it was argued that the use in s 310(7) of the words 'from time to time' implied that payments, to constitute 'income', must be periodical. This did not mean that payments had to be made at regular periodical intervals, but rather that they had to be shown to relate to money becoming due to the bankrupt regularly in respect of fixed periods. This was rejected by Evans-Lombe J who noted the definition of 'income' previously contained in the Bankruptcy Act 1914, s 51(2) and its predecessors,[173] and referred to *Affleck v Hammond* where the substantial question was whether a sum of £60 paid as commission to a bankrupt who was earning his living as a commission agent constituted personal earnings. In that case Buckley LJ had said:[174]

I am clearly of opinion that it is personal earnings; none the less because the money is the result of a single personal job with no element of periodicity, or periodical payment, about it. In fact, the distinction attempted to be founded on periodicity seems to me to be almost unintelligible.

Evans-Lombe J held that the payments made to the bankrupt were in any event 'income' and thus excluded from the ambit of s 307.[175] They could have been made the subject of an income payments order under s 310, but it was too late for the trustee to apply for such an order after the bankrupt's discharge.

In *Jones v Patel*,[176] Mr Richard Engelhart QC, the judge at first instance, did not in the end have to decide whether a redundancy payment and payment in lieu of notice constituted income for the purposes of s 310(7). However, he said:[177]

...the word "income" and the words "from time to time" in s.310(7) might suggest some kind of payment which is, or is capable of being, periodical in nature. The contrast is between after acquired income, which is covered by s.310, and after acquired property, which may be covered by s.307.

On the other hand, it can be said with some force that redundancy payments and payments in lieu of notice are in reality substitutes for periodic earnings from employment, and do indeed constitute payments "in respect of...employment".

In *Kilvert v Flackett*,[178] Mr Peter Scott QC, sitting as a High Court judge, held that a lump sum received by a bankrupt under an employees' pension scheme came within the statutory definition of 'income' for the purposes of s 310(7). Accordingly, where a bankrupt had sufficient income to provide for his and his family's reasonable domestic needs from other sources, there was, in principle, no reason why the whole sum could not be made the subject of an income

---

[172] [1999] BPIR 832. It may be noted that in *Supperstone* Evans Lombe J held that there will be no property within s 307 if the bankrupt has no contractual right to receive payments or no right under a trust created in his favour in respect of payments. See further Miller, 'Income Payments Orders' (2002) 18(2) IL & P 43.   [173] ibid 840–1.
[174] [1912] 3 KB 162, 171.   [175] [1999] BPIR 832, 840.   [176] [1999] BPIR 509.
[177] ibid 516.   [178] [1998] 2 FLR 806.

payments order. If the date on which the lump sum was payable had fallen after the discharge of the bankrupt then it would not have been subject to s 310. The judge said that while the timing of the receipt of the lump sum would determine, perhaps by chance, whether it came within s 310, the line had to be drawn somewhere and Parliament had drawn it.[179]

The form of the payment is not, therefore, conclusive, and its character may be determined more by the purpose for which it is made.

6.6.5 The standard of provision

6.6.5.1 *Reasonable needs*

An income payments order must not reduce the bankrupt's income 'below what appears to the court to be necessary for meeting the reasonable domestic needs of the bankrupt and his family'.[180] Different wording is used in s 283(2) in relation to property exempted from vesting in the trustee. Clothing, bedding, furniture, household equipment and provisions are exempted to the extent 'necessary for satisfying the basic needs of the bankrupt and his family'.[181] It may be argued that this implies that the standard to be applied when the court is considering, under s 310, the needs for which provision must be made out of income, is higher than that to be applied in determining the basic capital items exempted from vesting in the trustee.[182]

In *Re Rayatt*,[183] Mr Michael Hart QC, sitting as a High Court judge, said that it was not the object of the legislation that 'the debtor should become the slave of his creditors'. He went on to say:[184]

Implicit in this restriction is the notion that, within reasonable limits, the debtor should retain some freedom of choice as to the life style he adopts for himself and his family on the basis of the earnings which he is able to achieve by the deployment of his professional or other skills. He is not under any legal obligation to work at all. Even under the old law consideration of what was reasonably necessary was tempered by regard being had to the "occupation and station" of the particular bankrupt: see Tomlin J in *Re Walters*[185] ....

Whether particular expenditure could be described as necessary to meet the reasonable needs of the bankrupt or his family depended, in his view, on an examination of all the circumstances of the individual case. He rejected a general proposition that expenditure on private education could never, as a matter of principle, fall within that description. Clearly some expenditure in relation to the education of a child could be said to be both necessary and

---

[179] ibid 809.

[180] IA 1986, s 310(2). Contrast the wording of s 51 of the Bankruptcy Act 1914 which referred to the amount necessary for meeting the reasonable domestic needs of the bankrupt and his family.

[181] See also s 283(1) referring to items necessary for the use by the bankrupt in his employment, business or vocation. [182] See *Muir Hunter on Personal Insolvency*, para 3-1014.

[183] [1998] 2 FLR 264 quoting the Cork Committee, para 591. [184] ibid 271.

[185] [1929] 1 Ch 657, 653.

domestic. Even in the state system, parents could be expected to defray some expenses, for example the costs of travel to school, uniforms, where worn, dinner money, school trips, and so on. How much such expenditure could be described as meeting a reasonable domestic need was a subjective matter for the tribunal, highly dependent on the particular facts which had given rise to it. There is no presumption one way or the other as to whether a bankrupt will be allowed school fees as reasonable domestic needs. It all depends on the facts of the individual case.[186]

In *Re Rayatt*, a letter from the headmistress of the bankrupt's eldest daughter stated that the daughter would be seriously disadvantaged if she were to be moved from her present school at that juncture. The judge did not accept that there was a general rule against payment for private education and held that the letter established beyond doubt that the continuation of that daughter's education, at least until the completion of her GCSE course, was a reasonable domestic need. The existing income payments order was discharged though the trustee in bankruptcy remained free to make a fresh application for an order after the eldest daughter's current GCSE courses had finished.

In *Re Scott (a bankrupt)*,[187] the bankrupt's eldest child was in his last year at a private school, but his two other children had not been enrolled at their private schools until after the bankruptcy order. However, the judge concluded that because of a procedural and evidential muddle the bankrupt may have been deprived of a proper opportunity of putting relevant material before the court below and the case was remitted for a rehearing.

It may clearly be inappropriate for the bankrupt to continue living in more expensive accommodation than can be justified in the circumstances. Thus in *Malcolm v Official Receiver*,[188] Rattee J found it wholly unreasonable that the bankrupt should be living in a house on his own involving payments of £820 a month in mortgage instalments out of a net income of some £1100 a month. The payments were being made at least in part for the benefit of his wife as a joint owner of the property, while the substantial unsecured creditors were receiving nothing. Even so the actual order made by the district judge could not stand, for higher payments were not feasible until alternative accommodation was obtained.

In *Re Scott*, the judge accepted that the requirement to pay arrears of income tax was a 'domestic need' but it was a 'self-inflicted' need and the real question was whether it was 'reasonable' for the purposes of s 310(2). It was relevant to consider not only why the tax was not paid but also what happened to the money that was not put on one side out of the bankrupt's significant income during the period of the bankruptcy.

---

[186] See Mr Anthony Mann QC sitting as a High Court judge in *Re Scott (A Bankrupt)* [2003] All ER (D) 214, para 13 following *Re Rayatt*.   [187] [2003] All ER (D) 214.
[188] [1999] BPIR 97.

6.6.5.2 *The court's discretion*

The judge in *Re Rayatt* also noted that there are two discretionary elements in s 310.[189] First, the court must exercise its discretion under s 310(1) before any part of the bankrupt's income can be treated as vesting in the estate. Secondly, s 310(2) then 'operates by circumscribing that discretion and itself introduces a further discretionary element ("...what appears to the court to be necessary [etc]..."). The two discretionary elements are no doubt usually telescoped into one, but it is important not to allow a focus on the second element to obscure the existence of the initial discretion'. He went on to say that to the extent that the making of an income payments order would impose real hardship on a debtor or his family, there should be 'some reasonable proportionality between the hardship imposed and the benefit which will thereby be reaped by the creditors'.[190] This consideration was relevant to the exercise of the initial discretion under s 310(1). He concluded:[191]

Although I had no evidence about the effect of a change to the State system would have on these children (a daughter aged 12 at the same school as the eldest child and a son aged 8), it scarcely seems possible that the paltry sum which this approach yields for the trustee could justify the disruption to their lives which it would inevitably cause and the interference with the parental choice of education which it would involve.

In *Kilvert v Flackett*,[192] it was accepted by the judge that s 310(1) does enable the court to exercise a discretion as to whether or not to make an income payments order or to limit the ambit of any such order, even though the reason for refusing or limiting the order is not the one specified in s 310(2), ie that the effect of such an order would be to reduce the income of the bankrupt below what appears to be necessary for meeting the reasonable domestic needs of the bankrupt and his family. However, the court's discretion must be exercised by reference to the general purpose of the legislation. This is to vest in the trustee all property belonging to the bankrupt at the commencement of the bankruptcy, and after-acquired property in limited circumstances, and to provide that payments in the nature of income received between the bankruptcy and the discharge should also benefit the estate unless there are reasons to the contrary. Those reasons had to be truly relevant to the facts of the case. Without attempting to justify all such reasons, it seemed to the judge that 'the court's approach should be to seek to achieve proportionality between the creditors and the bankrupt, whilst not creating a situation in which the bankrupt is the slave of the creditors...'.[193]

These considerations involve looking at the position of the individual bankrupt, and not at what others, not in the unfortunate position of bankruptcy,

---

[189] [1998] 2 FLR 264, 270–1. [190] ibid 271. [191] ibid 273.
[192] [1998] 2 FLR 806.
[193] ibid 808, *per* Mr Peter Scott QC sitting as a High Court judge and referring to the Report of the Cork Committee.

141

might do with sums available to them under pension schemes or indeed other resources. Whilst some might use a lump sum to purchase an annuity, others might wish to pay off debts or simply expend the money in a variety of ways. There was no evidence as to what the bankrupt in that case would do with the money and it is not clear that any particular investment intention would have been relevant. Accordingly, 's 310(2) does not inevitably mean that the income of the [bankrupt] must be reduced to that required for his reasonable domestic needs and that of his family...'.[194] But in that case if only £10,000 were made the subject of an order then most of the lump sum would be available to enhance the bankrupt's income above that level even during the bankruptcy. Some reasonably plain justification ought to exist if that were to be the result, and there was no such justification. It might presumably have been otherwise if the evidence showed that the bankrupt's income from a pension after discharge would not be sufficient to meet his needs when the purchase of an annuity might be appropriate.

6.6.6 Income payments orders and orders in family proceedings

The assessment of the needs of the bankrupt and his family for the purposes of s 310 will be made by the bankruptcy court. In making such an assessment and determining the amount of any income payments order, the bankruptcy court is not bound by an assessment of the needs of the family already made by a family court making an order for periodical payments under the Matrimonial Causes Act 1973.[195] The bankrupt will, of course, be able to apply for a variation of the periodical payments order in the light of the order under s 310. If an order for periodical payments has not already been made under the 1973 Act, the family court on a subsequent application for such an order, will be bound by the income payments order which affects the amount of the bankrupt's income.[196]

6.7 THE EFFECT OF BANKRUPTCY

On bankruptcy an individual becomes subject to a number of restrictions, prohibitions, and disqualifications, but these are reduced in number and some of those that remain are altered in scope by the Enterprise Act 2002. A bankrupt has been disqualified from sitting or voting in the House of Lords and from being elected to, or sitting or voting in, the House of Commons.[197] The seat of a Member of Parliament has been vacated if he or she remained disqualified at the

---

[194] [1998] 2 FLR 809.

[195] *Albert v Albert (A Bankrupt)* [1996] BPIR 232, 235, *per* Millett LJ. A prior assessment/calculation under the Child Support Act 1991 will presumably be binding.

[196] See further ch 8, para 8.3 and Miller, 'The Effect of Insolvency on Applications for Financial Provision' (1998) 10 CFLQ 29, 32.   [197] IA 1986, s 427.

end of the period of six months from the date of his or her adjudication. As from the coming into force of the Enterprise Act 2002, a person is disqualified from membership of the House of Commons and from sitting or voting in the House of Lords only if a bankruptcy restrictions order is made in relation to him.[198] The seat of a Member of Parliament will be vacated as soon as the Member is disqualified by the making of a bankruptcy restrictions order.[199] Thus henceforth disqualification will be triggered not by a bankruptcy order, but only if a bankruptcy restrictions order is made on the basis of a sufficient degree of culpability on the part of the bankrupt. There are similar provisions in relation to membership of the assemblies in Wales, Scotland, and Northern Ireland. Similarly, the disqualification imposed in relation to membership of a local authority as a result of a bankruptcy order is replaced by disqualification only if a bankruptcy restrictions order or an interim order is made.[200] The disqualification from appointment as a justice of the peace was abolished by the 2002 Act.[201]

A bankrupt continues to be guilty of an offence if either alone or jointly with another person he obtains credit to the extent of the prescribed amount or more without giving the person from whom he obtains it the relevant information about his status, ie that he is an undischarged bankrupt.[202] He is also guilty of an offence if he engages (directly or indirectly) in any business under a name other than that in which he was adjudged bankrupt without disclosing to all persons with whom he enters into any business transaction the name in which he was so adjudged.[203] However, the impact of these restrictions is reduced for the majority of bankrupts as a result of the reduction in the period of bankruptcy to a maximum of one year,[204] though this may not ease the difficulty a bankrupt may face in obtaining credit. These restrictions will, however, continue to apply to a bankrupt after his discharge while a bankruptcy restrictions order is in force in respect of him.[205]

The position is similar in respect of a number of other statutory disqualifications. It is an offence for an undischarged bankrupt to act as a director of, or directly or indirectly to take part in or be concerned in the promotion, formation, or management of, a company without the leave of the court by which the bankruptcy order was made.[206] An undischarged bankrupt commits an offence if he acts as a receiver or manager of the property of a company on

---

[198] IA 1986, s 426A inserted by the Enterprise Act 2002, s 266.   [199] IA 1986, s 426A(2).

[200] Enterprise Act 2002, s 267 amending Local Government Act 1972, s 80.

[201] Enterprise Act 2002, s 265 repealing Justice of the Peace Act 1997, s 65.

[202] IA 1986, s 360(1)(a). As from 1 April 2004 the prescribed amount is £500: Insolvency Proceedings (Monetary Limits) (Amendment) Order 2004, SI 2004/547.

[203] IA 1986, s 360(1)(b). For the meaning of obtaining credit, see s 360(2).

[204] See paras 6.9 and 6.10 below.

[205] IA 1986, s 360(5) inserted by the Enterprise Act 2002, Sch 21. In which case the relevant information as to status is that a bankruptcy restrictions order is in force in respect of him (s 360(6)).

[206] Company Directors Disqualification Act 1986, s 11.

behalf of debenture holders unless he acts under an appointment made by the court.[207] An undischarged bankrupt is not qualified to act as an insolvency practitioner.[208] These provisions were amended by the Enterprise Act 2002 so as also to apply while a bankruptcy restrictions order is in force in respect of the person concerned.[209] A bankrupt is not guilty of an offence in respect of anything done after his discharge though proceedings may be instituted against him after his discharge in respect of an offence committed before his discharge.[210] This is now without prejudice to any provision applying to a person in respect of whom a bankruptcy restrictions order is in force. Finally, an undischarged bankrupt is disqualified from practising as a solicitor.[211]

Under s 371 of the Insolvency Act 1986, the court may order the re-direction of a bankrupt's mail to the official receiver or the trustee in bankruptcy.

6.8 BANKRUPTCY RESTRICTIONS ORDERS

The position of bankrupts generally has been alleviated by the Enterprise Act 2002, especially by the shortening of the period of bankruptcy. However, a minority of bankrupts may abuse the system or may have been dishonest or culpable so the court is empowered to make bankruptcy restrictions orders for the protection of the public and the business community.[212] The effect of such an order will be to continue various disqualifications and restrictions after the bankrupt's discharge and will provide the trigger for certain other disqualifications.[213]

The court may make a bankruptcy restrictions order on the application of the Secretary of State or the official receiver acting on the directions of the Secretary of State.[214] The court must grant such an application if it thinks it appropriate having regard to the conduct of the bankrupt whether before or after the making of the bankruptcy order. The court must, in particular, take into account any of the following kinds of behaviour on the part of the bankrupt:[215]

(a) failing to keep records which account for a loss of property by the bankrupt, or by a business carried on by him, where the loss occurred in the period beginning two years before petition and ending with the date of the application;[216]

---

[207] IA 1986, s 31.   [208] IA 1986, s 390.   [209] Section 257 and Sch 21 paras 1, 4, and 5.
[210] IA 1986, s 350(3).   [211] Solicitors Act 1974, s 15(1).
[212] Enterprise Act 2002, s 257 inserting s 281A into the Insolvency Act 1986 referring to Sch 4A inserted into the Act.
[213] See previous section and the Enterprise Act 2002, s 257 and Sch 21.
[214] Sch 4A, para 1.   [215] ibid para 2(2).
[216] Failure to keep proper accounts of a business was a criminal offence under s 361 of the Insolvency Act 1986. That was repealed by s 263 of the Enterprise Act 2002 so that such failure becomes a factor to be taken into account by the court in deciding whether to make a bankruptcy restrictions order.

(b) failing to produce records of that kind on demand by the official receiver or the trustee;

(c) entering into a transaction at an undervalue;[217]

(d) giving a preference;[218]

(e) making an excessive pension contribution;[219]

(f) a failure to supply goods or services which were wholly or partly paid for which gave rise to a claim provable in bankruptcy;

(g) trading at a time before commencement of the bankruptcy when the bankrupt knew or ought to have known that he was himself unable to pay his debts;

(h) incurring, before the commencement of the bankruptcy, a debt which the bankrupt had no reasonable expectation of being able to pay;

(i) failing to account satisfactorily to the court, the official receiver or the trustee for a loss of property or for an insufficiency of property to meet bankruptcy debts;

(j) carrying on any gambling, rash and hazardous speculation or unreasonable extravagance which may have materially contributed to or increased the extent of the bankruptcy or which took place between the presentation of the petition and commencement of the bankruptcy;[220]

(k) neglect of business affairs of a kind which may have materially contributed to or increased the extent of the bankruptcy;

(l) fraud or fraudulent breach of trust;

(m) failing to co-operate with the official receiver or the trustee.

The court must also, in particular, consider whether the bankrupt was an undischarged bankrupt at some time during the period of six years ending with the date of the bankruptcy to which the application relates.[221]

An application for a bankruptcy restrictions order in respect of a bankrupt must be made (a) before the end of the period of one year beginning with the date on which the bankruptcy commences, or (b) with the permission of the court.[222] An order comes into force when it is made, and ceases to have effect at

---

[217] 'Undervalue' is to be construed in accordance with s 339 of the Insolvency Act 1986. See ch 9.

[218] 'Preference' is to be construed in accordance with s 340 of the Insolvency Act 1986.

[219] 'Excessive pension contribution' is to be construed in accordance with s 342A of the 1986 Act inserted by the Pensions Act 1995, s 95(1) and amended by the Welfare Reform and Pensions Act 1999, s 15. See ch 9.

[220] Gambling, rash and hazardous speculations could amount to a criminal offence under s 362 of the Insolvency Act 1986. That is repealed by s 263 of the Enterprise Act 2002 so that such failure becomes a factor to be taken into account by the court in deciding whether to make a bankruptcy restrictions order.   [221] Sch 4A, para 2(3).

[222] Sch 4A, para 3. The period specified in (a) ceases to run in respect of a bankrupt while the period set for his discharge is suspended under s 279(3).

the end of a date specified in the order. The minimum period for an order is two years beginning with the date on which it is made and the maximum period is fifteen years beginning with that date.[223]

In many cases an application for a bankruptcy restrictions order may not have been determined before the bankrupt is discharged. Accordingly, the court may make an interim bankruptcy restrictions order if it thinks there are prima facie grounds to suggest that the application for the bankruptcy restrictions order will be successful, and it is in the public interest to make an interim order.[224] An interim order has the same effect as a bankruptcy restrictions order and comes into force when it is made. It will cease to have effect:

(a) on the determination of the application for the bankruptcy restrictions order,
(b) on the acceptance of a bankruptcy restrictions undertaking made by the bankrupt, or
(c) if the court discharges the interim order on the application of the person who applied for it or of the bankrupt.

A bankrupt may offer a bankruptcy restrictions undertaking to the Secretary of State to be bound by the restrictions that would be contained in an order thus avoiding the necessity for a court hearing.[225] In determining whether to accept such an undertaking the Secretary of State must have regard to the same matters as the court is required to take into account in determining whether to make an order. An undertaking comes into force on being accepted by the Secretary of State and ceases to have effect at the end of a date specified in the undertaking. The minimum period is again two years and the maximum period is fifteen years. On an application by the bankrupt the court may annul an undertaking or provide for it to cease to have effect before the date specified in the undertaking.

The Secretary of State is required to maintain a register of bankruptcy restrictions orders, interim bankruptcy restrictions orders, and bankruptcy restrictions undertakings.[226]

6.9 THE DURATION OF BANKRUPTCY

The bankruptcy of an individual against whom a bankruptcy order has been made commences with the day on which the order is made, and continues until the individual is discharged under the provisions of the Act as amended.[227] A bankruptcy order may also be annulled or rescinded.

---

[223] Sch 4A, para 4.   [224] ibid para 5   [225] ibid para 9.   [226] Sch 4A, para 12.
[227] IA 1986, s 278.

6.10 DISCHARGE FROM BANKRUPTCY

6.10.1 Automatic discharge

A bankrupt is automatically discharged from bankruptcy at the end of the period of one year beginning with the date on which the bankruptcy commences.[228] This is a significant reduction from the period of three years applicable before the Enterprise Act 2002 came into force.[229] However, discharge may occur before the end of that period if the official receiver files with the court a notice stating that investigation of the conduct and affairs of the bankrupt under s 289 is unnecessary or concluded. In that event the bankrupt is discharged when the notice is filed.[230] On the other hand, on the application of the official receiver or the trustee of the bankrupt's estate, the court may, if it is satisfied that the bankrupt has failed, or is failing, to comply with an obligation under the Act, order that the period of one year shall cease to run until the end of a specified period or the fulfilment of a specified condition.[231] Such an order must be made before the automatic discharge takes place if it is to be effective to suspend the automatic discharge. Once an automatic discharge has been obtained that discharge cannot be revoked so as to re-impose the bankruptcy. Although twenty-one days notice of such an application must generally be given to the bankrupt,[232] in *Bagnall v Official Receiver*,[233] it was held that the court has power to make an interim order suspending a bankrupt's automatic discharge, ex parte in a case where the court can properly regard the making of such an order as urgent.[234]

6.10.2 Discharge under an order of the court

Under the Insolvency Act 1986 when a bankrupt had been an undischarged bankrupt at any time in the period of fifteen years ending with the commencement of the bankruptcy, there was no automatic discharge.[235] It was

---

[228] IA 1986, s 279(1) as substituted by the Enterprise Act 2002, s 265.

[229] There are transitional provisions applicable to persons made bankrupt before the commencement of the 2002 Act who had not been discharged at that date. See Sch 19 to the Enterprise Act 2002 which provides that discharge will occur one year from the date of commencement or earlier if the three year period ends before that date. Where a bankruptcy order was made on the debtor's own petition and certain other conditions were satisfied then the court might issue a certificate of summary administration under s 275. In that event, if the certificate had not been revoked, the period before discharge was reduced from three years to two years (s 279(2)). The provisions relating to summary administration were repealed by the Enterprise Act 2002, s 269 and Sch 23.   [230] IA 1986, s 279(2).

[231] IA 1986, s 279(3)(4). A 'condition' includes a condition requiring that the court be satisfied of something: s 279(5).   [232] Insolvency Rules 1986, r 6.215.

[233] [2003] EWCA Civ 1925.   [234] See Insolvency Rules 1986, r 7.4(6).

[235] IA 1986, s 279(1).

necessary for the bankrupt to apply for an order of the court and such an application could be made only after the end of the period of five years beginning with the commencement of the bankruptcy.[236] If such a bankrupt was undischarged when the Enterprise Act 2002 came into force, he will be discharged five years from that date or earlier if an order for his discharge is made under s 280(2) of the Insolvency Act 1986 Act.[237]

6.10.3 Effect of discharge

When a bankrupt is discharged, the general principle is that discharge releases him from all bankruptcy debts.[238] A creditor's right of action is not revived by the discharge. A 'bankruptcy debt' means any of the following:[239]

(a) any debt or liability to which the bankrupt was subject at the commencement of the bankruptcy,

(b) any debt or liability to which he might have become subject after the commencement of the bankruptcy (including after his discharge from bankruptcy) by reason of any obligation incurred before the commencement of the bankruptcy,

(c) any interest provable in respect of a debt for a period prior to the commencement of the bankruptcy.[240]

There are a number of exceptions to the general rule:

Discharge has no effect on the functions of the trustee of his estate so far as they remain to be carried out, or on the operation of the Act for the purposes of the carrying out of those functions.[241] Discharge does not affect the right of any creditor of the bankrupt to prove in the bankruptcy for any debt from which the bankrupt is released. This means that a creditor may benefit from distributions out of property realized or becoming available after the discharge.

Discharge does not affect the right of any secured creditor of the bankrupt to enforce his security for the payment of a debt from which the bankrupt is released.[242]

Discharge does not release the bankrupt from any bankruptcy debt which he incurred in respect of, or forbearance in respect of which was secured by means of, any fraud or fraudulent breach of trust to which he was a party.[243]

---

[236] IA 1986, s 280(1)   [237] Enterprise Act 2002, Sch 19, para 5.

[238] IA 1986, s 281. If a debt is not a provable debt then it is not a debt which is released on discharge. The importance of this in relation to 'matrimonial debts' is considered in ch 8.

Discharge does not release any person other than the bankrupt from any liability (whether as partner or co-trustee of the bankrupt or otherwise) from which the bankrupt is released by the discharge, or from any liability as surety for the bankrupt or as a person in the nature of such a surety: s 281(7).   [239] IA 1986, s 382(1).

[240] See s 322(2).   [241] IA 1986, s 281(1).   [242] IA 1986, s 281(2).

[243] IA 1986, s 281(3).

Discharge does not release the bankrupt from any liability in respect of a fine imposed for an offence or from any liability under a recognisance except, in the case of a penalty imposed for an offence under an enactment relating to the public revenue or of a recognisance, with the consent of the Treasury.[244]

Discharge does not, except to such extent and on such conditions as the court may direct, release the bankrupt from any bankruptcy debt which:

(a) consists in a liability to pay damages for negligence, nuisance, or breach of a statutory, contractual or other duty, or to pay damages by virtue of Pt I of the Consumer Protection Act 1987 being in either case damages in respect of personal injuries to any person, or

(b) arises under any order made in family proceedings or under a maintenance calculation made under the Child Support Act 1991.[245]

Discharge does not release the bankrupt from such other bankruptcy debts, not being debts provable in his bankruptcy, as are prescribed.[246]

Discharge will also bring to an end various disqualifications and restrictions applicable during bankruptcy as outlined in an earlier section unless a bankruptcy restrictions order is made against the bankrupt.[247]

6.10.4 Annulment of the bankruptcy order

The court may annul a bankruptcy order under s 282 of the Insolvency Act 1986 which has the effect that the debtor is regarded as 'never have been bankrupt at all'.[248] The court may annul a bankruptcy order if it at any time appears to the court:

(a) that, on any grounds existing at the time the order was made, the order ought not to have been made, or

(b) that, to the extent required by the rules, the bankruptcy debts and the expenses of the bankruptcy have all, since the making of the order, been either paid or secured for to the satisfaction of the court.[249]

In relation to (a) the court must proceed in two stages.[250] First, it must ask whether at the time that the bankruptcy order was made, any ground existed on the basis of which the order ought not to have been made. The onus is on the

---

[244] IA 1986, s 281(4). The reference to a fine includes a reference to a confiscation order under Pts 2, 3, or 4 of the Proceeds of Crime Act 2002 (s 281(4A)).

[245] IA 1986, s 281(5). For the meaning of 'family proceedings', see s 281(8).

[246] IA 1986, s 281(6).   [247] See paras 6.7. and 6.8 above.

[248] Per Wilson J in Couvaras v Wolf [2002] 2 FLR 107, 112 referring to Aldous LJ in Choudhury v The Commissioners of Inland Revenue [2000] BPIR 246, 250. Nevertheless not all the consequences of the bankruptcy will be undone. See below. The court may annul a bankruptcy order whether or not the bankrupt has been discharged from the bankruptcy: s 282(3).   [249] IA 1986, s 282(1).

[250] Per Park J in Society of Lloyd's v Waters [2001] BPIR 698, 704.

applicant to establish that such a ground existed at the time the order was made. Secondly, if this is answered in the affirmative, the court has a discretion whether or not to annul the bankruptcy. The court has no duty to annul the bankruptcy order.[251] The court's power of annulment under (a) is therefore discretionary. In relation to (b) it will be noted that it is not necessary to show that all debts have actually been paid before a bankruptcy order can be annulled. It will be sufficient if all debts and expenses of the bankruptcy are adequately secured.

The court may also annul a bankruptcy order where a voluntary arrangement is approved by a creditors' meeting after a bankruptcy order was made.[252]

An annulment may, and of course usually will, be sought by the bankrupt himself, but where the bankrupt's marriage has broken down it may be necessary for the bankrupt's spouse to seek annulment of the bankruptcy order. The bankruptcy of one spouse may have serious consequences on applications in divorce proceedings for financial provision and property adjustment by the other spouse.[253] A spouse may be prepared to file his own petition in bankruptcy so as to take advantage of bankruptcy proceedings as a means of delaying or defeating the claims of the other spouse. In *F v F (Divorce: Insolvency: Annulment of Bankruptcy Order)*,[254] Thorpe J said:

The order was obtained on the husband's petition which presented a false picture of his financial circumstances. He omitted assets outside the jurisdiction that are cardinal to any evaluation of his true net worth. It was, in my judgment, a device in the intensification of the war between husband and wife in the aftermath of divorce. It was the product of the increasing bitterness and hostility developing between them.

He concluded that the husband's petition was an abuse of the processes of the court and the bankruptcy order should be set aside. More recently in *Couvaras v Wolf*[255] and *F v F (S Intervening) (Financial Provision: Bankruptcy: Reviewable Disposition)*,[256] it was found that the husband was not insolvent and that in each case the bankruptcy order ought not to have been made and was annulled.[257] However, even if the husband's main or sole motive was to baulk the claim his wife was making for a transfer of property order rather than to protect himself from undue pressure by creditors or to secure a fair distribution of his

---

[251] For examples of refusal of annulment see *Askew v Peter Dominic Ltd* [1997] BPIR 163 and *Re Coney* [1998] BPIR 333. See also Briggs and Sims, 'Escaping Bankruptcy—Applications to Annul' [2002] Insolvency Lawyer 2. [252] IA 1986, s 261.

[253] See ch 8.   [254] [1994] 1 FLR 359, 366.   [255] [2002] 2 FLR 107.

[256] [2002] EWHC 2814 (Fam), [2003] 1 FLR 911.

[257] In *Couvaras v Wolf*, Wilson J specifically referred to the transfer of the application to annul to the Family Division as being appropriate in view of the considerable amount of information which had been obtained in the proceedings there regarding the husband's financial circumstances. In *F v F (S Intervening)* the earlier decision of Coleridge J to stay the husband's bankruptcy petition and adjourning the wife's application to annul it to the conclusion of the ancillary relief hearing had been confirmed by the Court of Appeal ([2002] EWCA Civ 1527).

assets between them, his petition will not be an abuse of the process of the court if he is in fact unable to pay his debts. An annulment will therefore be inappropriate.[258]

Although the effect of an annulment is that the bankrupt is regarded as never having been bankrupt, any sale or other disposition of property, payment made or acts done, by or under the authority of the official receiver or a trustee of the bankrupt's estate or by the court before the annulment remain valid. Any of the bankrupt's estate vested in the trustee in bankruptcy at the date of annulment will vest in such persons as the court may appoint, such as the supervisor of a individual voluntary arrangement. In default of any such appointment, it will revert to the bankrupt on such terms (if any) as the court may direct.[259]

6.10.5 Effect of annulment of bankruptcy order on bankruptcy restrictions orders

Where a bankruptcy order is annulled under s 282(1)(a) on the basis that it appears to the court that on any ground existing at the time the order was made, the order ought not to have been made, then any bankruptcy restrictions order, interim order, or bankruptcy restrictions undertaking is also annulled. Further, no new bankruptcy restrictions order or interim order may be made in respect of the bankrupt and no new bankruptcy restrictions undertaking by the bankrupt may be accepted.[260] Where a bankruptcy order is annulled under s 282(1)(b) on the basis that the bankruptcy debts and expenses have all, since the making of the order, been either paid or secured to the satisfaction of the court, then the annulment will not affect any bankruptcy restrictions order, interim order, or undertaking in respect of the bankrupt. The court may make a bankruptcy restrictions order in relation to the bankrupt on an application instituted before the annulment and a bankruptcy restrictions undertaking offered before the annulment may be accepted. However, an application for a bankruptcy restrictions order or interim order in respect of the bankrupt may not be instituted after the annulment.[261]

6.10.6 Rescission

Courts exercising individual insolvency jurisdiction have power under s 375(1) to 'review, rescind or vary any order made by it in the exercise of that jurisdiction'. Rescission of a bankruptcy order may be appropriate where circumstances have changed since the order was properly made. Thus in *Fitch v Official Receiver*,[262] the Court of Appeal approved the rescission of bankruptcy

---

[258] See Re *Holliday* [1980] 3 All ER 385, 390, *per* Goff LJ.   [259] IA 1986, s 282(4).

[260] IA 1986, Sch 4A, para 10.

[261] ibid para 11. This also applies to an annulment under ss 261 or 263D (annulment following approval of a voluntary arrangement).   [262] [1996] 1 WLR 242.

orders made against a husband and wife where most of the creditors, including the petitioning creditor, had changed their attitude in the belief that the orders would prejudice the recovery of a substantial asset for their benefit.[263] However, the court emphasized that the discretion to rescind a bankruptcy order is to be exercised with caution and only in exceptional circumstances.

At first sight there seems little difference between annulment, the effect of which is that the bankruptcy order was never made at all, and rescission which is the retrospective termination of the bankruptcy. However, there is a difference which may be significant as in *Hoare v IRC*.[264] Mr Hoare had commercial arrangements with third parties containing clauses which might expose him to liability to pay a substantial sum of money triggered in the event of a bankruptcy order having been made. Peter Smith J set aside the rescinding of the bankruptcy order and annulled it instead.

6.11 DISTRIBUTION

6.11.1 The general principle

When the trustee has realized the assets of the bankrupt he must declare and distribute dividends among the creditors in respect of the debts which they have proved. This is subject to the retention of such sums as are necessary for the expenses of the bankruptcy.[265] While the longstanding general principle is that distribution should be made *pari passu*, ie rateably amongst the creditors who have proved, certain debts have been classified as preferential and are required to be paid in priority to other debts.[266] Preferential debts rank equally between themselves after the expenses of the bankruptcy and must be paid in full unless the bankrupt's estate is insufficient for meeting them. In that event they abate in equal proportions between themselves.[267] Remaining debts, subject to certain exceptions, also rank equally between themselves and, after the preferential debts, must be paid in full unless the bankrupt's estate is insufficient for meeting them. In that case these ordinary debts again abate in equal proportions.[268] Any surplus remaining after the payment of preferential and ordinary debts is to be applied in paying interest at the official rate on those debts in respect of the periods during which they have been outstanding since the commencement of the bankruptcy. Preferential and ordinary debts rank equally for this purpose.[269] Finally, certain debts are deferred debts and rank in priority after preferential and ordinary debtors.[270]

---

[263] The petitions were not dismissed and so could be restored for hearing.
[264] [2002] EWHC 775 (Ch).   [265] IA 1986, s 324.   [266] IA 1986, s 328(1).
[267] IA 1986, s 328(2).   [268] IA 1986, s 328(3).   [269] IA 1986, s 328(4)(5).
[270] IA 1986, s 329.

The amount available for all such unsecured creditors will be what is left after proprietary claims and secured creditors have been satisfied out of their security.

6.11.2 Preferred debts

Under the Insolvency Act 1986, the Crown had preferential status in respect of (a) debts due to the Inland Revenue in respect of tax deducted from emoluments in the twelve months prior to the relevant date, (b) debts due to Customs and Excise in respect of certain taxes referable to the six months prior to the relevant date and in respect of other taxes to the twelve months before that date, and (c) certain social security contributions for the twelve months prior to the relevant date.[271] The relevant date was generally the date of the making of the bankruptcy order.[272] The Enterprise Act 2002 abolishes the Crown's preferential status.[273] Preferential status will continue for (a) any sum owed by the bankrupt to which Sch 4 to the Pensions Schemes Act 1993 applies (contributions to occupational pensions schemes and state scheme premiums), (b) remuneration of employees or former employees for the period of four months next before the relevant date which is generally the date of the bankruptcy order, up to the amount prescribed by order made by the Secretary of State,[274] (c) an amount owed by way of accrued holiday remuneration, in respect of any period of employment before the relevant date, to a person whose employment by the bankrupt has been terminated, whether before, on or after that date, and (d) so much of any amount which is ordered (before or after the relevant date) to be paid by the debtor under the Reserve Forces (Safeguard of Employment) Act 1985 and is so ordered in respect of a default made by the debtor before that date in the discharge of his obligations under that Act. This is up to the limit prescribed by order made by the Secretary of State.[275]

6.11.3 Ordinary debts

These comprise all creditors who are neither preferential nor deferred creditors.

6.11.4 Deferred debts

Debts owed in respect of credit provided by a person who was the bankrupt's spouse at the commencement of the bankruptcy rank in priority after preferential and other ordinary debts.[276] This applies whether or not that person was the bankrupt's spouse at the time the credit was provided. Such deferred debts will therefore receive a distribution only after preferential and ordinary debts have been paid in full.

---

[271] IA 1986, s 386 and Sch 6.   [272] IA 1986, s 387(6).   [273] Section 251.
[274] This is currently £800.   [275] IA 1986, Sch 6.   [276] IA 1986, s 329.

If money has been advanced by way of a loan to a person engaged or about to engage in any business on the basis that the lender is to receive a share of the profits arising from the business, then although the lender may not thereby become a partner in the business, on the borrower's bankruptcy, the lender is not entitled to recover anything in respect of his loan until the claims of the other creditors of the borrower have been satisfied.[277]

---

[277] Partnership Act 1890, ss 2(3), and 3.

7

ALTERNATIVE METHODS OF
DEALING WITH INSOLVENCY

7.1 INTRODUCTION

The fact that a person is insolvent does not necessarily mean that bankruptcy is inevitable. There are a number of ways in which a debtor may obtain some relief from the pressure of his creditors while avoiding bankruptcy. The most obvious way is by reaching an agreement with his creditors without involving the formal procedure of an application to a court. Such informal agreements are likely to save the costs that would be incurred in a formal procedure and which would reduce the assets available for the creditors. However, if all the creditors are not prepared to co-operate then it will be necessary to turn to a procedure which will enable the wishes of the majority to prevail.

7.2 INFORMAL METHODS OF DEALING
WITH INSOLVENCY

A debtor may be able to enter into an agreement with one or more of his creditors to allow him more time to discharge his obligations or to accept less than the amount originally due or to provide additional credit. Such agreements are not without problems. Thus a simple agreement by one creditor to accept less than the amount originally due will be unenforceable for lack of consideration on the part of the debtor.[1] There must be some additional benefit to the creditor such as payment of the lesser sum at an earlier time than that originally required. However, where a debtor enters into an agreement with several creditors then this seems to be enforceable, though unless such a composition agreement has been made with all the debtor's creditors, there remains the problem that any creditor who is not a party to the agreement may take legal proceedings against the debtor including bankruptcy proceedings. This is so even though the creditors who are parties to the agreement are prevented from taking such steps.

7.3 DEEDS OF ARRANGEMENT

A deed of arrangement is an agreement by an individual debtor with his creditors to arrange his affairs without the need to resort to bankruptcy. This might consist of an assignment of property by the debtor to a trustee for the benefit of his creditors generally, or an agreement to pay to creditors a sum less than the full amount owing to them.[2] Although it is a contract between the debtor, the creditors, and the trustee of the deed, it is subject to regulation under the Deeds of Arrangement Act 1914. In particular, the deed must be registered with the Registrar of Deeds of Arrangement within seven days of execution and will be automatically void if not so registered.[3] The entry into a deed of arrangement whereby the debtor assigned his property for the benefit of his creditors was itself an act of bankruptcy upon which a petition for bankruptcy could be presented by a creditor who was not a party to the arrangement. The concept of an act of bankruptcy has been abolished, but such a creditor is likely to have little difficulty in successfully presenting a petition for bankruptcy on the basis that the debtor is unable to pay, or to have no reasonable prospect of being able to pay, the amount due to the creditor.[4] The use of deeds of arrangement has been in decline for many years and the Cork Report recommended the repeal of the Deeds of Arrangement Act.[5] This has not taken place, but little use is likely to be made of deeds of arrangement especially in view of the provisions relating to individual voluntary arrangements contained in the Insolvency Act 1986 and considered in detail in section 7.5 of this chapter.

---

[1] *Foakes v Beer* (1884) 9 App Cas 605; *D & C Builders Ltd v Rees* [1966] 2 QB 617; *Re Selectmove Ltd* [1995] 2 All ER 531.

[2] The definition of a deed of arrangement is rather wider and includes some documents that are not deeds. See the Deeds of Arrangement Act 1914, s 1.   [3] Section 2.

[4] See now s 267 (1) of the Insolvency Act 1986 considered in ch 6.

[5] (Cmnd 8585), para 399.

7.4 THE COUNTY COURT ADMINISTRATION ORDER

7.4.1 The scope of an order

Under the County Courts Act 1984 a county court may, on the application of a debtor, make an order providing for the administration of his estate if he (1) is unable to pay forthwith the amount of a judgment obtained against him, and (2) alleges that his whole indebtedness amounts to a sum not exceeding the county court limit, inclusive of the debt for which the judgment was obtained.[6] An administration order may provide for the payment of the debts of the debtor by instalments or otherwise, and either in full or to such extent as appears practicable to the court under the circumstances of the case. It may be made subject to any conditions as to his future earnings or income which the court may think just.[7] This offers a judgment debtor whose total debts are modest, but whose available assets are not sufficient to discharge those debts, a way of obtaining protection from action by his creditors while he repays his debts out of income. At the same time it provides an appropriate framework for ensuring an orderly payment of the debts. However, where there is no judgment debt and/or the total debts exceed the prescribed limit it will not be available, and the debtor may find it difficult to avoid bankruptcy in the absence of sufficient assets to make an individual voluntary arrangement attractive to his creditors.[8]

These restrictions are prospectively removed by the Courts and Legal Services Act 1990,[9] but the relevant provisions have not yet been brought into force. The prospectively substituted s 112(1) provides that where a debtor is unable to pay forthwith the amount of any debt owed by him, a county court may make an order providing for the administration of his estate. An administration order will then be possible:

(a) on the application of the debtor (whether or not a judgment debt has been obtained against him in respect of the debt or any of his debts),

(b) on the application of any creditor under a judgment obtained against the debtor, or

(c) of the court's own motion during the course of, or on the determination of, any enforcement or other proceedings.[10]

---

[6] Section 112(1). However, an administration order is not invalid by reason only that the total amount of the debts is found at any time to exceed the county court limit, but in that case the court may, if it thinks fit, set aside the order: s 112(5).　　　　　　　　　　　　[7] Section 112(6).

[8] In 2002, the number of administration orders granted was 6,330 being 16% less than in 2001: Judicial Statistics Annual Report (2002).　　　　　　　　　　　　[9] Section 13(1).

[10] Section 112(1A).

7.4.2 Procedure

A debtor who desires to obtain an administration order must file a request to that effect in the county court for the district in which he resides or carries on business.[11] He should provide a statement of his means and obligations and a list of his creditors. Where on his examination under the Civil Procedure Rules or otherwise, a debtor furnishes to the court on oath a list of his creditors and the amounts which he owes to them respectively, and sufficient particulars of his resources and needs, the court may proceed as if the debtor had filed a request for an administration order.[12]

The question whether an administration order should be made, and the terms of such an order, may be decided by the court officer. On the filing of a request or list of creditors under r 2, the court officer may, if he considers that the debtor's means are sufficient to discharge in full and within a reasonable period the total amount of the debts included in the list, determine the amount and frequency of the payments to be made under such an order. He must then inform the debtor of that proposed rate of payments requiring him to give written reasons for any objection he may have to the proposed rate within fourteen days of service of the notification upon him. He must also send to each creditor in the list provided by the debtor a copy of the debtor's request or of the list together with the proposed rate. He must require any such creditor to give written reasons for any objection he may have to the making of an administration order within fourteen days of service of the documents on him. Objections may be to the making of an order, to the proposed rate, or to the inclusion of a particular debt in the order. Where no objection is received within the time stated the court may make an administration order providing for payment in full of the total amount of the debts included in the list.[13]

Where the debtor or a creditor notifies the court of any objection within the time stated, the court officer must fix a day for a hearing at which the district judge will decide whether an administration order should be made. The debtor and each creditor mentioned in the list provided by the debtor must be given not less than fourteen days' notice of that day by the court officer.[14] Where the court officer is unable to fix a rate of payment whether because he considers that the debtor's means are insufficient or otherwise he must refer the request to the district judge.[15] Where the district judge considers that he is able to do so without the attendance of the parties, he may fix the proposed rate providing for the payment of the debts included in the list in full or to such extent and

---

[11] CCR Ord 39, r 2(1). The CCR are now included in Sch 2 to the Civil Procedure Rules 1998, SI 1998/3132.   [12] CCR Ord 39, r 2(2).

[13] CCR Ord 39, r 5(1), (2), and (3). The court officer may exercise the power of the court under s 5 of the Attachment of Earnings Act 1971 to make an attachment of earnings order to secure the payments required by the administration order (r 5(9)).   [14] ibid r 5(4).

[15] ibid r 5(5).

within such a period as appears practicable in the circumstances of the case.[16] Where the proposed rate is so fixed by the district judge then the procedure to be followed is similar to that which applies when the court officer determines the proposed rate.[17] Thus if no objection is received from the debtor or a creditor, the district judge may make an administration order. Where he does not fix the proposed rate he must direct the court officer to fix a day for a hearing at which the district judge will decide whether an administration order should be made. The court officer must give not less than fourteen days' notice of that day to the debtor and to each creditor mentioned in the list provided by the debtor.[18] Any creditor to whom notice has been given and who objects to any debt included in the list of debts must, not less than seven days before the day of the hearing, give notice of his objection to the court officer, the debtor, and the creditor to whose debt he objects, stating the grounds of his objection. No creditor may object to a debt unless he has given such notice of his objection, or with the permission of the court.[19]

At the hearing of the application any creditor may attend and prove his debt even though he was not on the list provided by the debtor.[20] Every debt included in the list is taken to be proved unless it is objected to by a creditor, or disallowed by the court, or required by the court to be supported by evidence. Any creditor whose debt is admitted or proved, and, with the permission of the court, any creditor the proof of whose debt has been adjourned, is entitled to be heard and to adduce evidence on the question whether an administration order should be made and, if so, in what terms.[21] The court may, on making an administration order or at any subsequent time, direct that the order shall be subject to review at such time or at such intervals as the court may specify.[22]

When an administration order is made, notice of the order must be sent to every person whose name the debtor notified to the court as being a creditor or who has proved.[23] Copies of the notice must also be sent to the debtor and to every other court in which, to the knowledge of the district judge, judgment has been obtained against the debtor or proceedings are pending in respect of any debt scheduled to the order.[24]

7.4.3 The effect of an order

When an administration order is made, no creditor is to have any remedy against the person or property of the debtor in respect of any debt (a) of which the debtor notified the appropriate court before the administration order was made, or (b) which has been scheduled to the order, except with leave of the appropriate court, and on such terms as the court may impose.[25] Any county court in which proceedings are pending against the debtor in respect of any debt

---

[16] ibid r 5(6).   [17] ibid r 5(7).   [18] ibid r 5(8).   [19] ibid r 6.   [20] ibid r 7(a).
[21] ibid r 7.   [22] ibid r 8.   [23] County Courts Act 1984, s 113(b).
[24] ibid s 113(a) and CCR Ord 39, r 9.   [25] ibid s 114(1).

so notified or scheduled must, on receiving notice of the administration order, stay the proceedings, but may allow costs already incurred by the creditor, and such costs may, on application, be added to the debt.[26]

The requirement to stay proceedings does not operate as a requirement that a county court in which proceedings in bankruptcy against the debtor are pending must stay those proceedings.[27] However, so long as an administration order is in force, a creditor whose name is included in the schedule to the order is not, without the leave of the court, entitled to present, or join in, a bankruptcy petition against the debtor unless three conditions are satisfied.[28] First, his name was notified to the court by the debtor before the administration order was made. Secondly, the debt by virtue of which he presents, or joins in, the petition, exceeds £1,500.[29] Thirdly, the notice given to the creditor prior to the making of the administration order was received within twenty-eight days immediately preceding the day on which the petition is presented.

Where it appears to the registrar of the court in which an administration order was made, and while the order is still in force, that property of the debtor exceeds in value a specified minimum amount, he must at the request of any creditor, and without any fee, issue execution against the debtor's goods.[30]

A landlord or other person to whom any rent is due from a debtor in respect of whom an administration order is made, may at any time, either before or after the date of the order, distrain upon the goods or effects of the debtor for the rent due to him from the debtor. However, if the distress for rent is levied after the date of the order, it is available only for six months' rent accrued due prior to the date of the order and is not be available for rent payable in respect of any period subsequent to the date when the distress was levied. The landlord or other person to whom the rent may be due from the debtor may prove under the order for the surplus due for which the distress may not have been available.[31]

The court may make an attachment of earnings order to secure payments under an administration order.[32]

7.4.4 Operation of the order

Money paid into court under an administration order must be appropriated (a) first in the satisfaction of the costs of administration (which must not exceed 10 pence in the pound on the total amount of the debts, and (b) then in liquidation of debts in accordance with the order.[33] In contrast to the position on

---

[26] County Courts Act 1984, s 114(2).   [27] ibid s 114(3).   [28] ibid s 112(4).
[29] The Secretary of State may by regulations increase or reduce the specified sum: s 112(7).
[30] ibid s 115. The minimum amount is at present £50 but this may be varied by statutory instrument.   [31] ibid s 116.
[32] Attachment of Earnings Act 1971, s 1(2)(c).   [33] ibid s 117(1).

bankruptcy, there are no preferential debts. Where the amount received is sufficient to pay (a) each creditor scheduled to the order to the extent provided by the order, (b) the costs of the plaintiff in the action in respect of which the order was made, and (c) the costs of the administration, then the order is superseded, and the debtor must be discharged from his debts to the scheduled creditors.[34] Under a provision in the Courts and Legal Services Act 1990, which has not yet been brought into force, an administration order will cease to have effect at the end of the period of three years beginning with the date on which it is made, or on such earlier date as may be specified in the order.[35]

7.4.5 Discharge, suspension, and revocation

Where it appears that the debtor is failing to make payments in accordance with the order, the court officer, either on his own initiative or on the application of a creditor, must send a notice to the debtor requiring him to make the payments as required by the order, or explain his reasons for failing to make the payments and make a proposal for payment of the amounts outstanding or make a request to vary the order. If the debtor fails to explain the reasons for his failure, or to make a proposal for payment or a request to vary the order, the court officer must revoke the administration order. If he does comply, then this must be referred to a district judge who may, without requiring the attendance of the parties, revoke or vary the order or suspend the operation of the order for such time and on such terms as he thinks fit. Alternatively, he may require the court officer to fix a day for the review of the administration order and to give the debtor and every creditor whose debt is scheduled to the order, not less than eight days' notice of that day.[36]

On the review of an administration order, the court may suspend the operation of the order for such time and on such terms as it thinks fit, if satisfied that the debtor is unable from any cause to pay any instalment due under the order. If the court is satisfied that there has been a material change in any relevant circumstances since the order was made, it may vary any provision of the order relating to manner and timing of payments. If the court is satisfied that the debtor has failed without reasonable cause to comply with any provision of the order, or that it is otherwise just and expedient to do so, it may revoke the order, either forthwith or on failure to comply with any condition specified by the court. The court may make an attachment of earnings order to secure the payments required by the administration order or vary or discharge any such attachment of earnings order already made.[37]

If the court revokes an administration order, it may also make an order directing that, for such period, not exceeding one year, as may be specified

---

[34] ibid s 117(2).   [35] ibid s 112(9) inserted by the Courts and Legal Services Act 1990, s 13(4).
[36] CCR Ord 39, r 13A.   [37] ibid r 14(1).

in the order, the debtor may not act as a director of a company or be directly or indirectly concerned in the management of a company without leave of the court.[38] The court may also provide that the debtor must not (a) either alone or jointly with another person, obtain credit to the extent of the amount prescribed for the purposes of s 306(1)(a) of the Insolvency Act 1986 or more, or (b) enter into any transaction in the course of, or for the purposes of, any business in which he is directly or indirectly engaged, without disclosing to the person from whom he obtains credit, or with whom the transaction is entered into, the fact that such an order has been made.[39] The power to impose such restrictions, which would normally apply on bankruptcy, is aimed at discouraging debtors from seeking to use the administration order procedure as a means of delaying the claims of creditors. A failure to comply with the provisions of an order under s 429 is a criminal offence.[40]

7.5 RESTRICTION ORDERS

An alternative to a full administration order is provided for in s 112A of the County Courts Act 1984 which was introduced by the Courts and Legal Services Act 1990,[41] but has not yet been brought into force. Under this provision where the court is satisfied (a) that it has power to make an administration order with the respect to the debtor concerned, but (b) that an order restricting enforcement would be a more satisfactory way of dealing with the case, it may make such an order instead of making an administration order.[42] Where an order restricting enforcement is made, no creditor specified in the order has any remedy against the person or property of the debtor in respect of any debt so specified, without leave of the court.[43] This would give the court an opportunity of considering the enforcement of a creditor's claim on its merits in the context of the debtor's financial position. While such an order has effect a creditor named in the schedule to the order who provides the debtor with mains gas, electricity, or water for the debtor's own domestic purposes may not stop providing such services or any associated services which it provides for its customers, without leave of the court. This does not apply if the reason for stopping

---

[38] Insolvency Act 1986, s 429(2) referring to s 12 of the Company Directors Disqualification Act 1986. The period of one year was substituted for the period of two years by the Enterprise Act 2002, s 269 and Sch 23, para 15 so as to bring the position into line with the reduced period of the duration of bankruptcy introduced by that Act.

[39] IA 1986, s 429(3). Although this provides that a person to whom s 429 applies 'shall' be subject to these disabilities, it is generally considered that the court has a discretion whether or not to include them in an order.   [40] IA 1986, s 429(5).

[41] Section 13(5).   [42] County Courts Act 1984, s 112A(1).   [43] ibid s 112A(2).

such services relates to the non-payment of charges incurred by the debtor after the making of the order or is unconnected with non-payment by him of any charges.[44]

7.6 INDIVIDUAL VOLUNTARY ARRANGEMENTS

7.6.1 Introduction

The Insolvency Act 1986[45] provides a statutory basis for an individual to enter into a voluntary arrangement ('IVA') with his creditors thereby enabling him to avoid bankruptcy and obtain relief from the actions of individual creditors while his debts are discharged under the provisions of the arrangement over a period of time. Such an arrangement will also need to be attractive for at least a majority of his creditors if they are to agree. Even after a bankruptcy order has been made such an arrangement may be attractive to the debtor and his creditors and thus provide a way out of bankruptcy. There are two basic forms which such an arrangement may take, namely a 'composition in satisfaction of his debts' and a 'scheme of arrangement of his affairs'. A 'composition with creditors' means that the debtor retains his assets and agrees to pay a specified sum to his creditors from the proceeds of the assets. Under a scheme of arrangement the debtor will transfer his assets to a trustee who will administer them under the terms of the scheme.

The Enterprise Act 2002 seeks to encourage greater use of individual voluntary arrangements and introduces a new 'fast track' procedure for use by debtors who are undischarged bankrupts.[46] This will be considered briefly after the ordinary procedure established by the Insolvency Act 1986 has been examined.[47] The procedure as originally introduced began in a formal sense with an application for an interim order, but under a provision introduced by the Insolvency Act 2000 it is now possible to make a proposal for a voluntary arrangement without first obtaining an interim order.[48]

7.6.2 The interim order

The first formal step in the procedure as originally introduced is to obtain an interim order from the court under s 252 which will provide a moratorium for the insolvent debtor while the details of the arrangement are formulated. The effect of an interim order is that during the period for which it is in force:

(i) no bankruptcy petition relating to the debtor may be presented or proceeded with;

---

[44] ibid s 112A(3)(4). This will also apply while an administration order is in force.
[45] Part VIII, ss 252–63.
[46] ibid s 264 and Sch 22, para 2 inserting ss 263A-263G into the Insolvency Act 1986.
[47] See para 7.6.14 below.   [48] See para 7.6.6 below.

(ii) no landlord or other person to whom rent is payable may exercise any right of forfeiture by peaceable re-entry in relation to premises let to the debtor in respect of a failure by the debtor to comply with any term or condition of his tenancy of such premises, except with leave of the court; and

(iii) no other proceedings, and no execution or other legal process, may be commenced or continued and no distress may be levied against the debtor or his property except with the leave of the court.[49]

It is further provided by s 254(1) that at any time when an *application* for an interim order is pending, the court may forbid the levying of any distress on the debtor's property or its subsequent sale, or both, and stay any action, execution, or other legal process against the property or person of the debtor. Any court in which proceedings are pending against an individual may, on proof that an application under that section has been made in respect of that individual, either stay the proceedings or allow them to continue on such terms as it thinks fit.[50]

An application for an interim order may be made where the debtor intends to make a proposal to his creditors for a voluntary arrangement, ie a composition in satisfaction of debts or a scheme of arrangement of his affairs.[51] If the debtor is an undischarged bankrupt an application may be made by the debtor, the trustee of his estate or the official receiver.[52] In any other case it may be made by the debtor.[53] An application must not be made while a bankruptcy petition presented by the debtor is pending, if the court has, under s 273, appointed an insolvency practitioner to inquire into the debtor's affairs and report.[54]

The court must not make an interim order on an application under s 253 unless it is satisfied:

(a) that the debtor intends to make a proposal under Pt VIII of the Act;
(b) that on the day of the making of the application the debtor was an undischarged bankrupt or was able to petition for his own bankruptcy;
(c) that no previous application has been made by the debtor for an interim order in the period of twelve months ending with that day; and
(d) that the nominee under the debtor's proposal is willing to act in relation to the proposal.[55]

---

[49] IA 1986, s 252(2) as amended by the Insolvency Act 2000, s 3 and Sch 3, para 2.

[50] As amended by the Insolvency Act 2000, s 3, and Sch 3, para 4. There is also a prohibition on the exercise by a landlord of any right of forfeiture by peaceable re-entry.

[51] IA 1986, s 253(1) as amended by the Insolvency Act 2000 s 3 and Sch 3, para 3.

[52] IA 1986, s 253(3)(a). An application cannot be made under this provision unless the debtor has given notice of his proposal (that is, the proposal to his creditors for a voluntary arrangement) to the official receiver and, if there is one, the trustee of his estate (s 253(4)).

[53] IA 1986, s 253(3)(b).   [54] IA 1986, s 253(5).

[55] IA 1986, s 255(1) as amended by the Insolvency Act 2000, s 3 and Sch 3, para 5.

If these conditions are satisfied the court may then make an order if it thinks that it would be appropriate to do so for the purpose of facilitating the consideration and implementation of the debtor's proposal.[56] Thus the court may consider the making of an order inappropriate if it seems that the debtor is merely seeking to gain time, or where there is a strong probability that the creditors' meeting would serve no useful purpose and would be a waste of money as no approval for the debtor's proposals would be obtained.[57]

Where the debtor is an undischarged bankrupt, the interim order may contain provision as to the conduct of the bankruptcy, and the administration of the bankrupt's estate, during the period for which the order is in force.[58]

7.6.3 The proposal for a voluntary arrangement

The proposal must provide for some person ('the nominee') to act in relation to the voluntary arrangement either as trustee or otherwise for the purpose of supervising its implementation. The nominee must be a person who is qualified to act as an insolvency practitioner, or authorized to act as nominee, in relation to the voluntary arrangement.[59] The Insolvency Rules set out specific requirements as to the contents of the proposal.[60] First, the proposal must provide a short explanation why, in the debtor's opinion, a voluntary arrangement under the Act is desirable and give reasons why his creditors may be expected to concur with such an arrangement.[61] This is likely to be because the arrangement will be more beneficial to them than a distribution in bankruptcy. Secondly, the rules specify that certain matters must be stated, or otherwise dealt with, in the proposal. These include, so far as within the debtor's immediate knowledge:

(i) his assets, with an estimate of their respective values;
(ii) the extent (if any) to which the assets are charged in favour of creditors;
(iii) the extent (if any) to which particular assets are to be excluded from the voluntary arrangement.

The proposal must also give particulars of any property, other than assets of the debtor himself, which it is proposed to include in the arrangement, the source of

---

[56] IA 1986, s 255(2).

[57] *Re Cove* [1990] 1 All ER 949, 956-7, *per* Scott J; *Re A Debtor (No 83 of 1988)* [1990] 1 WLR 708. This concerned an application for an extension of an interim order. See further *Greystoke v Hamilton-Smith* [1997] BPIR 24;*Hook v Jewson Ltd* [1997] BPIR 100; *Knowles v Coutts & Co* [1998] BPIR 96; and *Re O'Sullivan* [2001] BPIR 534 where an interim order was refused on the ground that the proposed fee for the nominee was too high.

[58] IA 1986, s 255(3). In that case the provision may include provision staying proceedings in the bankruptcy or modifying any provision in the Group of Parts of the Act relating to the Insolvency of Individuals and any provision of the rules in their application to the debtor's bankruptcy: s 255(4)(5).   [59] IA 1986, s 253(2) as amended by the Insolvency Act 2000, s 3 and Sch 3, para 3.

[60] Insolvency Rules 1986, SI 1986/1925 as amended by the Insolvency (Amendment) (No 2) Rules 2002, SI 2002/2712.   [61] ibid r 5.3(1).

such property and the terms on which it is to be made available for inclusion. It must also state the nature and amount of the debtor's liabilities (so far as within his immediate knowledge), the manner in which they are proposed to be met, modified, postponed, or otherwise dealt with by means of the arrangement.

The debtor must give to the intended nominee written notice of the proposal accompanied by a copy of the proposal.[62]

7.6.4 Duration of interim order

Generally, an interim order made on an application under s 253 ceases to have effect at the end of the period of fourteen days beginning with the day after the making of the order.[63] However, the court may, on the application of the nominee, extend the period for which the interim order has effect so as to enable the nominee to have more time to prepare his report.[64] In *Re Cove* Scott J said:[65]

The general intention of the legislative provisions was to provide a short period during which the affairs of the debtor could be looked into by an independent insolvency practitioner and to provide time for a voluntary arrangement regarding the affairs of the debtor to be considered by the debtor's creditors.

7.6.5 The nominee's report

Before the interim order ceases to have effect the nominee must submit a report to the court. This must state (i) whether, in his opinion, the voluntary arrangement which the debtor is proposing has a reasonable prospect of being approved and implemented, (ii) whether, in his opinion, a meeting of the debtor's creditors should be summoned to consider the debtor's proposal, and (iii) if in his opinion such a meeting should be summoned, the date on which, and time and place at which, he proposes the meeting should be held.[66] For the purpose of enabling the nominee to prepare his report the debtor must submit to the nominee a document setting out the terms of the proposed voluntary arrangement and a statement of his affairs.[67]

If the court is satisfied on receiving the nominee's report that a meeting of the debtor's creditors should be summoned to consider the debtor's proposal, the court must direct that the period for which the interim order has effect shall be extended for such further period as it may specify in the direction, for the purpose of enabling the debtor's proposal to be considered by his creditors.[68] If, on the other hand, the court is satisfied, on the application of the nominee, either

---

[62] Insolvency Rules 1986, r 5.4.   [63] IA 1986, s 255(6).   [64] IA 1986, s 256(4).
[65] [1990] 1 All ER 949, 950.
[66] IA 1986, s 256(1) as amended by the Insolvency Act 2000, s 3 and Sch 3, para 6. The nominee may be replaced by the court where he has failed to make a report, has died, or it is impracticable or inappropriate for him to continue to act: s 256(3) as substituted by para 6.
[67] IA 1986, s 256(2).   [68] IA 1986, s 256(5).

that the debtor has failed to comply with his obligations to provide the nominee with a copy of the proposal and statement of affairs, or that for any other reason it would be inappropriate for a meeting of the creditors to be summoned to consider the debtor's proposal, it may discharge the interim order.[69]

7.6.6 Proposal without an interim order

Under a provision introduced by the Insolvency Act 2000 it is now possible for a proposal for a voluntary arrangement to be made without an application first being made for an interim order.[70] In order to enable the nominee to prepare a report to the court, the debtor must submit to the nominee a document setting out the terms of the proposed voluntary arrangement together with a statement of his affairs.[71] If the nominee is of the opinion that the debtor is an undischarged bankrupt, or is able to petition for his own bankruptcy, he must submit a report to the court dealing with the same matters as are required in a report following the making of an interim order.[72]

7.6.7 The creditors' meeting

Where it has been reported to the court by the nominee that a meeting of the debtor's creditors should be summoned, the nominee must, unless the court otherwise directs, summon that meeting for the time, date, and place proposed in his report.[73] Where an interim order is in force, the date on which the meeting is to be held must be not less than fourteen days from that on which the nominee's report is filed in court nor more than twenty-eight days from that on which that report is considered by the court. Where an interim order has not been obtained, the date on which the meeting is to be held must be not less than fourteen days and not more than twenty-eight days from that on which the nominee's report is filed in court.[74] The persons to be summoned to the meeting are every creditor of the debtor of whose claim and address the person summoning the meeting is aware.[75] Notices must be sent at least fourteen days before the day fixed for it to be held.[76] For this purpose the creditors of a debtor who is an undischarged bankrupt include (a) every person who is a creditor of the bankrupt in respect of a bankruptcy debt, and (b) every person who would be such a creditor if the bankruptcy had commenced on the day on which notice of the meeting is given.

---

[69] IA 1986, s 256(6).

[70] IA 1986, s 256A inserted by Insolvency Act 2000, s 3 and Sch 3, paras 1 and 7. If the debtor is an undischarged bankrupt he must give notice of the proposal to the official receiver and, if there is one, the trustee of his estate.   [71] IA 1986, s 256A(2).

[72] IA 1986, s 256A(3).   [73] IA 1986, s 257(1).   [74] Insolvency Rules 1986, r 5.17.

[75] IA 1986, s 257(2).   [76] See further Insolvency Rules, rr 5.17 and 5.18.

The creditors' meeting summoned under s 257 must decide whether to approve the proposed voluntary arrangement.[77] The meeting may approve the proposed voluntary arrangement with modifications, but must not do so unless the debtor consents to each modification.[78] The meeting must not approve any proposal or modification which affects the right of a secured creditor of the debtor to enforce his security, except with the concurrence of the creditor concerned.[79] The meeting must not approve any proposal or modification under which a preferential creditor is prejudiced except with the concurrence of the preferential creditor concerned.[80]

The meeting is generally chaired by the nominee and is to be conducted in accordance with the rules.[81] These provide that in general every creditor who was given notice of the creditors' meeting is entitled to vote at the meeting or any adjournment of it either in person or by proxy.[82] In order for any resolution to pass approving any proposal or modification there must be a majority in excess of three quarters in value of the creditors present in person or by proxy and voting on the resolution. In respect of any other resolution proposed at the meeting the same applies, but substituting one half for three quarters.[83]

The creditors' meeting may from time to time be adjourned. If following any final adjournment of the meeting the proposal (with or without modifications) is not agreed to, it is deemed rejected.[84]

7.6.8 Report of decisions to the court

After the conclusion of the meeting of creditors in accordance with the rules, the chairman must report the result of the meeting to the court. Notice of the result must also be given to all those who were sent notice of the meeting, and, if the debtor is an undischarged bankrupt, to the official receiver and (if any) the trustee.[85] If the report is that the meeting has declined (with or without modifications) to approve the debtor's proposal, the court may discharge any interim order which is in force in relation to the debtor.[86]

7.6.9 Effect of approval of an arrangement

If the meeting approves the proposed voluntary arrangement (with or without modifications) then the approved arrangement:

(a) takes effect as if made by the debtor at the meeting, and
(b) binds every person who in accordance with the rules

---

[77] IA 1986, s 258(1).   [78] IA 1986, s 258(2).   [79] IA 1986, s 258(4).
[80] IA 1986, s 258(5).   [81] IA 1986, s 258(6).   [82] Insolvency Rules 1986, r 5.21.
[83] ibid r 5.23.   [84] ibid r 5.24.
[85] IA 1986, s 259(1) and Insolvency Rules 1986, r 5.27 where the contents of the report are also specified.   [86] IA 1986, s 259(2).

(i) was entitled to vote at the meeting (whether or not he was present or represented at it), or

(ii) would have been so entitled if he had had notice of it,

as if he were a party to the arrangement.[87]

Where a creditor is bound even though he did not have notice of the arrangement, then if any amount payable to him under the arrangement has not been paid when the arrangement ceases to have effect, the debtor then becomes liable to pay that amount to the creditor, provided the arrangement did not come to an end prematurely.[88]

Any interim order in force in relation to the debtor immediately before the end of the period of twenty-eight days beginning with the day on which the report with respect to the creditors' meeting was made to the court under s 259, ceases to have effect at the end of that period.[89] Where proceedings on a bankruptcy petition have been stayed by an interim order which thus ceases to have effect, that petition is deemed to have been dismissed unless the court otherwise orders.[90]

Where the debtor is an undischarged bankrupt then after approval of the voluntary arrangement the court must annul the bankruptcy order on an application by the bankrupt, or in default, by the official receiver. An application for annulment cannot be made during the period allowed for challenging the decision of the creditors' meeting under s 262, or while an application under that section is pending, or while an appeal in respect of an application under that section is pending or may be brought.[91]

Forthwith, after the approval of the voluntary arrangement, the debtor, or if he is an undischarged bankrupt, the official receiver must do all that is required for putting the supervisor into possession of the assets included in the arrangement.[92]

The chairman of the meeting of creditors is required to submit particulars to the Secretary of State.[93]

7.6.10 Challenging a decision of the meeting

Where an arrangement has been approved by the creditors' meeting its terms, or the manner in which it was approved, can be reviewed by the court on an

---

[87] IA 1986, s 260(1)(2). As amended by the Insolvency Act 2000, s 3 and Sch 3, para 10.

[88] IA 1986, s 260(2A) inserted by the Insolvency Act 2000, s 3 and Sch 3, para 10.

[89] IA 1986, s 260(4) except where the court otherwise directs where the decision of the meeting is challenged under s 262.   [90] IA 1986, s 260(5).

[91] IA 1986, s 261 as substituted by s 264 and Sch 22, para 1 of the Enterprise Act 2002. Applications to challenge the decision of a creditors' meeting under s 262 are considered in para 7.6.10 below.

[92] Insolvency Rules 1986, r 5.26. The duty of the supervisor in relation to the official receiver or trustee is further prescribed in the rule.   [93] ibid r 5.29.

application under s 262.[94] Unless challenged in such an application the approval is not invalidated by any irregularity at or in relation to the meeting.[95] An application under s 262 may be made to the court by the debtor, a person who was entitled to vote at the creditors' meeting, or would have been so entitled if he had had notice of it, the nominee, or, if the debtor is an undischarged bankrupt, by the trustee of his estate.[96] There are two grounds on which an application may be made.[97] The first is that the voluntary arrangement approved by the creditors' meeting unfairly prejudices the interests of a creditor of the debtor. The second is that there has been some material irregularity at or in relation to such a meeting. If the court is satisfied as to either of these grounds it may do one or both of the following, namely:[98]

(a) revoke or suspend any approval given by the meeting;
(b) give a direction to any person for the summoning of a further meeting of the debtor's creditors to consider any revised proposal he may make or, in a case where there has been a material irregularity, to reconsider his original proposal.

In the latter case it may also give a direction continuing or renewing the effect in relation to the debtor of an interim order.[99] If the court is subsequently satisfied that the debtor does not intend to submit a revised proposal as envisaged by the original direction, then it must revoke the direction and revoke or suspend any approval given at the previous meeting.[100] If the court gives a direction summoning a further meeting or revokes or suspends an approval, the court may give such supplemental directions as it thinks fit.[101]

An application under s 262 cannot generally be made after the end of the period of twenty-eight days beginning with the day on which the report of the creditors' meeting was made to the court under s 259.[102] The court may, however, grant an extension of time as occurred in *Re A Debtor, JP v A Debtor*.[103] In the case of a creditor who was not given notice of the creditors' meeting, an application under s 262 cannot be made after the end of the period of twenty-eight days beginning with the day on which he became aware that the meeting had taken place. However, subject to that, an application by such a person on the ground that the arrangement prejudices his interests may be made after the arrangement has ceased to have effect, unless it has come to an end prematurely.

---

[94] There is a parallel provision in s 263F where approval of an arrangement was obtained under s 263D under the 'fast track procedure'. See para 7.6.14 below.   [95] IA 1986, s 262(8).
[96] IA 1986, s 262(2) as amended by the Insolvency Act 2000, s 3 and Sch 3, para 11.
[97] IA 1986, s 262(1).   [98] IA 1986, s 262(4).   [99] IA 1986, s 262(6).
[100] IA 1986, s 262(5).   [101] IA 1986, s 262(7).
[102] IA 1986, s 262(3) as amended by the Insolvency Act 2000, s 3 and Sch 3, para 11.
[103] [1999] 1 FLR 926.

7.6.11 Implementation and supervision of an approved voluntary arrangement

The implementation and supervision of an approved voluntary arrangement is the responsibility of the supervisor. This will be the original nominee, unless he has been replaced by the court or the meeting of creditors.[104] The rules make provision in relation to the keeping of accounts and the making of reports by the supervisor, but close control of the supervisor is not envisaged.[105] However, the debtor, any of his creditors or any other person dissatisfied with any act, omission, or decision of the supervisor may apply to the court which may confirm, reverse, or modify any act or decision of the supervisor, give him directions, or make such other order as it thinks fit.[106]

7.6.12 Completion or termination of the arrangement

Not more than twenty-eight days after the final completion or termination of the voluntary arrangement, the supervisor must send to all creditors of the debtor who are bound by the arrangement, and to the debtor, a notice that the arrangement has been fully implemented or terminated.[107] With the notice he must send to each of those persons a copy of his report summarizing all receipts and payments made by him in pursuance of the arrangement and explaining any difference in the actual implementation of it as compared with the proposal as approved by the creditors' meeting. In the case of termination of the arrangement he must explain the reasons why the arrangement has not been implemented in accordance with the approved proposal. The supervisor must also, within the same period, send to the Secretary of State a copy of the notice and report.[108] No other formal act is required.

7.6.13 The position of secured creditors

The proposal for a voluntary arrangement is required to specify whether, and the extent to which, an asset of the debtor is charged in favour of a creditor.[109] The rights of a secured creditor to enforce his security are not to be affected without his concurrence,[110] and he would normally expect to obtain repayment of the amount due to him without participating in the voluntary arrangement. However, a secured creditor who has not yet realized his security may face a problem if

---

[104] IA 1986, s 263(2). Replacement by the court under s 256(3) and by the meeting of creditors under s 258(3). For the power of the court to make further appointments, see s 263(5)(6).

[105] See Insolvency Rules, r 5.31. He is accountable to the Secretary of State who, under r 5.32 may require him to produce records and accounts and other matters required by r 5.31.

[106] IA 1986, s 263(3).

[107] The IVA will usually provide that if the debtor becomes bankrupt, then assets held by the supervisor will be held for the benefit of creditors. See generally *Re NT Gallagher & Son Ltd* [2000] BCLC 133. [108] Insolvency Rules, r 5.34.

[109] ibid r 5.3(2)(a)(ii). [110] IA 1986, s 258(4).

it seems likely that the proceeds of sale of the property charged will be insufficient to discharge the amount due to him. He is not likely to wish to surrender his security, so he will only be able to participate in the distribution under the voluntary arrangement on the basis (which may turn out to be wrong) that part of his debt is unsecured. It will also be necessary to put a value on his security so as to quantify that part for the purposes of the calculation and payment of a dividend.

In *Whitehead v Household Mortgage Corporation*,[111] the Court of Appeal adopted an approach consistent with that applicable on bankruptcy. A secured creditor whose security may not be sufficient to satisfy the whole of his debt may be allowed to participate in a distribution of assets available to meet the claims of unsecured creditors on a provisional basis. If it turns out, on a realization of the security, that he has been paid too much out of the assets available to meet the claims of unsecured creditors, then he must repay the overpayment; but he is allowed to apply the proceeds of realization in or towards satisfaction of his secured debt.[112]

In that case a husband who, together with his wife, had charged the matrimonial home, subsequently made a proposal to his creditors for an IVA which was approved with modifications at a meeting of creditors. In support of his proposals the husband had obtained a valuation of the mortgaged property and in reliance on this valuation the nominee (as chairman of the meeting) treated the mortgagee's claim as secured to the extent of £75,500. He admitted the claim for the purposes of entitlement to vote at the creditors' meeting, at an amount of £25,046.06 that being the balance of the debt claimed. The mortgagee voted against the proposals, but they were approved by the votes of 76.2 per cent in value of the creditors present in person or by proxy. General condition (1) of the IVA stated that it was not proposed that anything in the proposal should affect the rights of any secured creditor to enforce its security. After the proposal was accepted, the mortgagee made a claim in the IVA for £37,109 being the difference between the total amount then shown as owing on the loan account (£102,109) and the figure at which it had valued its security (£65,000). It eventually received a dividend of a little over 5 per cent (£1,874) and credited the payment to the mortgage account. Subsequently the mortgaged property was sold for an amount in excess of the mortgage debt which stood at over £100,000. The proceeds of sale were applied by the mortgagee in satisfaction of the whole balance of the mortgage debt and not just the £65,000 at which it had previously valued its security.

The Court of Appeal held that the circumstances in which the mortgagee had made a claim in the debtor's IVA, and accepted a dividend in respect of that claim did not lead to the conclusion that it must be treated as having elected to abandon its security for any part of the mortgage debt; or as having agreed that it would not rely on its security for so much of the mortgage debt as exceeded £65,000 (or any other figure). It was entitled to insist that its security be redeemed for the full

---

[111] [2002] EWCA Civ 1657.   [112] ibid para [24].

amount of the mortgage debt. Chadwick LJ said that to imply a term into the IVA that, by claiming to participate in it and by accepting payment of a dividend under it in respect of part of the mortgage debt, the mortgagee had agreed to treat that part of its debt as unsecured 'would ignore both general condition (1) and the further provision, in the description of the husband's assets, that it was the shortfall to secured creditors that was to constitute an additional unsecured liability of the arrangement'. He said that it was '... plain that "shortfall to secured creditors" in that context, means "shortfall after realisation of the security"; it does not include a shortfall which arises as a result of a valuation of the security'.[113]

However, the position of the secured creditor will depend on the construction and effect of the agreement. In certain circumstances he may be deemed to have waived his security. This was the position in the earlier decision of the Court of Appeal in *Khan v Permayer*[114] which was distinguished in *Whitehead*. The secured debt of Mr Permayer had been specifically included amongst the unsecured debts who were to receive between them £7,500 over five years by six monthly instalments representing 12 per cent of the face value of their debts. The secured creditors were dealt with separately. Thus separate provision was made for payment to Barclays Bank plc in respect of its secured debt, based on the value of the property at the time of £50,000 and the unsecured balance of £110,000 in respect of which Barclays was to be paid £30,000 by monthly instalments over ten years. Morritt LJ said that in the circumstances Mr Permayer had agreed to be treated as an unsecured creditor. It would have been inconsistent with that treatment that he should, after the arrangement had been fully performed, seek to recover the original debt by the enforcement of the security for it. Once the arrangement had been fully implemented the original debt was discharged and the legal charge was thereby satisfied. Sir Christopher Staughton agreeing, said that it seemed a plain inference that the security was abandoned as part of the arrangement.

Nevertheless, in *Whitehead v Household Mortgage Corporation*,[115] Chadwick LJ said:

In the absence of an express term in the voluntary arrangement itself – or agreed between the supervisor and the secured creditor at the time when the creditor claims in the arrangement—I think that the court should be slow to imply a term which would lead to a result which differs in so material a respect from that to which the statutory code would have led in the bankruptcy for which the voluntary arrangement was proposed as a substitute.

7.6.14 The 'fast track' procedure

As noted earlier the Enterprise Act 2002 introduced a new 'fast track' procedure for use in the case of debtors who are undischarged bankrupts.[116] It also enables

---

[113] ibid para [26]   [114] CA, 22 June 2000.   [115] [2002] EWCA Civ 1657, para [24].

[116] See para 7.6.1 above. The provisions are to be found in s 264 and Sch 22, para 2 introducing ss 263A–263G into the Insolvency Act 1986. These provisions came into operation on 1 April 2004.

Official Receivers to act as nominees and supervisors for voluntary arrangements in such cases.[117]

The new procedure will operate where a debtor who is an undischarged bankrupt intends to make a proposal to his creditors for a voluntary arrangement, the official receiver is specified in the proposal as the nominee, and there is no application for an interim order.[118] The debtor may submit to the official receiver (a) a document setting out the terms of the voluntary arrangement which the debtor is proposing, and (b) a statement of his affairs containing such particulars as may be prescribed of his creditors, debts, other liabilities and assets and such other information as may be prescribed. If the official receiver thinks that the voluntary arrangement proposed has a reasonable prospect of being approved and implemented, he may make arrangements for inviting creditors to decide whether to approve it.[119] For this purpose a person is a creditor only if (a) he is a creditor of the debtor in respect of a bankruptcy debt, and (b) the official receiver is aware of his claim and his address.[120] Arrangements for inviting creditors to decide on a proposal may not include an opportunity for modifications to the proposed voluntary arrangement to be suggested or made.[121] As soon as is reasonably practical after the implementation of these arrangements the official receiver must report to the court whether the proposed voluntary arrangement has been approved or rejected.[122] Where he reports that it has been approved then the voluntary arrangement (a) takes effect, (b) binds the debtor, and (c) binds every person who was entitled to participate in the arrangements made for creditors to decide whether to approve the voluntary arrangement proposed.[123] The court must annul the bankruptcy order made in respect of the debtor on an application made by the official receiver.[124] However, such an application may not be made:

(a) in the period during which the voluntary arrangement may be revoked under s 263F;
(b) while an application under that section is pending, or
(c) while an appeal in respect of an application under that section is pending or may be brought.[125]

The court may give such directions about the conduct of the bankruptcy and the administration of the bankrupt's estate as it thinks appropriate for facilitating the implementation of the approved voluntary arrangement.[126] The provisions of s 263 of the Insolvency Act 1986 relating to the implementation and supervision of a voluntary arrangement approved by a creditors meeting are applied to voluntary arrangements taking effect under the 'fast track' procedure.[127]

---

[117] Sch 22, para 3 introducing s 389B into the Insolvency Act 1986.   [118] IA 1986, s 263A.
[119] IA 1986, s 263B(1)(2).   [120] IA 1986, s 263B(3).   [121] IA 1986, s 263B(4).
[122] IA 1986, s 263C.   [123] IA 1986, s 263D(1).   [124] IA 1986, s 263D(3).
[125] IA 1986, s 263D(4); s 263F is considered below.   [126] IA 1986, s 263D(5).
[127] IA 1986, s 263E.

An arrangement approved under this procedure can be revoked by the court on the ground (a) that it unfairly prejudices the interest of a creditor of the debtor, or (b) that a material irregularity occurred in relation to the arrangements made by the official receiver for inviting creditors to decide whether to approve the voluntary arrangement. Such an order can be made only on the application of the debtor, a person who was entitled to participate in the decision to approve the voluntary arrangement, the trustee of the bankrupt's estate, or the official receiver. No application can be made after the end of the period of twenty-eight days beginning with the date on which the official receiver makes his report to the court. However, a creditor who was not made aware of the arrangements made by the official receiver at the time when they were made may make an application during the period of twenty-eight days beginning with the date on which he becomes aware of the voluntary arrangement.[128]

7.6.15 Debts due to former spouses

When a debtor whose marriage has broken down proposes to enter into an IVA, special consideration needs to be given to any order for payment of a lump sum or transfer of property which may have been made against the debtor or which may be made against him in proceedings for ancillary relief under the Matrimonial Causes Act 1973.

Where the debtor's former spouse has obtained an order for, say, payment of a lump sum, then the amount due is not a provable debt in the debtor's bankruptcy though on his discharge from bankruptcy he is not released from his obligation to pay the lump sum.[129] In contrast if the debtor enters into an IVA his former spouse is a creditor who is entitled to receive notice of the meeting of creditors and to attend the meeting and vote on the proposal.[130] She may also participate in the distribution of assets under the IVA, but if she does so this will extinguish her claim even though the amount received falls far short of the lump sum due to her under the court order. A former wife may, therefore not wish to participate unless her special position is recognized. She 'may wish to preserve her claim in case other assets, not yet disclosed, come to light or in case the husband should have a more prosperous future'.[131]

---

[128] IA 1986, s 263F.   [129] See ch 8.

[130] *Re Bradley-Hole* [1995] 1 WLR 1097. The debtor is under a duty to disclose orders for lump sum payments and transfers of property.

[131] See Sir John Vinelott in *Re A Debtor; JP v A Debtor* [1995] 1 FLR 926, 936 summarizing the argument of counsel for the wife. He also noted that on the other side, it might equally be unfair to other creditors if a wife with a substantial claim for a lump sum should be in a position to frustrate a voluntary arrangement to which they all agree, or, to take an extreme case, that a wife with the preponderant debt should be in a position, in collaboration with her husband to force through a

Her special position is in fact recognized by para 20.1 of the standard conditions provided for incorporation into a proposal for a voluntary arrangement. This provides:

(a) Unless the proposal otherwise provides, no creditor whose claim falls within the definition of r 12.3(2) shall be entitled to vote in connection with or prove in the arrangement and any such creditor shall not be bound within the meaning of s 262 of the Act.

Care must therefore be taken to ensure that such a condition is not excluded without a consideration of the implications. In *Re A Debtor*, Sir John Vinelott found that para 20.1 was impliedly excluded by the terms of the proposal. Appendix 1 to the proposal set out details of the assets available to unsecured creditors under the arrangement and under the heading of 'Liabilities' specified an aggregate sum which included the lump sum and costs ordered to be paid to the wife. Paragraph 6 of the proposal stated that there would be 'a single distribution to creditors'. He concluded that it was 'impossible to escape the conclusion that the intention was that the wife would rank equally with the other creditors for dividend, and it must follow that the wife, like all the other creditors, would be bound to accept the dividend in satisfaction of that debt'.[132] He rejected the argument that standard conditions could only be excluded by a specific provision in the body of the proposal specifically referring to para 20.1, or alternatively providing in terms that a creditor with a specified debt falling within r 12.3(2), is to be bound by the arrangement as that imposed too strict a test.

If the special position of the debtor's former spouse is not recognized in the IVA then she may apply for an order under s 262 on the ground that the agreement unfairly prejudices her interests.[133] An order may revoke or suspend any approval given by the meeting or direct the summoning of a further meeting to consider a revised proposal.[134]

Where an order for payment of a lump sum or for the transfer of property has not yet been made against the debtor, then his former spouse will not be a creditor and therefore not entitled to attend or vote at the meeting of creditors that may take place. The former spouse will not be bound by the IVA and on obtaining an order for a lump sum payment could proceed to enforce payment without regard to the IVA. However, this may well lead to the bankruptcy of

---

voluntary arrangement against the wishes and interests of the other creditors, thereby, possibly, frustrating an investigation into the husband's affairs by the official receiver or an independent trustee.

[132] ibid 937.

[133] This might occur where the former spouse was not given notice of the meeting. It should be noted that as a result of the amendment of s 260 of the Insolvency Act 1986 by the Insolvency Act 2000, s 3, and Sch 3, paras 1 and 10, a creditor will be bound by the approval of an arrangement even though he or she had no notice of it. See further IA 1986, s 260(2A) and para 7.6.9 above for the consequences. [134] See para 7.6.10 above.

the debtor which may be disadvantageous to both the former spouse and the other creditors so that some form of compromise may be desirable.

7.6.16 An appraisal

An individual voluntary arrangement can provide a debtor with an attractive alternative to bankruptcy. It will provide relief from the claims of creditors without the restrictions that apply on bankruptcy. Provided it is approved by the appropriate majority of creditors it will be binding on all creditors including those who did not vote in favour of the arrangement. It may also allow specific arrangements to be made in relation to the family home. Creditors may also find such an arrangement more attractive than bankruptcy as there is likely to be a saving in costs and it is likely to give them a better return.

Their interests are safeguarded in a number of ways. The proposal for a voluntary arrangement must first be examined by a qualified insolvency practitioner and the court must be satisfied that it is an appropriate course to take. The arrangement must be approved by a majority of creditors at a meeting and the implementation of the arrangement will be supervised by a qualified practitioner. At the present time there are around 7,000 individual voluntary arrangements each year with only a small minority being entered into after bankruptcy has commenced.[135] It remains to be seen whether the new 'fast track' procedure will provide an attractive way out of bankruptcy.

---

[135] See the Explanatory Notes to the Enterprise Act 2002, para 763.

8

THE EFFECT OF INSOLVENCY ON APPLICATIONS FOR FINANCIAL PROVISION AND PROPERTY ADJUSTMENT

8.1 INTRODUCTION

The claims of creditors will almost invariably make it more difficult to achieve a satisfactory disposition of the parties' income and capital on the breakdown of a marriage. If the claims of the creditors lead to the bankruptcy of the husband he may be able to take advantage of bankruptcy proceedings as a means of delaying or defeating the claims of his wife; he may even be prepared to file his own petition in bankruptcy. In this event it may be possible and appropriate for his wife to seek annulment of the bankruptcy order. This was considered in

Chapter 6, para 6.10.4.[1] Even if the husband is not seeking to take advantage of his bankruptcy, the fact that he has become bankrupt will seriously affect the options open to the court seeking to exercise its powers to order financial provision and property adjustment for the wife and children.

The principles applicable in this situation were developed at a time when the powers of the court to order financial provision and adjust property rights were limited to maintenance in the form of periodical payments and the variation of pre-nuptial and post-nuptial settlements. Even the Matrimonial Causes Act 1973 does not address the questions that arise when orders for financial provision and property adjustment have not been made before the bankruptcy process commences or, if made, have not been completed. It is necessary to look to the Insolvency Act 1986 and the Insolvency Rules 1986. In particular r 12.3 of the Insolvency Rules 1986 provides that in bankruptcy all claims by creditors are provable as debts against the bankrupt, whether they are present or future, certain or contingent, ascertained or founding only in damages; but certain claims are not provable. These include any obligation arising under an order made in family proceedings or under a maintenance assessment or calculation made under the Child Support Act 1991.

8.2 THE GENERAL EFFECT OF BANKRUPTCY ON THE PROPERTY AND INCOME OF THE BANKRUPT

Once the bankruptcy of a spouse commences the distinction between his property and income becomes crucial in this context. Since the bankrupt's estate vests in the trustee in bankruptcy immediately on the trustee's appointment taking effect, or, in the case of the official receiver, on his becoming trustee, once the property has so vested no order under the Matrimonial Causes Act 1973 can affect it. Thus no transfer of property order, which must relate to specified property, can be made once property has vested in the trustee. Even if an order has been made before the commencement of the bankruptcy it is also necessary to consider whether it has become effective before the commencement of the bankruptcy. This is examined in paragraph 8.6 of this chapter. In contrast, a bankrupt's income remains available, at least to some extent, to meet the claims of his family for financial provision, subject to an income payments order or income payments agreement.

Under the previous law, the title of the trustee in bankruptcy to the bankrupt's property related back to the act of bankruptcy so that any disposition by the bankrupt during that period could have no effect because he had not been the owner of the property able to make it. Under the Insolvency Act 1986, the trustee acquires title to the bankrupt's estate, but not so as to relate back to the

---

[1] This chapter draws on an article by the author in the *Child and Family Law Quarterly* (1998) Vol 10, 29.

period before the order. Accordingly, provision is made in s 284 of the Insolvency Act that any disposition of property made by a bankrupt in the period beginning with the day of the presentation of the petition for the bankruptcy order and ending with the vesting of the bankrupt's estate in a trustee is void except to the extent that it is or was made with the consent of the court, or is or was subsequently ratified by the court.[2] This provision is considered further in paragraph 8.6.3.

8.3 ORDERS FOR PERIODICAL PAYMENTS

It has been long established that an order for periodical payments can be made, or continue to have effect, notwithstanding the bankruptcy of the spouse against whom it is made. Payment is a personal liability enforceable only against the personal earnings of the bankrupt.[3] A bankrupt's income remains available to meet the claim for periodical payments subject to any income payments order made against the bankrupt under s 310 of the Insolvency Act 1986. The effect of such an order is to claim for the bankrupt's estate a proportion of the income of the bankrupt, but the court must not make an order the effect of which would be to reduce the income of the bankrupt 'below what appears to the court to be necessary for meeting the reasonable domestic needs of the bankrupt *and his family*'.[4] This assessment of the needs of the bankrupt and his family under s 310 of the 1986 Act will be made by the bankruptcy court, and it is now established that in making an income payments order under s 310, the bankruptcy court is not bound by an assessment made by the family court.[5] The husband will, of course be able to apply for a variation of the periodical payments order in the light of the order under s 310. If an income payments order has already been made then the court in subsequent proceedings under the 1973 Act will be bound by that order which affects the amount of the bankrupt's income. In *Albert v Albert*,[6] Millett LJ said:

The Family Division is concerned with the division of the cake, but the size of the cake is liable to be diminished by any Order made by the Insolvency Court.

---

[2] It may also be noted that while s 39 of the Matrimonial Causes Act 1973 as amended refers to ss 339 and 340 of the Insolvency Act it makes no reference to s 284. See further ch 9.

[3] *Linton v Linton* (1885) 15 QBD 239; *Re Henderson* (1888) 20 QBD 508. See Rimer J in *Re Bradley-Hole (A Bankrupt)* [1995] 2 BCLC 163, 185 where the court was concerned with the rights of the former wife of a bankrupt who had previously entered into an IVA. See ch 7, para 7.6.15.

[4] See chapter 6, para 6.6. Italics added.

[5] In *Albert v Albert (A Bankrupt)* [1996] BPIR 232 at 235 Millett LJ said that if the trustee in bankruptcy subsequently applied for, and obtained, an income payments order, his application to the Insolvency Court would not be prejudiced or affected by an order in the Family Division for periodical payments against the bankrupt in favour of his wife. A prior assessment or calculation under the Child Support Act 1991 will presumably be binding. See the comment in *Re G (Children Act 1989, Schedule 1)* [1996] 2 FLR 171, 176 noted below.   [6] [1996] BPIR 232, 235.

In that case no application under s 310 had been made by the trustee in bankruptcy, and there was no evidence that he had ever considered such an application. The Court of Appeal held that, in the circumstances, there was no jurisdiction to join the husband's trustee in bankruptcy as an additional party to the wife's application for ancillary relief. The trustee's interest did not need to be protected from the risk of the court making an order for periodical payments.

Since the assessment of need involves a consideration of the resources of the non-bankrupt spouse and other members of the family, it is arguable that the family court would be better suited to the task which it is well used to performing. However, Millett LJ in *Albert v Albert*[7] said that:

...the last thing that would be just or convenient would be to bind the trustee in bankruptcy by a determination of the Family Division, on the evidence which the bankrupt and the wife chose to put before it, as to the extent or sources of the bankrupt's income. Nor is it desirable that the bankrupt should be bound, as against the trustee in bankruptcy, by any decision that may be made by the Family Division.

There is, of course, a danger of collusion between the spouses in the light of impending insolvency, but a failure to disclose the full extent or sources of the bankrupt's income to the family court seems unlikely to prejudice the trustee for it is likely to have resulted in lower periodical payments than would otherwise have been ordered. The discovery of further sources of income by the trustee provides greater justification for an income payments order and is more likely to place the wife in a disadvantageous position. However, there is a danger that a generous level of periodical payments will have been ordered by consent and for this reason it must be accepted that an order for periodical payments cannot be binding on the bankruptcy court. Nevertheless, the terse reference in s 310 to the 'reasonable domestic needs of the bankrupt and his family' is in marked contrast to the detailed criteria set out in ss 25 and 25A of the Matrimonial Causes Act. It must also be remembered that the bankrupt, far from colluding with his wife, may have gone to drastic lengths in an effort to frustrate her reasonable claims.[8]

Since the spouses will usually be separated, another possible difficulty, noted by Singer J in *Re G (Children Act 1989, Schedule 1)*,[9] is that 'family' for this purpose is somewhat restrictively defined by s 385(1) as 'the persons (if any) who are *living with* the bankrupt and are dependent on him'.[10] However, in that case the court was informed that as a matter of practice a Child Support Agency assessment, for instance, would be taken into account in the exercise of the court's discretion when considering an income payments order, and no income payments order made which would deprive the child of the benefit of an

---

[7] [1996] BPIR 232, 235.

[8] As is evident in those cases where the bankrupt has filed his own petition.

[9] [1996] 2 FLR 171, 176.   [10] Italics added.

assessment. Singer J considered that, by analogy, a bankruptcy court 'might well favourably view the liability under a lump sum order as falling within the category of reasonable demands upon the bankrupt's income'. Although he was concerned with a lump sum order, this view would seem to apply a fortiori in relation to a periodical payments order.

8.4 ORDERS FOR SECURED PERIODICAL PAYMENTS

Under s 23(1)(b) of the Matrimonial Causes Act 1973, the court may, on or after granting a decree of divorce, nullity, or judicial separation, make an order that either party to the marriage shall secure to the other to the satisfaction of the court such periodical payments for such term, as may be specified in the order. However, in the case of an order made on or after the granting of a decree of divorce or nullity neither the order nor any settlement made in pursuance of the order is to take effect unless the decree has been made absolute.[11] If the order provides for the periodical payments to be secured on identified property and for the security to be completed by the execution of a deed in appropriate form, this has the effect of creating an immediate equitable charge over the property pending the completion of the security in accordance with the order.[12] If the person against whom the order is made then becomes bankrupt, his trustee in bankruptcy will take the property subject to that equitable charge.

8.5 ORDERS FOR LUMP SUM PAYMENTS

8.5.1 General principles

An order for a lump sum payment need not specify a particular asset out of which payment is to be made, although it is likely that it will generally be envisaged that it will be paid out of capital. The bankruptcy of the person against whom such an order is made is therefore likely to raise practical difficulties to obstruct the making of such an order. Nevertheless, the power to make a lump sum order against a bankrupt has been affirmed in a number of cases, even though its enforceability has been shown to be problematic.[13] It was

---

[11] Section 23(5). Under s 23(1)(e) the court may order that a party to a marriage shall secure to such person as may be specified in the order for the benefit of such a child, or to such a child, to the satisfaction of the court, such periodical payments, for such term as may be specified in the order. Such an order takes effect even though the decree nisi of divorce or nullity has not been made absolute.

[12] *Maclurcan v Maclurcan* (1897) 77 LT 474; *In re Richardson's Will Trusts* [1958] 1 Ch 504.

[13] *Re G (Children Act 1989, Schedule 1)* [1996] 2 FLR 171; *Re Mordant, Mordant v Halls* [1996] 1 FLR 334; *Hellyer v Hellyer* [1996] 2 FLR 579. The difficulties of enforcement were highlighted in the earlier case of *Woodley v Woodley (No 2)* [1993] 2 FLR 477.

noted in Chapter 6 that a lump sum payable under such an order is not provable in bankruptcy, which is a reversal of the position that applied in the period between the introduction of the power to award lump sum payments in 1963 and the 1986 Act.[14] In *Russell v Russell*,[15] Chadwick J held that even though not provable in bankruptcy an order in favour of a wife for a lump sum payment could form the basis of a petition for bankruptcy against her husband.

In practice there appear to be two situations where a lump sum payment order may be made notwithstanding the bankruptcy of the person against whom it is made.[16]

8.5.2 As a claim on income of the bankrupt

First, a lump sum payment may be ordered on the basis that payment will be made out of income. In *Re G (Children Act 1989, Schedule 1)*,[17] Singer J held that there was jurisdiction to make an order for a lump sum payment against the father of a child under the Children Act 1989, though there was no power to make a periodical payments order in relation to the child because of the Child Support Act 1991. The argument was not whether the court had the power to make the order, but whether it was appropriate in the circumstances. Singer J said that the fact that there might be no short term anticipation on the part of the father that he would have an income did not seem to him, in the circumstances of the case, to be a good reason for not making the order. It would on the contrary, be quite wrong in view of the history which he had outlined, for the mother and, of course, in particular, the child, to be left with no order simply because a third party had got round to the exercise of their rights to obtain a bankruptcy order against the father. Whether or not mother and child would derive any satisfaction from the order the future alone would tell, but it would, in his view, be a mockery if no order were made in the circumstances of this case.[18]

Where a lump sum order is made on the basis that it is to be paid out of income regard must, of course, be had to the provisions of s 310 of the Insolvency Act 1986 under which 'surplus' income of the bankrupt is liable to be diverted for the benefit of his creditors. However, as already noted Singer J considered that in exercising its discretion the bankruptcy court is required to take account of the needs of the bankrupt's family and that a lump sum might fall within the reasonable demands upon the bankrupt's income at least when it is intended to provide support.

---

[14] The power to award lump sum payments was introduced by the Matrimonial Causes Act 1963, s 5.

[15] [1998] 1 FLR 936.

[16] See Miller, 'The Effect of Insolvency on Applications for Financial Provision' (1998) 10 C & FLQ 29. [17] [1996] 2 FLR 171.

[18] ibid 177.

8.5.3 Where there is likely to be a surplus

An order for payment of a lump sum may be considered appropriate where the court considers that there is likely to be a surplus at the termination of the bankruptcy. In *Re Mordant*,[19] Rattee J had made an order for payment of a lump sum by the husband to the wife shortly after the presentation of a bankruptcy petition against the husband. The judge had formed an adverse view of the husband whose behaviour had made it virtually impossible to form any reliable picture of his financial dealings. However, Rattee J concluded that once the proceedings were determined, the husband would have ready access to large sums of money from his mother on account of a share of his father's estate worth some £1.5 million. The judge had observed that the bankruptcy proceedings were within the husband's own control, because he had the means to pay off the building society which was the petitioning creditor. Sir Donald Nicholls V-C said:[20] 'The husband, in other words, was using continuing non-payment of his debts to the building society as a means to delay, or defeat, payment to the wife.'[21]

In *Hellyer v Hellyer*,[22] the Court of Appeal upheld an order against the husband, who was a bankrupt, for payment of a lump sum of £450,000 to the wife. Aldous LJ said:[23]

... there is no reason in principle as to why such an order should not be made by a judge exercising his jurisdiction under s 25 of the Matrimonial Causes Act. The fact that the bankrupt cannot pay at that time is irrelevant. However, such an order should only be made when the judge has a clear picture of the assets and liabilities of the bankrupt and the expenses of the bankruptcy. It is only then he can decide that in the foreseeable future there will be assets to pay the sum ordered. That of course only applies to a money order. Nothing in the Insolvency Act or the rules suggest that such an order should not be made.

The court was required to take into account assets to which the husband would be entitled in the foreseeable future. On this basis he had rightly concluded that there would be a surplus at the end of the bankruptcy which would be a financial resource on which to calculate a lump sum payment. Although there were errors the figure he had arrived at was appropriate.

8.6 TRANSFER OF PROPERTY ORDERS

8.6.1 Power to make orders for the transfer of property

On the appointment of a trustee in bankruptcy taking effect or, in the case of the official receiver, on his becoming trustee, the bankrupt's estate vests immediately

---

[19] [1996] 1 FLR 334.   [20] ibid 338.
[21] *Re Mordant* is considered further in para 8.11 below.   [22] [1996] 2 FLR 579.
[23] ibid 584.

in the trustee without any conveyance, assignment, or transfer.[24] The consequence is that as such property is no longer vested in the bankrupt, no transfer of property order can be made under the Matrimonial Causes Act 1973.

Moreover, although a bankrupt's property may remain vested in him before it vests in the trustee in bankruptcy, once a petition has been presented the ability of the bankrupt to deal with that property and, hence the power to make a transfer of property order affecting it, is restricted by s 284 of the Insolvency Act 1986.[25]

A transfer of property order which has been made and become effective against a party to a marriage is not rendered invalid by the subsequent presentation of a bankruptcy petition against him though it is vulnerable to a later application by the trustee in bankruptcy under s 339 of the Insolvency Act 1986 as a transaction at an undervalue. This is considered in Chapter 9.

8.6.2 When does a transfer of property become effective?

In determining when a transfer of property becomes effective there are two provisions of the Matrimonial Causes Act to take into consideration.

First, not only can no property adjustment order in favour of a spouse be made under the Matrimonial Causes Act 1973 unless a decree of divorce or of nullity or a decree of judicial separation has been granted, but no such order made on or after the granting of a decree nisi of divorce or of nullity can take effect unless the decree has been made absolute.[26]

Secondly, the wording of s 24(1)(a) indicates that the party against whom it is made must transfer to the other party the specified property 'being property to which the first mentioned party is entitled, either in possession or reversion'. Until that transfer is made it would seem that the order is incomplete and the property remains that of the party against whom it was made and the order will be ineffective. Although a different view had been expressed in *Re Flint*[27] the more general view was that until an order had been carried into effect by the execution of an appropriate transfer the order was not effective.[28] Following the view expressed by Butler-Sloss J in *Burton v Burton*,[29] Jonathan Parker J in *Beer v Higham*[30] held that a transfer of property order did not itself effect the transfer of the beneficial interest in the property concerned and a formal transfer was necessary to make the transfer effective on the bankruptcy of the party against whom it was made. However, in *Mountney v Treharne*,[31] the Court of Appeal took a different view.

---

[24] IA 1986, s 306(1)(2). See ch 6, para 6.5.   [25] See further para 8.6.3 below.
[26] Section 24(3).   [27] [1993] Ch 319.
[28] An order will commonly provide for execution of the appropriate transfer by a nominated person in the event of default on the part of the party against whom the order is made. See also Supreme Court Act 1981, s 39 and the County Courts Act 1984, s 38.
[29] [1986] 2 FLR 419, 425.   [30] [1997] BPIR 349.   [31] [2002] EWCA Civ 1174.

In *Mountney v Treharne*, the former matrimonial home had been purchased in the sole name of Mr Mountney, and following his wife's petition for divorce, on 6 July 2000, the District Judge made a property adjustment order under s 24 requiring the husband to transfer the property to Mrs Mountney forthwith subject to the existing mortgage. In the event of the bankrupt failing to sign and return the transfer documents within fourteen days, the documents might be signed by the District Judge. On 13 July decree absolute was pronounced, but no transfer documents had been signed before the following day when a bankruptcy order was made against the husband on his own petition. It was not argued that s 284 applied although there is no express mention of when the petition was presented. In the subsequent case of *Treharne v Forrester*,[32] Lindsay J noted that the practice is that where it is the debtor's own petition that is before the court, as it was in *Mountney v Treharne*, the adjudication is made on the very day of presentation. Lindsay J said that it could be 'taken that the presentation of the petition was on 14 July, namely after the property adjustment order and after it had become uncontingent on 13 July'.

The District Judge subsequently made an order declaring that the property vested in the trustee in bankruptcy by virtue of s 306. Stanley Burnton J held that the property adjustment order did not, of itself, create any proprietary interest in the property. It gave the wife a personal right and subjected the husband to a personal obligation to execute the necessary transfer documents. If the order had been carried out then she would have acquired a proprietary interest and the property would have ceased to be part of the bankrupt's estate. That had not occurred.[33]

In the Court of Appeal Jonathan Parker LJ said that the issue was whether by virtue of the property adjustment order Mrs Mountney acquired rights in relation to which the trustee in bankruptcy took subject, as provided by s 283(5) of the Insolvency Act.[34] That issue raised two sub-issues: (1) What rights did Mrs Mountney acquire in relation to the property by virtue of the order? and (2) Did the property vest in the trustee subject to those rights?[35]

In relation to the first sub-issue, Jonathan Parker LJ accepted that a line of decisions starting with *Maclurcan v Maclurcan*[36] was clear authority for the proposition that where the court makes an order for secured periodical payments, with provision for the security to be embodied in a deed, and the

---

[32] [2003] EWHC 2784 (Ch), para [23]. Under r 6.42(6) of the Insolvency Rules 1986 in the case of a debtor's petition the court 'may hear the petition forthwith'. If it does not do so it must fix a venue for the hearing. [33] [2002] 2 FLR 406.

[34] Section 283(5) provides that property comprised in the bankrupt's estate is so comprised subject to the rights of any person other than the bankrupt (whether as a secured creditor of the bankrupt or otherwise) in relation thereto. [35] [2002] EWCA Civ 1174, para [39].

[36] (1897) 77 LT 474. The other decisions were *Hyde v Hyde* [1948] P 198; *In re Richardson's Will Trusts* [1958] 1 Ch 504. The decision in *Mosey v Mosey and Barker* [1956] P 26 was also consistent with that decision.

property to be provided by way of security had been identified, the effect of the order was to create an equitable charge over that property pending execution of the requisite deed.[37] It seems that the *Maclurcan* line of authority had not been cited to the court in *Beer v Higham*, or, it seems in the earlier decision in *Burton v Burton*. The fact that the order in *Maclurcan* was made under the predecessor of s 23(1)(b) dealing with secured periodical payments, was an immaterial distinction for this purpose. The ratio was directly applicable to an order made under s 24(1)(a).[38]

Jonathan Parker LJ concluded that, applying *Maclurcan*, 'the order in the instant case had the effect of conferring on Mrs Mountney an equitable interest in property at the moment when the order took effect (i.e. on the making of the decree absolute)'.[39] On that basis she was, if anything, in a better position than a purchaser of the property under a specifically enforceable contract in that by making the order under s 24(1)(a) the court had in effect already made a decree of specific performance in her favour. All that remained was for her to enforce it. His earlier decision in *Beer v Higham* was wrong and the same applied to the observations of Butler-Sloss J in *Burton v Burton*.[40]

In relation to the second sub-issue, he held that since s 283(5) applied to proprietary rights it followed from the conclusion in relation to the first sub-issue that the trustee took subject to Mrs Mountney's equitable interest under the order and that she was accordingly entitled to enforce the order against the trustee (subject always to the trustee's right, preserved by s 39 of the 1973 Act, to challenge the transaction as being a transaction at an undervalue).[41] Aldous and Laws LJJ agreed with Jonathan Parker LJ although Laws LJ thought the result to be unsatisfactory.[42]

Accordingly, the present position is that when the court has made a transfer of property order which has become effective under the Matrimonial Causes Act 1973 on the making of the decree absolute, the person in whose favour the order is made has an equitable interest on the basis that equity looks on that as done which ought to have been done. When a bankruptcy petition is subsequently presented against the person against whom the order is made and he is adjudged bankrupt, his property will vest in his trustee in bankruptcy subject to that equitable interest notwithstanding that no formal transfer has been executed. It is important to emphasize, however, that this will not be the case if the decree nisi of divorce has not been made absolute before the property vests in the trustee in bankruptcy.

---

[37] [2002] EWCA Civ 1174, para [55].   [38] ibid para [75].   [39] ibid para [76].
[40] ibid para [77].   [41] ibid para [80].
[42] Laws LJ said that *Maclurcan* was binding on the court but it assumed or implied what seemed to him to be a very doubtful proposition, namely that equity may be called in aid of a statute. He did not see how the evolution of equity could touch the operation of a statutory order as it may touch the operation of a common law rule, ibid para [84].

8.6.3 The effect of s 284

Under the 1986 Act, the trustee's title to the bankrupt's estate no longer relates back to the presentation of the petition as it did under the previous law.[43] In the absence of a special provision a disposition made by the debtor during this period between the presentation of a petition and the making of a bankruptcy order would be effective to pass title to the property disposed of subject to a subsequent application by the trustee when appointed for an order under ss 339 or 340. Accordingly, it is provided by s 284 that where a person is adjudged bankrupt any disposition of property made by him in the period beginning with the day of the presentation of the petition for the bankruptcy order and ending with the vesting of the bankrupt's estate in a trustee is void except to the extent that it is or was made with the consent of the court or is or was subsequently ratified by the court. This means the court exercising insolvency jurisdiction.[44]

It may be argued that although a transfer of property order made by the court is a disposition, as was established in *Mountney v Treharne*, it is not a disposition by the bankrupt for the purpose of s 284. Such an argument was rejected in *Re Flint* by Mr Nicholas Stewart QC sitting as a deputy judge in the Chancery Division. This question was considered in some detail by Lindsay J in *Treharne v Forrester* who noted that although the order in *Re Flint* had been made by consent the deputy judge had made it clear that this was not material to his decision. His conclusion would have been the same even if the relevant parts of the order had been the result of a contested application. Lindsay J reached the same conclusion and added that the actual instrument of transfer completed by the judge upon the husband's failure to do so was inescapably a disposition by the husband.[45]

In relation to the exercise of the court's powers to give consent or ratify a disposition it may be that guidance can be obtained from decisions on a similar provision in s 227 of the Companies Act 1948 which is now contained in s 127 of the Insolvency Act 1986.[46] Those decisions show that in exercising its discretion under s 227, and by analogy under s 284, the court should consider what is just and fair in all the circumstances, having particular regard to good faith and honest intentions.[47] In *Re AI Levy (Holdings) Ltd*, the court authorized a sale of a lease after the commencement of winding up proceedings against the lessee company where the landlord would have been entitled to forfeit the lease if the lessee company had been compulsorily wound up. It may be that a disposition of an item of the bankrupt's property, such as his matrimonial home, at a favourable price would justify consent to a sale.

---

[43] IA 1986, s 306. See *Re Flint* [1993] Ch 319, 325.
[44] IA 1986, ss 337 and 385.   [45] [2003] EWHC 2784 (Ch), para [54].
[46] See *Re Flint* [1993] 1 WLR 319, 328; *Treharne v Forrester* [2003] EWHC 2784, para [56].
[47] See *Re AI Levy (Holdings) Ltd* [1964] Ch 19; *Re Gray's Inn Construction Co Ltd* [1980] 1 WLR 711.

In relation to s 284, the reported cases provide limited guidance as to the approach to be adopted in relation to the ratification of an order made by the family court under the Matrimonial Causes Act 1973. In *Treharne v Forrester*,[48] Lindsay J said that ratification 'should occur only when matters can be looked at in the round'. In the earlier case of *Re Flint*,[49] Mr Nicholas Stewart QC, sitting as a deputy judge in the Chancery Division, found that there were no grounds for interfering with the decision of the judge who had refused ratification of an order made in favour of Mrs Flint under s 24 of the 1973 Act. He rejected the argument that the judge had failed to take account of the fact that Mrs Flint took on liabilities of Mr Flint's estate and that it was for the benefit of the estate that the position was crystallized, particularly with regard to possible future maintenance payments. The judge had had before him the order made by the court under s 24 and it was clear on the face of the order what liabilities were being taken over by Mrs Flint. He also had before him an affidavit by Mrs Flint which contained information about the financial background. Accordingly the judge could see the financial implications of the order made under s 24 in sufficient detail for the purposes of the exercise of his discretion under s 284. He had also heard oral evidence by Mrs Flint. There was 'no indication that the judge failed to consider the overall effect of the [transfer of property] order and give it proper weight'.[50] His decision was not perverse or obviously wrong. Indeed he said that would have been 'a rather startling proposition in circumstances where . . . a man owing over £120,000 makes a disposition of about £20,000 . . . six days before being made bankrupt'.[51] Moreover, although it was not suggested that the consent order involved any scheme on the part of Mr and Mrs Flint, in the sense of anything underhand, it was 'a fact that the impending risk of bankruptcy was known to Mrs Flint (and of course to Mr Flint) at the time the [transfer of property] order was made'.[52] The crucial question, however, is whether value was given by her and if so was it significantly less than £20,000. Unfortunately no details of the liabilities taken over by Mrs Flint or of the assessment of the value given by her appear in the report.[53]

---

[48] [2003] EWHC 2784 (Ch), para [61].

[49] [1993] 1 WLR 319. In *Re Mordant* [1996] 1 FLR 334, the District Judge dismissed the wife's application under s 284 that the court should give its approval to the payment of £385,000 to the wife as ordered by Rattee J in the Family Division. On appeal Sir Donald Nicholls V-C did not find it necessary to deal with the application under s 284 since he found that money held by the husband's solicitors as a result of the order made by Rattee J had ceased to be part of the husband's own estate. This is considered further in para 8.11 below. For subsequent proceedings relating to an order for costs against the building society see *Re Mordant* [1995] 2 BCLC 647 and *Mordant v The Trustee of the Estate of Mordant* (CA, 8 November 1995).   [50] [1993] 1 WLR 319, 329.

[51] ibid.   [52] ibid.

[53] The Deputy Judge said (329) that the 'slightly surprising proposition' that 'as a result of the [transfer of property] order Mr Flint's creditors were better off than they otherwise would have been' did not bear close examination.

In contrast in *Treharne v Forrester*,[54] Lindsay J considered it convenient to adjourn the issue of ratification. He was reluctant to make any order for ratification without a better view than was then available to him regarding the composition and value of the estate and of the creditors or other competitors seeking recourse to it. The trustee in bankruptcy could not yet be sure of what the estate consisted and still less had it been collected. The liabilities of the estate were also unresolved. He did not say that no ratification could ever be granted whilst every penny of the assets and every penny of the liabilities of the estate were unknown, but the picture was far from settled. He could not ratify the transfer of property orders on the footing that they represented a considered view by the Family Division of what was appropriate in all surrounding circumstances because a highly material factor, namely that the husband had a bankruptcy petition pending based on debts of over £1.5 million in which a bankruptcy order would very shortly be made, was not known to the Family Division Court.

A particular matter making an adjournment convenient was termed the 'windfall argument'.[55] This arose on the basis that the wife had spent a good deal of money, possibly as high as £115,000, with some success in seeking to find what were the husband's assets, where they were and, so far as possible, to prevent their dissipation. She was of course doing so with her own interests in mind. Lindsay J did not wish to discourage such steps which were not uncommon. In the circumstances he was not willing to rule out ratification to the extent at least to which expenditure by the wife had been reasonable in amount, had conduced to the identification, collection, or preservation of the husband's assets and had done so in such a way that either the outgoings of the trustee in bankruptcy had probably been reduced or the estate had in some other way probably been enlarged or not reduced. The extent of this was unknown. Some ratification might therefore be justified, but this could only be determined when the court had before it a more settled view of the estate and of its creditors and of any benefit which the wife's efforts to ascertain, collect, and preserve assets, had produced for the estate.[56]

8.7 ORDERS FOR THE SETTLEMENT OF PROPERTY

Under s 24(1)(b) of the Matrimonial Causes Act 1973, the court may make an order for the settlement of property specified in the order to which a party to the marriage is entitled, for the benefit of the other party to the marriage and of the children of the family or either or any of them. Such an order does not take effect unless the decree nisi has been made absolute. The effect of the bankruptcy of the person ordered to make a settlement appears to be the same as in the case of an order for the transfer of property considered in the previous section.

---

[54] [2003] EWHC 2784 (Ch), paras [61]–[62].   [55] ibid paras [57]–[60].   [56] ibid para [63].

8.8 ORDERS FOR THE VARIATION OF ANTE- OR POST-NUPTIAL SETTLEMENTS

Two powers relating to ante- or post-nuptial settlements are conferred upon the court by s 24 of the Matrimonial Causes Act 1973. They are as follows:

(c) an order varying for the benefit of the parties to the marriage and of the children of the family or either or any of them any ante-nuptial or post-nuptial settlement (including such a settlement made by will or codicil) made on the parties to the marriage;[57]

(d) an order extinguishing or reducing the interest of either of the parties to the marriage under such a settlement, other than one in the form of a pension arrangement.

The power to make an order under (d) is designed to make it clear that the court has power to extinguish the interest of a spouse under any ante- or post-nuptial settlement notwithstanding that this does not benefit the other spouse or children. Where an order is made under (c) or (d) on or after granting a decree of divorce or nullity of marriage, neither the order not any settlement made in pursuance of the order is to have effect unless the decree has been made absolute.[58]

An order made under s 24(1)(c) or (d) varying, extinguishing, or reducing the interest of a party under an ante- or post-nuptial settlement has an immediate effect on a beneficial interest provided the decree of divorce or nullity has been made absolute. Thus where the court has made an order transferring or extinguishing the beneficial interest of a spouse who subsequently becomes bankrupt, the order will be effective against the trustee in bankruptcy even though the order has not been fully implemented.

In *Harper v O'Reilly*,[59] following dissolution of the parties' marriage, an order was made by consent in relation to the former matrimonial home to which they were entitled beneficially in equal shares. The order provided that the property should be sold and the net proceeds of sale paid to the petitioner wife. Some months later the husband presented a petition for his own bankruptcy and a bankruptcy order was made against him. Mr Michael Hart QC, sitting as High Court judge, said that in the light of the powers conferred by ss 23 and 24, the least artificial way of interpreting the direction that the net proceeds of sale should be paid to the wife was that she was to be entitled to the net proceeds of sale as sole beneficiary. That must have been on the basis that the pre-existing shares of the parties in what was conceded to be a post-nuptial settlement were to be varied by the order itself. There was no reason to interpret

---

[57] The court may make an order varying a settlement under (c) notwithstanding that there are no children of the family.   [58] Matrimonial Causes Act 1973, s 24(3).

[59] [1997] 2 FLR 816.

the order as deferring the effective date of that variation to the date on which the sale itself was completed.[60]

While it was true that the order contemplated that the husband would continue to have a say in matters relating to the property pending sale, this was clearly because an early sale would affect the husband's obligations (by elimination or reduction respectively) in respect of outgoings and periodical payments. He therefore had an interest in having some control over the timing of the sale, but otherwise was not interested in the price at which a sale was achieved. There was no conceivable reason for the order to preserve for him some beneficial interest in the property pending sale.

8.9 FAILURE TO SPECIFY THE RELEVANT PARAGRAPH

In *Burton v Burton*,[61] Butler-Sloss J emphasized that when the interests of third parties are involved, it is vital to know under which subsection of the Act the order is actually made. This comment was made when it was considered that a distinction existed between orders for the transfer or settlement of property on the one hand and orders varying ante- or post-nuptial settlements on the other hand. While this distinction is no longer correct in the light of the decision in *Mountney v Treharne*,[62] it clearly remains desirable to specify the relevant paragraph of s 24(1) under which an order is made.

8.10 PENSION SHARING ORDERS

In the light of the changes made by the Welfare Reform and Pensions Act 1999, the power of the court to make pension sharing orders in relation to the future pension of a spouse are in the majority of cases unlikely to be affected by the bankruptcy of the person entitled to the pension. In relation to approved schemes, pension rights are excluded from the bankrupt's estate vesting in the trustee in bankruptcy.[63] In certain prescribed circumstances pension rights under unapproved schemes are capable of protection in the same way.[64] Moreover, the trustees or managers of a pension scheme are no longer able to forfeit pension rights on a member's bankruptcy.[65]

8.11 PRESERVING THE POSITION PENDING DETERMINATION OF A SPOUSE'S CLAIM

There is a possibility that a spouse may make a disposition of property or otherwise take some action with a view to defeating a claim for financial provision by

---

[60] ibid 822.   [61] [1986] 2 FLR 419, 426.   [62] [2002] EWCA Civ 1174.
[63] Section 11.   [64] Section 12.   [65] Section 14.

the other spouse which is pending or has not been finally determined by the court. Thus as noted in paragraph 8.5.3 above, in *Re Mordant*[66] Rattee J in the Family Division observed that the bankruptcy proceedings against the husband were within his own control because he had the means to pay off the debt to the petitioning creditor if he chose. The husband was using continuing non-payment of his debt as a means to delay, or defeat, payment to the wife. The position of the spouse applying for financial provision may, however, be protected.

In *Re Mordant*, Rattee J in the Family Division, when reserving judgment on the wife's application for financial provision until a further hearing, also ordered the husband to transfer to his solicitors to the order of the court a sum of £275,000 standing to the husband's credit in a bank account in Ireland. A further sum of £109,000 was also paid to the solicitors on the same basis. Sir Donald Nicholls V-C in the Chancery Division subsequently concluded that the money held by the husband's solicitors as a result of the order made by Rattee J had ceased to be part of the husband's own estate. He said that 'when making this order the purpose of the judge was to afford the wife protection in respect of her claim similar to the protection she would have enjoyed had he ordered payment of the money into court'. He considered that the judge's order was effective to achieve the purpose.[67] Since the order had been made before the issue of the bankruptcy petition the trustee in bankruptcy had no right to claim the money.[68]

Protection may also be achieved by an application under s 37(2) of the Matrimonial Causes Act 1973. This provides:

(2) Where proceedings for financial relief are brought by one person against another, the court may, on the application of the first-mentioned person—

    (a) if it is satisfied that the other party to the proceedings is, with the intention of defeating the claim for financial relief, about to make any disposition or to transfer out of the jurisdiction or otherwise deal with any property, make such order as it thinks fit for restraining the other party from so doing or otherwise for protecting the claim;

In *Re Mordant*,[69] Sir Donald Nicholls V-C pointed out that the words 'or otherwise for protecting the claim' are wide. He could see no justification for

---

[66] The proceedings in the Family Division are not reported but details are given in the report of proceedings in the Chancery Division: [1996] 1 FLR 334.

[67] ibid 341. He pointed out that a *Mareva* injunction does not confer on the plaintiff any proprietary interest in the defendant's assets or any charge over them even if it relates only to a particular asset. However, he said, 'it is well established that where a sum is paid into court by a defendant, either voluntarily under Ord 22 in satisfaction of the plaintiff's cause of action, or involuntarily, for instance under Ord 14 as a condition of leave to defend, the plaintiff is treated as a secured creditor in the defendant's bankruptcy to the extent of the money paid in' (339–40).

[68] ibid 342. This conclusion was not queried in the Court of Appeal hearing an appeal against an order for costs against the petitioning creditor made by the Vice Chancellor in proceedings reported at [1995] 2 BCLC 647.   [69] [1996] 1 FLR 334, 340.

cutting them down so as to exclude the power to make an order which, when carried out, will have the effect of making property security for the claim in the same way as a payment into court under Ord 14 or Ord 22. He said: 'For instance, the judge may direct that a sum shall be paid into court to await the outcome of a claim for financial provision.' He recognized that when ordering a lump sum payment, the 1973 Act only gives express power to direct that the payment must be secured when payment is to be made in instalments,[70] and that security may also be ordered in respect of periodical payments.[71] In his view, this was not a good reason for cutting down the width of the protection which the court may order under s 37(2)(a). He concluded that that provision applied to all forms of financial relief, including property adjustment orders. That indicated that a wider rather than a narrower meaning should be given to the provision.

8.12 INSOLVENCY OF THE APPLICANT

Where an applicant is bankrupt this will not preclude the court making an order for periodical payments in his or her favour. The bankrupt will be entitled to receive payments under the order as his or her income which does not vest in the trustee in bankruptcy. However, the trustee may seek an income payments order under s 310 of the Insolvency Act 1986 for the benefit of the bankrupt's estate though such an order must not have the effect of reducing the income of the bankrupt below what appears to the court to be necessary for meeting the reasonable domestic needs of the bankrupt and his or her family. The relationship between this power and the powers of the court to order periodical payments under the Matrimonial Causes Act was considered in paragraph 8.3 above. It seems unlikely to be appropriate for an order for periodical payments to make provision beyond what is necessary for this purpose and which would only be for the benefit of the recipient's creditors.

Any lump sum paid or property transferred to the bankrupt in accordance with an order under the 1973 Act will pass to his or her trustee in bankruptcy for the benefit of his or her creditors. In *Davy-Chiesman v Davy-Chiesman*,[72] May LJ said in relation to an application for a lump sum payment that in these circumstances 'any application for such an order would be bound to fail'. The position would be the same in relation to a transfer of property order. However, the court might utilize capital of the non-bankrupt spouse to make provision for the bankrupt by making an order for the settlement of property. In so far as a settlement provided for payment of income to the bankrupt it would be subject to the power of the bankruptcy court to make an income payments order. An order might provide for a sum to be settled on trustees, and thus not be available to the trustee in bankruptcy, to purchase a suitable home for the bankrupt husband.

---

[70] Section 23(3)(c).   [71] Section 23(1)(b).   [72] [1984] Fam 48, 64.

Where an applicant has entered into a voluntary arrangement, the effect of an order for financial provision or property adjustment will depend upon the terms of the agreement. This has been considered in relation to an application under the Inheritance (Provision for Family and Dependants) Act 1975 in *Re Abram deceased*.[73] In that case the applicant had entered into an IVA a term of which provided that any capital sum he received from his mother's estate on her death should be paid for the benefit of his creditors. He succeeded in establishing a claim against the estate under the 1975 Act, but such a claim is only for maintenance. Judge Roger Cooke sitting as a judge of the High Court said that he could not see how the provision of funds to pay off creditors could be said to be proper provision for maintenance.[74] The only way that the settlement of debts might be justified was on the basis that it would enable an applicant to establish himself in business, but very clear evidence would be required as to the objective and as to the amount of maintenance it might eventually produce.[75]

An order for payment of a capital sum with the object of paying off the debts under the IVA was, therefore, not appropriate. The terms of the IVA itself also made any capital sum inappropriate, since any such sum was to be applied to pay the applicant's debts and not by way of maintenance. Moreover, the applicant was unable to ask for any other order because he would break the terms of the IVA and a bankruptcy petition under s 276 was the likely outcome. The applicant clearly needed maintenance and the court made an order under s 2(1)(d) of the 1975 Act directing a settlement of an appropriate proportion of the estate on the applicant for life on protective trusts so that if he went bankrupt or sought to alienate his interest, the life interest would determine and would be replaced by a discretionary trust for him and his immediate family

8.13 POSTPONING AN APPLICATION

Where a husband is bankrupt at the time of divorce it may be pointless to seek any order for a lump sum at that stage. However, circumstances may change and after the husband's discharge from bankruptcy such an application may be feasible. It will, of course, be necessary to seek leave to apply out of time but the circumstances may justify this. Thus in *Pearce v Pearce*,[76] the wife, having been granted leave to apply out of time for a lump sum payment was awarded a lump sum of £12,000 following the receipt by the former husband of some £15,000 from his father's estate, some nine years after dissolution of the marriage. An important factor was that, at the time of the divorce, the husband had been an undischarged bankrupt and no lump sum had been applied for as it was pointless to do so. A nominal order for maintenance was all that had been feasible. The husband had made no provision for the wife and the two children who had been supported by social security.

---

[73] [1996] 2 FLR 379.   [74] ibid 396.   [75] See *Re Dennis deceased* [1981] 2 All ER 140.
[76] (1980) 1 FLR 261.

9

THE EFFECT OF INSOLVENCY
ON PRIOR TRANSACTIONS

9.1 THE BACKGROUND

An obvious way of protecting assets from the claims of creditors or potential creditors is to transfer assets to another in whose hands the transferor may continue to enjoy their benefit. There has long been statutory provision to enable the effect of such transfers to be reversed for the benefit of creditors in certain circumstances. The need for such provisions is clear when the transferor's marriage is ongoing as the likely benefit to him of a transfer into his wife's name is obvious. However, even when the marriage has broken down the impact of such provisions is important even though the transferor may appear to derive no benefit personally. Property may have been transferred by a husband, usually to comply with an order of the court in discharge of his obligations to his family and/or by way of an appropriate division of assets between the spouses. The claims of the transferor's family are thus brought into conflict with those of his creditors.

The Insolvency Act 1986 contains two provisions designed to recover for the benefit of a person's creditors property which has been transferred. Section 339 is applicable only in the event of the transferor's bankruptcy.[1] Section 423 is not so limited, but it may be conveniently considered at this point as the two sections have certain concepts in common such as that of a 'transaction at an undervalue'.

Resort to these statutory provisions may be unnecessary if the transfer was not genuine.

If the transfer was a sham then nothing was transferred by the transferor. The assets which he purported to transfer remain vested in him and can be reached by his creditors.[2] On the other hand, if there has been an effective transfer of the assets, it becomes necessary to determine the extent to which the transferor received value in return for the assets transferred. If the transferor received full value for the assets transferred, then the creditors should not be prejudiced. However, in the context of family transfers the question of value is often a difficult one.

This chapter will first consider the statutory provisions under which a transfer of assets may be attacked and will then consider their impact on orders for financial provision and property adjustment under the Matrimonial Causes Act 1973.

9.2 RECOVERING PROPERTY ON BANKRUPTCY

9.2.1 Transactions at an undervalue

Where an individual is adjudged bankrupt and has, within the period of five years ending with the day of the presentation of the bankruptcy petition on which the individual is adjudged bankrupt, entered into a transaction at an undervalue, the trustee of the bankrupt's estate may apply to the court for an order under s 339 of the Insolvency Act 1986 with respect to that transaction.[3] On such an application the court must make such order as it thinks fit for restoring the position to what it would have been if the bankrupt had not entered into that transaction.[4] Such an order may affect the property of, or impose an obligation on, a person even though he is not the person with whom the bankrupt entered into the transaction at an undervalue. However, the order must not prejudice any interest in property acquired from a person other than

---

[1] Section 238 contains a similar provision applicable where a company goes into liquidation and some of the cases in which the concept of a transaction at an undervalue is discussed arise under that section. Account may also need to be taken of s 340 of the Insolvency Act 1986 which in certain circumstances enables the court to restore the position to what it would have been if a bankrupt had not given a preference to one of his creditors.

[2] Midland Bank plc V Wyatt [1995] 1 FLR 696. See also *Abdel Rahman v Chase Bank (C I) Trust Co Ltd* [1991] JLR 103 and the discussion of the concept of 'sham' by Lee, 'The Concept of Sham: A Fiction or Reality?' (1996) 47 Northern Ireland LQ 377.   [3] IA 1986,ss 339(1) and 341(1).

[4] IA 1986, s 339(2). Without prejudice to the generality of that provision, s 342 sets out a list of orders that the court can make in exercising its power under s 339.

the bankrupt and which was acquired in good faith and for value, or prejudice any interest deriving from such an interest.[5]

Where the individual bankrupt entered into the transaction at an undervalue more than two years before the end of the five year period, the court cannot make an order unless the individual (a) was insolvent at the time of the transaction, or (b) became insolvent in consequence of the transaction.[6] An individual is insolvent for this purpose if (a) he is unable to pay his debts as they fall due, or (b) the value of his assets is less than the amount of his liabilities, taking into account his contingent and prospective liabilities.[7] This requirement will be presumed to be satisfied, unless the contrary is shown, in relation to any transaction at an undervalue which is entered into by an individual with a person who is an associate of his (otherwise than by reason only of his being an employee).[8] A lengthy definition of 'associate' is to be found in s 435 of the Act. In particular, it should be noted that a person is an associate of an individual if that person is the individual's husband or wife—or is a relative, or the husband or wife of a relative, of the individual or of the individual's husband or wife.[9]

A 'transaction' for this purpose includes, except where the context otherwise requires, a gift, agreement, or arrangement, and references to entering into a transaction must be construed accordingly.[10] It is clearly a wide concept, but it is important to identify the relevant transaction. In *Clarkson v Clarkson*,[11] the Court of Appeal held that the exercise of a power of appointment by trustees over a life insurance policy in favour of the bankrupt's wife was not the relevant transaction for the purposes of s 339. The policy had been taken out by the bankrupt and he had paid the premiums until his bankruptcy after which his family kept them up on his behalf. Hoffman LJ said that the wife had indeed received a gift from her husband but the gift was not the appointment to her by the trustees, but the creation of the settlement of the policy. Since it had been made more than two years before the bankruptcy petition at a time when the bankrupt had been solvent, it was no longer vulnerable to attack under s 339.

It is essential for the application of s 339 that the relevant transaction was entered into by the bankrupt. In *Re Brabon*,[12] it was held that s 339 did not apply to a sale of property by the bankrupt's wife as mortgagee.

---

[5] IA 1986, s 342(2) as amended by the Insolvency (No 2) Act 1994, s 2. See further s 342(2A)(4), (5), and (6). [6] IA 1986, s 341(2).

[7] IA 1986, s 341(3). [8] IA 1986, s 341(2).

[9] IA 1986, s 435(2). A 'relative' is defined in subs (8). See *Re Schuppan (A Bankrupt)(No 2)* [1997] 1 BCLC 256. [10] IA 1986, s 436.

[11] [1994] BCC 921.

[12] [2000] BPIR 537. The court was satisfied that the transaction was not a conveyancing device to disguise a disposal by the bankrupt. But contrast *DEFRA v Feakins and Hawkins* [2002] BPIR 281 in relation to s 423 where Penry Davey J looked at the 'reality of the transaction' and the actual sale was by a mortgagee.

9.2.2 Preferences

Similar provisions apply where the bankrupt has given a preference to one of his creditors or a surety or guarantor or done any thing which has the effect of putting such a person in a better position than that in which he would have been if that thing had not been done.[13] These might be applicable where the bankrupt had discharged a debt due to a spouse or other family member in preference to other creditors.[14]

9.2.3 Extortionate credit transactions

Where a person who is adjudged bankrupt is or has been a party to a transaction for, or involving, the provision to him of credit, then if that transaction is or was extortionate, the court may, on the application of the trustee of the bankrupt's estate make an order under s 343 of the Insolvency Act 1986 in respect of that transaction provided it was not entered into more than three years before the commencement of the bankruptcy. An order under s 343 may contain such one or more of the provisions set out in subsection (4) as the court thinks fit. These are:

(a) provision setting aside the whole or part of any obligation created by the transaction;

(b) provision otherwise varying the terms of the transaction or varying the terms on which any security for the purposes of the transaction is held;

(c) provision requiring any person who is or was a party to the transaction to pay to the trustee any sums paid by the bankrupt to that person under the transaction;

(d) provision requiring any person to surrender to the trustee any property held by him as security for the purposes of the transaction; and

(e) provision directing accounts to be taken between any persons.

Any sums or property which are required to be paid or surrendered to the trustee in accordance with an order under s 343 will form part of the bankrupt's estate.[15]

A transaction is extortionate for this purpose if, having regard to the risk accepted by the person providing credit, the terms of the transaction were or are such as to require grossly exorbitant payments to be made in respect of the provision of the credit,[16] or the transaction otherwise grossly contravened ordinary principles of fair dealing. There is a presumption that a transaction

---

[13] IA 1986, s 340.

[14] See *Doyle v Saville and Hardwick* [2002] BPIR 947 where the trustee failed to show that the bankrupt had preferred or intended to prefer a close family friend who was a creditor.

[15] IA 1986, s 343(5).   [16] Whether unconditionally or in certain contingencies.

which is the subject of an application under s 343 is or was extortionate unless the contrary is proved.[17]

The powers conferred by s 343 are exercisable in relation to any transaction concurrently with any powers exercisable under this Act in relation to that transaction as a transaction at an undervalue.[18]

9.3 TRANSACTIONS DEFRAUDING CREDITORS

9.3.1 The scope of s 423 of the Insolvency Act 1986

Where a person enters into a transaction with another person at an undervalue, the court may, on the application of a victim of the transaction, and if certain conditions are satisfied, make such order as it thinks fit for (a) restoring the position to what it would have been if the transaction had not been entered into, and (b) protecting the interests of persons who are victims of the transaction.[19] Unlike s 339, which is an integral part of the bankruptcy code and was considered in para 9.2, the availability of s 423 is not limited to situations where the transferor has become bankrupt. Moreover, s 423 is aimed at improper, if not dishonest, conduct by a debtor towards a creditor or creditors while the intention of the bankrupt is irrelevant in an application under s 339, which is aimed at transactions within a limited period before bankruptcy.[20]

Three conditions must be satisfied for the application of s 423:

(1) it must be shown that the impugned transaction was at an undervalue;
(2) it must be shown that it was entered into with the necessary intention, and
(3) the applicant must be a victim of the transaction.

If these conditions are satisfied the court has a discretion as to the form of order it can make.

9.3.2 A transaction at an undervalue

The concept of a transaction at an undervalue is also relevant to applications under s 339 and is considered further in paragraph 9.4.

---

[17] IA 1986, s 343(3).
[18] IA 1986, s 343(6). An application under s 139(1)(a) of the Consumer Credit Act 1974 for the re-opening of an extortionate credit agreement by which credit was provided to the bankrupt cannot be made by the trustee of the bankrupt's estate or by the undischarged bankrupt. See further ch 2, para 2.3.
[19] IA 1986, s 423. This topic was discussed by the author in an article ('Transactions Prejudicing Creditors') published in The Conveyancer and Property Lawyer [1998] 362.
[20] See the Report of the Cork Committee on *Insolvency Law and Practice* (Cmnd 8558), para 1209.

9.3.3 A victim of the transaction

An application under s 423 can be made by a person who is a victim of the transaction unless the person entering into the transaction is bankrupt or, in the case of a company, is being wound up or is subject to an administration order. In those situations an application can be made by the official receiver or trustee in bankruptcy of an individual, or the liquidator or administrator of the company, but by a victim of a transaction only with leave of the court.[21] Subsection (5) provides that in relation to a transaction at an undervalue references to a victim of the transaction are to 'a person who is, or is capable of being, prejudiced by it; ...' In *Pinewood Joinery v Starelm Properties Ltd,*[22] the court held that this is sufficiently wide 'to enable a person who is a litigant in proceedings and who has a chance of success in those proceedings to qualify as a victim of a transaction as a person capable of being prejudiced by the transaction'.[23] An applicant is not required to establish that the purpose of the transaction was to put assets beyond his reach in particular.[24] On the other hand, the section is not intended to be confined to transactions which may prejudice the body of creditors as a whole. It can be invoked by a particular creditor who is the intended victim of the transaction.[25] It is not necessary for the applicant to have been a victim of the transaction at the time of the transaction if he comes within that category at the time of the application.[26] If the requirements of s 423 are satisfied then there is no time limit after which the transaction becomes immune from an application.[27]

---

[21] IA 1986, s 424. See *The Mercantile Group (Europe) AG v Aiyela* [1993] FSR 745, 757 and *National Bank of Kuwait v Menzies* [1994] 2 BCLC 306 for examples of the need to obtain leave. If the victim of a transaction is bound by an approved voluntary arrangement then application can be made by the supervisor of the voluntary arrangement.   [22] [1994] 2 BCLC 412, 418.

[23] The applicant must, of course, be prejudiced by the transaction. An application will fail if the applicant is in no worse a position as a result of the transaction as was the case in *Pinewood Joinery*.

[24] *Per* Evans-Lombe J in *Jyske Bank (Gibraltar) Ltd v Spjeldnaes* [1999] 2 BCLC 101, 121.

[25] *Per* Neuberger J in *National Westminster Bank plc v Jones* [2001] 1 BCLC 98, 120, para 73. He said it was possible that in that case other creditors of the defendants might have benefited from the transaction.

[26] In *Law Society v Southall* [2001] BPIR 303, 311, Hart J considered the position of a transferor who, being solvent at the time of the transfer, is contemplating some activity which might expose him to financial risk. It was arguable that the wording of s 423 left open the question whether the only creditors who can apply under s 423 are those who have become creditors as a result of the particular risky activity which the debtor had in contemplation. On the other hand, the view that anyone who is subsequently prejudiced by the transaction may claim to be a victim is supported by the fact that the definition of a 'victim of the transaction' exists independently of any consideration of the purpose of the transaction. That would mean that there 'need be no nexus between the type of debacle which the debtor had in mind at the date of the disposition and that which eventually (it may be many years later) happens'. There had been no argument on the point and he expressed no view upon it.

[27] See *Mackay v Douglas* (1872) 14 Eq 106 and *Re Butterworth* (1882) 18 ChD 588 in relation to earlier legislation.

9.3.4 The requisite intent

A transfer at an undervalue may be made for perfectly proper reasons. The transferor may wish to provide for his family or to achieve genuine business objectives. A transaction is not necessarily open to attack under s 423 simply because it has the effect of reducing the value of his estate available for his creditors. An order can only be made if it can be shown that the person entering into the transaction did so for the purpose:

(a) of putting the assets beyond the reach of a person who is making, or may at some time make, a claim against him, or

(b) of otherwise prejudicing the interests of such a person in relation to the claim which he is making or may make.[28]

This requirement of a relevant purpose is an essential feature of s 423 and is additional to the requirement of a transaction at an undervalue in subsection (1). This means that the fact that the transfer was made for no consideration does not by itself establish the requisite purpose of defeating creditors. In *Royscot Spa Leasing Ltd v Lovett*[29] Sir Christopher Slade said that 'The test is not solely an objective one.'

However, the fact that the transferor did not have a dishonest motive will not prevent the application of s 423 if the intention of the transferor was in fact to place the assets transferred beyond the reach of his creditors.[30] Thus in *Arbuthnot Leasing International Ltd v Havelet Leasing Ltd (No 2)*,[31] Scott J said that the 'fact that lawyers may have advised that the transaction is proper or can be carried into effect does not by itself mean that the purpose of the transaction was not the subsection (3) purpose'. In that case the motive of the person responsible for a transfer of assets by a company was to save the business and though this was 'not necessarily a dishonest motive,' it was consistent with an intention to put the assets out of the reach of a creditor who had initiated litigation against the transferor.[32] Thus a court may find that the purpose of a transaction was to place assets beyond the reach of creditors even though the reason or motive for the transfer may be understandable and unobjectionable.

In *Chohan v Saggar*,[33] Mr Edward Evans-Lombe QC sitting as a High Court judge said:

As Lord Oliver in the well-known case of *Brady v. Brady*[34] acknowledged, the word "purpose" is a word of wide content. But he went on to say that it must be construed bearing in mind the mischief against which the section in which that word appears is

---

[28] IA 1986, s 423(3).   [29] [1995] BCC 502, 507.

[30] In *Midland Bank plc v Wyatt* [1995] 1 FLR 696, 698, Mr DEM Young QC, sitting as a High Court judge, said that in relation to s 423 it was 'common ground that proof of dishonesty is not a requirement, merely proof of avoidance of creditors whether they be existing or future creditors'.

[31] [1990] BCC 636, 644.   [32] ibid.   [33] [1992] BCC 306, 321.

[34] [1989] 1 AC 755, 779.

aimed. Here, the purpose or mischief against which the section is aimed, namely s 423, is the removal of assets by their owner, in anticipation of claims being made or contemplated, out of the reach of such claimants if those claims ultimately prove to be successful. It would defeat that purpose if it were possible successfully to contend that if the owner was able to point to another purpose, such as the benefit of his family, friends or the advantage of business associates, the section could not be applied.

This approach was approved by the Court of Appeal in *Royscot Spa Leasing Ltd v Lovett*.[35]

9.3.5 More than one purpose

A difficult question therefore arises as to the circumstances in which the existence of another purpose will prevent the application of s 423 despite the fact that the transaction has the effect of removing assets from the reach of creditors.

One view was that it is necessary for a person attacking a transaction under s 423 to show that the dominant purpose of the transaction was to place assets beyond the reach of creditors even though there might be other purposes underlying the transfer.[36] This was doubted by Judge Moseley QC in *Pinewood Joinery*[37] though in that case he was in any event satisfied that the dominant purpose for the transfer was to gain tax advantages which had been negotiated with the tax authorities rather than to put the property beyond the reach of creditors. Any suggestion that it is necessary to establish a sole purpose was rejected 'without hesitation' by Sir Christopher Slade in *Royscot Spa Leasing Ltd v Lovett*.[38] He said:

For the purposes of this appeal, though without deciding the point, I am content to assume in favour of the plaintiffs that the relevant purpose which has to be established in the application of section 423 is substantial purpose, rather than the stricter test of dominant purpose.

In that case a matrimonial home had been vested in the joint names of a husband and wife subject to a mortgage in favour of a building society and a second mortgage in favour of the National Westminster Bank. The bank had suggested that as a means of raising further funds the property should be re-mortgaged, but the proposed new mortgagee would not accept the husband as a mortgagor. Accordingly the husband and wife transferred the property into the joint names of the wife and her son. Three days later the plaintiffs obtained a summary judgement against the husband. The Court of Appeal held that a prima facie case that a substantial purpose of the execution of the transfer had

---

[35] [1995] BCC 502.

[36] *Chohan v Saggar* [1992] BCC 306, 321. See also *Re Schuppan (A Bankrupt)(No 2)* [1997] BCLC 256, 271.　　　　　　　　　　　　　　　　　　　　[37] [1994] 2 BCLC 412, 419.

[38] [1995] BCC 502, 507.

been to put assets beyond the reach of the plaintiffs or otherwise prejudice their interests had not been established. The available evidence was equally consistent with the conclusion that the purpose of the husband in making the transfer had been to keep a home for himself and his family by satisfying the bank, which was pressing for payment.[39]

The question was reviewed by the Court of Appeal in *IRC v Hashmi*,[40] where the question was whether the purpose shown must be a dominant purpose. Arden LJ said:

Accordingly, in my judgment, the section does not require the inquiry to be made whether the purpose was a dominant purpose. It is sufficient if the statutory purpose can properly be described as a purpose and not merely as a consequence, rather than something which was indeed positively intended.

She agreed with the observation of Hart J at first instance 'that it will often be the case that the motive to defeat creditors and the motive to secure family protection will co-exist in such a way that even the transferor himself may be unable to say what was uppermost in his mind'. She went on to emphasize that for something to be a purpose it must be a real substantial purpose; it is not sufficient to quote something which is a by-product of the transaction under consideration or to show that it was simply a result of it, as in *Royscot Spa Leasing v Lovett* itself or an element which made no contribution of importance to the debtor's purpose of carrying out the transaction under consideration. Trivial purposes must be excluded.[41]

Accordingly, the present position appears to be that if a substantial purpose of a transaction was to place assets beyond the reach of creditors then the fact that the transferor also had another purpose will not prevent the application of s 423.

9.3.6 Establishing the necessary intent

The onus is on the applicant to establish the necessary intent.[42] It has already been noted that in *Royscot Spa Leasing Ltd v Lovett*[43] Sir Christopher Slade said that '... result cannot be equated with purpose', and that it is not sufficient to show that the result of a transfer is to place assets beyond the reach of creditors or otherwise prejudice their interests. However, although 'result cannot be equated with purpose' it may in fact be crucial in establishing the necessary purpose. It will often be difficult for an applicant to obtain direct

---

[39] See also *Aiglon v Gau Shan* [1993] 1 Lloyd's Rep 164.
[40] [2002] EWCA Civ 981, para [23], [2002] 2 BCLC 489. [41] ibid para [25].
[42] The Cork Committee (Cmnd 8585), para 1215 had recommended that it should be made clear that the necessary intent might be inferred 'whenever this is the natural and probable consequence of the debtor's actions, in the light of the financial circumstances of the debtor at the time, as known, or taken to have been known, to him'. However, the Act contains no express provision to this effect.
[43] [1995] BCC 502, 509.

evidence of the purpose of the transferor in entering into a transaction so that the critical factor in establishing a prima facie case under s 423 may be the inferences which can be drawn from the circumstances in which the transfer was made. This may be necessary in order to obtain discovery of documents subject to professional privilege. In *Barclays Bank plc v Eustice*,[44] Schiemann LJ said:

Once one accepts that there is a strong prima facie case that the bank's security has been transferred to members of the family at a time when action by the creditor was clearly anticipated by the debtor and that these transfers were at an undervalue and that what remains in the hands of the debtor barely if at all covers the debt, there is in my judgment a strong prima facie case that the purpose of the transactions was to prejudice the interests of the creditor.[45]

In the absence of direct evidence as to the purpose of the transferor in entering into the transaction, the existence of debts owed by him or claims against him may be a significant factor in establishing the necessary purpose. On the other hand, even if the transferor had no debts and there were no claims against him at the time of the transfer, it may be apparent that the purpose of the transfer was to avoid the claims of potential creditors. Thus a person who is about to set up in business may seek to safeguard his assets against the claims of future and perhaps unknown creditors in the event that his business proves unsuccessful. This was established in relation to an earlier statutory provision in cases such as *Mackay v Douglas*[46] and *Re Butterworth*.[47] It was reaffirmed in relation to s 423 in the more recent case of *Midland Bank plc v Wyatt*,[48] where the settlement had been made some nine months before the settlor established a fabrics business in the form of a limited liability company. Mr DEM Young QC, sitting as a High Court judge, rejected the contention that the principle to be derived from these cases was that a settlement is voidable only where the settlor is about to enter into a business involving a high degree of risk either as a sole practitioner or as a partner. He said:[49]

I consider that if the purpose of the transaction can be shown to put assets beyond the reach of future creditors, s 423 will apply whether or not the transferor was about to enter into a hazardous business or whether his business was as a sole practitioner or as a partner or as a participant in a limited liability company. It is a question of proof of intention or purpose underlying the transaction. Clearly, the more hazardous the

---

[44] [1995] 1 WLR 1238, 1248. See also *Aiglon v Gau Shan* [1993] 1 Lloyd's Rep 164.

[45] Schiemann LJ accepted that there could easily be cases where part of the security is transferred at an undervalue and thus the security is reduced in value and yet still amply covers the debt. In such cases there may well be an argument that the transactions do not prejudice the interests of the creditor: ibid. [46] (1872) 14 Eq 106.

[47] (1882) 18 Ch D 588. See the points raised by Hart J in *The Law Society v Southall* [2001] BPIR 303, 313 in relation to possible victims of a transaction set out in n 26 above.

[48] [1995] 1 FLR 696. [49] ibid 709.

business being contemplated is, the more readily the court will be satisfied of the intention of the settlor or transferor.

Although Mr Wyatt intended to carry on his business through a limited liability company, the judge accepted that the setting up of any new business 'would no doubt...involve risks of a personal nature such as personal guarantees'. Indeed such long-term risks of a personal nature were being contemplated by Mr Wyatt as he had stated in his affidavit that that was one of the reasons for transferring his assets. The judge had also found that Mr Wyatt had no intention when he executed the settlement of endowing his children with his interest in the property concerned which at the time was his only real asset. He considered that it was not to be acted upon 'but to put in the safe for a rainy day...as a safeguard to protect his family from long term commercial risk should he set up his own company'. It was in fact a sham.[50]

9.3.7 The form of order

If the conditions set out in s 423 are satisfied the court *may* make such order as it thinks fit for restoring the position to what it would have been if the transaction had not been entered into, and protecting the interests of persons who are victims of the transaction.[51] This confers a very wide discretion as to the form of order and it may refuse to make any order against the transferor.[52] However, the discretion must be exercised with the objective of the section in mind. In *Arbuthnot Leasing International Ltd v Havelet Leasing Ltd (No 2)*,[53] Scott J said that 'the courts must set their faces against transactions which are designed to prevent plaintiffs in proceedings, creditors with unimpeachable debts, from obtaining the remedies by way of execution that the law would normally allow them.'

It will be noted that s 423 does not confer upon the court a power to set aside the transaction as this would be inappropriate in view of the sophisticated and often complex transactions that may now come before the courts. It is also necessary to take into account interests that may have been acquired by third parties. Without prejudice to the generality of this provision the court is empowered to include in an order a number of specific provisions set out in s 425. An order under s 423 may affect the property of, or impose any obligation on, any person whether or not he is the person with whom the debtor entered into the transaction. However, this is

---

[50] [1995] 1 FLR 707. The judge did not accept that it was necessary for both Mr and Mrs Wyatt to have had a common intention that the settlement was to be a sham: ibid 700.

[51] IA 1986, s 423(2).

[52] *Per* Sir Donald Nicholls V-C in *Re Paramount Airways Ltd (No 2)* [1992] BCC 416, 425 and Neuberger J in *National Westminster Bank plc v Jones* [2001] 1 BCLC 98 at 121. Such a discretion has been seen as a safeguard against the wide ambit of the section. In particular, if a foreign element is involved.   [53] [1990] BCC 636, 645.

specifically restricted in two ways in relation to persons other than the transferee.[54] First, such an order must not prejudice any interest in property which was acquired from a person other than the debtor and was acquired in good faith, for value and without notice of the relevant circumstances, or prejudice any interest deriving from such an interest. Secondly, it must not require a person who received a benefit from the transaction in good faith, for value and without notice of the relevant circumstances to pay any sum unless he was a party to the transaction.

In *Chohan v Saggar*,[55] Nourse LJ pointed out that provided the power conferred by s 423(2) 'is exercised in order to restore the position and protect the interests of the victims of the transaction so far as practicable..., the whole or any part of the transaction may be set aside'. He said:[56]

Thus, for example, where the transaction is made up of more than one component the power may be exercised by setting aside one component and not the other or others of them. Any lingering doubt on this question is dispelled by a consideration of the wide range of possible orders specified in s 425(1).

The Court of Appeal held that the judge had not been wrong to refuse to set aside the transfer of property by the debtor to Mrs Saggar, since that would have prejudiced the mortgagee. However, he had also not been wrong to set aside a declaration of trust of the property subsequently made by Mrs Saggar. Nourse LJ said:[57]

It is not a power to restore the position generally, but in a such a way as to protect the victims' interests; in other words, by restoring assets to the debtor to make them available for execution by the victims. So the first question the judge must ask himself is what assets have been lost to the debtor. His order should, so far as practicable, restore that loss.

The result of the order was that the transferee, Mrs Saggar, held the property on trust for herself and the debtor, the share of the debtor being such as to cover the loss to him (and hence his creditors) resulting from the transaction at an undervalue.

In *Moon v Franklin*,[58] a husband had made a gift of £65,000 to his wife and transferred to her his interest in a house. Mervyn Davies J made a declaration that the purpose of these transactions was to put assets beyond the reach of the applicant. However, the wife was not ordered to restore the property to her husband. First, she was restrained from dealing with the legal or beneficial interest in the house. Secondly, it was ordered that such part of the money as was still traceable in the wife's bank account should be held jointly by her and the applicant's solicitors pending the outcome of a negligence action against the husband.[59]

---

[54] IA 1986, s 425(2).   [55] [1994] BCLC 706.   [56] ibid 713.
[57] ibid 714.   [58] [1996] BPIR 196.
[59] See also *Arbuthnot* [1990] BCC 636 where assets were ordered to be held on trust.

9.4 A TRANSACTION AT AN UNDERVALUE

An essential concept in both s 339 and s 423 is that of a transaction at an undervalue.[60] This is defined in identical terms in both sections.[61] A person enters into a transaction at an undervalue with another person if:

(a) he makes a gift to the other person or he otherwise enters into a transaction with the other on terms that provide for him to receive no consideration;

(b) he enters into a transaction with the other in consideration of marriage; or

(c) he enters into a transaction with the other for a consideration the value of which, in money or money's worth, is significantly less than the value, in money or money's worth, of the consideration provided by himself.

A transaction 'includes a gift, agreement or arrangement...'[62] and is clearly a wide concept.

Difficulty is most likely to arise where some consideration was received by the transferor and it becomes necessary to determine whether that consideration was significantly less than the value of the consideration provided by him.

In *Agricultural Mortgage Corporation plc v Woodward*,[63] which was concerned with s 423, Sir Christopher Slade said that 'An assessment of the value in money or money's worth of the consideration provided by each of the respective parties to the transaction is thus of crucial importance.' The difficulty involved in that task has been amply illustrated in recent cases from which it also appears that the valuation of the consideration involved may well depend on identifying the full scope of the transaction or transactions involved. Indeed in *National Westminster Bank plc v Jones*,[64] Mummery LJ delivering the judgment of the court said that three relevant questions must be answered in determining whether a transaction was at an undervalue for the purposes of s 423. These are:

(i)   What is the relevant transaction?
(ii) What was the consideration for the transaction?
(iii) Was the value of the consideration provided by the transferee 'significantly less' than the value provided by the transferor?

---

[60] As noted earlier, a 'transaction at an undervalue' is also a key concept in s 238 which is the corresponding section to s 339 dealing with companies.

[61] IA 1986, ss 339(3) and 423(1). The definition in s 238 is similar but obviously omits the reference to marriage consideration. The courts appear to have treated the concept of a transaction at an undervalue as the same in relation to all three sections.   [62] IA 1986, s 436.

[63] [1995] 1 BCLC 1, 6.   [64] [2001] EWCA Civ 1541, [2002] 1 BCLC 55.

The identification of the relevant transaction will often cause little difficulty, but where there are a number of linked arrangements this task may become more difficult. It is also likely to become crucial in determining what can be regarded as consideration and hence whether there is in fact a transaction at an undervalue.[65]

In *Agricultural Mortgage Corporation plc v Woodward*, the defendant farmer had charged his farm to the plaintiffs to secure a loan of £700,000. Shortly before the expiration of a deadline for mortgage arrears to be cleared he entered into a tenancy agreement with his wife. The effect of the agreement on the plaintiff's security was serious because whereas the value of the farm with vacant possession was over £1 million, its value subject to the tenancy was less than £500,000. The principal issue before the Court of Appeal was whether the tenancy agreement was a transaction 'entered into at an undervalue' within s 423(1)(c). On the basis of an assessment of the value in money or money's worth of the consideration provided by each of the parties to the transaction, the transaction did not appear to be at an undervalue because the annual rent payable by the wife was equal to the market value and was the best rent reasonably obtainable. Accordingly, the two considerations appeared to be equal in money or money's worth provided the incidental detriment resulting from the loss of vacant possession was disregarded.[66] The Court of Appeal accepted the argument that by the grant of the tenancy agreement Mrs Woodward acquired the benefit of the surrender value which placed her in 'a ransom position' in any future dealings with the mortgagee.[67] On the facts of the case, it was not necessary for the court to calculate the precise surrender value, but it was bound to be a substantial sum in view of the existence of the mortgage, quite apart from any value which might be attributed to the securing of the family home and the acquisition of a debt free business. It was necessary to look at the transaction as a whole and the tenancy agreement could not be considered in isolation. Sir Christopher Slade said:[68]

Accepting that she agreed to pay for her yearly tenancy a rent which was the best rent reasonably obtainable for that tenancy viewed in isolation, and that she undertook the other tenant's obligations imposed by the tenancy agreement, it seems to me nevertheless

---

[65] Consideration need not move directly from the transferor to the transferee or vice versa. See in relation to s 423 *Phillips v Brewin Dolphin Bell Lawrie* [2001] UKHL 2, para [20], [2001] 1 WLR 143, 150. However, involvement of a third party may make identification of the transaction more difficult and contentious.

[66] The Court of Appeal left open the question whether benefits or detriments could be taken into account only if they were part of the bargain as opposed to being merely an incidental result of the transaction. See [1995] 1 BCLC 1, 10.

[67] The facts were similar in *Barclays Bank plc v Eustice* [1995] 1 WLR 1238 where the ransom point was also accepted as showing that the transferees were obtaining more than they were paying for. However, the point was not needed for provisions for deferred payment of consideration and the payment of rent in arrears were enough to lead to a strong prima facie case that the transactions were at an undervalue. [68] [1995] 1 BCLC 1, 10.

clear that, when the transactions are viewed as a whole, the benefits which the first defendant thereby conferred on her were significantly greater in value, far greater in value, in money or money's worth than the value of the consideration provided by her. To hold otherwise would seem to me to fly in the face of reality and common sense.

This may be compared with *National Westminster Bank plc v Jones*,[69] where a husband and wife carried on a farming business in partnership on freehold land the title to which was vested in them subject to a mortgage and floating charges over other assets. When the bank demanded payment they granted a lease of the land to a company which they formed and of which Mr and Mrs Jones were the beneficial owners and only directors. The lease for twenty years reserved not only the full market rent, but also charged the base rent. This was said to represent a payment by the company to the defendants primarily for the benefit of obtaining the surrender and/or ransom values referred to in *Woodward*. They also sold the farming assets to the company.[70]

The Court of Appeal dismissed an appeal from the decision of Neuberger J setting aside the tenancy agreement and the asset sale agreement on the grounds that they were transactions at an undervalue. The relevant transactions were the tenancy agreement and the sale agreement which had been entered into for the admitted purpose of putting assets beyond the reach of the bank. The acquisition of the company and the issue of the shares in it was not a relevant transaction within s 423. The consideration for the tenancy agreement was the obligation to pay rent and the consideration for the sale agreement was the sum to be paid for the farm assets. The issue of shares in the company was not consideration for either transaction and the fact that the two transactions caused the shares in the company to increase in value was irrelevant. On this basis Mr and Mrs Jones had entered into the relevant transactions at an undervalue and the decision setting them aside was upheld.

In *National Westminster Bank plc v Jones*, the Court of Appeal also addressed the question of valuing the consideration which had been identified. Approval was given to the statement of Millett J in *Re MC Bacon Ltd*[71] that in making a comparison between the value of the consideration received by the transferor for the transaction and the value of the consideration provided by the transferor, both values must be measured in money or in money's worth, and both must be considered from the transferor's point of view. Mummery LJ said that s 423 requires a comparison to be made between two figures and for that purpose the court must arrive at a conclusion on actual values. There is no express or implied reference in s 423 to the concept of a 'band or range of values', such as is used by the courts when determining the liability of a valuer for professional negligence.[72]

---

[69] [2001] EWCA Civ 1541.
[70] They did not obtain the consent of the bank as required by the mortgage.
[71] [1990] BCLC 324, 340.   [72] [2001] EWCA Civ 1541, para [28].

The value of the consideration provided by either party in money or money's worth must be assessed as at the date of the transaction. If at that date value is dependent on the occurrence or non-occurrence of some event and that event occurs before the assessment of value has been completed, then the valuer may have regard to it. However, the valuer is entitled, indeed bound, to take account of all other matters relevant to the determination of value as at the date of the transaction.[73]

9.5 TRANSFER OF ASSETS WITHIN THE FAMILY

It is evident that a transfer of assets from one member of a family to another may be vulnerable to attack under s 339 or s 423 by the trustee in bankruptcy or a creditor of the transferor respectively. Thus a transfer of the family home from one spouse to the other in consideration of 'natural love and affection' will almost certainly constitute a transaction at an undervalue within both statutory provisions. It will also be clear that the acquisition of property in the name of one member of a family may constitute a transfer of assets by the person providing the whole of the purchase price for that property. Where the property is vested in the joint names of spouses or cohabitants, but the spouse or cohabitant providing the purchase price acquires only a share of the beneficial interest that spouse or cohabitant will have entered into a transaction at an undervalue. In some cases the respective contributions of the parties will have been less clear, and in others the property will have been vested in the name of only one of the spouses or cohabitants even though both have made contributions to its acquisition. It may then be necessary to distinguish between a share acquired as a result of a resulting trust and a share acquired by the imposition of a constructive trust. A share to which a person is entitled under a resulting trust, being based upon the contribution of that person to the acquisition of the property, will be effective against the trustee in bankruptcy or creditors of the other party. However, where a constructive trust is imposed, the share of one party may be larger than the share which could be justified on the basis of his or her contributions. To the extent that it exceeds the share appropriate to those contributions, it is vulnerable to attack by the trustee in bankruptcy or creditors of the other party as a transaction at an undervalue. This was the situation in *Re Densham*.[74]

In a number of cases it has been argued by the debtor's spouse that she already had a beneficial interest in the property transferred to her by the debtor.

---

[73] *Per* Sir Andrew Morritt V-C in *Re Thoars deceased* [2002] EWHC 2416 (Ch), para [17] following the statement of Lord Scott in *Phillips v Brewin Dolphin Bell Lawrie* [2001] UKHL 2, paras [26] and [27]. For subsequent proceedings in *Re Thoars* which concerned an application under s 339, see [2003] EWHC 1999 (Ch).   [74] [1975] 1 WLR 1519.

In *Kubiangha v Ekpenyong*,[75] Mr Ekpenyong had transferred the matrimonial home into the name of his wife some two weeks after receiving a letter from solicitors acting for the claimants who had recovered damages against him and others seeking payment. He failed in his contention that the entire beneficial interest in the property was already vested in his wife as a result of a constructive trust arising from an intended but ineffective gift of the property in 1985. The judge concluded that a constructive trust had indeed arisen under which the wife was entitled to a beneficial interest in the property. There had been an express understanding between the spouses when the property was purchased that it was to be a joint acquisition and the wife had then contributed directly to the purchase price by her payments towards the mortgage instalments. Her substantial expenditure on repairs and improvements also pointed strongly towards a common understanding that they should both have a stake in the property. He considered that 50 percent was the appropriate size of the wife's share. It was agreed that any order should not seek to re-vest the property in the husband but should rather declare that the beneficial interest should be held by the wife subject to the building society's mortgage on trust for Mr and Mrs Ekpenyong in equal shares. If it became necessary to sell the property in order to enforce the claimant's judgment and if the husband's half share would otherwise be insufficient for that purpose, the burden of the building society mortgage was to be borne as to 50 per cent by the wife's share in the property in exoneration of the husband's share. In other words for the purpose of protecting the claimants' interests, but not further or otherwise, only one half of the burden of the building society charge was to be treated as a first charge on the proceeds of sale of the property and, subject thereto the whole of the husband's half share was to be available, if necessary, to satisfy the judgment against him.

9.6 THE EFFECT ON FINANCIAL PROVISION AND PROPERTY ADJUSTMENT ORDERS

9.6.1 The competing claims

A transfer of assets from one spouse to another may have been made as a result of an order for financial provision or property adjustment under the Matrimonial Causes Act 1973 following divorce. This creates a potential conflict between the claims of the transferor's spouse and family on the one hand and the claims of his creditors on the other. The Law Commission expressed their views in relation to these competing claims in their Report on *Financial*

---

[75] [2002] EWHC 1567 (Ch). See also *Simms v Oakes* [2002] EWCA Civ 08, and *Re Schuppan (No 2)* [1997] 1 BCLC 256 where the judge said that if the wife could establish an interest, this interest ought not to be defeated by the property being acquired or held by a company owned by her husband instead of being owned by him direct.

Provision in Matrimonial Proceedings which preceded the Matrimonial Proceedings and Property Act 1970 the relevant provisions of which are now contained in the 1973 Act.[76] They said:

Whether the claims of the family should prevail over those of creditors is essentially a question of social policy. The answer given by the Matrimonial Homes Act 1967 is that the claims of a spouse should be subordinated to those of creditors, and this is the view which we favour. Marriage is a form of partnership and, on normal partnership principles, neither partner should compete with the partner's creditors.[77]

Following the recommendation of the Law Commission, s 39 of the Matrimonial Causes Act 1973 provided that the fact that a settlement or transfer of property had to be made in order to comply with a property adjustment order should not prevent that settlement or transfer from being a settlement for the purposes of s 42 of the Bankruptcy Act 1914. This was subsequently amended so as to replace the reference to a settlement for the purposes of s 42 with a reference to a transaction in respect of which an order may be made under ss 339 or 340 of the Insolvency Act 1986.

9.6.2 Orders for secured periodical payments

The provision of security for periodical payments may involve a transfer of capital, but on the basis of the wording of s 39 of the 1973 Act, this appears to be protected from attack under s 339 if the transferor subsequently becomes bankrupt.[78]

9.6.3 Orders for lump sum payments

The implication of s 39 of the 1973 Act is that a lump sum payment made by virtue of a court order is also not vulnerable to attack under s 339 of the Insolvency Act 1986, but there is no decision to this effect. This would reflect the fact that the lump sum payment was seen primarily as an alternative method of providing maintenance especially when difficulty in the enforcement of periodical payments was envisaged. The lump sum continues to perform this function and has become of importance in effecting a clean break. This feature is clearly apparent when it is calculated on the basis of capitalizing an annual sum. However, this is no longer the only function of a lump sum. It is now also frequently used as the means of awarding the recipient her share of the family assets on the basis of the contributions she 'has made or is likely in

---

[76] Law Com No 25 (1969), para 78.

[77] The Insolvency Act 1985, s 171(2) reversed the provisions of the Matrimonial Homes Act 1967, s 2(7) whereby statutory rights of occupation conferred by the 1967 Act were not binding on the entitled spouse's trustee in bankruptcy even though protected by registration in the appropriate manner. [78] See *Platt v Platt* (1976) 120 SJ 199 in relation to s 42 of the Bankruptcy Act 1914.

the foreseeable future to make to the welfare of the family, including any contribution by looking after the home or caring for the family'.[79] Often these two elements will not be clearly distinguishable.[80] While it may be desirable from the standpoint of the family that this dual function should not affect the apparent immunity of a lump sum payment from attack, the contrasting position in relation to orders for the transfer or settlement of property may operate unfairly.

9.6.4 Property adjustment orders

An order for the transfer of property under s 24 of the Matrimonial Causes Act 1973 will be effective against the trustee in bankruptcy of the spouse against whom it was made provided the order was made before the bankruptcy petition was presented and provided the decree nisi of divorce had been made absolute before that date.[81] The same would seem to apply to an order for the settlement of property. However, by virtue of s 39 of the 1973 Act, such orders are vulnerable to adjustment on an application by the trustee in bankruptcy under s 339 of the 1986 Act.[82] In *Jackson v Bell*,[83] the Court of Appeal gave permission to appeal to raise the question, inter alia, of whether a property adjustment order could be a transaction at an undervalue. In *Treharne v Forrester*,[84] Lindsay J noted that unfortunately the question had not been answered because it seemed that the permission to appeal was not taken up. He said that '[I]n any event the Court of Appeal presumably took it to be a possible view that property orders might well not be vulnerable as transactions at an undervalue . . . '.

Assuming that such orders are vulnerable under s 339, the concept of valuable consideration is not easy to apply.[85] What is required is an assessment in monetary terms of the consideration provided by each spouse. While the value of the property transferred or settled will generally be clear,[86] the consideration provided by the party in whose favour the order is made will generally be

---

[79] Matrimonial Causes Act 1973, s 25(2)(f). See Lord Denning MR in *Trippas v Trippas* [1973] Fam 134, 140.

[80] It may sometimes be necessary to distinguish between the two elements in a lump sum order, for example for the purposes of the Civil Jurisdiction and Enforcement of Judgments Act 1982. See *Van den Boogaard v Laumen* [1997] QB 759 considered in ch 10, para 10.6.2.

[81] *Mountney v Treharne* [2002] EWCA Civ 1174. See ch 8, para 8.6.2.

[82] Orders made after the party against whom they are made is adjudicated bankrupt will be void and so no application under s 339 will be necessary. Orders made between presentation of a bankruptcy petition and adjudication are governed by s 284 of the Insolvency Act 1986. See ch 8, para 8.6.3. [83] [2001] EWCA Civ 387, [2002] BPIR 612.

[84] [2003] EWHC 2784 (Ch), para [47].

[85] See Miller, 'The Effect of Insolvency on Financial Provision and Property Adjustment on Divorce' [1994] 10 (3) IL & P 66 from which material has been drawn.

[86] If the value of their shares in jointly owned property is not clear an assessment may have to be made as in *Re Densham* [1975] 1 WLR 1519. See para 6.5 above.

difficult to represent in monetary terms. There may be cases where the person making the transfer or settlement receives compensation in the form of a lump sum payment, but in most cases the consideration will have to be found in the compromise and dismissal of a claim or the assumption of a responsibility.

9.6.4.1 *The assumption of responsibility*

Where a transfer of property order provides for the transfer of a husband's share in the former matrimonial home to the wife, then sole liability for the mortgage may be assumed by the wife who will covenant to indemnify the husband against liability under the mortgage. In *In re Windle*,[87] it was established that where there was an equity of redemption of significant value a mere covenant of indemnity against liability under the mortgage could not be regarded as valuable consideration for the purposes of s 42 of the Bankruptcy Act 1914. However, s 42 contained no provision such as that now contained in s 339(3)(c) of the 1986 Act for comparing the respective values of consideration moving in each direction. The difference proved to be of little practical significance in *Re Kumar*[88] where the husband had transferred his interest in the matrimonial home to his wife though not in pursuance of an order under s 24. It was not disputed that even if the assumption of liability under the mortgage did constitute relevant consideration, so leading to a need to evaluate the case under paragraph (c), it would not by itself be enough to prevent there being a significant difference in value for the purposes of paragraph (c).[89]

The circumstances in which an assumption of liability would be sufficient consideration are not clear. Presumably there would be sufficient consideration if there was a negative equity even though this might mean that the wife would get the benefit of earlier contributions made by the husband whether to the original purchase price or towards the mortgage. The same might be thought to apply where the valuation of the house at the time of the transfer left it in doubt whether a sale would produce sufficient to discharge the mortgage. If it was not at that time a transfer at an undervalue, a subsequent rise in value should not make the transfer liable to adjustment under s 339.

9.6.4.2 *Compromise and dismissal of a claim*

In relation to the previous legislation it was held in *Re Pope*[90] that it was not essential that money or physical property should have been given to the debtor and that the release of a right or the compromise of a claim could amount to valuable consideration. In that case the fact that the wife had agreed to refrain from taking proceedings in the divorce court was held to be sufficient to constitute her a purchaser for valuable consideration in relation to the settlement in her favour made by her husband.

---

[87] [1975] 1 WLR 1628.   [88] [1993] 1 WLR 224.   [89] ibid 235.   [90] [1908] 2 KB 169.

This was followed in *Re Abbott*[91] where a compromise of an application for a property adjustment order in relation to the jointly owned matrimonial home following divorce, provided for the sale of the house and payment to the wife out of the proceeds of sale of the sum of £18,000 and one half of any excess. On the subsequent bankruptcy of the husband his trustee argued that there had been a settlement of £9,000 on the wife within s 42 of the Bankrupty Act 1914. However, it was held that the wife was a purchaser for valuable consideration and that there was no need for the consideration moving from the 'purchaser' to replace in the hands of the debtor the consideration moving from the debtor.[92] It will be noted that while the order in *Re Abbott* was the result of a compromise of an application by the wife for a transfer of property order under s 24 in respect of the matrimonial home, the consequence of the order was the payment of a sum of money. If the compromise had been effected by a lump sum order then, on the interpretation of s 39 of the 1973 Act adopted above, s 42 would not have been applicable, but this point does not appear to have been raised.

In *Harman v Glencross*,[93] Balcombe LJ noted that in the case before him the wife had given up her claim for periodical payments and it seemed to him 'that this constituted valuable consideration on her part which would preclude a trustee in bankruptcy of the husband from maintaining that the transfer of property order was void against him; see *Re Abbott* . . . .' Certainly the contrary was not so clear as to support the contention that there was no point in transferring the husband's interest in the property concerned to the wife.

The decision in *Re Abbott* and the views expressed in *Harman v Glencross* must now be viewed in the light of the difference between s 42 and s 339 of the 1986 Act. Under s 42, it was possible that as long as the consideration provided by the person in whose favour it was made was not merely nominal, it was not necessary to weigh it against the value of the property settled. Under s 339, it is necessary to determine whether the value of the consideration provided by the person in whose favour the transfer of property is made is significantly less than the value of the property transferred under the order.

An order for the transfer of property under s 24 will generally be either part of an overall compromise agreed by the parties or the result of an overall assessment of the financial position of the parties by the court. In some cases it will be accompanied by a dismissal of the wife's claim for periodical payments so as to achieve a clean break. In other cases there will also be an order for

---

[91] [1983] Ch 45.

[92] There was a suggestion by counsel that if the claim had not been compromised, but the application had been contested and the court had made an order in the same terms as the consent order, the wife could not have been described as a purchaser and she had therefore improved her position by reaching a compromise. Peter Gibson J thought it unnecessary and perhaps undesirable to decide the point, but was by no means convinced that counsel's premise was correct.

[93] [1986] Fam 81, 97.

periodical payments in her favour which may be substantive or nominal and for a limited term or without specified limit. Will the termination of a wife's right to periodical payments be regarded as consideration that is not significantly less than the value of, say, the share of the former matrimonial home transferred to her by her husband to achieve a clean break? Had an order for periodical payments been made in her favour this could have continued in existence despite the husband's subsequent bankruptcy. One of the objects of periodical payments is likely to be to assist with the provision for accommodation, but it will often be the case that this is more effectively provided by a capital payment or by a property adjustment order.[94] If it takes the form of a property adjustment order rather than an order for a lump sum payment it is vulnerable under s 339 even though the wife can no longer go back to the court for period-ical payments to cover her accommodation needs. Where the wife's entitlement to periodical payments continues in existence even if only in the form of a nominal order, it seems more difficult to argue that the wife has provided consideration or at any rate sufficient consideration. On the other hand, even where her claim is dismissed this may be because of the assessment of her earning capacity so that her claim for support was in any event limited or even non existent.

Unfortunately, *Re Kumar* is also of limited assistance in relation to the effect of dismissal of a wife's claim for financial provision. There appears to have been no dismissal of the wife's potential claim for periodical payments, probably because such a claim was not made or likely to be made in view of the fact that she had greater earning capacity than her husband. In relation to capital pro-vision Ferris J found that there was nothing to support the contention that the home had been transferred to the wife in return for an agreeement on her part not to seek further capital provision under ss 23 or 24. The husband 'sought nothing from her in return and . . . he received nothing'.[95] However, he did say that although *Re Abbott* was a decision on s 42, it was applicable to s 339 to the extent that it decides that a compromise of a claim to provision in matrimonial proceedings is capable of being consideration in money or money's worth. Nevertheless, even if the transfer had been found to be in consideration of the dismissal of her claim, there would have been a substantial difference in value. The transfer of the husband's interest in the property was a disposal of his only remaining capital asset of any significance. Ferris J could not 'believe that any divorce court would have so exercised its jurisdiction under s 24 . . . as to require [the husband] to transfer to the [wife], who had superior earning capacity, substantially the whole of his capital, leaving him without the means to contribute from capital to the cost of acquiring a separate home for himself'.[96]

---

[94] As in *Mullard v Mullard* (1982) 3 FLR 330.   [95] [1993] 1 WLR 224, 239.
[96] ibid 240–1.

This suggests that an assessment must be made of the strength of the wife's claim under the 1973 Act at least for support. In *Re Kumar*, the wife had superior earning capacity and her claim was not regarded as significant and so could not be sufficient consideration to prevent the transfer being at an undervalue. If, on the other hand, the wife has little or no earning capacity, but the enforcement of periodical payments is fraught with difficulty, then if the court orders a lump sum payment which has been paid it seems that this will be protected from attack under s 339. If the court orders the transfer of the husband's interest to her as the only realistic way of providing something for her support then, while the transfer is not protected from attack under s 339, it seems possible that it may well clear the hurdle provided by that section. However, the assessment of the value provided by the wife must be made by the court exercising bankruptcy jurisdiction and not by the divorce court which has adjudicated upon the wife's claim. It is unfortunate that uncertainty remains about the effect of a transfer of property order in these circumstances, especially where a dismissal of the wife's claim for periodical payments seems desirable in order to achieve a clean break.

This is to consider only the wife's claim for support, but orders under s 24 are also concerned to provide the wife with a share of the assets appropriate to her contribution to the marriage and family. Since the decision of the House of Lords in *White v White*[97] this has been accorded greater recognition as between a husband and wife but it remains to be seen what effect it will have in relation to the claims of the husband's creditors. If the contribution is recognized by the award of a lump sum payment, then if the husband subsequently becomes bankrupt this will not be vulnerable to an application by the husband's trustee in bankruptcy under s 339. However, in so far as the wife's contribution to the family is recognized by the transfer to her of, say the husband's interest in the former matrimonial home, it will be subject to an application under s 339 when the value of the wife's contribution will be put in issue. Are such contributions to be accorded the same recognition as financial contributions to the acquisition of property?

9.7 A TRANSFER OF ASSETS AS A PREFERENCE

It is arguable that a spouse in whose favour a property adjustment order has been made is creditor for the purposes of ss 382 and 383 of the Insolvency Act 1986 so that a transaction in her favour might be a preference within s 340. In *Jackson v Bell*,[98] Sir Andrew Morritt V-C in the Court of Appeal said that there was substance in this point which, with other points, justified granting leave to appeal. However, that appeal does not seem to have proceeded.

---

[97] [2001] 1 AC 596.   [98] [2001] EWCA Civ 387.

9.8 BANKRUPTCY, PENSIONS, AND ORDERS RELATING TO PENSIONS

9.8.1 Bankruptcy petitions presented before 29 May 2000

In Chapter 6, it was noted that in relation to bankruptcy petitions presented before 29 May 2000 the rights to sums payable in the future under a pension policy or scheme to the bankrupt vested in the trustee in bankruptcy.[99] This applied even though the relevant sums whether in the form of an annuity or a lump sum payment did not become payable until the bankrupt's retirement after his discharge from bankruptcy. Moreover, prior to the Pensions Act 1995, which introduced 'earmarking', the courts had no special power under the Matrimonial Causes Act 1973 to deal with future pension rights on divorce and there was no power to transfer pension benefits between spouses on divorce. They could only attempt to make provision for the spouse of a person entitled to future payments under a pension scheme by exercising their general powers to order financial provision or property adjustment.

The provisions relating to 'earmarking' orders, now known as 'attachment orders', are to be found in ss 25B to 25D of the Matrimonial Causes Act 1973. Such an order directs that part or all of any lump sum or pension becoming payable on the retirement of one spouse be paid to the other spouse. In *T v T (Financial Relief: Pensions)*,[100] Singer J rejected the argument that earmarking orders against pension providers were distinct from the other and pre-existing orders that can be made under s 23. Thus the court's power of variation in relation to orders for periodical payments applies to such an order directed to pension providers as it does to a conventional order against the paying spouse. Moreover, he observed that:

the newly inserted paragraph represented by s 31(2)(dd) of the 1973 Act upon a variation application gives the court complete control over any deferred lump sum order that includes provision made by virtue of either s 25B(4) or s 25C. Therefore the obligation to pay a lump sum in future may, before it takes effect, be varied in amount (obviously up as well as down), discharged or temporarily suspended.[101]

In these circumstances it seems difficult, at first sight, to see how a earmarking order in respect of a lump sum payment could be regarded as taking effect as an immediate assignment which might be effective against the trustee in bankruptcy of the spouse entitled to the pension.

In *Roberts v Nunn*,[102] the court had to consider the effect of the bankruptcy of the husband on what had been a common form of order where it was sought to achieve a 'clean break'. In that case a consent order had been made in 1994

---

[99] Para 6.5.4 above.   [100] [1998] 1 FLR 1072, 1085.

[101] ibid 1089. Para (dd) reads 'any order made by virtue of s 23(3)(c) (lump sums) which includes provision made by virtue of (i) s 25B(4) or (ii) s 25C (provision in respect of pension rights)'.

[102] [2004] All ER (D) 233, 26 January 2004.

which provided for the division of the proceeds of the matrimonial home and for nominal maintenance until the receipt by the husband of benefits under his pension policies. It then provided that on 10 August 2000, or such other date or dates as the husband elected to take the benefit under the pension policies, he would pay to the wife (a) one half of the lump sum received by him under each of the pension policies, and (b) thereafter pay to her an annual sum equivalent to one half of the annual payment or payments due to him under each of the policies. The husband was made bankrupt in September 1996 and his trustee in bankruptcy received tax free lump sums payable in respect of the pension policies and held one half of those sums pending determination of the question whether the former wife's contingent right to the half share of the pension lump sums was property which had vested in the trustee at the commencement of the former husband's bankruptcy under s 283(1) of the Insolvency Act 1986.

Mr Nicholas Strauss QC, sitting as a deputy judge of the High Court, held that the contingent right to the half share in the fund created by payment of the pension lump sums was not part of the bankrupt's estate, by virtue of s 283(5) which provides that property comprised in the bankrupt's estate is so comprised 'subject to the rights of any [other] person whether as a secured creditor of the bankrupt or otherwise in relation thereto'. The deputy judge said that in 'relation to the provision for payment of one half of the lump sums the order was intended to have immediate effect as an assignment and, if it had that effect, the assignor became a bare trustee to hold one half of the fund when received and the assignee thereby acquired security for the payment of the lump sum'.[103]

However, he went on to hold that the court had no jurisdiction to make an order for payment of the lump sums in any form which created an equitable interest or security. Section 23(1)(b) gives the court an express power to secure periodical payments, but the only similar powers in relation to lump sum orders are those set out in s 23(1)(f) and (3)(c), that is in cases involving children and where payment by instalments is ordered. Neither applied in the case before him. The words 'without prejudice to the generality' in s 23(3) did not assist because there is no general power earlier in the section to order security. This meant that if the husband had not been made bankrupt he would have been entitled to have the order set aside, at least to the extent that it was invalid. An application by the husband's trustee in bankruptcy to have the order set aside would 'inevitably succeed' thereby reversing any finding that the former wife was entitled to a half share pending the setting aside of the order. Accordingly, needless expense would be incurred if the former wife were to succeed.[104]

---

[103] Following *Mountney v Treharne* [2003] Ch 135. Insofar as the order referred to the lump sums payable under the policies it referred to an identifiable fund.

[104] The judge reached his decision without enthusiasm and thought that the absence of a power to order security for lump sum payable in the future was due to an oversight. Moreover, it could be avoided by, eg providing for £1 to be paid immediately on receipt and the balance on the following day or vice versa: para [11].

9.8.2 Bankruptcy petitions presented on or after 29 May 2000

In relation to bankruptcy petitions presented on or after 29 May 2000, approved pension arrangements are excluded from a bankrupt's estate and will not vest in the trustee in bankruptcy.[105] The Act also contains provision for rights under unapproved pension arrangements to be excluded from the bankrupt's estate by agreement or by an order of the court.[106] This new protection for the pension rights might provide an incentive for an individual to pay substantial sums into pension arrangements where they would be protected from the claims of his creditors on his bankruptcy. Accordingly, provision is made for a trustee in bankruptcy to recover excessive contributions to a pension scheme in certain circumstances.[107] These provisions came into force on 6 April 2002.[108]

Another important change is that where a petition for divorce or nullity is filed on or after 1 December 2000, the court will be able to make a pension sharing order under the provisions added to the Matrimonial Causes Act 1973 by the Welfare Reform and Pensions Act 1999.[109] Section 21A(1) of the 1973 Act provides that a pension sharing order is one which provides that a party's shareable rights under a specified pension arrangement or shareable state scheme rights be subject to pension sharing for the benefit of the other party and specifies the percentage value to be transferred. This means that the spouse in whose favour the order is made will acquire part of the pension rights of the other spouse under the pension arrangement either by becoming a member of that scheme or by having the specified percentage transferred into his or her own pension scheme. The share to be transferred must be expressed in percentage rather than cash terms. The Welfare Reform and Pensions Act 1999 provides that on the day on which the order takes effect, the transferor's shareable rights under the relevant arrangement becomes subject to a debit of the appropriate amount, and the transferee becomes entitled to a credit of that amount as against the person responsible for that arrangement.[110]

A pension sharing order is obviously intended to have immediate effect in transferring a percentage of one spouse's pension rights to the other and in that respect is not directly affected by the subsequent bankruptcy of the transferor spouse. However, where the pension arrangement which was the subject of the pension sharing order has benefited from excessive contributions, the trustee in bankruptcy of the transferor spouse may in certain circumstances recover an appropriate amount in respect of what are called 'unfair contributions' on the

---

[105] Welfare Reform and Pensions Act 1999, s 11 and SI 2000/1382. See ch 6.

[106] Section 12. Under s 14 the persons responsible for the pension scheme are no longer able to forfeit pension rights on a member's bankruptcy.   [107] Section 15. See para 9.9 below.

[108] SI 2002/153.   [109] See Matrimonial Causes Act 1973, ss 21A and 24B–24D.

[110] Section 29(1).

basis that the pension sharing order was a transaction at an undervalue within s 339, or a preference under s 340 of the Insolvency Act 1986.[111]

9.9 RECOVERY OF EXCESSIVE PENSION CONTRIBUTIONS

9.9.1 The power to make recovery orders

Where an individual who is adjudged bankrupt has rights under an approved pension arrangement, or excluded rights under an unapproved pension arrangements, these rights will not vest in his trustee in bankruptcy.[112] However, if the trustee considers that the bankrupt's contributions to a pension arrangement were excessive he may apply to the court for an order under s 342A of the Insolvency Act 1986.[113] The court may make such order as it thinks fit for restoring the position to what it would have been had the excessive contributions not been made if it is satisfied on two matters. First, that the rights under the arrangement are to any extent, and whether directly or indirectly, the fruits of relevant contributions, that is contributions which have at any time been made by or on behalf of the individual. Secondly, that the making of the excessive contributions has unfairly prejudiced the individual's creditors.[114]

In determining whether it is satisfied that contributions have unfairly prejudiced the individual's creditors the court must consider two matters in particular. First, it must consider whether any of the contributions were made for the purpose of putting assets beyond the reach of the individual's creditors or any of them. It is suggested that it will be relevant to refer to the case law in relation to a similar requirement in s 423 of the Insolvency Act considered earlier.[115] Secondly, it must consider whether the total amount of any contributions (i) made by or on behalf of the individual to pension arrangements, and (ii) represented (whether directly or indirectly) by rights under approved pension arrangements or excluded rights under unapproved pension arrangements, is an amount which is excessive in view of the individual's circumstances

---

[111] See para 9.9.3 below.

[112] See ch 6. For the meaning of 'approved pension arrangement' and 'unapproved pension arrangement' see respectively ss 11 and 12 of the Welfare Reform and Pensions Act 1999. For the purposes of the recovery provisions (ss 342A, 342B, and 342C) rights of an individual under an unapproved pension arrangement are excluded rights if they are rights which are excluded from his estate by virtue of regulations under s 12 of the Welfare Reform and Pensions Act 1999.

[113] By s 15 of the Welfare Reform and Pensions Act 1999 the present form of ss 342A–342C of the Insolvency Act 1986 replaced the form inserted by the Pensions Act 1995, s 95(1). They came into force 6 April 2002. The person responsible for a pension arrangement under which a bankrupt has or has had rights must, on the bankrupt's trustee in bankruptcy making a written request, provide the trustee with such information about the arrangement and rights as the trustee may reasonably require for, or in connection with, the making of applications under s 342A: s 342C(1).

[114] IA 1986, s 342A(1), (2), and (5).   [115] See para 9.3.4 above.

when those contributions were made.[116] If these requirements are satisfied the court has a discretion to make an order.

9.9.2 Contents of an order under s 342A

If the court decides to make an order under s 342A restoring the position to what it would have been had the excessive contributions not been made, the order may include provision on a number of matters.[117] First, it may include provision requiring the person responsible for the pension arrangement to pay an amount to the individual's trustee in bankruptcy.[118] Where an order requires the person responsible for the arrangement to pay a sum to the trustee in bankruptcy, then that sum is comprised in the bankrupt's estate.[119] Secondly, it may provide for adjusting the liabilities of the pension arrangement in respect of the individual bankrupt and this includes reducing the amount of any benefit or future benefit to which the individual is entitled under the arrangement. Thirdly, it may provide for adjusting any liabilities of the arrangement in respect of any other person that derive, directly or indirectly, from rights of the individual bankrupt under the arrangement. This again includes in particular reducing the amount of any benefit or future benefit to which that person is entitled under the arrangement. However, this does not include reducing the liabilities of the arrangement in respect of a person which result from giving effect to a pension sharing order or pension sharing agreement within s 28(1) of the Welfare Reform and Pensions Act 1999.[120] The maximum amount which the person responsible for a pension arrangement may be required to pay by an order under s 342A is the lesser of:

(a) the amount of the excessive contributions, and
(b) the value of the individual's rights under the arrangement (if the arrangement is an approved pension arrangement) or of his excluded rights under the arrangement (if the arrangement is an unapproved pension arrangement).[121]

An order under s 342A which requires the person responsible for an arrangement to pay an amount ('the restoration amount') to the individual's trustee in bankruptcy must provide for the liabilities of the arrangement to be correspondingly reduced.[122] An order under s 342A in respect of a pension arrangement is binding on the person responsible for the arrangement and overrides

---

[116] IA 1986, s 342A(6).   [117] IA 1986, s 342B(1), (2), and (3).

[118] The persons responsible for a pension arrangement are (a) the trustees, managers or provider of the arrangement, or (b) the person having functions in relation to the arrangement corresponding to those of a trustee, manager or provider: s 342C(6).   [119] IA 1986, s 342C(3).

[120] IA 1986, s 342B(3). Recovery from a former spouse of the bankrupt is dealt with in ss 342D to 342F considered in para 9.9.3 below.   [121] IA 1986, s 342B(4).

[122] IA 1986, s 342B(5).

provisions of the arrangement to the extent that they conflict with the provisions of the order.[123]

9.9.3 Excessive contributions and pension sharing

Where a pension sharing order has previously been made against an individual bankrupt then his or her pension entitlement will have been reduced by the debit in favour of his or her former spouse.[124] Where the bankrupt's contributions to the pension arrangement are considered to have been excessive then the trustee in bankruptcy may in certain circumstances reach the pension share of the bankrupt's former spouse to recover an appropriate proportion of excessive contributions.

First, it is provided that where the court is satisfied that the value of the rights under the pension arrangement is less than it would otherwise have been as a result of the rights of the individual under the arrangement having at any time become subject to a debit giving effect to a pension sharing order, then any relevant contributions which were represented by the rights which became subject to the debit are to be taken to be contributions of which the rights under the arrangement are the fruits. Secondly, where the relevant contributions represented by the rights under the arrangement are not all excessive contributions, relevant contributions which are represented by the rights under the arrangement not subject to a debit are to be treated as excessive contributions before any which are subject to a debit.[125] The effect of these provisions is that the amount of the excessive contributions will be recovered first from the bankrupt's remaining share of the pension arrangement. Only if it is not sufficient to enable a full recovery of the excessive contributions will the trustee be entitled to seek recovery from the share transferred to the bankrupt's former spouse. If all the contributions are found to be excessive, then recovery of the appropriate proportion may in any event be sought from the share transferred to the bankrupt's former spouse. It is not envisaged that the relative shares of the bankrupt and his or her spouse under the pension sharing order will be altered, so if the latter was awarded a one third share of the pension rights then that cannot be altered though its value may be reduced to the extent that contributions giving rise to those rights are found to be excessive contributions.

---

[123] IA 1986, s 342B(7). A court exercising its powers under s 342A is not affected by certain statutory provisions preventing assignment and the making of orders that restrain a person from receiving anything which he is prevented from assigning or by any corresponding provision: s 342C(2).   [124] See ch 8 and para 9.8.2, above.

[125] IA 1986, s 342A(3) and (4). As noted above s 342B(1) provides that an order under s 342A may include a provision adjusting any liabilities of the arrangement in respect of any person other than the bankrupt that derive from the bankrupt's rights under the arrangement. Section 342B(3)provides that this does not include liabilities in respect of a person which result from giving effect to a pension sharing order or agreement.

In order to seek recovery in respect of such excessive contributions as against the entitlement of the bankrupt's former spouse under the share of the bankrupt's pension transferred to him or her under a pension order sharing order or agreement, a trustee in bankruptcy may resort to the provisions of s 339 relating to transactions at an undervalue or s 340 relating to preferences.

For the purposes of an application under s 339 a pension sharing transaction is to be taken to be a transaction, entered into by the transferor with the transferee, by which the appropriate amount is transferred by the transferor to the transferee. A 'pension sharing transaction' means a pension sharing order or agreement within s 28(1) of the Welfare Reform and Pensions Act 1999. The 'transferee' means the person for whose benefit the transaction is made and the 'transferor' means the person to whose rights the transaction relates. Such a pension sharing transaction is to be capable of being a transaction entered into at an undervalue only so far as it is a transfer of so much of the appropriate amount as is recoverable. The 'appropriate amount' means the appropriate amount in relation to that transaction for the purposes of s 29(1) of the 1999 Act which is concerned with the creation of pension credits and debits.[126]

For the purposes of s 340, a pension sharing transaction is to be taken to be something (namely a transfer of the appropriate amount to the transferee) done by the transferor. It is to be capable of being a preference given to the transferee only so far as it is a transfer of so much of the appropriate amount as is recoverable.[127]

On an application under ss 339 or 340 any question as to whether, or the extent to which, the appropriate amount in the case of a pension sharing transaction is recoverable is to be determined as provided in s 342D.

First, the court must determine the extent (if any) to which the transferor's rights under the shared arrangement at the time of the transaction appear to have been (whether directly or indirectly) the fruits of contributions (personal contributions) which the transferor has at any time made on his or her own behalf or which have at any time been made on the transferor's behalf to the shared arrangement or any other pension arrangement.[128]

Secondly, where it appears that those rights were to any extent the fruits of personal contributions, the court must then determine the extent (if any) to which those rights appear to have been the fruits of personal contributions whose making unfairly prejudiced the transferor's creditors.[129] Such contributions are referred to as 'the unfair contributions' rather than 'excessive contributions'. In making this determination the court must consider in particular:

(a) whether any of the personal contributions were made for the purpose of putting assets beyond the reach of the transferor's creditors or any of them, and

---

[126] IA 1986, s 342D(1) and (9). [127] IA 1986, s 342D(2) and (9).
[128] IA 1986, s 342D(4). [129] IA 1986, s 342D(5).

(b) whether the total amount of any personal contributions represented, at the time the pension sharing transaction was made, by rights under pension arrangements is an amount which is excessive in view of the transferor's circumstances when those contributions were made.[130]

Thirdly, if it appears to the court that the extent to which those rights were the fruits of the unfair contributions is such that the transfer of the appropriate amount to the bankrupt's former spouse could have been made out of rights under the shared arrangement which were not the fruits of the unfair contributions, then the appropriate amount is not recoverable.[131] If it appears to the court that the transfer of the appropriate amount to the bankrupt's former spouse could not have been wholly made out of rights which were not the fruits of unfair contributions, then the appropriate amount is recoverable to the extent to which it appears to the court that the transfer could not have been so made.[132]

Sections 342E and 342F apply where the court is making an order under ss 339 or 340 in a case where (a) the transaction or preference is, or is any part of, a pension sharing transaction, and (b) the transferee has rights under a pension arrangement ('the destination arrangement') that are derived, directly or indirectly, from the pension sharing transaction.[133] A 'destination arrangement' may be either the shared arrangement where the effect of the pension sharing is that the bankrupt's former spouse became a member of the bankrupt's pension arrangement, or any other pension arrangement where the pension sharing took the form of a transfer of the allocated percentage into the former spouse's own scheme. Without prejudice to the generality of s 339(2), s 340(2) or of s 342 the order may include provision on a number of matters.[134] First, it may include a provision requiring the person responsible for the destination arrangement to pay an amount to the transferor's trustee in bankruptcy. Secondly it may include a provision adjusting the liabilities of the destination arrangement in respect of the transferee, or in respect of any other person that derive, directly or indirectly, from the rights of the transferee under the destination arrangement. This includes reducing the amount of any benefit or future benefit to which that person is entitled under the arrangement.[135] It may also provide for the costs of persons responsible for affected pension arrangements incurred in complying with obligations to provide information imposed by s 342F or giving effect to an order.[136]

The maximum amount which the person responsible for the destination arrangement may be required to pay by the order is the smallest of:

(a) so much of the appropriate amount as is recoverable,
(b) so much (if any) of the amount of the unfair contributions as is not recoverable by way of an order under s 342A containing a provision requiring

---

[130] IA 1986, s 342D(8).   [131] IA 1986, s 342D(6).   [132] IA 1986, s 342D(7).
[133] IA 1986, s 342E(1).   [134] IA 1986, s 342E(2).   [135] IA 1986, s 342E(3).
[136] For the obligations to provide information, see s 342F(1), (2), and (3).

the person responsible for the arrangement to pay an amount to the bankrupt's trustee, and

(c) the value of the transferee's rights under the destination arrangement so far as they are derived, directly or indirectly, from the pension sharing transaction.[137]

If the order requires the person responsible for the destination arrangement to pay an amount to the transferor's trustee in bankruptcy it must provide for the liabilities of the arrangement to be correspondingly reduced.[138] An order is binding on the person responsible for the destination arrangement and over-rides provisions of the destination arrangement to the extent that they conflict with the provisions of the order.[139] Provisions or enactments preventing the assignment of pension rights do not apply to a court exercising its powers under ss 339 or 340.[140]

---

[137] IA 1986, s 342E(4).   [138] IA 1986, s 342E(5).   [139] IA 1986, s 342E(7).
[140] IA 1986, s 342F(5).

10

INSOLVENCY AND THE ENFORCEMENT OF ORDERS FOR FINANCIAL PROVISION

10.1 EFFECT OF INSOLVENCY ON THE ENFORCEMENT OF ORDERS FOR FINANCIAL PROVISION AND PROPERTY ADJUSTMENT

The bankruptcy of a person against whom an order for financial provision or property adjustment has been made may create serious difficulties for the person in whose favour such an order has been made. An order for periodical payments involves a continuing obligation on the part of the person against whom it is made with the continuing risk of insolvency and bankruptcy on his part and the position is often aggravated by the accumulation of arrears. The obligations imposed by other forms of provision are normally expected to be discharged within a short time of the making of the order by the provision of security, the payment of a lump sum, or the transfer or settlement of property as the case may be, but the person against whom such orders are made may become bankrupt before they have been completed or become effective.

On the other hand, while the bankruptcy of the person against whom an order is made will generally be viewed with apprehension by the intended recipient, the latter may in some cases wish to resort to bankruptcy as a means of enforcement.

The threat of bankruptcy may be thought to be a potent weapon against a former spouse who is resorting to every possible means to avoid payment of a lump sum or the transfer of property. This chapter will also consider the extent to which bankruptcy remains a weapon against a recalcitrant former spouse.

10.2 PERIODICAL PAYMENTS

It was noted in Chapter 8 that an order for periodical payments can be made and continue to have effect, notwithstanding the bankruptcy of the spouse against whom it is made.[1] In the event of default, enforcement can only be against the bankrupt's income which he retains subject to an income payments order.[2]

Debts representing arrears of maintenance have been held to be excluded from proof in bankruptcy.[3] An order for periodical payments is not a final judgment and it may be varied or discharged by the court so that it is not capable of valuation. Even arrears of periodical payments cannot be recovered as an ordinary debt for they are not enforceable as of right. The court has a discretion and may allow time to pay, or allow payment by instalments, and may even remit arrears in whole or in part.[4] On the other hand, while claims under such orders are not provable in bankruptcy they are enforceable in other ways notwithstanding the bankruptcy of the person against whom they are made, and liability under such orders continues notwithstanding discharge from bankruptcy.[5]

A husband's obligation to make payments under a maintenance agreement comes to an end on his bankruptcy. However, a wife may prove in the bankruptcy of her husband for the value of the payments due to her under a covenant by him in a separation deed, but she cannot take proceedings against him for arrears, whether they accrued before or after the bankruptcy, even though she has elected not to prove.[6]

10.3 LUMP SUM PAYMENTS

If a spouse against whom an order for payment of a lump sum is made becomes bankrupt before complying with the order, then enforcement will no longer be possible against the capital assets of the bankrupt as they will have vested in his

---

[1] See para 8.3.

[2] It is likely that any after-acquired property will be claimed by the trustee in bankruptcy under s 307 during the period of the bankruptcy. See para 6.5.12

[3] *Linton v Linton* (1885) 15 QBD 239; *Re Henderson* (1888) 20 QBD 508. See Cmnd 8558, para 1296.   [4] *Robins v Robins* [1907] 2 KB 13; *Kerr v Kerr* [1897] 2 QB 439.

[5] See Rimer J in *Re Bradley-Hole* [1995] 2 BCLC 163, 185, and Miller, 'Financial Provision and Insolvency' [1999] Private Client Business 381, 382.   [6] *Victor v Victor* [1912] 1 KB 247.

trustee in bankruptcy. By virtue of r 12.3 of the Insolvency Rules 1986, a lump sum payment is not a debt provable in bankruptcy. In *Re G (Children Act 1989, Schedule 1)*, Singer J said:[7]

Whatever the rationale for the inclusion of, for present purposes, a lump sum order, in the category of debts not provable in bankruptcy, the consequence of creating a debt which is not provable in bankruptcy is that the creditor is not precluded by s 285(3) from any remedies which they may find would be effective against the person of the bankrupt, or indeed against the bankrupt's after-acquired property before it is claimed by the trustee, or indeed against the bankrupt's future income.

The person in whose favour an order is made may therefore seek to enforce payment out of the bankrupt's income though it must be borne in mind that the trustee in bankruptcy may seek an income payments order under s 310 of the Insolvency Act 1986. The difficulties of enforcement were highlighted in *Woodley v Woodley (No 2)*[8] and the problems were vividly illustrated by the litigation culminating in the Court of Appeal decision in *Mubarak v Mubarak*.[9] In that case the wife in whose favour the order for a lump sum payment of £4,875,000 was made, sought, unsuccessfully, to enforce payment by means of a judgment summons under the Debtors Act 1869. Jacob J said:[10]

Since the Debtors Act 1869, a Victorian Act, many more remedies have been devised which enable creditors—that would include people entitled to payments under orders made in the Family Division—to obtain their money in one way or another. A freezing order, with all the disclosure that can be obtained, is an extremely powerful weapon. The remedies available extend to constructive trusts and the obtaining of information from bankers.

However, it should be remembered that a lump sum order is not discharged on bankruptcy and enforcement may become possible at a later date.

10.4 PROPERTY ADJUSTMENT ORDERS

Since the property of the bankrupt vests in his trustee in bankruptcy, enforcement of an order for the transfer or settlement of property against specific property will no longer be possible. The precise time at which such an order became effective is therefore crucial and was considered in Chapter 8.[11] An order made against a party to a marriage before the presentation of a bankruptcy petition against him or her will be effective provided the decree nisi of divorce has been made absolute. An order made after the presentation of a bankruptcy petition but before the making of a bankruptcy order will be void without the consent or ratification of the court under s 284 of the Insolvency Act 1986.[12]

---

[7] [1996] 2 FLR 171, 176.   [8] [1993] 2 FLR 477.   [9] [2001] 1 FLR 698.
[10] ibid 713.   [11] Para 8.6.2.   [12] Para 8.6.3.

10.5 BANKRUPTCY AS A MEANS OF ENFORCEMENT IN FAMILY PROCEEDINGS

10.5.1 Availability as a means of enforcement

The possible use of bankruptcy as a means of enforcement has arisen in relation to an order for the payment of a lump sum.[13] When the divorce court was given power to order payment of a lump sum in 1963, one of the perceived advantages was the fact that it could be enforced by bankruptcy proceedings.[14] The Insolvency Act 1986 provides that discharge from bankruptcy does not release the bankrupt from any bankruptcy debt which arises under any order made in family proceedings.[15] More significantly for the question of enforcement, r 12.3 of the Insolvency Rules 1986 provides that any obligation 'arising under an order made in family proceedings' or under a maintenance assessment or calculation made under the Child Support Act is not provable in bankruptcy. Reservations about the validity of r 12.3 were expressed in *Woodley v Woodley,*[16] but the Court of Appeal proceeded on the basis that r 12.3 was valid and its validity was confirmed by the Court of Appeal in *Woodley v Woodley (No 2).*[17]

Although it seemed that a wife could no longer resort to bankruptcy as a weapon to enforce payment of a lump sum to her, in *Russell v Russell,*[18] Chadwick J held that an order for a lump sum payment in favour of a wife could form the basis of a petition for bankruptcy against her husband even though it did not give rise to a debt provable in his bankruptcy. There was no doubt that the wife was a creditor for the purposes of s 264(1) of the Insolvency Act 1986 and so was a person entitled to present a bankruptcy petition against the husband, provided the other requirements of Pt IX of that Act were satisfied. He went on to say that generally there would be little purpose in making a bankruptcy order on the petition of a wife in such a case because the trustee would have no functions to perform in relation to the wife and would be in no position to distribute any part of the estate to her. Indeed, the effect of the order would be to postpone the wife to the other creditors whose debts could be proved in bankruptcy. It would, therefore, not usually be appropriate to make a bankruptcy order in such cases unless there were special circumstances.

In *Levy v Legal Services Commission,*[19] the Court of Appeal agreed with Chadwick J in *Russell v Russell* that, since the Act plainly allows a creditor with

---

[13] See further Miller 'Bankruptcy as a Means of Enforcement in Family Proceedings' [2002] 32 Fam Law 21 from which material has been drawn.

[14] Report on *Financial Provision in Matrimonial Proceedings*, Law Com No 25 (1969), para 9. See also Danckwerts LJ in *Curtis v Curtis* [1969] 1 WLR 422, 429 and the Report of the Committee on 'Insolvency Law and Practice' (The Cork Report) (Cmnd 8558, 1982), para 235 where the importance of the court's investigative powers in bankruptcy was stressed.

[15] IA 1986, s 281(5).   [16] [1992] FLR 417, 422–3.   [17] [1993] 2 FLR 477, 485.
[18] [1998] 1 FLR 936.   [19] [2000] 1 FLR 435.

a non-provable debt to present a bankruptcy petition based upon that debt, it must follow that the court had jurisdiction under the Act to make a bankruptcy order on such a petition. However, Jonathan Parker LJ said that 'a bankruptcy order made on a petition which is based on a non-provable debt is an anomaly, since . . . the trustee has, by definition, no functions to perform in relation to the petitioner'.[20] Only in special circumstances would a bankruptcy order be made. Where there is no realistic prospect of a bankruptcy order being made, the statutory demand may be set aside as in *Levy*.

10.5.2 Orders for costs

It may also be necessary to consider whether bankruptcy can be used as a means of enforcement in relation to an order for costs made in proceedings for ancillary relief. In *Levy v Legal Services Commission*,[21] Jonathan Parker LJ could see 'no scope whatever for construing the words "any obligation arising under an order made in family proceedings" . . . in r 12.3(2)(a) as excluding a particular type of obligation arising under an order made in family proceedings'.[22] He stressed the word 'any' and went on to say that there was much to be said for the view that it was logical that they should be treated in the same way as lump sum orders. There was risk that the overall balance between the parties intended to be reflected in the order for financial provision would be significantly distorted if it was necessary for the party in whose favour the order had been made to prove in the bankruptcy of the other party for the costs of the proceedings.[23]

In *Levy v Legal Services Commission*, the Legal Services Commission (then known as the Legal Aid Board) had itself served a statutory demand on the husband seeking payment of the sum due under an order for costs in favour of the wife. It was not disputed that where an order is made for payment of costs to an assisted person, the Legal Services Commission is entitled to serve a statutory demand in its own name and to present a bankruptcy petition based upon it.[24] However, this was of no avail unless there were special circumstances justifying the making of a bankruptcy order.

10.5.3 Special circumstances

Since the court will not exercise its jurisdiction to make a bankruptcy order on the basis of a debt, such as a lump sum payment, which is not provable, it is necessary to consider what will amount to special circumstances for this purpose.

---

[20] ibid 443.
[21] [2000] 1 FLR 435, approving of the view of Sir John Vinelott in *Re A Debtor, JP v A Debtor* [1999] 1 FLR 926, 935. [22] At p 442.
[23] ibid.
[24] Civil Legal Aid (General) Regulations 1989, reg 91(1)(b). In *Re A Debtor* [1998] 4 All ER 779, Jonathan Parker J had held that the Legal Aid Board had power under reg 91(2) to authorize the service of a statutory demand by a wife who was an assisted person in whose favour an order for costs had been made against her husband in proceedings for ancillary relief.

In *Russell v Russell*,[25] Chadwick J identified three special circumstances in that case, all, in essence, based on misconduct of the debtor. The husband had been found to be less than frank to the court in disclosing particulars of his income and capital; he had failed to pay the costs ordered in other proceedings; and he had failed to pay the costs which had been taxed in the matrimonial proceedings. In *Wheatley v Wheatley*,[26] the making of a bankruptcy order on the petition of a wife was held to be justified on the basis of the husband's failure to pay £47,500 to the wife in return for her share in the matrimonial home and in a nursing home business, the presence of other creditors, and the fact that the trustee in bankruptcy would have wider powers than the wife to recover assets for distribution.

In *Levy v Legal Services Commission*,[27] Jonathan Parker LJ found it difficult to see why misconduct by the debtor should be relevant in this context. However badly or irresponsibly the debtor may have behaved, the position still remains that the petitioning creditor has no financial interest in the bankruptcy process. Nor in his judgment, did the failure or refusal to pay other debts (whether provable or non-provable) constitute a 'special circumstance' in this context. If the debts are non-provable, then non-payment of them is a matter outside the bankruptcy regime; if they are provable, then the creditor concerned has his remedy.

He found it extremely difficult to foresee the wholly exceptional cases in which the court, in its discretion, would be persuaded to exercise the jurisdiction which he had to accept existed, but which he considered to be wholly anomalous.[28] He also rejected the argument that a petitioning creditor with a non-provable debt might nevertheless have a legitimate interest in initiating a bankruptcy if there is a prospect of a surplus being available after all proving creditors are paid in full. It would be an abuse of the bankruptcy process to have recourse to it for that purpose.[29]

10.5.4 Judicial criticism

The present position is that in practice bankruptcy is unlikely to be available as a means of enforcement of an order for payment of a lump sum. There has been judicial criticism of the present position and of r 12.3 on a number of occasions. In *Woodley v Woodley (No 2)*,[30] Balcombe LJ invited the Insolvency Rules Committee to consider whether a lump sum order made in family proceedings should be provable in bankruptcy, as was the case before the Insolvency Rules 1986 came into force. This criticism was endorsed by Sir Donald Nicholls V-C

---

[25] [1998] 1 FLR 936, 942–3.   [26] [1999] 2 FLR 205.   [27] [2001] 1 FLR 435, 444.

[28] He mentioned the possibility of a case where a supporting creditor with a provable debt obtains a change of carriage order pursuant to r 6.31.   [29] ibid 445.

[30] [1993] 2 FLR 477, 488–9.

in *Re Mordant*[31] and more recently in *Cartwright v Cartwright (No 2)*[32] Arden LJ repeated the invitation made by Balcombe LJ in *Woodley v Woodley (No 2)* for the position to be reconsidered. She said that the present position was 'an anomaly for which there is no obvious policy justification'.

In *Woodley v Woodley (No 2)*,[33] Balcombe LJ thought that the change brought about by r 12.3 might have been due to the fact that it was considered that as a debt arising from an order made in family proceedings is not released upon discharge of the bankrupt,[34] therefore it should not be provable. However, he pointed out that there is no necessary or logical link between a debt being provable in bankruptcy and its release on discharge. Thus 'a liability to pay damages in respect of personal injuries is a provable debt in bankruptcy, but is not released on discharge from bankruptcy.[35] Any link between provability and release was, in his view, a matter of policy and he could see 'good policy grounds for saying that a lump sum order made in family proceedings should (like damages for personal injuries) be both provable in bankruptcy and yet not released on discharge'.

The decision of the Court of Appeal in *Levy* is indicative of a different view of the appropriateness of bankruptcy in this context.[36] It may be that the use of bankruptcy as a means of enforcement may not sit easily with the principles that may be thought to underlie the law of bankruptcy, though it is understandable that a frustrated judgment creditor should turn to bankruptcy in the apparent absence of any other effective means of enforcement of an order against an obstructive and determined debtor.

10.6 FOREIGN ORDERS

10.6.1 The general position

Where a spouse has obtained an order against the other spouse in an overseas jurisdiction for payment of a capital sum he or she may seek to enforce payment in England and Wales by serving a statutory demand to be followed by a petition for bankruptcy in the event of default. It then becomes necessary to consider whether the foreign debt is provable in bankruptcy and this depends on the scope of r 12.3 of the Insolvency Rules 1986 which, as noted earlier, excludes any obligation 'arising under an order made in family proceedings'. This in turn has made it necessary to consider the meaning of 'family proceedings' for this purpose.

---

[31] [1996] 1 FLR 334, 338. [32] [2002] 2 FLR 610, 615, para [21].
[33] [1993] 2 FLR 477, 488–9. [34] IA 1986, s 281(5)(b). [35] IA 1986, s 281(5)(a).
[36] See also the view of Mr Registrar James in *Wehmeyer v Wehmeyer* [2001] 2 FLR 84, 87, referred to in para 10.6 below, that a bankruptcy petition is not an enforcement procedure.

The definition of 'family proceedings' is to be found in s 281(8) of the Insolvency Act 1986 which provides:[37]

"family proceedings" means—

(a) proceedings within the meaning of the Magistrates Courts Act 1980 and any proceedings which would be such proceedings but for section 65(1)(ii) of that Act (proceedings for variation of order for periodical payments), and

(b) family proceedings within the meaning of Part V of the Matrimonial and Family Proceedings Act 1984.

There are therefore two possible statutory provisions under which a foreign order may be regarded as made in 'family proceedings' and therefore excluded from proof in bankruptcy by r 12.3.

10.6.2 The Magistrates' Courts Act 1980

Section 65(1) of the Magistrates' Courts Act 1980 provides that 'family proceedings' means proceedings under a number of listed statutory provisions. Two of the listed provisions may be especially relevant in the present context, namely: '(f) Part I of the Maintenance Orders (Reciprocal Enforcement) Act 1972;' and '(m) Part I of the Civil Jurisdiction and Judgments Act 1982, so far as that Part relates to the recognition or enforcement of maintenance orders...'

Part I of the 1972 Act makes provision for the reciprocal enforcement of maintenance orders made in the United Kingdom and in countries which have been designated by Order in Council as 'reciprocating' for the purpose of the Act. An order made in a reciprocating country may be registered in a court in England and Wales, and it may then be enforced as if it had been made by the court of registration. A 'maintenance order' for this purpose includes an order 'which provides for the payment of a lump sum or the making of periodical payments towards the maintenance of any person, ...'.[38] Under the 1982 Act a maintenance order made in one contracting state may be registered in the appropriate court of another contracting state and is then of the same force and effect and enforceable in the same way as if it had been originally made by that court. However, 'maintenance' must be distinguished from 'matters relating to matrimonial property' and the latter are excluded from the scope of the Act. This is important in relation to orders providing for capital payments as it has been held by the European Court that a court in another member state considering an application for the enforcement of an order made under the Matrimonial Causes Act 1973 must distinguish between those aspects of an order which relate to rights of property arising out of a matrimonial relationship and those which relate to maintenance, 'having regard in each particular case to the specific aim of the decision rendered'.[39]

---

[37] Definition substituted by the Children Act 1989, s 92(11), Sch 11, Pt II, para 11(2).

[38] Section 21(1) as amended by the Civil Jurisdiction and Judgments Act 1982, Sch 11, para 4.

[39] *Van den Boogaard v Laumen* [1997] QB 759, 784.

Section 65(1) then goes on to provide two exceptions. First paragraph (i) provides that the term 'family proceedings' does not include proceedings for the enforcement of any order made, confirmed, or registered under any of the listed enactments.[40] This was considered in *Wehmeyer v Wehmeyer*[41] where the wife had presented a petition in bankruptcy against her former husband on the basis of a maintenance order made in Germany and registered in the High Court. The maintenance order fell within the definition of family proceedings under s 65(1)(m) of the Magistrates' Courts Act 1980 and was therefore within r 12.3(2)(a) and non-provable.[42] Mr Registrar James held that the debt was not caught by the exception in paragraph (i) of s 65 because a petition in bankruptcy is not a proceeding for the enforcement of an order. He said that: 'A bankruptcy petition seeks an adjudication in the nature of a declaration of insolvency, the consequence of which is the imposition upon the insolvent's estate of a statutory scheme for the distribution of his assets among his creditors.'[43] Secondly, paragraph (ii) excludes from the term 'family proceedings' any proceedings for the variation of any provision for the periodical payment of money contained in an order made, confirmed or registered under any of those enactments, but this exclusion does not apply under s 281(8) of the Insolvency Act.

Thus if a foreign maintenance order is registered under the 1972 Act it is an 'order made in family proceedings' and therefore falls within the ambit of r 12.3(2)(a) and is not provable in bankruptcy. On the other hand, a foreign maintenance order which has not been registered under the Act has not become an 'order made in family proceedings' and is not prevented from being a provable debt.[44] The same applies to an order which cannot be so registered.

---

[40] Subject to subs(2).   [41] [2001] 2 FLR 84.

[42] He also found that there were no special circumstances justifying the court in exercising its jurisdiction to make a bankruptcy order on a petition based on a non-provable debt.

[43] Para [13]. In *Cartwright v Cartwright (No 2)* [2002] 2 FLR 610 it was common ground that the exception in s 65(1) did not apply.

[44] See Neuberger J in *Cadwell v Jackson* [2001] BPIR 966 where he pointed out that if an order for maintenance is registered under Pt I of the Maintenance Orders Reciprocal Enforcement Act 1972, then the effect is not merely that the order is enforceable in England, but also that the English courts have jurisdiction to vary the order in the same way as they can amend or vary orders made in domestic proceedings. He could, therefore, see why the legislature thought it right to provide for only registered foreign maintenance orders to be within the ambit of r 12.3(2)(a) and not unregistered orders.

In *Wehemeyer v Wehemeyer* [2001] 2 FLR 84, para [16], Mr Registrar James said that ' ... it is contrary to public policy that a foreign maintenance order which would be a non-provable debt if registered in this jurisdiction were to be treated as a provable debt if it were not so registered. Both the underlying policy of the statute and common sense dictate that a foreign maintenance order which is capable of being registered but is not registered in this jurisdiction should be treated as a non-provable debt'.

In *Cartwright v Cartwright* [2002] 1 FLR 919, 926, at first instance Rimer J said the case was distinguishable from *Wehemeyer* in that in *Cartwright* the Hong Kong order could not have been registered under any of the provisions listed in s 65(1). It could have been registered under the Administration of Justice Act 1920 but that is not listed in s 65(1). In *Wehemeyer*, the orders had been registered under the 1982 Act which is listed in s 65(1). Rimer J was not convinced that the

In *Cartwright v Cartwright*,[45] Rimer J found that a consent order for financial provision made in Hong Kong divorce proceedings was not capable of being registered under either (f) or (m) and was not for that reason an order made in family proceedings for the purposes of r 12.3. It was therefore provable in the bankruptcy of the husband.[46]

In the Court of Appeal, it was held that the Hong Kong order was a maintenance order for the purposes of s 21 of the 1972 Act insofar as it provided for periodical payments.[47] However, a provision for payment of a lump sum could not, under s 21, constitute a maintenance order unless the lump sum was for the maintenance of a person falling within the description given in the definition. This makes it necessary to distinguish those parts of an order for payment of a lump sum dealing with maintenance from those which deal with rights of property.[48] In the instant case, since there was separate provision for periodical payments, the lump sum payment was by way of division of property between Mr and Mrs Cartwright and did not fall within r 12.3(2)(a).[49]

With regard to r 12.3(3)[50] it was held that the court had to assume that the order for periodical payments was variable by the court in Hong Kong where it was made and so constituted a debt unenforceable in the United Kingdom,[51] and a debt which was not provable in bankruptcy. On the other hand, the provision for a lump sum payment was not variable and there was no impediment to its being enforced at common law.

The bankruptcy order was set aside and the case remitted to the bankruptcy court where it would be necessary to determine whether the lump sum remained unpaid in whole or in part in the light of payments which had been made by Mr Cartwright. It would be necessary to establish whether these payments had been tendered and accepted in payment of periodical payments due or the lump sum.

10.6.3 The Matrimonial and Family Proceedings Act 1984

Part V of the Matrimonial and Family Proceedings Act 1984 is headed 'Family Business: Distribution and Transfer' and s 32 defines 'family business' to mean

---

Registrar's generalized assertion was correct. Whether or not an unregistered foreign maintenance order is an order made in 'family proceedings' is a matter of statutory interpretation and cannot depend on some ill-defined concept of public policy or the even less defined concept of common sense. There was no disapproval of his comments in the Court of Appeal.

[45] [2002] 1 FLR 919.

[46] He noted that it could have been registered under the Administration of Justice Act 1920 but this had not been done.   [47] [2002] 2 FLR 610.

[48] As in *Van den Boogaard v Laumen* [1977] QB 759 for the purposes of the Civil Jurisdiction and Judgments Act 1982.

[49] Arden LJ said that an order which could be registered under the 1972 Act, but which has not been so registered, does not fall within r 12.3(2)(a).

[50] This provides that 'Nothing in the Rules prejudices any enactment or rule of law under which a particular kind of debt is not provable, whether on grounds of public policy or otherwise'.

[51] *Harrop v Harrop* [1920] 3 KB 386.

'proceedings which are family business'. It then defines 'family business' to mean 'business of any description which in the High Court is for the time being assigned to the Family Division and to no other Division by or under section 61 of (and Schedule 1 to) the Supreme Court Act 1981'. In *Cadwell v Jackson*,[52] Neuberger J held that even if the nature of proceedings in Florida in which a former husband had obtained judgment against his former wife was such that they would have been 'family proceedings' if they had been brought in England and Wales, that was irrelevant because the definition in s 32 did not encompass proceedings in foreign jurisdictions. He said that if one looked at the definition of 'family proceedings' in s 32 it was impossible to contend that it extends to proceedings outside the United Kingdom. He went on to hold that even if s 32 did have such an extra-territorial effect, the nature of the issues in the Florida proceedings was such they should anyway not be regarded as satisfying the definition of 'family proceedings' in s 32. The main judgment was described as determining all matters in controversy between the parties including all property rights and obligations, all claims for spousal support and all matters not disposed of by virtue of the dissolution of marriage judgment. The judgment provided that the proceeds of certain specified shares having a value of $1,824,000 were a non-marital asset belonging solely to Mr Cadwell and that to effectuate an equitable allocation Mrs Cadwell should pay to Mr Cadwell the sum of $1,694,00 and interest. Mr Cadwell subsequently obtained a further judgment against Mrs Cadwell in the same proceedings, apparently for costs. Before his death Mr Caldwell had assigned both judgments to different companies who submitted proofs in Mrs Caldwell's bankruptcy. Neuberger J said that the fact that 'family proceedings' are defined as proceedings which are family business, rather than being defined as proceedings in the Family Division is of relevance and indicates that the court has to take a rather more critical view of whether a particular aspect of a composite claim is within 'family proceedings' or not.

He noted that a claim by a husband against a wife for shares in a company, or the value of the proceeds of those shares would not normally be thought of as 'family business'. Indeed such a claim could not normally be brought in the Family Division although in the context of divorce proceedings and associated 'maintenance proceedings,' the Family Division will often have jurisdiction to consider disputes between husband and wife which are not family business within the very limited definition in s 32 of the 1984 Act. Accordingly, bearing in mind both the policy behind r 12.3(2)(a) and the fact that the limitation on provable debts should be read narrowly rather than widely, and taking the natural meaning of the definition imported into r 12.3(2)(a), it seemed to him that it was necessary to ask in relation to any particular debt whether the debt arose from family proceedings. In other words, was the order made in the Family Division, or would it have been made in the Family Division if the

---

[52] [2001] BPIR 966.

proceedings had been brought in this country? It was then necessary to ask 'whether, looking at the precise nature of the debt, and the facts and legal argument leading up to the order, the nature of the claim which gave rise to the order was really family proceedings, ie was a claim which, taken on its own, would have had to be brought in the Family Division, and in no other division'.[53] He accepted that Mr Cadwell's claim arose in the context of family proceedings and would, on the basis of arguments he had heard, have arisen in the Family Division if the matrimonial dispute which did exist between Mr and Mrs Cadwell was in this jurisdiction. However, her obligation to pay that sum was not an obligation arising under an order in proceedings which would have been assigned to the Family Division and to no other division. The debt was therefore rightly admitted to proof.

---

[53] [2001] BPIR 966.

11

EQUITABLE ACCOUNTING AND THE EQUITY OF EXONERATION

11.1 INTRODUCTION

The general principle is that only the debtor's property can be reached by his creditors. Thus the debtor's spouse is entitled to retain her own property and in the event of a sale of joint property to satisfy the husband's creditors she is entitled to receive her share of the proceeds of sale. This assumes that her property or her share in jointly owned property is easily identifiable, but this will not always be the case. She may find it necessary to establish that she has acquired a beneficial interest in property vested in her husband's name by relying on the principles of resulting trust, constructive trust, or proprietary estoppel. A detailed consideration of these principles is beyond the scope of this book, but it should be noted that the position of the debtor's spouse may differ vis-à-vis the creditors depending upon the basis of her claim to a beneficial interest. Thus a share to which a person is entitled under a resulting trust, being based upon the contributions of that person to the acquisition of the property, will be effective against the trustee in bankruptcy of the party in whom the legal title is vested. However, where a constructive trust is imposed to give effect to the common intention of the parties, the share of the spouse may be larger than the share which could be justified on the basis of his or her contributions. To the extent that it exceeds the share appropriate to those contributions it is vulnerable to attack by the trustee in bankruptcy of the other party under the Insolvency Act 1986 as a transaction at an undervalue.[1]

---

[1] See *Re Densham* [1975] 1 WLR 1519 and ch 9.

In addition to establishing the beneficial interests in the property, it may also be necessary for an account to be taken between the spouses for money spent by the wife on such items as improvements to the property and mortgage instalments. The same applies as between cohabitants and other co-owners. Equitable accounting is considered in the next section of this chapter.

The last section of this chapter examines other situations when the burden of one co-owner's debt is to be borne primarily by his beneficial interest rather than by the interest of his spouse, cohabitant, or other co-owner.

11.2 EQUITABLE ACCOUNTING

11.2.1 The general principle

Where two persons are beneficially entitled to property which they have occupied as a home, it will often be appropriate for an account to be taken on a sale of the property, or when one party buys the other out, following the separation of the parties. Thus one party may have had the benefit of sole occupation for a period following separation so that some form of occupation rent may be appropriate. Again a party may have expended money on the property by way of mortgage instalments or in effecting improvements so that some credit may be appropriate in the division of the proceeds of the property. Such adjustments do not alter the beneficial interests in the property but result in an adjustment of the amounts payable to each party.[2]

In *Bernard v Josephs*,[3] Lord Denning explained the position as follows:

After ascertaining the shares, the next problem arises when it is to be turned into money. Usually one of the parties stays in the house, paying the mortgage instalments and the rates and other outgoings. The house also increases in value greatly owing to inflation. None of that alters the shares of the parties in the house itself. But it does mean that when the house is sold—or one buys the other out—there have to be many adjustments made. The value of the house itself is taken at the value at the time of sale or buying out. There must be deducted from it all money needed to redeem the mortgage. Then the one in possession must be given credit for paying the other's share of the mortgage instalments and be debited with an occupation rent for using the other's share of the house. Other adjustments may be needed for other outgoings. Then the net amount must be divided according to the shares.

More recently Millett J said:[4]

The guiding principle of the Court of equity is that the proportions in which the entirety should be divided between former co-owners must have regard to any increase in its value which has been brought about by means of expenditure by one of them.

---

[2] In relation to improvements regard should be had to the possibility of an increased share on the basis of s 37 of the Matrimonial Proceedings and Property Act 1970.   [3] [1982] Ch 391, 400.

[4] In *Re Pavlou* [1993] 1 WLR 1046, 1048.

The principles of equitable accounting apply equally to beneficial tenancies in common and beneficial joint tenancies. The argument that equitable accounting is only available between tenants in common was rejected by Millett J in *Re Pavlou*.[5] In *Byford v Butler*,[6] Lawrence Collins J held that the principles of equitable accounting applied as between a wife and her husband's trustee in bankruptcy even though there had been no breakdown in the marriage and the bankrupt husband remained in occupation of the matrimonial home with the wife until his death.

11.2.2 Improvements

On a sale of jointly owned property a co-owner who has expended money on repairs or improvements to the property will be entitled to a credit as against the other co-owner or his trustee in bankruptcy. He or she will be entitled 'to credit only for one half of the lesser of the actual expenditure and any increase in the value realised' by the sale.[7] This recognizes that not all expenditure on property is reflected in any increase in value and most expenditure on property results in a much smaller increase in value than the amount expended. Thus if an unmarried couple, A and B, own their home in equal shares, and A has expended £15,000 on improvements to the home, it may be that this would be reflected in the proceeds of sale of the property only to the extent of, say £10,000. As against B or his trustee in bankruptcy, A will be entitled to a credit of £5,000 with the following effect:

Net proceeds of sale		£50,000
A and B are each entitled to		£25,000
One half of the actual expenditure	£7,500	
One half of increase in value	£5,000	
Therefore deduct from B's share	£5,000	
A is entitled to £30,000 and B or his trustee is entitled to £20,000		

This course was adopted in *Re Gorman*[8] where Vinelott J said that it was common ground that on sale the wife would 'be entitled to be credited, in the division of the net proceeds after repaying the balance of the mortgage debt and any outstanding interest, with one half of the sums spent by her in improving the property, to the extent that the improvements have enhanced the value of the property and the sum realised on sale'.[9]

---

[5] ibid. See also Lawrence Collins J in *Byford v Butler* [2003] EWHC 1267 (Ch).

[6] [2003] EWHC 1267 (Ch), [2004] 1 FLR 56.

[7] *Per* Millett J in *Re Pavlou* [1993] 1 WLR 1046, 1048.   [8] [1990] 2 FLR 284, 292.

[9] See Cooke, 'Equitable Accounting Between Co-owners' [1993] Fam Law 695, where it is pointed out that the same result can be achieved by deducting the whole sum attributable to the improvements from the net proceeds of sale and dividing the resulting figure between the parties. The sum attributable to the improvements is then added to the share of the party who paid for the improvements.

11.2.3 Occupation rent

Generally one tenant in common in sole occupation of jointly owned premises is not liable to pay an occupation rent where the other co-owner voluntarily chooses not to exercise a right of occupation. However, if the non-occupying co-owner has been excluded from the premises the court will order payment of an occupation rent if it is necessary to do justice between the parties. In *Re Pavlou*,[10] Millett J, after reviewing the earlier cases, said that:

a court of equity will order an inquiry and payment of occupation rent, not only in the case where the co-owner in occupation has ousted the other, but in any other case in which it is necessary in order to do equity between the parties that an occupation rent should be paid. The fact that there has not been an ouster or forceful exclusion is far from conclusive.

Further, where it is a matrimonial home and the marriage has broken down, the party who leaves the property will, in most cases, be regarded as excluded from the family home, so that an occupation rent should be paid by the co-owner who remains. That, he said, was not a rule of law but merely a statement of the prima facie conclusion to be drawn from the facts. He said:

The true position is that if a tenant in common leaves the property voluntarily, but would be welcome back and would be in a position to enjoy his or her right to occupy, it would normally not be fair or equitable to the remaining tenant in common to charge him or her with an occupation rent which he or she never expected to pay.

In *Byford v Butler*,[11] Lawrence Collins J had to apply these principles to a situation in which the marriage of the co-owners had not broken down and both remained in occupation of the home after the bankruptcy of the husband in 1991. They were still in occupation at the husband's death in 2000, the outgoings having been paid by the wife. On an application by the trustee in bankruptcy for an order for sale and a declaration that the estate was beneficially entitled to half the equity in the property the judge at first instance held that the wife was entitled to credit for improvements and mortgage interest payments, but the trustee was entitled to a set-off for an occupation rent by the wife. Lawrence Collins J dismissed the wife's appeal noting that while the wife was in occupation the trustee could not reside in or obtain any financial benefit from the property. Moreover, although the trustee could have taken action earlier, the wife had benefited considerably from the continued use of the property.

It should be noted that in *Re Gorman*[12] Vinelott J accepted that Mrs Gorman was only liable for an occupation rent for the period after the making of the receiving order. Prior to the making of the receiving order Mr Gorman had been ordered to pay maintenance to Mrs Gorman and to pay the mortgage

---

[10] [1993] 1 WLR 1046, 1050.   [11] [2003] EWHC 1267 (Ch).   [12] [1990] 2 FLR 284, 294–5.

instalments and other outgoings on the house and so could not himself have asserted any equity to charge her an occupation rent on the taking of an account after sale of the house. The trustee in bankruptcy could be in no better position.

If it is appropriate for the occupying co-owner to make a payment it is not strictly 'rent' though the term 'occupation rent' is commonly used. In calculating a fair 'rent' as between co-owners Arnold P in *Dennis v McDonald*[13] pointed out that a co-owner occupies the property by right of his beneficial interest and not because he has been able to negotiate in the market and obtain it. Some allowance should be made for this, and it was difficult to see what justification there was for charging a co-owner with such extra payment as a tenant would have to make by reason of the scarcity of relevant accommodation in the market. Accordingly, he said:[14]

If one is setting out to achieve a fair solution in a situation in which plainly the defendant has to pay something, I can think of no better way of regulating that than by doing one's best to assess a fair rent for the property, with all its advantages and defects, and eliminating the scarcity element.

In the circumstances of the case the order provided for the occupying defendant to pay one half of such sum as represented a fair payment for the exclusive use and occupation of the said property (unfurnished) upon the principles of valuation laid down in respect of regulated tenancies under s 70 of the Rent Act 1977, but without regard to any other provisions of the Act. However, it was inappropriate to provide for annual assessment of such a rent as the cost would be disproportionate to the sum involved.

11.2.4 Mortgage payments

Where one spouse or other co-owner has continued to pay mortgage instalments after the other has left he or she is prima facie entitled to credit for those payments when an equitable account is taken. A distinction must generally be drawn between the capital element and the interest element in such instalments for the former increases the value of the equity while the latter does not. The co-owner making the payments will thus be entitled to credit for one half of the capital element in the instalments and this also applies as against the trustee in bankruptcy of the other spouse. (That co-owner's share of the equity will in any event have been increased by the other half of the capital payments which he or she will be deemed to have been making on his or her own behalf.) The party making the payments will also be entitled to credit in relation to the interest element but account may need to be taken of the fact that he or she has had the benefit of occupation of the property. In practice, therefore, in 'some cases, to avoid the necessity of expensive and protracted inquiries and accounts, the

---

[13] [1982] Fam 63.   [14] ibid 82.

courts have treated mortgage interest paid by a' co-owner 'who has been in sole occupation as equal to an occupation rent, leaving only an appropriate proportion of any capital repayments to be credited to him'.[15]

That was the course taken in *Suttill v Graham*[16] where Stamp LJ referred to this as 'normal practice' certainly 'where the husband was in occupation, although it may not always have been the case where the wife and particularly the children, were in occupation'. However, in *Re Gorman* Vinelott J said:[17]

> That practice is not, of course, a rule of law to be applied in all circumstances, irrespective of, on the one hand, the amount of the mortgage debt and the instalments paid and, on the other hand, the value of the property and the amount of the occupation rent that ought fairly to be charged. It is a rule of convenience and more readily applies between husband and wife, or cohabitees, than between a spouse and the trustee in bankruptcy of the other co-owner.

In that case the wife of the bankrupt was held to be entitled to equitable accounting on a sale of the former matrimonial home on the application of the trustee in bankruptcy. In default of agreement between the parties there would have to be an inquiry into the amount of the proper occupation rent between the making of the receiving order and the sale of the property and an account of all the mortgage instalments paid by Mrs Gorman before and after the receiving order was made. The amount of the mortgage was comparatively small, some £5,000, and the property, which was situated in a commuter area and worth more than £100,000 might well command, even on the most conservative basis, an occupation rent substantially larger than the mortgage instalments. The court hoped that the trustee would renew the offer to set the occupation rent against the interest and encouraged the wife to give serious consideration to it.

In *Byford v Butler*,[18] Lawrence Collins J held that the wife was entitled to credit for the mortgage interest payments and that the trustee was entitled to a set off for occupation rent from the wife.

11.3 THE EQUITY OF EXONERATION

11.3.1 The context

Where jointly owned property, such as the family home, is mortgaged to secure a loan to be used in the business or to discharge the debts of one of the joint owners, usually the husband, a number of questions may arise if he subsequently defaults in repayment or becomes bankrupt. The first question is whether the other joint owner, usually the wife, is bound by the mortgage in view of the possibility that she was persuaded to join in the mortgage as a result

---

[15] Vinelott J in *Re Gorman* [1990] 2 FLR 284, 293.   [16] [1977] 1 WLR 819.
[17] [1990] 2 FLR 284, 294.   [18] [2003] EWHC 1267 (Ch).

of the undue influence, misrepresentation or other wrongful conduct on the part of the husband. This was considered in Chapter 3. In cases where the wife is bound by the mortgage, she will be in the position of a surety and the burden of the debt as between the joint owners may be affected by the equity of exoneration. If this is applicable it may have serious implications for the mortgagee or other third parties.

11.3.2 The right to indemnity

Where a wife charges her property or, as joint owner, has joined in a mortgage to secure a loan for the benefit of her husband, then as a surety, she will be entitled to be indemnified by the husband. This may, of course, be of little or no assistance especially if the husband becomes bankrupt. The wife will be entitled to prove in her husband's bankruptcy, but by virtue of s 329 of the Insolvency Act 1986 payment of her debt will be postponed until preferential and ordinary creditors have been paid in full.[19] The right of indemnity will also apply where the roles of the spouses are reversed and the husband is surety.[20]

11.3.3 The right to exoneration

A more significant entitlement of the surety in this situation will be the right to have the secured debt discharged as far as possible out of the beneficial interest of the debtor to the exoneration of the surety's beneficial interest.[21] In *In re Pittortou*, Scott J said:[22]

As a general proposition, if there is found to be a charge on property jointly owned, to secure the debts of one only of the joint owners, the other joint owner, being in the position of a surety, is entitled, as between the two joint owners, to have the secured indebtedness discharged so far as possible out of the equitable interest of the debtor.

The effect of the equity of exoneration in such a case is to enhance the proprietary interest of the surety which will be important where the debtor has become bankrupt so that the surety's personal right of indemnity is likely to be of limited value.[23] Thus if the joint owners of a property worth £200,000 and subject to a mortgage of £50,000 in favour of a building society, charge the property to a bank to secure a loan of £50,000 for the business of the husband, the application of the doctrine will mean that the debt of £50,000 in favour of the bank will be discharged entirely from the husband's share of the equity of £150,000 leaving the wife with her share of £75,000 and the husband or his trustee in bankruptcy with £25,000.

---

[19] See *In re Cronmire* [1901] 1 QB 480.
[20] *Gray v Dowman* (1858) 27 LJ Ch 702.
[21] *In re A Debtor, ex p Marley* [1976] 1 WLR 952.
[22] [1985] 1 WLR 58, 61.
[23] ibid.

Although the equity is of particular importance in the context of bankruptcy, it can apply in other circumstances, such as the administration of estates.[24] It is not limited to spouses, but can apply as between other joint owners such as a father and son as in *In re A Debtor, ex p Marley*.[25] In *R v Posener*,[26] the doctrine was applied when a confiscation order was sought against a husband who had been convicted of fraudulent evasion of VAT. The only potential realizable asset of the husband was his share in the matrimonial home which was registered in the joint names of himself and his wife. The property had a value of £230,000, and there was an outstanding balance of £102,088 on a joint mortgage account with the Halifax Building Society. This was referable to four advances the first of which had been in respect of the property itself. The other three advances, amounting in total to £63,000, were each applied for the benefit of the husband's then business. There were two further advances repayable out of the husband's share in the equity, but the critical question was whether the £63,000 advanced and used in the husband's business affairs fell to be repaid from the equity in the whole of the property or from the husband's half share in the equity. In the former case there remained a sum in excess of £30,000 available to the husband which could be the subject of a confiscation order. In the latter case his share of the equity would be exhausted, but the wife's share of the equity would be larger. The Court of Appeal held that the doctrine applied so that the husband's equity in the property was extinguished and a confiscation order therefore inappropriate.

11.3.4 Requirements for application of the doctrine

There are three requirements for the application of the doctrine:[27]

(1) The wife must have charged her property or, if she is a joint owner of the property with her husband, she must have joined in a mortgage of the property.
(2) The wife must have done so for the purposes of the husband or otherwise for his benefit.
(3) The money borrowed must have been applied for the purposes of the husband or otherwise for his benefit.

Little difficulty seems likely to arise in relation to the first requirement. However, the second requirement may well be disputed and in such cases may be difficult to distinguish from the third requirement. This is because inferences as to the purpose of the loan may be drawn from evidence of its actual application.

---

[24] *In re Cronmire* [1901] 1 QB 480.   [25] [1976] 1 WLR 952.   [26] [2001] EWCA Crim 14.

[27] The same principles will apply where a husband is in the position of a surety in respect of a loan for the purposes of his wife and also as between cohabitants or other co-owners.

11.3.4.1 *The loan must be for the benefit of one joint owner alone*

The essential basis for the application of the equity of exoneration is that one joint owner has entered into a mortgage to secure a loan obtained for the benefit or purposes of the other joint owner. Unless it can be shown that the former was in the position of a mere surety there can be no question of exoneration. Thus in the case of a loan which is clearly for the joint purposes of the spouses, such as to purchase the matrimonial home, there can be no question of exonerating the wife's share—though equitable accounting is another matter.

However, where it is clear that only part of the loan was obtained for the joint benefit of the parties and part applied 'exclusively' for the benefit of one party alone, then the loan may be divided and the equity of exoneration applied only to the latter part. Thus in the Australian case of *Farrugia v Official Receiver in Bankruptcy*,[28] a sum of $23,000 was borrowed by a husband and wife on the security of their joint property. The sum of $12,500 was applied for the joint benefit of the husband and wife in discharging the previous mortgage under which they were jointly liable and only the balance of $10,500 was applied for the benefit of the husband alone. Deane J in the Federal Court of Australia said:[29]

> It seems to me that where the joint property is charged partially for the benefit of the husband alone and partly for the benefit of both husband and wife and it is possible to apportion the principal between the two, there is room for the application of the equitable doctrine of exoneration and the wife is, in the absence of agreement to the contrary, entitled to exoneration to the extent of what was borrowed and applied for the benefit of the husband alone ....[30]

The identification of that part of the loan to be applied for the husband's business was clear from the outset, namely that part not needed to discharge the earlier mortgage. The division may not be so easy to make, but an examination of the manner in which the loan was dealt with may enable the doctrine to be applied to that part used for the benefit of the bankrupt as in the leading case *In re Pittortou*,[31] which is considered further below.

11.3.4.2 *The intention of the parties*

It must have been the intention of the parties at the time of the loan that it was to be satisfied primarily from the share of the joint owner for whose benefit the loan was obtained. In the absence of any evidence of an express intention it will be necessary to infer what the intention must have been. In the past there has been some uncertainty as to the burden of proof and as to whether there is a presumption in favour of a wife.[32] The present position appears to be that if it

---

[28] (1982) 43 ALR 700.   [29] ibid 702–3.
[30] Referring to 22 Halsbury (4th edn, para 1073); *Gee v Smart* (1857) 8 El & Bl 313, 319; 120 ER 116, 119.   [31] [1985] 1 WLR 58.
[32] Thus in *Paget v Paget* [1898] 1 Ch 470, Lindley MR said that the authorities establishing the doctrine showed that it was based on an inference to be drawn from the circumstances of each

can be shown by the wife that the loan was clearly for the *purposes* of the husband, then a presumption will arise that it was the *intention* of the parties that exoneration was to apply. It will then be necessary to see whether there is evidence to rebut that presumption.

In *R v Posener*, the judge at first instance took the view that when the wife, who was a solicitor specializing in conveyancing, signed the relevant charges, she would have appreciated that she was going to benefit because the loans were to enable her husband to maintain his business. The equity of exoneration was not therefore applicable. However, the Court of Appeal held that the judge had failed to apply the correct test, in that he failed to consider the intention of the parties at the time of the advances. Henriques J said:

The fact that the appellant's wife was a solicitor does not, in our judgment, make it any more likely that she was agreeing that their indebtedness should be discharged equally out of each share in the equity, as opposed to being discharged, so far as possible, out of the appellant's share of the equity. Indeed, the fact that she is a solicitor with some knowledge of commerce, well able to assess her husband's competence or otherwise, militates towards a conclusion that she would be less likely than otherwise to agree to their indebtedness being discharged equally.

However, it was unnecessary to speculate. It was necessary to consider only what evidence there was as to the intention of the parties when the money was advanced. There was no such evidence and accordingly there was a presumption that the wife meant to charge her property merely by way of security and was in the position of surety and entitled to throw the debt primarily onto her husband's estate to the exoneration of her own.[33] As noted earlier the result was that the husband's equity was extinguished and a confiscation order therefore inappropriate.

The presumption will, of course, arise only if it can be shown that the loan was for the benefit of the husband and for him alone. The purpose for which the loan was obtained may be unclear. In the absence of clear evidence of the intention of the parties as to the purpose of the loan an inference may have to be drawn from their subsequent conduct in relation to the proceeds of the loan.

---

particular case with the prima facie inference being that the wife's assistance should be limited to the necessity of the case. However, to say that there was a presumption in favour of the wife, and that it was for the husband to rebut it was in his view, to go too far (474). In *Hall v Hall* [1911] 1 Ch 487, 499, Warrington J interpreted the judgment of Lindley MR as meaning that if a married woman charged her property for the purpose of paying her husband's debts and the money raised was so applied, then there was a prima facie inference to be drawn from those facts, but not a legal presumption in the strict sense, in favour of the wife, and, unlike a legal presumption, the court was entitled to go into all the facts of the case to see whether there was or was not that prima facie inference.

[33] Contrast *Rhoden v Josephs* (ChD, 6 September 1990) where the judge was satisfied in relation to arrangements between an unmarried couple, that although the man had, and was intended to have, the primary benefit, the woman was quite agreeable to the purchase of a car being acquired out of their joint assets and resources including a loan. Moreover she did have some benefit.

Insofar as the loan has been used for the purposes of the husband the equity of exoneration will apply unless there is evidence to rebut it.

In *In re Pittortou*,[34] Scott J said:

> ...the equity of exoneration is a principle of equity which depends upon the presumed intention of the parties. If the circumstances of a particular case do not justify the inference, or indeed if the circumstances negate the inference, that it was the joint intention of the joint mortgagors that the burden of the secured indebtedness should fall primarily on the share of that one of them who was the debtor, then that consequence will not follow.

In that case, the husband and wife had charged their matrimonial home to secure any indebtedness to a bank on an account intended to be used, amongst other things, for the purpose of the restaurant business which the husband took over from members of his family. That charge was paid off when the home was subsequently sold and replaced by a charge on the new home purchased in the joint names of the spouses. This was a second charge which secured the bank account which was used not only in relation to the restaurant business, but also to some extent for the payment of expenses in connection with the matrimonial home. The parties subsequently separated and were divorced and the husband became bankrupt. Scott J found that until the separation of the spouses, the family had acted as a family unit in its family and business affairs. The wife had worked in the restaurants which the Pittortou family conducted, for long hours and without pay. 'In that respect, her conduct was similar to the conduct of many wives assisting their husbands in the conduct of the business on which the livelihood and support of the family depend.' He concluded that payments made out of the husband's bank account for the benefit of the family were of a character as to make it impossible to impute to the parties the intention that as between the husband and wife the payments should be regarded as falling only on the share in the mortgaged property of the husband. In his view 'the equity of exoneration should be confined to payments out of the account which do not have the character of payments made for the joint benefit of the household'. However, 'save for payments made for the joint benefit of the household', it did not seem to Scott J:

> that the equity of exoneration has any less part to play now than it had in the days when the equitable doctrine was being formulated. Accordingly, payments made by the husband for business purposes and, a fortiori, any payments made by the husband for the purposes of the second establishment it seems he was supporting, should as between the bankrupt and the second respondent be treated as charged primarily on the bankrupt's half share in the mortgaged property.[35]

Even if the loan was raised to discharge liabilities of the husband, it will not necessarily be appropriate to infer that the wife is entitled to the equity of exoneration. Thus the court refused to draw such an inference in

---

[34] [1985] 1 WLR 58, 62.   [35] ibid 62–3.

Paget v Paget[36] where the wife had charged her property to secure loans needed to pay debts for which the husband was legally liable, but which were the result of the extravagant life style which they had both enjoyed.

Whether a wife has or will receive a benefit as a result of the loan may be a matter of dispute or at least be unclear. It has been argued that even where a loan secured on the wife's property has been obtained to pay the husband's business debts or for his business purposes there is a substantial common benefit. This means that the wife has substantially benefited at least indirectly as the business provides the means of support for the family.[37] The approach of the New Zealand Court of Appeal in *Re Berry*[38] has been said to illustrate this view.

In that case, at the time when the matrimonial home was purchased, the parties had, according to the wife, sufficient funds from the proceeds of their former home to pay the full price in cash, but the husband was in difficulties with his building business and their joint account was substantially overdrawn. This account had started as a normal domestic arrangement, but it became increasingly confined to the business and over the relevant period any domestic or personal dealings were insignificant. It was decided to use the property as security for a bank overdraft for the business and both parties signed the usual form of bank mortgage over the property for overdraft facilities in the joint account up to a certain figure. Subsequently this overdraft was repaid from another loan raised on mortgage over the property and the bank mortgage discharged and other business debts paid. The Court of Appeal held that it was not a case where a wife had charged her property and the husband had received the loan monies. They had entered into the transaction jointly. They were jointly liable and they incurred liability in consideration of advances made and accommodation given to them jointly. There was nothing to justify any implication that one was the principal debtor and the other a secondary debtor.

Richardson J, while noting that the loans had been arranged on the husband's initiative said: 'But her purpose and his was that funds would thus become available for use in his business and in a broader way for the benefit of the family.'[39] Somers J said:[40]

While as between strangers the simple question, who got the money, may afford a ready and just solution, its potency as a solvent in the case of a joint account of a housewife and mother in New Zealand in the 1970's is not so apparent. It necessarily involves the proposition that husband and wife intended to enter into legal relations, such intent being an actual intention or–denied in *Paget v Paget* . . . – a presumed intent.

However, it can be said that the case simply illustrates the difficulty of ascertaining the intention of husband and wife especially when the loan is paid into a

---

[36] [1898] 1 Ch 470, CA.

[37] See Briggs, 'A Wife's "Equity of Exoneration": The Doctrine Revisited' (2000) 14 Insolvency Intelligence 33 and 43.   [38] [1978] 2 NZLR 373.

[39] ibid 379.   [40] ibid 385.

joint bank account which may have been used for domestic as well as business purposes. Richardson J said that 'in terms of the matrimonial sharing arrangements adopted by this husband and wife the family home was a joint asset and the joint account and the mortgages were joint responsibilities'.[41] It does not lend support to the argument that when a wife joins in a mortgage to secure a loan which is clearly paid to and used for the separate business of the husband the equity of exoneration is excluded because the wife and family are supported by the income from the business. Even when there is a mixed purpose or use of a loan the decision in *In re Pittortou* shows that the court is prepared to separate the business element from the domestic element.

It is suggested that if the loan was clearly for the purpose of the husband's business, then the mere fact that the wife and family have been supported from the income produced by that business will not, by itself, be enough to displace the inference in favour of exoneration.

In the Australian case of *Parsons v McBain*,[42] the wives of two brothers had each mortgaged their shares in their respective matrimonial homes to secure the borrowing of the brothers' business. The trial judge had denied that the principle applied because each wife had received 'a tangible benefit' from the loan. The benefit, which the Full Court thought could be more accurately described as 'an expected benefit' was that by putting money into the partnership business, the business might survive and that would bring 'home money to put food on the table and clothe the children'. On appeal it was acknowledged by the Full Court that if a surety receives a benefit from the loan, then the equity of exoneration may be defeated. Thus if the borrowed funds are applied to discharge the surety's debts, the surety could not claim exoneration, at least in respect of the benefit received. However, the court said that the benefit must be from the loan itself and referred to the question suggested by the Lord Chancellor of Ireland in *In re Kiely*:[43] 'Who got the money?' They noted that in *Paget v Paget*[44] both husband and wife 'got the money' and this prevented the wife claiming exoneration. The court continued:

The "tangible benefit" referred to by the trial judge will not defeat the equity. It is too remote. In any event, the exoneration to which a surety is entitled could hardly be defeated by a benefit which is incapable of valuation, and even if it were so capable, the value is unlikely to bear any relationship to the amount received by the principal debtor.

Finally, even if the original purpose of the loan was clearly for the husband's benefit, the presumption may be rebutted by evidence that the money was in fact spent for the benefit of the wife or for the joint benefit of the parties. Money used for general household and family living expenses will be treated as being used for their joint benefit as *In re Pittortou* shows.

---

[41] ibid 379.   [42] (2001) 109 FCR 120, 127.   [43] (1857) Ir Ch Rep 394, 405.
[44] [1898] 1 Ch 470.

THE MATRIMONIAL CAUSES ACT 1973

PART II
FINANCIAL RELIEF FOR PARTIES TO MARRIAGE AND CHILDREN OF FAMILY

Financial provision and property adjustment orders

21. Financial provision and property adjustment orders

(1) The financial provision orders for the purposes of this Act are the orders for periodical or lump sum provision available (subject to the provisions of this Act) under section 23 below for the purpose of adjusting the financial position of the parties to a marriage and any children of the family in connection with proceedings for divorce, nullity of marriage or judicial separation and under section 27(6) below on proof of neglect by one party to a marriage to provide, or to make a proper contribution towards, reasonable maintenance for the other or a child of the family, that is to say—

(a) any order for periodical payments in favour of a party to a marriage under section 23(1)(a) or 27(6)(a) or in favour of a child of the family under section 23(1)(d), (2) or (4) or 27(6)(d);

(b) any order for secured periodical payments in favour of a party to a marriage under section 23(1)(b) or 27(6)(b) or in favour of a child of the family under section 23(1)(e), (2) or (4) or 27(6)(e); and

(c) any order for lump sum provision in favour of a party to a marriage under section 23(1)(c) or 27(6)(c) or in favour of a child of the family under section 23(1)(f), (2) or (4) or 27 (6)(f);

and references in this Act (except in paragraphs 17(1) and 23 of Schedule 1 below) to periodical payments orders, secured periodical payments orders, and orders for the payment of a lump sum are references to all or some of the financial provision orders requiring the sort of financial provision in question according as the context of each reference may require.

(2) The property adjustment orders for the purposes of this Act are the orders dealing with property rights available (subject to the provisions of this Act) under section 24 below for the purpose of adjusting the financial position of the parties to a marriage and any children of the family on or after the grant of a decree of divorce, nullity of marriage or judicial separation, that is to say—

(a) any order under subsection (1)(a) of that section for a transfer of property;

(b) any order under subsection (1)(b) of that section for a settlement of property; and

(c) any order under subsection (1)(c) or (d) of that section for a variation of settlement.

21A. Pension sharing orders

(1) For the purposes of this Act, a pension sharing order is an order which—
    (a) provides that one party's—
        (i) shareable rights under a specified pension arrangement, or
        (ii) shareable state scheme rights,
    be subject to pension sharing for the benefit of the other party, and
    (b) specifies the percentage value to be transferred.
(2) In subsection (1) above—
    (a) the reference to shareable rights under a pension arrangement is to rights in relation to which pension sharing is available under Chapter I of Part IV of the Welfare Reform and Pensions Act 1999, or under corresponding Northern Ireland legislation,
    (b) the reference to shareable state scheme rights is to rights in relation to which pension sharing is available under Chapter II of Part IV of the Welfare Reform and Pensions Act 1999, or under corresponding Northern Ireland legislation, and
    (c) 'party' means a party to a marriage.

Ancillary relief in connection with divorce proceedings, etc

22. Maintenance pending suit

On a petition for divorce, nullity of marriage or judicial separation, the court may make an order for maintenance pending suit, that is to say, an order requiring either party to the marriage to make to the other such periodical payments for his or her maintenance and for such term, being a term beginning not earlier than the date of the presentation of the petition and ending with the date of the determination of the suit, as the court thinks reasonable.

23. Financial provision orders in connection with divorce proceedings, etc

(1) On granting a decree of divorce, a decree of nullity of marriage or a decree of judicial separation or at any time thereafter (whether, in the case of a decree of divorce or of nullity of marriage, before or after the decree is made absolute), the court may make any one or more of the following orders, that is to say—
    (a) an order that either party to the marriage shall make to the other such periodical payments, for such term, as may be specified in the order;
    (b) an order that either party to the marriage shall secure to the other to the satisfaction of the court such periodical payments, for such term, as may be so specified;
    (c) an order that either party to the marriage shall pay to the other such lump sum or sums as may be so specified;
    (d) an order that a party to the marriage shall make to such person as may be specified in the order for the benefit of a child of the family, or to such a child, such periodical payments, for such term, as may be so specified;

(e) an order that a party to the marriage shall secure to such person as may be so specified for the benefit of such a child, or to such a child, to the satisfaction of the court, such periodical payments, for such term as may be so specified;

(f) an order that a party to the marriage shall pay to such person as may be so specified for the benefit of such a child, or to such a child, such lump sum as may be so specified;

subject, however, in the case of an order under paragraph (d), (e) or (f) above, to the restrictions imposed by section 29(1) and (3) below on the making of financial provision orders in favour of children who have attained the age of eighteen.

(2) The court may also, subject to those restrictions, make any one or more of the orders mentioned in subsection (1)(d), (e) and (f) above—

(a) in any proceedings for divorce, nullity of marriage or judicial separation, before granting a decree; and

(b) where any such proceedings are dismissed after the beginning of the trial, either forthwith or within a reasonable period after the dismissal.

(3) Without prejudice to the generality of subsection (1)(c) or (f) above—

(a) an order under this section that a party to a marriage shall pay a lump sum to the other party may be made for the purpose of enabling that other party to meet any liabilities or expenses reasonably incurred by him or her in maintaining himself or herself or any child of the family before making an application for an order under this section in his or her favour;

(b) an order under this section for the payment of a lump sum to or for the benefit of a child of the family may be made for the purpose of enabling any liabilities or expenses reasonably incurred by or for the benefit of that child before the making of an application for an order under this section in his favour to be met; and

(c) an order under this section for the payment of a lump sum may provide for the payment of that sum by instalments of such amount as may be specified in the order and may require the payment of the instalments to be secured to the satisfaction of the court.

(4) The power of the court under subsection (1) or (2)(a) above to make an order in favour of a child of the family shall be exercisable from time to time; and where the court makes an order in favour of a child under subsection (2)(b) above, it may from time to time, subject to the restrictions mentioned in subsection (1) above, make a further order in his favour of any of the kinds mentioned in subsection (1)(d), (e) or (f) above.

(5) Without prejudice to the power to give a direction under section 30 below for the settlement of an instrument by conveyancing counsel, where an order is made under subsection (1)(a), (b) or (c) above on or after granting a decree of divorce or nullity of marriage, neither the order nor any settlement made in pursuance of the order shall take effect unless the decree has been made absolute.

(6) Where the court—

(a) makes an order under this section for the payment of a lump sum; and

(b) directs—

(i) that payment of that sum or any part of it shall be deferred; or

(ii) that that sum or any part of it shall be paid by instalments, the court may order that the amount deferred or the instalments shall carry interest at such rate as may be specified by the order from such date, not earlier than the date of the order, as may be so specified, until the date when payment of it is due.

24. Property adjustment orders in connection with divorce proceedings, etc.

(1) On granting a decree of divorce, a decree of nullity of marriage or a decree of judicial separation or at any time thereafter (whether, in the case of a decree of divorce, or of nullity of marriage, before or after the decree is made absolute), the court may make any one or more of the following orders, that is to say—

  (a) an order that a party to the marriage shall transfer to the other party, to any child of the family or to such person as may be specified in the order for the benefit of such a child such property as may be so specified, being property to which the first-mentioned party is entitled, either in possession or reversion;

  (b) an order that a settlement of such property as may be so specified, being property to which a party to the marriage is so entitled, be made to the satisfaction of the court for the benefit of the other party to the marriage and of the children of the family or either or any of them;

  (c) an order varying for the benefit of the parties to the marriage and of the children of the family or either or any of them any ante-nuptial or post-nuptial settlement (including such a settlement made by will or codicil) made on the parties to the marriage, other than one in the form of a pension arrangement (within the meaning of section 25D below);

  (d) an order extinguishing or reducing the interest of either of the parties to the marriage under any such settlement, other than one in the form of a pension arrangement (within the meaning of section 25D below);

subject, however, in the case of an order under paragraph (a) above, to the restrictions imposed by section 29(1) and (3) below on the making of orders for a transfer of property in favour of children who have attained the age of eighteen.

(2) The court may make an order under subsection (1)(c) above notwithstanding that there are no children of the family.

(3) Without prejudice to the power to give a direction under section 30 below for the settlement of an instrument by conveyancing counsel, where an order is made under this section on or after granting a decree of divorce or nullity of marriage, neither the order nor any settlement made in pursuance of the order shall take effect unless the decree has been made absolute.

24A. Orders for sale of property

(1) Where the court makes under section 23 or 24 of this Act a secured periodical payments order, an order for the payment of a lump sum or a property adjustment order, then, on making that order or at any time thereafter, the court may make a further order for the sale of such property as may be specified in the order, being property in which or in the proceeds of sale of which either or both of the parties to the marriage has or have a beneficial interest, either in possession or reversion.

(2) Any order made under subsection (1) above may contain such consequential or supplementary provisions as the court thinks fit and, without prejudice to the

generality of the foregoing provision, may include—

(a) provision requiring the making of a payment out of the proceeds of sale of the property to which the order relates, and

(b) provision requiring any such property to be offered for sale to a person, or class of persons, specified in the order.

(3) Where an order is made under subsection (1) above on or after the grant of a decree of divorce or nullity of marriage, the order shall not take effect unless the decree has been made absolute.

(4) Where an order is made under subsection (1) above, the court may direct that the order, or such provision thereof as the court may specify, shall not take effect until the occurrence of an event specified by the court or the expiration of a period so specified.

(5) Where an order under subsection (1) above contains a provision requiring the proceeds of sale of the property to which the order relates to be used to secure periodical payments to a party to the marriage, the order shall cease to have effect on the death or re-marriage of that person.

(6) Where a party to a marriage has a beneficial interest in any property, or in the proceeds of sale thereof, and some other person who is not a party to the marriage also has a beneficial interest in that property or in the proceeds of sale thereof, then, before deciding whether to make an order under this section in relation to that property, it shall be the duty of the court to give that other person an opportunity to make representations with respect to the order; and any representations made by that other person shall be included among the circumstances to which the court is required to have regard under section 25(1) below.

24B. Pension sharing orders in connection with divorce proceedings, etc

(1) On granting a decree of divorce or a decree of nullity of marriage or at any time thereafter (whether before or after the decree is made absolute), the court may, on an application made under this section, make one or more pension sharing orders in relation to the marriage.

(2) A pension sharing order under this section is not to take effect unless the decree on or after which it is made has been made absolute.

(3) A pension sharing order under this section may not be made in relation to a pension arrangement which—

(a) is the subject of a pension sharing order in relation to the marriage, or

(b) has been the subject of pension sharing between the parties to the marriage.

(4) A pension sharing order under this section may not be made in relation to shareable state scheme rights if—

(a) such rights are the subject of a pension sharing order in relation to the marriage, or

(b) such rights have been the subject of pension sharing between the parties to the marriage.

(5) A pension sharing order under this section may not be made in relation to the rights of a person under a pension arrangement if there is in force a requirement imposed by virtue of section 25B or 25C below which relates to benefits or future benefits to which he is entitled under the pension arrangement.

24C. Pension sharing orders: duty to stay

(1) No pension sharing order may be made so as to take effect before the end of such period after the making of the order as may be prescribed by regulations made by the Lord Chancellor.

(2) The power to make regulations under this section shall be exercisable by statutory instrument which shall be subject to annulment in pursuance of a resolution of either House of Parliament.

24D. Pension sharing orders: apportionment of charges

If a pension sharing order relates to rights under a pension arrangement, the court may include in the order provision about the apportionment between the parties of any charge under section 41 of the Welfare Reform and Pensions Act 1999 (charges in respect of pension sharing costs), or under corresponding Northern Ireland legislation.

25. Matters to which court is to have regard in deciding how to exercise its powers under sections 23, 24 and 24A

(1) It shall be the duty of the court in deciding whether to exercise its powers under sections 23, 24, 24A or 24B above and, if so, in what manner, to have regard to all the circumstances of the case, first consideration being given to the welfare while a minor of any child of the family who has not attained the age of eighteen.

(2) As regards the exercise of the powers of the court under section 23(1)(a), (b) or (c), 24, 24A or 24B above in relation to a party to the marriage, the court shall in particular have regard to the following matters—

    (a) the income, earning capacity, property and other financial resources which each of the parties to the marriage has or is likely to have in the foreseeable future, including in the case of earning capacity any increase in that capacity which it would in the opinion of the court be reasonable to expect a party to the marriage to take steps to acquire;

    (b) the financial needs, obligations and responsibilities which each of the parties to the marriage has or is likely to have in the foreseeable future;

    (c) the standard of living enjoyed by the family before the breakdown of the marriage;

    (d) the age of each party to the marriage and the duration of the marriage;

    (e) any physical or mental disability of either of the parties to the marriage;

    (f) the contributions which each of the parties has made or is likely in the foreseeable future to make to the welfare of the family, including any contribution by looking after the home or caring for the family;

    (g) the conduct of each of the parties, if that conduct is such that it would in the opinion of the court be inequitable to disregard it;

    (h) in the case of proceedings for divorce or nullity of marriage, the value to each of the parties to the marriage of any benefit which, by reason of the dissolution or annulment of the marriage, that party will lose the chance of acquiring.

(3) As regards the exercise of the powers of the court under section 23(1)(d), (e) or (f), (2) or (4), 24 or 24A above in relation to a child of the family, the court shall in particular have regard to the following matters—

    (a) the financial needs of the child;

(b) the income, earning capacity (if any), property and other financial resources of the child;

(c) any physical or mental disability of the child;

(d) the manner in which he was being and in which the parties to the marriage expected him to be educated or trained;

(e) the considerations mentioned in relation to the parties to the marriage in paragraphs (a), (b), (c) and (e) of subsection (2) above.

(4) As regards the exercise of the powers of the court under section 23(1)(d), (e) or (f), (2) or (4), 24 or 24A above against a party to a marriage in favour of a child of the family who is not the child of that party, the court shall also have regard—

(a) to whether that party assumed any responsibility for the child's maintenance, and, if so, to the extent to which, and the basis upon which, that party assumed such responsibility and to the length of time for which that party discharged such responsibility;

(b) to whether in assuming and discharging such responsibility that party did so knowing that the child was not his or her own;

(c) to the liability of any other person to maintain the child.

25A. Exercise of court's powers in favour of party to marriage on decree of divorce or nullity of marriage

(1) Where on or after the grant of a decree of divorce or nullity of marriage the court decides to exercise its powers under section 23(1)(a),(b) or (c), 24, 24A or 24B above in favour of a party to the marriage, it shall be the duty of the court to consider whether it would be appropriate so to exercise those powers that the financial obligations of each party towards the other will be terminated as soon after the grant of the decree as the court considers just and reasonable.

(2) Where the court decides in such a case to make a periodical payments or secured periodical payments order in favour of a party to the marriage, the court shall in particular consider whether it would be appropriate to require those payments to be made or secured only for such term as would in the opinion of the court be sufficient to enable the party in whose favour the order is made to adjust without undue hardship to the termination of his or her financial dependence on the other party.

(3) Where on or after the grant of a decree of divorce or nullity of marriage an application is made by a party to the marriage for a periodical payments or secured periodical payments order in his or her favour, then, if the court considers that no continuing obligation should be imposed on either party to make or secure periodical payments in favour of the other, the court may dismiss the application with a direction that the applicant shall not be entitled to make any further application in relation to that marriage for an order under section 23 (1)(a) or (b) above.

25B. Pensions

(1) The matters to which the court is to have regard under section 25(2) above include—

(a) in the case of paragraph (a), any benefits under a pension arrangement which a party to the marriage has or is likely to have, and

(b) in the case of paragraph (h), any benefits under a pension arrangement which by reason of the dissolution or annulment of the marriage, a party to the marriage will lose the chance of acquiring,

and, accordingly, in relation to benefits under a pension arrangement, section 25(2)(a) above shall have effect as if 'in the foreseeable future' were omitted.

(3) The following provisions apply where, having regard to any benefits under a pension arrangement, the court determines to make an order under section 23 above.

(4) To the extent to which the order is made having regard to any benefits under a pension arrangement, the order may require the person responsible for the pension arrangement in question, if at any time any payment in respect of any benefits under the arrangement becomes due to the party with pension rights, to make a payment for the benefit of the other party.

(5) The order must express the amount of any payment required to be made by virtue of subsection (4) above as a percentage of the payment which becomes due to the party with pension rights.

(6) Any such payment by the person responsible for the arrangement—

(a) shall discharge so much of his liability to the party with pension rights as corresponds to the amount of the payment, and

(b) shall be treated for all purposes as a payment made by the party with pension rights in or towards the discharge of his liability under the order.

(7) Where the party with pension rights has a right of commutation under the arrangement, the order may require him to exercise it to any extent; and this section applies to any payment due in consequence of commutation in pursuance of the order as it applies to other payments in respect of benefits under the arrangement.

(7A) The power conferred by subsection (7) above may not be exercised for the purpose of commuting a benefit payable to the party with pension rights to a benefit payable to the other party.

(7B) The power conferred by subsection (4) or (7) above may not be exercised in relation to a pension arrangement which—

(a) is the subject of a pension sharing order in relation to the marriage, or

(b) has been the subject of pension sharing between the parties to the marriage.

(7C) In subsection (1) above, references to benefits under a pension arrangement include any benefits by way of pension, whether under a pension arrangement or not.

25C. Pensions: lump sums

(1) The power of the court under section 23 above to order a party to a marriage to pay a lump sum to the other party includes, where the benefits which the party with pension rights has or is likely to have under a pension arrangement include any lump sum payable in respect of his death, power to make any of the following provision by the order.

(2) The court may—

(a) if the person responsible for the pension arrangement in question has power to determine the person to whom the sum, or any part of it, is to be paid, require him to pay the whole or part of that sum, when it becomes due, to the other party,

(b) if the party with pension rights has power to nominate the person to whom the sum, or any part of it, is to be paid, require the party with pension rights to nominate the other party in respect of the whole or part of that sum,

(c) in any other case, require the person responsible for the pension arrangement in question to pay the whole or part of that sum, when it becomes due, for the benefit of the other party instead of to the person to whom, apart from the order, it would be paid.

(3) Any payment by the person responsible for the arrangement under an order made under section 23 above by virtue of this section shall discharge so much of his liability in respect of the party with pension rights as corresponds to the amount of the payment.

(4) The powers conferred by this section may not be exercised in relation to a pension arrangement which—

(a) is the subject of a pension sharing order in relation to the marriage, or

(b) has been the subject of pension sharing between the parties to the marriage.

25D. Pensions: supplementary

(1) Where—

(a) an order made under section 23 above by virtue of section 25B or 25C above imposes any requirement on the person responsible for a pension arrangement ('the first arrangement') and the party with pension rights acquires rights under another pension arrangement ('the new arrangement') which are derived (directly or indirectly) from the whole of his rights under the first arrangement, and

(b) the person responsible for the new arrangement has been given notice in accordance with regulations made by the Lord Chancellor,

the order shall have effect as if it had been made instead in respect of the person responsible for the new arrangement.

(2) The Lord Chancellor may by regulations—

(a) in relation to any provision of sections 25B or 25C above which authorises the court making an order under section 23 above to require the person responsible for a pension arrangement to make a payment for the benefit of the other party, make provision as to the person to whom, and the terms on which, the payment is to be made,

(ab) make, in relation to payment under a mistaken belief as to the continuation in force of a provision included by virtue of section 25B or 25C above in an order under section 23 above, provision about the rights or liabilities of the payer, the payee or the person to whom the payment was due,

(b) require notices to be given in respect of changes of circumstances relevant to such orders which include provision made by virtue of sections 25B and 25C above,

(ba) make provision for the person responsible for a pension arrangement to be discharged in prescribed circumstances from a requirement imposed by virtue of section 25B or 25C above,

(c) make provision about calculation and verification in relation to the valuation of—

(i) benefits under a pension arrangement, or

(ii) shareable state scheme rights,

for the purposes of the court's functions in connection with the exercise of any of its powers under this Part of this Act.

(2A) Regulations under subsection (2)(e) above may include—

    (a) provision for calculation or verification in accordance with guidance from time to time prepared by a prescribed person, and

    (b) provision by reference to regulations under section 30 or 49(4) of the Welfare Reform and Pensions Act 1999.

(2B) Regulations under subsection (2) above may make different provision for different cases

(2C) Power to make regulations under this section shall be exercisable by statutory instrument which shall be subject to annulment in pursuance of a resolution of either House of Parliament.

(3) In this section and sections 25B and 25C above—

    'occupational pension scheme' has the same meaning as in the Pension Schemes Act 1993;

    'the party with pension rights' means the party to the marriage who has or is likely to have benefits under a pension arrangement and 'the other party' means the other party to the marriage;

    'pension arrangement' means—

    (a) an occupational pension scheme,

    (b) a personal pension scheme,

    (c) a retirement annuity contract,

    (d) an annuity or insurance policy purchased, or transferred, for the purpose of giving effect to rights under an occupational pension scheme or a personal pension scheme, and

    (e) an annuity purchased, or entered into, for the purpose of discharging liability in respect of a pension credit under section 29(1)(b) of the Welfare Reform and Pensions Act 1999 or under corresponding Northern Ireland legislation;

    'personal pension scheme' has the same meaning as in the Pension Schemes Act 1993;

    'prescribed' means prescribed by regulations;

    'retirement annuity contract' means a contract or scheme approved under Chapter III of Part XIV of the Income and Corporation Taxes Act 1988;

    'shareable state scheme rights' has the same meaning as in section 21A(1) above;

    'trustees or managers', in relation to an occupational pension scheme or a personal pension scheme means—

    (a) in the case of a scheme established under a trust, the trustees of the scheme, and

    (b) in any other case, the managers of the scheme.

(4) In this section and sections 25B and 25C above, references to the person responsible for a pension arrangement are—

    (a) in the case of an occupational pension scheme or a personal pension scheme, to the trustees or managers of the scheme,

    (b) in the case of a retirement annuity contract or an annuity falling within paragraph (d) or (e) of the definition of 'pension arrangement' above, the provider of the annuity, and

    (c) in the case of an insurance policy falling within paragraph (d) of the definition of that expression, the insurer.

26. Commencement of proceedings for ancillary relief, etc

(1) Where a petition for divorce, nullity of marriage or judicial separation has been presented, then, subject to subsection (2) below, proceedings for maintenance pending suit under section 22 above, for a financial provision order under section 23 above, or for a property adjustment order may be begun, subject to and in accordance with rules of court at any time after the presentation of the petition.

(2) Rules of court may provide, in such cases as may be prescribed by the rules—

    (a) that applications for any such relief as is mentioned in subsection (1) above shall be made in the petition or answer; and

    (b) that applications for any such relief which are not so made, or are not made until after the expiration of such period following the presentation of the petition or filing of the answer as may be so prescribed, shall be made only with the leave of the court.

[…]

30. Direction for settlement of instrument for securing payments or effecting property adjustment

Where the court decides to make a financial provision order requiring any payments to be secured or a property adjustment order—

    (a) it may direct that the matter be referred to one of the conveyancing counsel of the court for him to settle a proper instrument to be executed by all necessary parties; and

    (b) where the order is to be made in proceedings for divorce, nullity of marriage or judicial separation it may, if it thinks fit, defer the grant of the decree in question until the instrument has been duly executed.

APPENDIX 2

INSOLVENCY ACT 1986

THE SECOND GROUP OF PARTS
INSOLVENCY OF INDIVIDUALS; BANKRUPTCY
PART VIII
INDIVIDUAL VOLUNTARY ARRANGEMENTS

Moratorium for insolvent debtor

252. Interim order of court

(1) In the circumstances specified below, the court may in the case of a debtor (being an individual) make an interim order under this section.

(2) An interim order has the effect that, during the period for which it is in force—

    (a) no bankruptcy petition relating to the debtor may be presented or proceeded with,

    (aa) no landlord or other person to whom rent is payable may exercise any right of forfeiture by peaceable re-entry in relation to premises let to the debtor in respect of a failure by the debtor to comply with any term or condition of his tenancy of such premises, except with the leave of the court, and

    (b) no other proceedings, and no execution or other legal process, may be commenced or continued and no distress may be levied against the debtor or his property except with the leave of the court.

253. Application for interim order

(1) Application to the court for an interim order may be made where the debtor intends to make a proposal under this Part, that is, a proposal to his creditors for a composition in satisfaction of his debts or a scheme of arrangement of his affairs (from hereon referred to, in either case, as a 'voluntary arrangement').

(2) The proposal must provide for some person ('the nominee') to act in relation to the voluntary arrangement either as trustee or otherwise for the purpose of supervising its implementation and the nominee must be a person who is qualified to act as an insolvency practitioner, or authorised to act as nominee, in relation to the voluntary arrangement.

(3) Subject as follows the application may be made-

    (a) if the debtor is an undischarged bankrupt, by the debtor, the trustee of his estate, or the official receiver, and

    (b) in any other case, by the debtor.

(4) An application shall not be made under subsection (3)(a) unless the debtor has given notice of the proposal to the official receiver and, if there is one, the trustee of his estate.

(5) An application shall not be made while a bankruptcy petition presented by the debtor is pending, if the court has, under section 273 below, appointed an insolvency practitioner to inquire into the debtor's affairs and report.

254. Effect of application

(1) At any time when an application under section 253 for an interim order is pending,
    (a) no landlord or other person to whom rent is payable may exercise any right of forfeiture by peaceable re-entry in relation to premises let to the debtor in respect of a failure by the debtor to comply with any term or condition of his tenancy of such premises, except with the leave of the court, and
    (b) the court may forbid the levying of any distress on the debtor's property or its subsequent sale, or both, and stay any action, execution or other legal process against the property or person of the debtor.

(2) Any court in which proceedings are pending against an individual may, on proof that an application under that section has been made in respect of that individual, either stay the proceedings or allow them to continue on such terms as it thinks fit.

255. Cases in which interim order can be made

(1) The court shall not make an interim order on an application under section 253 unless it is satisfied—
    (a) that the debtor intends to make a proposal under this Part;
    (b) that on the day of the making of the application the debtor was an undischarged bankrupt or was able to petition for his own bankruptcy;
    (c) that no previous application has been made by the debtor for an interim order in the period of 12 months ending with that day; and
    (d) that the nominee under the debtor's proposal is willing to act in relation to the proposal.

(2) The court may make an order if it thinks that it would be appropriate to do so for the purpose of facilitating the consideration and implementation of the debtor's proposal.

(3) Where the debtor is an undischarged bankrupt, the interim order may contain provision as to the conduct of the bankruptcy, and the administration of the bankrupt's estate, during the period for which the order is in force.

(4) Subject as follows, the provision contained in an interim order by virtue of subsection (3) may include provision staying proceedings in the bankruptcy or modifying any provision in this Group of Parts, and any provision of the rules in their application to the debtor's bankruptcy.

(5) An interim order shall not, in relation to a bankrupt, make provision relaxing or removing any of the requirements of provisions in this Group of Parts, or of the rules, unless the court is satisfied that that provision is unlikely to result in any significant diminution in, or in the value of, the debtor's estate for the purposes of the bankruptcy.

(6) Subject to the following provisions of this Part, an interim order made on an application under section 253 ceases to have effect at the end of the period of 14 days beginning with the day after the making of the order.

256. Nominee's report on debtor's proposal

(1) Where an interim order has been made on an application under section 253, the nominee shall, before the order ceases to have effect, submit a report to the court stating—
>   (a) whether, in his opinion, the voluntary arrangement which the debtor is proposing has a reasonable prospect of being approved and implemented,
>   (aa) whether, in his opinion, a meeting of the debtor's creditors should be summoned to consider the debtor's proposal, and
>   (b) if in his opinion such a meeting should be summoned, the date on which, and time and place at which, he proposes the meeting should be held.

(2) For the purpose of enabling the nominee to prepare his report the debtor shall submit to the nominee—
>   (a) a document setting out the terms of the voluntary arrangement which the debtor is proposing, and
>   (b) a statement of his affairs containing—
>>   (i) such particulars of his creditors and of his debts and other liabilities and of his assets as may be prescribed, and
>>   (ii) such other information as may be prescribed.

(3) The court may—
>   (a) on an application made by the debtor in a case where the nominee has failed to submit the report required by this section or has died, or
>   (b) on an application made by the debtor or the nominee in a case where it is impracticable or inappropriate for the nominee to continue to act as such,
>
>   direct that the nominee shall be replaced as such by another person qualified to act as an insolvency practitioner, or authorised to act as nominee, in relation to the voluntary arrangement.

(3A) The court may on an application made by the debtor in a case where the nominee has failed to submit the report required by this section, direct that the interim order shall continue, or (if it has ceased to have effect) be renewed, for such further period as the court may specify in the direction.

(4) The court may, on the application of the nominee, extend the period for which the interim order has effect so as to enable the nominee to have more time to prepare his report.

(5) If the court is satisfied on receiving the nominee's report that a meeting of the debtor's creditors should be summoned to consider the debtor's proposal, the court shall direct that the period for which the interim order has effect shall be extended, for such further period as it may specify in the direction, for the purposes of enabling the debtor's proposal to be considered by his creditors in accordance with the following provisions of this Part.

(6) The court may discharge the interim order if it is satisfied, on the application of the nominee—
>   (a) that the debtor has failed to comply with his obligations under subsection (2), or
>   (b) that for any other reason it would be inappropriate for a meeting of the debtor's creditors to be summoned to consider the debtor's proposal.

256A. Debtor's proposal and nominee's report

(1) This section applies where a debtor (being an individual)—
>   (a) intends to make a proposal under this Part (but an interim order has not been made in relation to the proposal and no application for such an order is pending), and

(b) if he is an undischarged bankrupt, has given notice of the proposal to the official receiver and, if there is one, the trustee of his estate,

unless a bankruptcy petition presented by the debtor is pending and the court has, under section 273, appointed an insolvency practitioner to inquire into the debtor's affairs and report.

(2) For the purpose of enabling the nominee to prepare a report to the court, the debtor shall submit to the nominee—
    (a) a document setting out the terms of the voluntary arrangement which the debtor is proposing, and
    (b) a statement of his affairs containing—
        (i) such particulars of his creditors and of his debts and other liabilities and of his assets as may be prescribed, and
        (ii) such other information as may be prescribed.

(3) If the nominee is of the opinion that the debtor is an undischarged bankrupt, or is able to petition for his own bankruptcy, the nominee shall, within 14 days (or such longer period as the court may allow) after receiving the document and statement mentioned in subsection (2), submit a report to the court stating—
    (a) whether, in his opinion, the voluntary arrangement which the debtor is proposing has a reasonable prospect of being approved and implemented,
    (b) whether, in his opinion, a meeting of the debtor's creditors should be summoned to consider the debtor's proposal, and
    (c) if in his opinion such a meeting should be summoned, the date on which, and time and place at which, he proposes the meeting should be held.

(4) The court may—
    (a) on an application made by the debtor in a case where the nominee has failed to submit the report required by this section or has died, or
    (b) on an application made by the debtor or the nominee in a case where it is impracticable or inappropriate for the nominee to continue to act as such,

direct that the nominee shall be replaced as such by another person qualified to act as an insolvency practitioner, or authorised to act as nominee, in relation to the voluntary arrangement.

(5) The court may, on an application made by the nominee, extend the period within which the nominee is to submit his report.

257. Summoning of creditors' meeting

(1) Where it has been reported to the court under section 256 or 256A that a meeting of the debtor's creditors should be summoned, the nominee (or his replacement under section 256(3) or 256A(4)) shall, unless the court otherwise directs, summon that meeting for the time, date and place proposed in his report.

(2) The persons to be summoned to the meeting are every creditor of the debtor of whose claim and address the person summoning the meeting is aware.

(3) For this purpose the creditors of a debtor who is an undischarged bankrupt include—
    (a) every person who is a creditor of the bankrupt in respect of a bankruptcy debt, and
    (b) every person who would be such a creditor if the bankruptcy had commenced on the day on which notice of the meeting is given.

Consideration and implementation of debtor's proposal

258. Decisions of creditors' meeting

(1) A creditors' meeting summoned under section 257 shall decide whether to approve the proposed voluntary arrangement.

(2) The meeting may approve the proposed voluntary arrangement with modifications, but shall not do so unless the debtor consents to each modification.

(3) The modifications subject to which the proposed voluntary arrangement may be approved may include one conferring the functions proposed to be conferred on the nominee on another person qualified to act as an insolvency practitioner or authorised to act as nominee, in relation to the voluntary arrangement.

But they shall not include any modification by virtue of which the proposal ceases to be a proposal under this Part.

(4) The meeting shall not approve any proposal or modification which affects the right of a secured creditor of the debtor to enforce his security, except with the concurrence of the creditor concerned.

(5) Subject as follows, the meeting shall not approve any proposal or modification under which—

   (a) any preferential debt of the debtor is to be paid otherwise than in priority to such of his debts as are not preferential debts, or

   (b) a preferential creditor of the debtor is to be paid an amount in respect of a preferential debt that bears to that debt a smaller proportion than is borne to another preferential debt by the amount that is to be paid in respect of that other debt.

However, the meeting may approve such a proposal or modification with the concurrence of the preferential creditor concerned.

(6) Subject as above, the meeting shall be conducted in accordance with the rules.

(7) In this section 'preferential debt' has the meaning given by section 386 in Part XII and 'preferential creditor' is to be construed accordingly.

259. Report of decisions to court

(1) After the conclusion in accordance with the rules of the meeting summoned under section 257, the chairman of the meeting shall report the result of it to the court and, immediately after so reporting, shall give notice of the result of the meeting to such persons as may be prescribed.

(2) If the report is that the meeting has declined (with or without modifications) to approve the debtor's proposal, the court may discharge any interim order which is in force in relation to the debtor.

260. Effect of approval

(1) This section has effect where the meeting summoned under section 257 approves the proposed voluntary arrangement (with or without modifications).

(2) The approved arrangement—

   (a) takes effect as if made by the debtor at the meeting, and

   (b) binds every person who in accordance with the rules—

      (i) was entitled to vote at the meeting (whether or not he was present or represented at it), or

(ii) would have been so entitled if he had had notice of it,

as if he were a party to the arrangement.

(2A) If—

(a) when the arrangement ceases to have effect any amount payable under the arrangement to a person bound by virtue of subsection (2)(b)(ii) has not been paid, and

(b) the arrangement did not come to an end prematurely,

the debtor shall at that time become liable to pay to that person the amount payable under the arrangement.

(3) The Deeds of Arrangements Act 1914 does not apply to the approved voluntary arrangement.

(4) Any interim order in force in relation to the debtor immediately before the end of the period of 28 days beginning with the day on which the report with respect to the creditors' meeting was made to the court under section 259 ceases to have effect at the end of that period.

This subsection applies except to such extent as the court may direct for the purposes of any application under section 262 below.

(5) Where proceedings on a bankruptcy petition have been stayed by an interim order which ceases to have effect under subsection (4), the petition is deemed, unless the court otherwise orders, to have been dismissed.

261. Additional effect on undischarged bankrupt

(1) This section applies where—

(a) the creditors' meeting summoned under section 257 approves the proposed voluntary arrangement (with or without modifications), and

(b) the debtor is an undischarged bankrupt.

(2) Where this section applies the court shall annul the bankruptcy order on an application made—

(a) by the bankrupt, or

(b) where the bankrupt has not made an application within the prescribed period, by the official receiver.

(3) An application under subsection (2) may not be made—

(a) during the period specified in section 262(3)(a) during which the decision of the creditors' meeting can be challenged by application under section 262,

(b) while an application under that section is pending, or

(c) while an appeal in respect of an application under that section is pending or may be brought.

(4) Where this section applies the court may give such directions about the conduct of the bankruptcy and the administration of the bankrupt's estate as it thinks appropriate for facilitating the implementation of the approved voluntary arrangement.

262. Challenge of meeting's decision

(1) Subject to this section, an application to the court may be made, by any of the persons specified below, on one or both of the following grounds, namely—

(a) that a voluntary arrangement approved by a creditors' meeting summoned under section 257 unfairly prejudices the interests of a creditor of the debtor;

(b) that there has been some material irregularity at or in relation to such a meeting.

(2) The persons who may apply under this section are—

    (a) the debtor;

    (b) a person who—

        (i) was entitled, in accordance with the rules, to vote at the creditors' meeting, or

        (ii) would have been so entitled if he had had notice of it;

    (c) the nominee (or his replacement under section 256(3), 256A(4) or 258(3)); and

    (d) if the debtor is an undischarged bankrupt, the trustee of his estate or the official receiver.

(3) An application under this section shall not be made—

    (a) after the end of the period of 28 days beginning with the day on which the report of the creditors' meeting was made to the court under section 259, or

    (b) in the case of a person who was not given notice of the creditors' meeting, after the end of the period of 28 days beginning with the day on which he became aware that the meeting had taken place,

but (subject to that) an application made by a person within subsection (2)(b)(ii) on the ground that the arrangement prejudices his interests may be made after the arrangement has ceased to have effect, unless it has come to an end prematurely.

(4) Where on an application under this section the court is satisfied as to either of the grounds mentioned in subsection (1), it may do one or both of the following, namely—

    (a) revoke or suspend any approval given by the meeting;

    (b) give a direction to any person for the summoning of a further meeting of the debtor's creditors to consider any revised proposal he may make or, in a case falling within subsection (1)(b), to reconsider his original proposal.

(5) Where at any time after giving a direction under subsection (4)(b) for the summoning of a meeting to consider a revised proposal the court is satisfied that the debtor does not intend to submit such a proposal, the court shall revoke the direction and revoke or suspend any approval given at the previous meeting.

(6) Where the court gives a direction under subsection (4)(b), it may also give a direction continuing or, as the case may require, renewing, for such period as may be specified in the direction, the effect in relation to the debtor of any interim order.

(7) In any case where the court, on an application made under this section with respect to a creditors' meeting, gives a direction under subsection (4)(b) or revokes or suspends an approval under subsection (4)(a) or (5), the court may give such supplemental directions as it thinks fit and, in particular, directions with respect to—

    (a) things done since the meeting under any voluntary arrangement approved by the meeting, and

    (b) such things done since the meeting as could not have been done if an interim order had been in force in relation to the debtor when they were done.

(8) Except in pursuance of the preceding provisions of this section, an approval given at a creditors' meeting summoned under section 257 is not invalidated by any irregularity at or in relation to the meeting.

[...]

263. Implementation and supervision of approved voluntary arrangement

(1) This section applies where a voluntary arrangement approved by a creditors' meeting summoned under section 257 has taken effect.

(2) The person who is for the time being carrying out, in relation to the voluntary arrangement, the functions conferred by virtue of the approval on the nominee (or

his replacement under section 256(3), 256A(4) or 258(3)) shall be known as the supervisor of the voluntary arrangement.

(3) If the debtor, any of his creditors or any other person is dissatisfied by any act, omission or decision of the supervisor, he may apply to the court; and on such an application the court may—

    (a) confirm, reverse or modify any act or decision of the supervisor,

    (b) give him directions, or

    (c) make such other order as it thinks fit.

(4) The supervisor may apply to the court for directions in relation to any particular matter arising under the voluntary arrangement.

(5) The court may, whenever—

    (a) it is expedient to appoint a person to carry out the functions of the supervisor, and

    (b) it is inexpedient, difficult or impracticable for an appointment to be made without the assistance of the court,

make an order appointing a person who is qualified to act as an insolvency practitioner or authorised to act as a supervisor, in relation to the voluntary arrangement, either in substitution for the existing supervisor or to fill a vacancy.

This is without prejudice to section 41(2) of the Trustee Act 1925 (power of court to appoint trustees of deeds of arrangement).

(6) The power conferred by subsection (5) is exercisable so as to increase the number of persons exercising the functions of the supervisor or, where there is more than one person exercising those functions, so as to replace one or more of those persons.

'Fast-track voluntary arrangement'

263A. Availability

Section 263B applies where an individual debtor intends to make a proposal to his creditors for a voluntary arrangement and—

    (a) the debtor is an undischarged bankrupt,

    (b) the official receiver is specified in the proposal as the nominee in relation to the voluntary arrangement, and

    (c) no interim order is applied for under section 253.

263B. Decision

(1) The debtor may submit to the official receiver—

    (a) a document setting out the terms of the voluntary arrangement which the debtor is proposing, and

    (b) a statement of his affairs containing such particulars as may be prescribed of his creditors, debts, other liabilities and assets and such other information as may be prescribed.

(2) If the official receiver thinks that the voluntary arrangement proposed has a reasonable prospect of being approved and implemented, he may make arrangements for inviting creditors to decide whether to approve it.

(3) For the purposes of subsection (2) a person is a creditor only if—

    (a) he is a creditor of the debtor in respect of a bankruptcy debt, and

(b) the official receiver is aware of his claim and his address.
(4) Arrangements made under subsection (2)—
    (a) must include the provision to each creditor of a copy of the proposed voluntary arrangement,
    (b) must include the provision to each creditor of information about the criteria by reference to which the official receiver will determine whether the creditors approve or reject the proposed voluntary arrangement, and
    (c) may not include an opportunity for modifications to the proposed voluntary arrangement to be suggested or made.
(5) Where a debtor submits documents to the official receiver under subsection (1) no application under section 253 for an interim order may be made in respect of the debtor until the official receiver has—
    (a) made arrangements as described in subsection (2), or
    (b) informed the debtor that he does not intend to make arrangements (whether because he does not think the voluntary arrangement has a reasonable prospect of being approved and implemented or because he declines to act).

263C. Result

As soon as is reasonably practicable after the implementation of arrangements under section 263B(2) the official receiver shall report to the court whether the proposed voluntary arrangement has been approved or rejected.

263D. Approval of voluntary arrangement

(1) This section applies where the official receiver reports to the court under section 263C that a proposed voluntary arrangement has been approved.
(2) The voluntary arrangement—
    (a) takes effect,
    (b) binds the debtor, and
    (c) binds every person who was entitled to participate in the arrangements made under section 263B(2).
(3) The court shall annul the bankruptcy order in respect of the debtor on an application made by the official receiver.
(4) An application under subsection (3) may not be made—
    (a) during the period specified in section 263F(3) during which the voluntary arrangement can be challenged by application under section 263F(2),
    (b) while an application under that section is pending, or
    (c) while an appeal in respect of an application under that section is pending or may be brought.
(5) The court may give such directions about the conduct of the bankruptcy and the administration of the bankrupt's estate as it thinks appropriate for facilitating the implementation of the approved voluntary arrangement.
(6) The Deeds of Arrangement Act 1914 (c.47) does not apply to the voluntary arrangement.
(7) A reference in this Act or another enactment to a voluntary arrangement approved under this Part includes a reference to a voluntary arrangement which has effect by virtue of this section.

263E. Implementation

Section 263 shall apply to a voluntary arrangement which has effect by virtue of section 263D(2) as it applies to a voluntary arrangement approved by a creditors' meeting.

263F. Revocation

(1) The court may make an order revoking a voluntary arrangement which has effect by virtue of section 263D(2) on the ground—
  (a) that it unfairly prejudices the interests of a creditor of the debtor, or
  (b) that a material irregularity occurred in relation to the arrangements made under section 263B(2).
(2) An order under subsection (1) may be made only on the application of—
  (a) the debtor,
  (b) a person who was entitled to participate in the arrangements made under section 263B(2),
  (c) the trustee of the bankrupt's estate, or
  (d) the official receiver.
(3) An application under subsection (2) may not be made after the end of the period of 28 days beginning with the date on which the official receiver makes his report to the court under section 263C.
(4) But a creditor who was not made aware of the arrangements under section 263B(2) at the time when they were made may make an application under subsection (2) during the period of 28 days beginning with the date on which he becomes aware of the voluntary arrangement.

263G. Offences

(1) Section 262A shall have effect in relation to obtaining approval to a proposal for a voluntary arrangement under section 263D.
(2) Section 262B shall have effect in relation to a voluntary arrangement which has effect by virtue of section 263D(2) (for which purposes the words 'by a creditors' meeting summoned under section 257' shall be disregarded).

PART IX
BANKRUPTCY
CHAPTER I
BANKRUPTCY PETITIONS; BANKRUPTCY ORDERS

Preliminary

264. Who may present a bankruptcy petition

(1) A petition for a bankruptcy order to be made against an individual may be presented to the court in accordance with the following provisions of this Part—
  (a) by one of the individual's creditors or jointly by more than one of them,
  (b) by the individual himself,
  (ba) by a temporary administrator (within the meaning of Article 38 of the EC Regulation),

    (bb) by a liquidator (within the meaning of Article 2(b) of the EC Regulation) appointed in proceedings by virtue of Article 3(1) of the EC Regulation,

    (c) by the supervisor of, or any person (other than the individual) who is for the time being bound by, a voluntary arrangement proposed by the individual and approved under Part VIII, *or*

    [...]

(2) Subject to those provisions, the court may make a bankruptcy order on any such petition.

265. Conditions to be satisfied in respect of debtor

(1) A bankruptcy petition shall not be presented to the court under section 264(1)(a) or (b) unless the debtor—

    (a) is domiciled in England and Wales

    (b) is personally present in England and Wales on the day on which the petition is presented, or

    (c) at any time in the period of 3 years ending with that day—

        (i) has been ordinarily resident, or has had a place of residence, in England and Wales, or

        (ii) has carried on business in England and Wales.

(2) The reference in subsection (1)(c) to an individual carrying on business includes—

    (a) the carrying on of business by a firm or partnership of which the individual is a member, and

    (b) the carrying on of business by an agent or manager for the individual or for such a firm or partnership.

(3) This section is subject to Article 3 of the EC Regulation.

266. Other preliminary conditions

(1) Where a bankruptcy petition relating to an individual is presented by a person who is entitled to present a petition under two or more paragraphs of section 264(1), the petition is to be treated for the purposes of this Part as a petition under such one of those paragraphs as may be specified in the petition.

(2) A bankruptcy petition shall not be withdrawn without the leave of the court.

(3) The court has a general power, if it appears to it appropriate to do so on the grounds that there has been a contravention of the rules or for any other reason, to dismiss a bankruptcy petition or to stay proceedings on such a petition; and, where it stays proceedings on a petition, it may do so on such terms and conditions as it thinks fit.

[...]

Creditor's petition

267. Grounds of creditor's petition

(1) A creditor's petition must be in respect of one or more debts owed by the debtor, and the petitioning creditor or each of the petitioning creditors must be a person to whom the debt or (as the case may be) at least one of the debts is owed.

(2) Subject to the next three sections, a creditor's petition may be presented to the court in respect of a debt or debts only if, at the time the petition is presented—

(a) the amount of the debt, or the aggregate amount of the debts, is equal to or exceeds the bankruptcy level,

(b) the debt, or each of the debts, is for a liquidated sum payable to the petitioning creditor, or one or more of the petitioning creditors, either immediately or at some certain, future time, and is unsecured,

(c) the debt, or each of the debts, is a debt which the debtor appears either to be unable to pay or to have no reasonable prospect of being able to pay, and

(d) there is no outstanding application to set aside a statutory demand served (under section 268 below) in respect of the debt or any of the debts.

[...]

(4) 'The bankruptcy level' is £750; but the Secretary of State may by order in a statutory instrument substitute any amount specified in the order for that amount or (as the case may be) for the amount which by virtue of such an order is for the time being the amount of the bankruptcy level.

(5) An order shall not be made under subsection (4) unless a draft of it has been laid before, and approved by a resolution of, each House of Parliament.

268. Definition of 'inability to pay', etc; the statutory demand

(1) For the purposes of section 267(2)(c), the debtor appears to be unable to pay a debt if, but only if, the debt is payable immediately and either—

(a) the petitioning creditor to whom the debt is owed has served on the debtor a demand (known as 'the statutory demand') in the prescribed form requiring him to pay the debt or to secure or compound for it to the satisfaction of the creditor, at least 3 weeks have elapsed since the demand was served and the demand has been neither complied with nor set aside in accordance with the rules, or

(b) execution or other process issued in respect of the debt on a judgment or order of any court in favour of the petitioning creditor, or one or more of the petitioning creditors to whom the debt is owed, has been returned unsatisfied in whole or in part.

(2) For the purposes of section 267(2)(c) the debtor appears to have no reasonable prospect of being able to pay a debt if, but only if, the debt is not immediately payable and—

(a) the petitioning creditor to whom it is owed has served on the debtor a demand (also known as 'the statutory demand') in the prescribed form requiring him to establish to the satisfaction of the creditor that there is a reasonable prospect that the debtor will be able to pay the debt when it falls due,

(b) at least 3 weeks have elapsed since the demand was served, and

(c) the demand has been neither complied with nor set aside in accordance with the rules.

269. Creditor with security

(1) A debt which is the debt, or one of the debts, in respect of which a creditor's petition is presented need not be unsecured if either—

(a) the petition contains a statement by the person having the right to enforce the security that he is willing, in the event of a bankruptcy order being made, to give up his security for the benefit of all the bankrupt's creditors, or

(b) the petition is expressed not to be made in respect of the secured part of the debt and contains a statement by that person of the estimated value at the date of the petition of the security for the secured part of the debt.

(2) In a case falling within subsection (1)(b) the secured and unsecured parts of the debt are to be treated for the purposes of sections 267 and 270 as separate debts.

270. Expedited petition

In the case of a creditor's petition presented wholly or partly in respect of a debt which is the subject of a statutory demand under section 268, the petition may be presented before the end of the 3-week period there mentioned if there is a serious possibility that the debtor's property or the value of any of his property will be significantly diminished during that period and the petition contains a statement to that effect.

271. Proceedings on creditor's petition

(1) The court shall not make a bankruptcy order on a creditor's petition unless it is satisfied that the debt, or one of the debts, in respect of which the petition was presented is either—
   (a) a debt which, having been payable at the date of the petition or having since become payable, has been neither paid nor secured or compounded for, or
   (b) a debt which the debtor has no reasonable prospect of being able to pay when it falls due.

(2) In a case in which the petition contains such a statement as is required by section 270, the court shall not make a bankruptcy order until at least 3 weeks have elapsed since the service of any statutory demand under section 268.

(3) The court may dismiss the petition if it is satisfied that the debtor is able to pay all his debts or is satisfied—
   (a) that the debtor has made an offer to secure or compound for a debt in respect of which the petition is presented,
   (b) that the acceptance of that offer would have required the dismissal of the petition, and
   (c) that the offer has been unreasonably refused;
   and, in determining for the purposes of this subsection whether the debtor is able to pay all his debts, the court shall take into account his contingent and prospective liabilities.

(4) In determining for the purposes of this section what constitutes a reasonable prospect that a debtor will be able to pay a debt when it falls due, it is to be assumed that the prospect given by the facts and other matters known to the creditor at the time he entered into the transaction resulting in the debt was a reasonable prospect.

(5) Nothing in sections 267 to 271 prejudices the power of the court, in accordance with the rules, to authorise a creditor's petition to be amended by the omission of any creditor or debt and to be proceeded with as if things done for the purposes of those sections had been done only by or in relation to the remaining creditors or debts.

Debtor's petition

272. Grounds of debtor's petition

(1) A debtor's petition may be presented to the court only on the grounds that the debtor is unable to pay his debts.

(2) The petition shall be accompanied by a statement of the debtor's affairs containing —
   (a) such particulars of the debtor's creditors and of his debts and other liabilities and of his assets as may be prescribed, and
   (b) such other information as may be prescribed.

273. Appointment of insolvency practitioner by the court

(1) Subject to the next section, on the hearing of a debtor's petition the court shall not make a bankruptcy order if it appears to the court—
   (a) that if a bankruptcy order were made the aggregate amount of the bankruptcy debts, so far as unsecured, would be less that the small bankruptcies level,
   (b) that if a bankruptcy order were made, the value of the bankrupt's estate would be equal to or more than the minimum amount,
   (c) that within the period of 5 years ending with the presentation of the petition the debtor has neither been adjudged bankrupt nor made a composition with his creditors in satisfaction of his debts or a scheme of arrangement of his affairs, and
   (d) that it would be appropriate to appoint a person to prepare a report under section 274.

'The minimum amount' and 'the small bankruptcies level' mean such amounts as may for the time being be prescribed for the purposes of this section.

(2) Where on the hearing of the petition, it appears to the court as mentioned in subsection (1), the court shall appoint a person who is qualified to act as an insolvency practitioner in relation to the debtor—
   (a) to prepare a report under the next section, and
   (b) subject to section 258(3) in Part VIII, to act in relation to any voluntary arrangement to which the report relates either as trustee or otherwise for the purpose of supervising its implementation.

274. Action on report of insolvency practitioner

(1) A person appointed under section 273 shall inquire into the debtor's affairs and, within such period as the court may direct, shall submit a report to the court stating whether the debtor is willing, for the purposes of Part VIII, to make a proposal for a voluntary arrangement.

(2) A report which states that the debtor is willing as above mentioned shall also state—
   (a) whether, in the opinion of the person making the report, a meeting of the debtor's creditors should be summoned to consider the proposal, and
   (b) if in that person's opinion such a meeting should be summoned, the date on which, and the time and place at which, he proposes the meeting should be held.

(3) On considering a report under this section the court may—
   (a) without any application, make an interim order under section 252, if it thinks that it is appropriate to do so for the purpose of facilitating the consideration and implementation of the debtor's proposal, or
   (b) if it thinks it would be inappropriate to make such an order, make a bankruptcy order.

(4) An interim order made by virtue of this section ceases to have effect at the end of such period as the court may specify for the purpose of enabling the debtor's proposal to be considered by his creditors in accordance with the applicable provisions of Part VIII.

(5) Where it has been reported to the court under this section that a meeting of the debtor's creditors should be summoned, the person making the report shall, unless the court otherwise directs, summon that meeting for the time, date and place proposed in his report.

The meeting is then deemed to have been summoned under section 257 in Part VIII, and subsections (2) and (3) of that section, and sections 258 to 263 apply accordingly.

275. Summary administration

Repealed by the Enterprise Act 2002, ss 269, 278(2), Sch 23, paras 1.2, Sch 26 with effect from 1 April 2004.

Other cases for special consideration

276. Default in connection with voluntary arrangement

(1) The court shall not make a bankruptcy order on a petition under section 264(1)(c) (supervisor of, or person bound by, voluntary arrangement proposed and approved) unless it is satisfied—

    (a) that the debtor has failed to comply with his obligations under the voluntary arrangement, or

    (b) that information which was false or misleading in any material particular or which contained material omissions—

        (i) was contained in any statement of affairs or other document supplied by the debtor under Part VIII to any person, or

        (ii) was otherwise made available by the debtor to his creditors at or in connection with a meeting summoned under that Part, or

    (c) that the debtor has failed to do all such things as may for the purposes of the voluntary arrangement have been reasonably required of him by the supervisor of the arrangement.

(2) Where a bankruptcy order is made on a petition under section 264(1)(c), any expenses properly incurred as expenses of the administration of the voluntary arrangement in question shall be a first charge on the bankrupt's estate.

Commencement and duration of bankruptcy; discharge

278. Commencement and continuance

The bankruptcy of an individual against whom a bankruptcy order has been made—

    (a) commences with the day on which the order is made, and

    (b) continues until the individual is discharged under the following provisions of this Chapter.

279. Duration

(1) A bankrupt is discharged from bankruptcy at the end of the period of one year beginning with the date on which the bankruptcy commences.

(2) If before the end of that period the official receiver files with the court a notice stating that investigation of the conduct and affairs of the bankrupt under section 289 is unnecessary or concluded, the bankrupt is discharged when the notice is filed.

(3) On the application of the official receiver or the trustee of a bankrupt's estate, the court may order that the period specified in subsection (1) shall cease to run until—
   (a) the end of a specified period, or
   (b) the fulfilment of a specified condition.

(4) The court may make an order under subsection (3) only if satisfied that the bankrupt has failed or is failing to comply with an obligation under this Part.

(5) In subsection 3(b) 'condition' includes a condition requiring that the court be satisfied of something.

(6) In the case of an individual who is adjudged bankrupt on a petition under section 264(1)(d)—
   (a) subsections (1) to (5) shall not apply, and
   (b) the bankrupt is discharged from bankruptcy by an order of the court under section 280.

(7) This section is without prejudice to any power of the court to annul a bankruptcy order.

280. Discharge by order of the court

(1) An application for an order of the court discharging an individual from bankruptcy in a case falling within section 279(6) may be made by the bankrupt at any time after the end of the period of 5 years beginning with the date on which the bankruptcy commences.

(2) On an application under this section the court may—
   (a) refuse to discharge the bankrupt from bankruptcy,
   (b) make an order discharging him absolutely, or
   (c) make an order discharging him subject to such conditions with respect to any income which may subsequently become due to him, or with respect to property devolving upon him, or acquired by him, after his discharge, as may be specified in the order.

(3) The court may provide for an order falling within subsection (2)(b) or (c) to have immediate effect or to have its effect suspended for such period, or until the fulfilment of such conditions (including a condition requiring the court to be satisfied as to any matter), as may be specified in the order.

281. Effect of discharge

(1) Subject as follows, where a bankrupt is discharged, the discharge releases him from all the bankruptcy debts, but has no effect—
   (a) on the functions (so far as they remain to be carried out) of the trustee of his estate, or
   (b) on the operation, for the purposes of the carrying out of those functions, of the provisions of this Part;
   and, in particular, discharge does not affect the right of any creditor of the bankrupt to prove in the bankruptcy for any debt from which the bankrupt is released.

(2) Discharge does not affect the right of any secured creditor of the bankrupt to enforce his security for the payment of a debt from which the bankrupt is released.

(3) Discharge does not release the bankrupt from any bankruptcy debt which he incurred in respect of, or forbearance in respect of which was secured by means of, any fraud or fraudulent breach of trust to which he was a party.

(4)   Discharge does not release the bankrupt from any liability in respect of a fine imposed for an offence or from any liability under a recognisance except, in the case of a penalty imposed for an offence under an enactment relating to the public revenue or of a recognisance, with the consent of the Treasury.

(4A) In subsection (4) the reference to a fine includes a reference to a confiscation order under Part 2, 3 or 4 of the Proceeds of Crime Act 2002.

(5)   Discharge does not, except to such extent and on such conditions as the court may direct, release the bankrupt from any bankruptcy debt which—

      (a) consists in a liability to pay damages for negligence, nuisance or breach of a statutory, contractual or other duty, or to pay damages by virtue of Part I of the Consumer Protection Act 1987, being in either case damages in respect of personal injuries to any person, or

      (a) arises under any order made in family proceedings or under a maintenance calculation made under the Child Support Act 1991.

(6)   Discharge does not release the bankrupt from such other bankruptcy debts, not being debts provable in his bankruptcy, as are prescribed.

(7)   Discharge does not release any person other than the bankrupt from any liability (whether as partner or co-trustee of the bankrupt or otherwise) from which the bankrupt is released by the discharge, or from any liability as surety for the bankrupt or as a person in the nature of such a surety.

(8)   In this section—

      'family proceedings' means—

        (a) family proceedings within the meaning of the Magistrates' Courts Act 1980 and any proceedings which would be such proceedings but for section 65(1)(ii) of that Act (proceedings for variation of order for periodical payments); and

        (b) family proceedings within the meaning of Part V of the Matrimonial and Family Proceedings Act 1984; and

      'fine' means the same as in the Magistrates' Courts Act 1980; and

      'personal injuries' includes death and any disease or other impairment of a person's physical or mental condition.

281A. Post-discharge restrictions

Schedule 4A to this Act (bankruptcy restrictions order and bankruptcy restrictions undertaking) shall have effect.

282. Court's power to annul bankruptcy order

(1)   The court may annul a bankruptcy order if it at any time appears to the court—

      (a) that, on the grounds existing at the time the order was made, the order ought not to have been made, or

      (b) that, to the extent required by the rules, the bankruptcy debts and the expenses of the bankruptcy have all, since the making of the order, been either paid or secured for to the satisfaction of the court.

(2)   Prospectively repealed by Criminal Justice Act 1988

(3)   The court may annul a bankruptcy order whether or not the bankrupt has been discharged from the bankruptcy.

(4) Where the court annuls a bankruptcy order (whether under this section or under section 261 or 263D in Part VIII)—

    (a) any sale or other disposition of property, payment made or other thing duly done, under any provision in this Group of Parts, by or under the authority of the official receiver or a trustee of the bankrupt's estate or by the court is valid, but

    (b) if any of the bankrupt's estate is then vested, under any such provision, in such a trustee, it shall vest in such person as the court may appoint or, in default of any such appointment, revert to the bankrupt on such terms (if any) as the court may direct;

and the court may include in its order such supplemental provisions as may be authorised by the rules.

CHAPTER II
PROTECTION OF BANKRUPT'S ESTATE
AND INVESTIGATION OF HIS AFFAIRS

283. Definition of bankrupt's estate

(1) Subject as follows, a bankrupt's estate for the purposes of any of this Group of Parts comprises—

    (a) all property belonging to or vested in the bankrupt at the commencement of the bankruptcy, and

    (b) any property which by virtue of any of the following provisions of this Part is comprised in that estate or is treated as falling within the preceding paragraph.

(2) Subsection (1) does not apply to—

    (a) such tools, books, vehicles and other items of equipment as are necessary to the bankrupt for use personally by him in his employment, business or vocation;

    (b) such clothing, bedding, furniture, household equipment and provisions as are necessary for satisfying the basic domestic needs of the bankrupt and his family.

This subsection is subject to section 308 in Chapter IV (certain excluded property reclaimable by trustee).

(3) Subsection (1) does not apply to—

    (a) property held by the bankrupt on trust for any other person, or

    (b) the right of nomination to a vacant ecclesiastical benefice.

(3A) Subject to section 308A in Chapter IV, subsection (1) does not apply to—

    (a) a tenancy which is an assured tenancy or an assured agricultural occupancy, within the meaning of Part I of the Housing Act 1988, and the terms of which inhibit an assignment as mentioned in section 127(5) of the Rent Act 1977, or

    (b) a protected tenancy, within the meaning of the Rent Act 1977, in respect of which, by virtue of any provision of Part IX of that Act, no premium can lawfully be required as a condition of assignment, or

    (c) a tenancy of a dwelling-house by virtue of which the bankrupt is, within the meaning of the Rent (Agriculture) Act 1976, a protected occupier of the dwelling-house, and the terms of which inhibit an assignment as mentioned in section 127(5) of the Rent Act 1977, or

   (d) a secure tenancy, within the meaning of Part IV of the Housing Act 1985, which is not capable of being assigned, except in cases mentioned in section 91(3) of that Act.

(4) References in any of this Group of Parts to property, in relation to a bankrupt, include references to any power exercisable by him over or in respect of property except in so far as the power is exercisable over or in respect of property not for the time being comprised in the bankrupt's estate and—

   (a) is so exercisable at a time after either the official receiver has had his release in respect of that estate under section 299(2) in Chapter III or a meeting summoned by the trustee of that estate under section 331 in Chapter IV has been held, or

   (b) cannot be so exercised for the benefit of the bankrupt;

and a power exercisable over or in respect of property is deemed for the purposes of any of this Group of Parts to vest in the person entitled to exercise it at the time of the transaction or event by virtue of which it is exercisable by that person (whether or not it becomes so exercisable at that time).

(5) For the purposes of any such provision in this Group of Parts, property comprised in a bankrupt's estate is so comprised subject to the rights of any person other than the bankrupt (whether as a secured creditor of the bankrupt or otherwise) in relation thereto, but disregarding—

   (a) any rights in relation to which a statement such as is required by section 269(1)(a) was made in the petition on which the bankrupt was adjudged bankrupt, and

   (b) any rights which have been otherwise given up in accordance with the rules.

(6) This section has effect subject to the provisions of any enactment not contained in this Act under which any property is to be excluded from a bankrupt's estate.

283A. Bankrupt's home ceasing to form part of estate

(1) This section applies where property comprised in the bankrupt's estate consists of an interest in a dwelling-house which at the date of the bankruptcy was the sole or principal residence of—

   (a) the bankrupt,

   (b) the bankrupt's spouse, or

   (c) a former spouse of the bankrupt.

(2) At the end of the period of three years beginning with the date of the bankruptcy the interest mentioned in subsection (1) shall—

   (a) cease to be comprised in the bankrupt's estate, and

   (b) vest in the bankrupt (without conveyance, assignment or transfer).

(3) Subsection (2) shall not apply if during the period mentioned in that subsection—

   (a) the trustee realises the interest mentioned in subsection (1),

   (b) the trustee applies for an order for sale in respect of the dwelling-house,

   (c) the trustee applies for an order for possession of the dwelling-house,

   (d) the trustee applies for an order under section 313 in Chapter IV in respect of that interest, or

   (e) the trustee and the bankrupt agree that the bankrupt shall incur a specified liability to his estate (with or without the addition of interest from the date of the agreement) in consideration of which the interest mentioned in subsection (1) shall cease to form part of the estate.

(4) Where an application of a kind described in subsection (3)(b) to (d) is made during the period mentioned in subsection (2) and is dismissed, unless the court orders otherwise the interest to which the application relates shall on the dismissal of the application—

(a) cease to be comprised in the bankrupt's estate, and

(b) vest in the bankrupt (without conveyance, assignment or transfer).

(5) If the bankrupt does not inform the trustee or the official receiver of his interest in a property before the end of the period of three months beginning with the date of the bankruptcy, the period of three years mentioned in subsection (2)—

(a) shall not begin with the date of the bankruptcy, but

(b) shall begin with the date on which the trustee or official receiver becomes aware of the bankrupt's interest.

(6) The court may substitute for the period of three years mentioned in subsection (2) a longer period—

(a) in prescribed circumstances, and

(b) in such other circumstances as the court thinks appropriate.

(7) The rules may make provision for this section to have effect with the substitution of a shorter period for the period of three years mentioned in subsection (2) in specified circumstances (which may be described by reference to action to be taken by a trustee in bankruptcy).

(8) The rules may also, in particular, make provision—

(a) requiring or enabling the trustee of a bankrupt's estate to give notice that this section applies or does not apply;

(b) about the effect of a notice under paragraph (a);

(c) requiring the trustee of a bankrupt's estate to make an application to the Chief Land Registrar.

(9) Rules under subsection (8)(b) may, in particular—

(a) disapply this section;

(b) enable a court to disapply this section;

(c) make provision in consequence of a disapplication of this section;

(d) enable a court to make provision in consequence of a disapplication of this section;

(e) make provision (which may include provision conferring jurisdiction on a court or tribunal) about compensation.

284. Restrictions on disposition of property

(1) Where a person is adjudged bankrupt, any disposition of property made by that person in the period to which this section applies is void except to the extent that it is or was made with the consent of the court, or is or was subsequently ratified by the court.

(2) Subsection (1) applies to a payment (whether in cash or otherwise) as it applies to a disposition of property and, accordingly, where any payment is void by virtue of that subsection, the person paid shall hold the sum paid for the bankrupt as part of his estate.

(3) This section applies to the period beginning with the day of the presentation of the petition for the bankruptcy order and ending with the vesting, under Chapter IV of this Part, of the bankrupt's estate in a trustee.

(4) The preceding provisions of this section do not give a remedy against any person—

    (a) in respect of any property or payment which he received before the commencement of the bankruptcy in good faith, for value and without notice that the petition had been presented, or

    (b) in respect of any interest in property which derives from an interest in respect of which there is, by virtue of this subsection, no remedy.

(5) Where after the commencement of his bankruptcy the bankrupt has incurred a debt to a banker or other person by reason of the making of a payment which is void under this section, that debt is deemed for the purposes of any of this Group of Parts to have been incurred before the commencement of the bankruptcy unless—

    (a) that banker or person had notice of the bankruptcy before the debt was incurred, or

    (b) it is not reasonably practicable for the amount of the payment to be recovered from the person to whom it was made.

(6) A disposition of property is void under this section notwithstanding that the property is not or, as the case may be, would not be comprised in the bankrupt's estate; but nothing in this section affects any disposition made by a person of property held by him on trust for any other person.

285. Restriction on proceedings and remedies

(1) At any time when proceedings on a bankruptcy petition are pending or an individual has been adjudged bankrupt the court may stay any action, execution or other legal process against the property or person of the debtor or, as the case may be, of the bankrupt.

(2) Any court in which proceedings are pending against any individual may, on proof that a bankruptcy petition has been presented in respect of that individual or that he is an undischarged bankrupt, either stay the proceedings or allow them to continue on such terms as it thinks fit.

(3) After the making of a bankruptcy order no person who is a creditor of the bankrupt in respect of a debt provable in the bankruptcy shall—

    (a) have any remedy against the property or person of the bankrupt in respect of that debt, or

    (b) before the discharge of the bankrupt, commence any action or other legal proceedings against the bankrupt except with the leave of the court and on such terms as the court may impose.

This is subject to sections 346 (enforcement procedures) and 347 (limited right to distress).

(4) Subject as follows, subsection (3) does not affect the right of a secured creditor of the bankrupt to enforce his security.

(5) Where any goods of an undischarged bankrupt are held by any person by way of pledge, pawn or other security, the official receiver may, after giving notice in writing of his intention to do so, inspect the goods.

Where such a notice has been given to any person, that person is not entitled, without leave of the court, to realise his security unless he has given the trustee of the bankrupt's estate a reasonable opportunity of inspecting the goods and of exercising the bankrupt's right of redemption.

(6) References in this section to the property or goods of the bankrupt are to any of his property or goods, whether or not comprised in his estate.

[...]

287. Receivership pending appointment of trustee

(1) Between the making of a bankruptcy order and the time at which the bankrupt's estate vests in a trustee under Chapter IV of this Part, the official receiver is the receiver and (subject to section 370 (special manager)) the manager of the bankrupt's estate and is under a duty to act as such.

(2) The function of the official receiver while acting as receiver or manager of the bankrupt's estate under this section is to protect the estate; and for this purpose
  (a) he has the same powers as if he were a receiver or manager appointed by the High Court, and
  (b) he is entitled to sell or otherwise dispose of any perishable goods comprised in the estate and any other goods so comprised the value of which is likely to diminish if they are not disposed of.

(3) The official receiver while acting as receiver or manager of the estate under this section—
  (a) shall take all such steps as he thinks fit for protecting any property which may be claimed for the estate by the trustee of that estate,
  (b) is not, except in pursuance of directions given by the Secretary of State, required to do anything that involves his incurring expenditure,
  (c) may, if he thinks fit (and shall, if so directed by the court) at any time summon a general meeting of the bankrupt's creditors.

(4) Where—
  (a) the official receiver acting as receiver or manager of the estate under this section seizes or disposes of any property which is not comprised in the estate, and
  (b) at the time of the seizure or disposal the official receiver believes, and has reasonable grounds for believing, that he is entitled (whether in pursuance of an order of the court or otherwise) to seize or dispose of that property,
  the official receiver is not to be liable to any person in respect of any loss or damage resulting from the seizure or disposal except in so far as that loss or damage is caused by his negligence; and he has a lien on the property, or the proceeds of its sale, for such of the expenses of the bankruptcy as were incurred in connection with the seizure or disposal.

(5) This section does not apply where by virtue of section 297 (appointment of trustee; special cases) the bankrupt's estate vests in a trustee immediately on the making of the bankruptcy order.

[. . .]

289. Investigatory duties of official receiver

(1) The official receiver shall
  (a) investigate the conduct and affairs of each bankrupt (including his conduct and affairs before the making of the bankruptcy order), and
  (b) make such report (if any) to the court as the official receiver thinks fit.

(2) Subsection (1) shall not apply to a case in which the official receiver thinks an investigation under that subsection unnecessary.

(3) Where a bankrupt makes an application for discharge under section 280—
  (a) the official receiver shall make a report to the court about such matters as may be prescribed, and
  (b) the court shall consider the report before determining the application.

(4) A report by the official receiver under this section shall in any proceedings be prima facie evidence of the facts stated in it.

[...]

291. Duties of bankrupt in relation to official receiver

(1) Where a bankruptcy order has been made, the bankrupt is under a duty—

    (a) to deliver possession of his estate to the official receiver, and

    (b) to deliver up to the official receiver all books, papers and other records of which he has possession or control and which relate to his estate and affairs (including any which would be privileged from disclosure in any proceedings).

(2) In the case of any part of the bankrupt's estate which consists of things possession of which cannot be delivered to the official receiver, and in the case of any property that may be claimed for the bankrupt's estate by the trustee, it is the bankrupt's duty to do all such things as may reasonably be required by the official receiver for the protection of those things or that property.

(3) Subsections (1) and (2) do not apply where by virtue of section 297 below the bankrupt's estate vests in a trustee immediately on the making of a bankruptcy order.

(4) The bankrupt shall give the official receiver such inventory of his estate and such other information, and shall attend on the official receiver at such times, as the official receiver may reasonably require—

    (a) for a purpose of this Chapter, or

    (b) in connection with the making of a bankruptcy restrictions order.

(5) Subsection (4) applies to a bankrupt after his discharge.

(6) If the bankrupt without reasonable excuse fails to comply with any obligation imposed by this section, he is guilty of a contempt of court and liable to be punished accordingly (in addition to any other punishment to which he may be subject).

[...]

CHAPTER IV
ADMINISTRATION BY TRUSTEE

Preliminary

305. General functions of trustee

(1) This Chapter applies in relation to any bankruptcy where either—

    (a) the appointment of a person as trustee of a bankrupt's estate takes effect, or

    (b) the official receiver becomes trustee of a bankrupt's estate.

(2) The function of the trustee is to get in, realise and distribute the bankrupt's estate in accordance with the following provisions of this Chapter; and in the carrying out of that function and in the management of the bankrupt's estate the trustee is entitled, subject to those provisions, to use his own discretion.

(3) It is the duty of the trustee, if he is not the official receiver—

    (a) to furnish the official receiver with such information,

    (b) to produce to the official receiver, and permit inspection by the official receiver of, such books, papers and other records, and

    (c) to give the official receiver such other assistance,

as the official receiver may reasonably require for the purpose of enabling him to carry out his functions in relation to the bankruptcy.

(4) The official name of the trustee shall be 'the Trustee of the estate of ...., a bankrupt' (inserting the name of the bankrupt); but he may be referred to as 'the trustee in bankruptcy' of the particular bankrupt.

Acquisition, control and realisation of bankrupt's estate

306. Vesting of bankrupt's estate in trustee

(1) The bankrupt's estate shall vest in the trustee immediately on his appointment taking effect or, in the case of the official receiver, on his becoming trustee.

(2) Where any property which is, or is to be, comprised in the bankrupt's estate vests in the trustee (whether under this section or under any other provisions in this Part), it shall so vest without any conveyance, assignment or transfer.

[...]

307. After-acquired property

(1) Subject to this section and section 309, the trustee may by notice in writing claim for the bankrupt's estate any property which has been acquired by, or has devolved upon, the bankrupt since the commencement of the bankruptcy.

(2) A notice under this section shall not be served in respect of—
  (a) any property falling within subsection (2) or (3) of section 283 in Chapter II,
  (aa) any property vesting in the bankrupt by virtue of section 283A in Chapter II,
  (b) any property which by virtue of any other enactment is excluded from the bankrupt's estate, or
  (c) without prejudice to section 280(2)(c) (order of court on application for discharge), any property which is acquired by, or devolves upon, the bankrupt after his discharge.

(3) Subject to the next subsection, upon the service on the bankrupt of a notice under this section the property to which the notice relates shall vest in the trustee as part of the bankrupt's estate; and the trustee's title to that property has relation back to the time at which the property was acquired by, or devolved upon, the bankrupt.

(4) Where, whether before or after service of a notice under this section—
  (a) a person acquires property in good faith, for value and without notice of the bankruptcy, or
  (b) a banker enters into a transaction in good faith and without such notice,
  the trustee is not in respect of that property or transaction entitled by virtue of this section to any remedy against that person or banker, or any person whose title to any property derives from that person or banker.

(5) References in this section to property do not include any property which, as part of the bankrupt's income, may be the subject of an income payments order under section 310.

308. Vesting in trustee of certain items of excess value

(1) Subject to section 309, where—
  (a) property is excluded by virtue of section 283(2) (tools of trade, household effects, etc.) from the bankrupt's estate, and

(b) it appears to the trustee that the realisable value of the whole or any part of that property exceeds the cost of a reasonable replacement for that property or that part of it,

the trustee may by notice in writing claim that property or, as the case may be, that part of it for the bankrupt's estate.

(2)   Upon the service on the bankrupt of a notice under this section, the property to which the notice relates vests in the trustee as part of the bankrupt's estate; and, except against a purchaser in good faith, for value and without notice of the bankruptcy, the trustee's title to that property has relation back to the commencement of the bankruptcy.

(3)   The trustee shall apply funds comprised in the estate to the purchase by or on behalf of the bankrupt of a reasonable replacement for any property vested in the trustee under this section; and the duty imposed by this subsection has priority over the obligation of the trustee to distribute the estate.

(4)   For the purposes of this section property is a reasonable replacement for other property if it is reasonably adequate for meeting the needs met by the other property.

309. Time-limit for notice under s.307 or 308

(1)   Except with the leave of the court, a notice shall not be served—
   (a) under section 307, after the end of the period of 42 days beginning with the day on which it first came to the knowledge of the trustee that the property in question had been acquired by, or had devolved upon, the bankrupt;
   (b) under section 308 or section 308A, after the end of the period of 42 days beginning with the day on which the property or tenancy in question first came to the knowledge of the trustee.

(2)   For the purposes of this section—
   (a) anything which comes to the knowledge of the trustee is deemed in relation to any successor of his as trustee to have come to the knowledge of the successor at the same time; and
   (b) anything which comes (otherwise than under paragraph (a)) to the knowledge of a person before he is the trustee is deemed to come to his knowledge on his appointment taking effect or, in the case of the official receiver, on his becoming trustee.

310. Income payments orders

(1)   The court may make an order ('an income payments order') claiming for the bankrupt's estate so much of the income of the bankrupt during the period for which the order is in force as may be specified in the order.

(1A)   An income payments order may be made only on an application instituted—
   (a) by the trustee, and
   (b) before the discharge of the bankrupt.

(2)   The court shall not make an income payments order the effect of which would be to reduce the income of the bankrupt when taken together with any payments to which subsection (8) applies below what appears to the court to be necessary for meeting the reasonable domestic needs of the bankrupt and his family.

(3)   An income payments order shall, in respect of any payment of income to which it is to apply, either—

    (a) require the bankrupt to pay the trustee an amount equal to so much of that payment as is claimed by the order, or

    (b) require the person making the payment to pay so much of it as is so claimed to the trustee, instead of to the bankrupt.

(4)   Where the court makes an income payments order it may, if it thinks fit, discharge or vary any attachment of earnings order that is for the time being in force to secure payments by the bankrupt.

(5)   Sums received by the trustee under an income payments order form part of the bankrupt's estate.

(6)   An income payments order must specify the period during which it is to have effect; and that period—

    (a) may end after the discharge of the bankrupt, but

    (b) may not end after the period of three years beginning with the date on which the order is made.

(6A) An income payments order may (subject to subsection (6)(b)) be varied on the application of the trustee or the bankrupt (whether before or after discharge).

(7)   For the purposes of this section the income of the bankrupt comprises every payment in the nature of income which is from time to time made to him or to which he from time to time becomes entitled, including any payment in respect of the carrying on of any business or in respect of any office or employment and (despite anything in section 11 or 12 of the Welfare Reform and Pensions Act 1999) any payment under a pension scheme but excluding any payment to which subsection (8) applies.

(8)   This subsection applies to—

    (a) payments by way of guaranteed minimum pension; and

    (b) payments giving effect to the bankrupt's protected rights as a member of a pension scheme.

(9)   In this section, 'guaranteed minimum pension' and 'protected rights' have the same meaning as in the Pension Schemes Act 1993.

310A. Income payments agreement

(1)   In this section 'income payments agreement' means a written agreement between a bankrupt and his trustee or between a bankrupt and the official receiver which provides—

    (a) that the bankrupt is to pay to the trustee or the official receiver an amount equal to a specified part or proportion of the bankrupt's income for a specified period, or

    (b) that a third person is to pay to the trustee or the official receiver a specified proportion of money due to the bankrupt by way of income for a specified period.

(2)   A provision of an income payments agreement of a kind specified in subsection (1)(a) or (b) may be enforced as if it were a provision of an income payments order.

(3)   While an income payments agreement is in force the court may, on the application of the bankrupt, his trustee or the official receiver, discharge or vary an attachment of earnings order that is for the time being in force to secure payments by the bankrupt.

(4) The following provisions of section 310 shall apply to an income payments agreement as they apply to an income payments order—
   (a) subsection (5) (receipts to form part of estate), and
   (b) subsections (7) to (9) (meaning of income).

(5) An income payments agreement must specify the period during which it is to have effect; and that period –
   (a) may end after the discharge of the bankrupt, but
   (b) may not end after the period of three years beginning with the date on which the agreement is made.

(6) An income payments agreement may (subject to subsection (5)(b)) be varied—
   (a) by written agreement between the parties, or
   (b) by the court on an application made by the bankrupt, the trustee or the official receiver.

(7) The court—
   (a) may not vary an income payments agreement so as to include provision of a kind which could not be included in an income payments order, and
   (b) shall grant an application to vary an income payments agreement if and to the extent that the court thinks variation necessary to avoid the effect mentioned in section 310(2).

311. Acquisition by trustee of control

(1) The trustee shall take possession of all books, papers and other records which relate to the bankrupt's estate or affairs and which belong to him or are in his possession or under his control (including any which would be privileged from disclosure in any proceedings).

(2) In relation to, and for the purpose of acquiring or retaining possession of, the bankrupt's estate, the trustee is in the same position as if he were a receiver of property appointed by the High Court; and the court may, on his application, enforce such acquisition or retention accordingly.

(3) Where any part of the bankrupt's estate consists of stock or shares in a company, shares in a ship or any other property transferable in the books of a company, office or person, the trustee may exercise the right to transfer the property to the same extent as the bankrupt might have exercised it if he had not become bankrupt.

(4) Where any part of the estate consists of things in action, they are deemed to have been assigned to the trustee; but notice of the deemed assignment need not be given except so far as it is necessary, in a case where the deemed assignment is from the bankrupt himself, for protecting the priority of the trustee.

(5) Where any goods comprised in the estate are held by any person by way of pledge, pawn or other security and no notice has been served in respect of those goods by the official receiver under subsection (5) of section 285 (restriction on realising security), the trustee may serve such a notice in respect of the goods; and whether or not a notice has been served under this subsection or that subsection, the trustee may, if he thinks fit, exercise the bankrupt's right of redemption in respect of any such goods.

(6) A notice served by the trustee under subsection (5) has the same effect as a notice served by the official receiver under section 285(5).

312. Obligation to surrender control to trustee

(1) The bankrupt shall deliver up to the trustee possession of any property, books, papers or other records of which he has possession or control and of which the trustee is required to take possession.

This is without prejudice to the general duties of the bankrupt under section 333 in this Chapter.

(2) If any of the following is in possession of any property, books, papers or other records of which the trustee is required to take possession, namely—

(a) the official receiver,

(b) a person who has ceased to be trustee of the bankrupt's estate, or

(c) a person who has been the supervisor of a voluntary arrangement approved in relation to the bankrupt under Part VIII,

the official receiver or, as the case may be, that person shall deliver up possession of the property, books, papers or records to the trustee.

(3) Any banker or agent of the bankrupt or any other person who holds any property to the account of, or for, the bankrupt shall pay or deliver to the trustee all property in his possession or under his control which forms part of the bankrupt's estate and which he is not by law entitled to retain as against the bankrupt or trustee.

(4) If any person without reasonable excuse fails to comply with any obligation imposed by this section, he is guilty of a contempt of court and liable to be punished accordingly (in addition to any other punishment to which he may be subject).

313. Charge on bankrupt's home

(1) Where any property consisting of an interest in a dwelling-house which is occupied by the bankrupt or by his spouse or former spouse is comprised in the bankrupt's estate and the trustee is, for any reason, unable for the time being to realise that property, the trustee may apply to the court for an order imposing a charge on the property for the benefit of the bankrupt's estate.

(2) If on an application under this section the court imposes a charge on any property, the benefit of that charge shall be comprised in the bankrupt's estate and is enforceable, up to the charged value from time to time, for the payment of any amount which is payable otherwise than to the bankrupt out of the estate and of interest on that amount at the prescribed rate.

(2A) In subsection (2) the charged value means—

(a) the amount specified in the charging order as the value of the bankrupt's interest in the property at the date of the order, plus

(b) interest on that amount from the date of the charging order at the prescribed rate.

(2B) In determining the value of an interest for the purposes of this section the court shall disregard any matter which it is required to disregard by the rules.

(3) An order under this section made in respect of property vested in the trustee shall provide, in accordance with the rules, for the property to cease to be comprised in the bankrupt's estate and, subject to the charge (and any prior charge), to vest in the bankrupt.

(4) Subsections (1) and (2) and (4) to (6) of section 3 of the Charging Orders Act 1979 (supplemental provisions with respect to charging orders) have effect in relation to orders under this section as in relation to charging orders under that Act.

(5) But an order under section 3(5) of that Act may not vary a charged value.

313A. Low value home: application for sale, possession or charge

(1) This section applies where—

    (a) property comprised in the bankrupt's estate consists of an interest in a dwelling-house which at the date of the bankruptcy was the sole or principal residence of—

        (i) the bankrupt,

        (ii) the bankrupt's spouse, or

        (iii) a former spouse of the bankrupt, and

    (b) the trustee applies for an order for the sale of the property, for an order for possession of the property or for an order under section 313 in respect of the property.

(2) The court shall dismiss the application if the value of the interest is below the amount prescribed for the purposes of this subsection.

(3) In determining the value of an interest for the purposes of this section the court shall disregard any matter which it is required to disregard by the order which prescribes the amount for the purposes of subsection (2).

Disclaimer of onerous property

315. Disclaimer (general power)

(1) Subject as follows, the trustee may, by the giving of the prescribed notice, disclaim any onerous property and may do so notwithstanding that he has taken possession of it, endeavoured to sell it or otherwise exercised rights of ownership in relation to it.

(2) The following is onerous property for the purposes of this section, that is to say—

    (a) any unprofitable contract, and

    (b) any other property comprised in the bankrupt's estate which is unsaleable or not readily saleable, or is such that it may give rise to a liability to pay money or perform any other onerous act.

(3) A disclaimer under this section—

    (a) operates so as to determine, as from the date of the disclaimer, the rights, interests and liabilities of the bankrupt and his estate in or in respect of the property disclaimed, and

    (b) discharges the trustee from all personal liability in respect of that property as from the commencement of his trusteeship,

but does not, except so far as is necessary for the purpose of releasing the bankrupt, the bankrupt's estate and the trustee from liability, affect the rights or liabilities of any other person.

(4) A notice of disclaimer shall not be given under this section in respect of any property that has been claimed for the estate under section 307 (after-acquired property) or 308 or 308A (personal property of bankrupt exceeding reasonable replacement value) except with the leave of the court.

(5) Any person sustaining loss or damage in consequence of the operation of a disclaimer under this section is deemed to be a creditor of the bankrupt to the extent of the loss or damage and accordingly may prove for the loss or damage as a bankruptcy debt.

318. Disclaimer of dwelling-house

Without prejudice to section 317, the disclaimer of any property in a dwelling-house does not take effect unless a copy of the disclaimer has been served (so far as the trustee is aware of their addresses) on every person in occupation of or claiming a right to occupy the dwelling-house and either—

    (a) no application under section 320 is made with respect to the property before the end of the period of 14 days beginning with the day on which the last notice served under this section was served, or

    (b) where such an application has been made, the court directs that the disclaimer is to take effect.

Distribution of bankrupt's estate

332. Saving for bankrupt's home

(1) This section applies where—

    (a) there is comprised in the bankrupt's estate property consisting of an interest in a dwelling-house which is occupied by the bankrupt or by his spouse or former spouse, and

    (b) the trustee has been unable for any reason to realise that property.

(2) The trustee shall not summon a meeting under section 331 unless either—

    (a) the court has made an order under section 313 imposing a charge on that property for the benefit of the bankrupt's estate, or

    (b) the court has declined, on an application under that section, to make such an order, or

    (c) the Secretary of State has issued a certificate to the trustees stating that it would be inappropriate or inexpedient for such an application to be made in the case in question.

Supplemental

333. Duties of bankrupt in relation to trustee

(1) The bankrupt shall—

    (a) give to the trustee such information as to his affairs,

    (b) attend on the trustee at such times, and

    (c) do all such other things,

as the trustee may for the purposes of carrying out his functions under any of this Group of Parts reasonably require.

(2) Where at any time after the commencement of the bankruptcy any property is acquired by, or devolves upon, the bankrupt or there is an increase of the bankrupt's income, the bankrupt shall, within the prescribed period, give the trustee notice of the property or, as the case may be, of the increase.

(3) Subsection (1) applies to a bankrupt after his discharge.

(4) If the bankrupt without reasonable excuse fails to comply with any obligation imposed by this section, he is guilty of a contempt of court and liable to be punished accordingly (in addition to any other punishment to which he may be subject).

[...]

335A. Rights under trusts of land

(1) Any application by a trustee of a bankrupt's estate under section 14 of the Trusts of Land and Appointment of Trustees Act 1996 (powers of court in relation to trusts of

land) for an order under that section for the sale of land shall be made to the court having jurisdiction in relation to the bankruptcy.

(2) On such an application the court shall make such order as it thinks just and reasonable having regard to—

    (a) the interests of the bankrupt's creditors;

    (b) where the application is made in respect of land which includes a dwelling-house which is or has been the home of the bankrupt or the bankrupt's spouse or former spouse—

        (i) the conduct of the spouse or former spouse, so far as contributing to the bankruptcy,

        (ii) the needs and financial resources of the spouse or former spouse, and

        (iii) the needs of any children; and

    (c) all the circumstances of the case other than the needs of the bankrupt.

(3) Where such an application is made after the end of the period of one year beginning with the first vesting under Chapter IV of this Part of the bankrupt's estate in a trustee, the court shall assume, unless the circumstances of the case are exceptional, that the interests of the bankrupt's creditors outweigh all other considerations.

(4) The powers conferred on the court by this section are exercisable on an application whether it is made before or after the commencement of this section.

CHAPTER V
EFFECT OF BANKRUPTCY ON CERTAIN RIGHTS TRANSACTIONS, ETC

Rights of occupation

336. Rights of occupation etc. of bankrupt spouse

(1) Nothing occurring in the initial period of the bankruptcy (that is to say, the period beginning with the day of the presentation of the petition for the bankruptcy order and ending with the vesting of the bankrupt's estate in a trustee) is to be taken as having given rise to any matrimonial home rights under Part IV of the Family Law Act 1996 in relation to a dwelling-house comprised in the bankrupt's estate.

(2) Where a spouse's matrimonial home rights under the Act of 1996 are a charge on the estate or interest of the other spouse, or of trustees for the other spouse, and the other spouse is adjudged bankrupt—

    (a) the charge continues to subsist notwithstanding the bankruptcy and, subject to the provisions of that Act, binds the trustee of the bankrupt's estate and persons deriving title under that trustee, and

    (b) any application for an order under section 33 of that Act shall be made to the court having jurisdiction in relation to the bankruptcy.

(3) [...]

(4) On such an application as is mentioned in subsection (2) ... the court shall make such order under section 33 of the Act of 1996 ... as it thinks just and reasonable having regard to—

    (a) the interests of the bankrupt's creditors,

    (b) the conduct of the spouse or former spouse, so far as contributing to the bankruptcy,

(c) the needs and financial resources of the spouse or former spouse,

(d) the needs of any children, and

(e) all the circumstances of the case other than the needs of the bankrupt.

(5) Where such an application is made after the end of the period of one year beginning with the first vesting under Chapter IV of this Part of the bankrupt's estate in a trustee, the court shall assume, unless the circumstances of the case are exceptional, that the interests of the bankrupt's creditors outweigh all other considerations.

337. Rights of occupation of bankrupt

(1) This section applies where—

(a) a person who is entitled to occupy a dwelling-house by virtue of a beneficial estate or interest is adjudged bankrupt, and

(b) any persons under the age of 18 with whom that person had at some time occupied that dwelling-house had their home with that person at the time when the bankruptcy petition was presented and at the commencement of the bankruptcy.

(2) Whether or not the bankrupt's spouse (if any) has matrimonial home rights under Part IV of the Family Law Act 1996—

(a) the bankrupt has the following rights as against the trustee of his estate—

(i) if in occupation, a right not to be evicted or excluded from the dwelling-house or any part of it, except with the leave of the court,

(ii) if not in occupation, a right with the leave of the court to enter into and occupy the dwelling-house, and

(b) the bankrupt's rights are a charge, having the like priority as an equitable interest created immediately before the commencement of the bankruptcy, on so much of his estate or interest in the dwelling-house as vests in the trustee.

(3) The Act of 1996 has effect, with the necessary modifications, as if—

(a) the rights conferred by paragraph (a) of subsection (2) were matrimonial home rights under that Act,

(b) any application for such leave as is mentioned in that paragraph were an application for an order under section 33 of that Act, and

(c) any charge under paragraph (b) of that subsection on the estate or interest of the trustee were a charge under that Act on the estate or interest of a spouse.

(4) Any application for leave such as is mentioned in subsection (2)(a) or otherwise by virtue of this section for an order under section 33 of the Act of 1996 shall be made to the court having jurisdiction in relation to the bankruptcy.

(5) On such an application the court shall make such order under section 33 of the Act of 1996 as it thinks just and reasonable having regard to the interests of the creditors, to the bankrupt's financial resources, to the needs of the children and to all the circumstances of the case other than the needs of the bankrupt.

(6) Where such an application is made after the end of the period of one year beginning with the vesting (under Chapter IV of this Part) of the bankrupt's estate in a trustee, the court shall assume, unless the circumstances of the case are exceptional, that the interests of the bankrupt's creditors outweigh all other considerations.

338. Payments in respect of premises occupied by bankrupt

Where any premises comprised in a bankrupt's estate are occupied by him (whether by virtue of the preceding section or otherwise) on condition that he makes payments

298

towards satisfying any liability arising under a mortgage of the premises or otherwise towards the outgoings of the premises, the bankrupt does not by virtue of those payments, acquire any interest in the premises.

Adjustment of prior transactions, etc.

339. Transactions at an undervalue

(1) Subject as follows in this section and sections 341 and 342, where an individual is adjudged bankrupt and he has at a relevant time (defined in section 341) entered into a transaction with any person at an undervalue, the trustee of the bankrupt's estate may apply to the court for an order under this section.

(2) The court shall, on such an application, make such order as it thinks fit for restoring the position to what it would have been if that individual had not entered into that transaction.

(3) For the purposes of this section and sections 341 and 342, an individual enters into a transaction with a person at an undervalue if—

(a) he makes a gift to that person or he otherwise enters into a transaction with that person on terms that provide for him to receive no consideration,

(b) he enters into a transaction with that person in consideration of marriage, or

(c) he enters into a transaction with that person for a consideration the value of which, in money or money's worth, is significantly less than the value, in money or money's worth, of the consideration provided by the individual.

340. Preferences

(1) Subject as follows in this and the next two sections, where an individual is adjudged bankrupt and he has at a relevant time (defined in section 341) given a preference to any person, the trustee of the bankrupt's estate may apply to the court for an order under this section.

(2) The court shall, on such an application, make such order as it thinks fit for restoring the position to what it would have been if that individual had not given that preference.

(3) For the purposes of this and the next two sections, an individual gives a preference to a person if—

(a) that person is one of the individual's creditors or a surety or guarantor for any of his debts or other liabilities, and

(b) the individual does anything or suffers anything to be done which (in either case) has the effect of putting that person into a position which, in the event of the individual's bankruptcy, will be better than the position he would have been in if that thing had not been done.

(4) The court shall not make an order under this section in respect of a preference given to any person unless the individual who gave the preference was influenced in deciding to give it by a desire to produce in relation to that person the effect mentioned in subsection (3)(b) above.

(5) An individual who has given a preference to a person who, at the time the preference was given, was an associate of his (otherwise than by reason only of being his employee) is presumed, unless the contrary is shown, to have been influenced in deciding to give it by such a desire as is mentioned in subsection (4).

(6) The fact that something has been done in pursuance of the order of a court does not, without more, prevent the doing or suffering of that thing from constituting the giving of a preference.

341. 'Relevant time' under ss 339, 340

(1) Subject as follows, the time at which an individual enters into a transaction at an undervalue or gives a preference is a relevant time if the transaction is entered into or the preference given—

    (a) in the case of a transaction at an undervalue, at a time in the period of 5 years ending with the day of the presentation of the bankruptcy petition on which the individual is adjudged bankrupt,

    (b) in the case of a preference which is not a transaction at an undervalue and is given to a person who is an associate of the individual (otherwise than by reason only of being his employee), at a time in the period of 2 years ending with that day, and

    (c) in any other case of a preference which is not a transaction at an undervalue, at a time in the period of 6 months ending with that day.

(2) Where an individual enters into a transaction at an undervalue or gives a preference at a time mentioned in paragraph (a), (b) or (c) of subsection (1) (not being, in the case of a transaction at an undervalue, a time less than 2 years before the end of the period mentioned in paragraph (a)), that time is not a relevant time for the purposes of sections 339 and 340 unless the individual—

    (a) is insolvent at that time, or

    (b) becomes insolvent in consequence of the transaction or preference;

but the requirements of this subsection are presumed to be satisfied, unless the contrary is shown, in relation to any transaction at an undervalue which is entered into by an individual with a person who is an associate of his (otherwise than by reason only of being his employee).

(3) For the purposes of subsection (2), an individual is insolvent if—

    (a) he is unable to pay his debts as they fall due, or

    (b) the value of his assets is less than the amount of his liabilities, taking into account his contingent and prospective liabilities.

[...]

342. Orders under ss 339, 340

(1) Without prejudice to the generality of section 339(2) or 340(2), an order under either of those sections with respect to a transaction or preference entered into or given by an individual who is subsequently adjudged bankrupt may (subject as follows)—

    (a) require any property transferred as part of the transaction, or in connection with the giving of the preference, to be vested in the trustee of the bankrupt's estate as part of that estate;

    (b) require any property to be so vested if it represents in any person's hands the application either of the proceeds of sale of property so transferred or of money so transferred;

    (c) release or discharge (in whole or in part) any security given by the individual;

(d) require any person to pay, in respect of benefits received by him from the individual, such sums to the trustee of his estate as the court may direct;

(e) provide for any surety or guarantor whose obligations to any person were released or discharged (in whole or in part) under the transaction or by the giving of the preference to be under such new or revived obligations to that person as the court thinks appropriate;

(f) provide for security to be provided for the discharge of any obligation imposed by or arising under the order, for such an obligation to be charged on any property and for the security or charge to have the same priority as a security or charge released or discharged (in whole or in part) under the transaction or by the giving of the preference; and

(g) provide for the extent to which any person whose property is vested by the order in the trustee of the bankrupt's estate, or on whom obligations are imposed by the order, is to be able to prove in the bankruptcy for debts or other liabilities which arose from, or were released or discharged (in whole or in part) under or by, the transaction or the giving of the preference.

(2) An order under section 339 or 340 may affect the property of, or impose any obligation on, any person whether or not he is the person with whom the individual in question entered into the transaction or, as the case may be, the person to whom the preference was given; but such an order—

(a) shall not prejudice any interest in property which was acquired from a person other than that individual and was acquired in good faith and for value, or prejudice any interest deriving from such an interest, and

(b) shall not require a person who received a benefit from the transaction or preference in good faith and for value to pay a sum to the trustees of the bankrupt's estate, except where he was a party to the transaction or the payment is to be in respect of a preference given to that person at a time when he was a creditor of that individual.

(2A) Where a person has acquired an interest in property from a person other than the individual in question, or has received a benefit from the transaction or preference, and at the time of that acquisition or receipt—

(a) he had notice of the relevant surrounding circumstances and of the relevant proceedings, or

(b) he was an associate of, or was connected with, either the individual in question or the person with whom that individual entered into the transaction or to whom that individual gave the preference,

then, unless the contrary is shown, it shall be presumed for the purposes of paragraph (a) or (as the case may be) paragraph (b) of subsection (2) that the interest was acquired or the benefit was received otherwise than in good faith.

(3) Any sums required to be paid to the trustee in accordance with an order under section 339 or 340 shall be comprised in the bankrupt's estate.

(4) For the purposes of subsection (2A)(a), the relevant surrounding circumstances are (as the case may require)—

(a) the fact that the individual in question entered into the transaction at an undervalue; or

(b) the circumstances which amounted to the giving of the preference by the individual in question.

(5) For the purposes of subsection (2A)(a), a person has notice of the relevant proceedings if he has notice—

  (a) of the fact that the petition on which the individual in question is adjudged
  bankrupt has been presented; or

  (b) of the fact the individual in question has been adjudged bankrupt.

(6) Section 249 in Part VII of this Act shall apply for the purposes of subsection (2A)(b)
as it applies for the purposes of the first Group of Parts.

342A. Recovery of excessive pension contributions

(1) Where an individual who is adjudged bankrupt—

  (a) has rights under an approved pension arrangement, or

  (b) has excluded rights under an unapproved pension arrangement,

  the trustee of the bankrupt's estate may apply to the court for an order under this
  section.

(2) If the court is satisfied—

  (a) that the rights under the arrangement are to any extent, and whether directly or
  indirectly, the fruits of relevant contributions, and

  (b) that the making of any of the relevant contributions ('the excessive contributions') has unfairly prejudiced the individual's creditors,

  the court may make such order as it thinks fit for restoring the position to what it
  would have been had the excessive contributions not been made.

(3) Subsection (4) applies where the court is satisfied that the value of the rights under
the arrangement is, as a result of rights of the individual under the arrangement or
any other pension arrangement having at any time become subject to a debit under
section 29(1)(a) of the Welfare Reform and Pensions Act 1999 (debits giving effect to
pension-sharing), less than it would otherwise have been.

(4) Where this subsection applies—

  (a) any relevant contributions which were represented by the rights which became
  subject to the debit shall, for the purposes of subsection (2), be taken to be
  contributions of which the rights under the arrangement are the fruits, and

  (b) where the relevant contributions represented by the rights under the arrangement
  (including those so represented by virtue of paragraph (a)) are not all excessive
  contributions, relevant contributions which are represented by the rights under the
  arrangement otherwise than by virtue of paragraph (a) shall be treated as excessive
  contributions before any which are so represented by virtue of that paragraph.

(5) In subsections (2) to (4) 'relevant contributions' means contributions to the arrangement or any other pension arrangement—

  (a) which the individual has at any time made on his own behalf, or

  (b) which have at any time been made on his behalf.

(6) The court shall, in determining whether it is satisfied under subsection (2)(b), consider in particular—

  (a) whether any of the contributions were made for the purpose of putting assets
  beyond the reach of the individual's creditors or any of them, and

  (b) whether the total amount of any contributions—

    (i) made by or on behalf of the individual to pension arrangements, and

    (ii) represented (whether directly or indirectly) by rights under approved pension
    arrangements or excluded rights under unapproved pension arrangements,

is an amount which is excessive in view of the individual's circumstances when those contributions were made.

(7) For the purposes of this section and sections 342B and 342C ('the recovery provisions'), rights of an individual under an unapproved pension arrangement are excluded rights if they are rights which are excluded from his estate by virtue of regulations under section 12 of the Welfare Reform and Pensions Act 1999.

(8) In the recovery provisions—

'approved pension arrangement' has the same meaning as in section 11 of the Welfare Reform and Pensions Act 1999;

'unapproved pension arrangement' has the same meaning as in section 12 of that Act.

342B. Orders under section 342A

(1) Without prejudice to the generality of section 342A(2), an order under section 342A may include provision—

(a) requiring the person responsible for the arrangement to pay an amount to the individual's trustee in bankruptcy,

(b) adjusting the liabilities of the arrangement in respect of the individual,

(c) adjusting any liabilities of the arrangement in respect of any other person that derive, directly or indirectly, from rights of the individual under the arrangement,

(d) for the recovery by the person responsible for the arrangement (whether by deduction from any amount which that person is ordered to pay or otherwise) of costs incurred by that person in complying in the bankrupt's case with any requirement under section 342C(1) or in giving effect to the order.

(2) In subsection (1), references to adjusting the liabilities of the arrangement in respect of a person include (in particular) reducing the amount of any benefit or future benefit to which that person is entitled under the arrangement.

(3) In subsection (1)(c), the reference to liabilities of the arrangement does not include liabilities in respect of a person which result from giving effect to an order or provision falling within section 28(1) of the Welfare Reform and Pensions Act 1999 (pension sharing orders and agreements).

(4) The maximum amount which the person responsible for an arrangement may be required to pay by an order under section 342A is the lesser of—

(a) the amount of the excessive contributions, and

(b) the value of the individual's rights under the arrangement (if the arrangement is an approved pension arrangement) or of his excluded rights under the arrangement (if the arrangement is an unapproved pension arrangement).

(5) An order under section 342A which requires the person responsible for an arrangement to pay an amount ('the restoration amount') to the individual's trustee in bankruptcy must provide for the liabilities of the arrangement to be correspondingly reduced.

(6) For the purposes of subsection (5), liabilities are correspondingly reduced if the difference between—

(a) the amount of the liabilities immediately before the reduction, and

(b) the amount of the liabilities immediately after the reduction,

is equal to the restoration amount.

(7) An order under section 342A in respect of an arrangement—
    (a) shall be binding on the person responsible for the arrangement, and
    (b) overrides provisions of the arrangement to the extent that they conflict with the provisions of the order.

342C. Orders under section 342A: supplementary

(1) The person responsible for—
    (a) an approved pension arrangement under which a bankrupt has rights,
    (b) an unapproved pension arrangement under which a bankrupt has excluded rights, or
    (c) a pension arrangement under which a bankrupt has at any time had rights,
shall, on the bankrupt's trustee in bankruptcy making a written request, provide the trustee with such information about the arrangement and rights as the trustee may reasonably require for, or in connection with, the making of applications under section 342A.

(2) Nothing in—
    (a) any provision of section 159 of the Pensions Schemes Act 1993 or section 91 of the Pensions Act 1995 (which prevent assignment and the making of orders that restrain a person from receiving anything which he is prevented from assigning),
    (b) any provision of any enactment (whether passed or made before or after the passing of the Welfare Reform and Pensions Act 1999) corresponding to any of the provisions mentioned in paragraph (a), or
    (c) any provision of the arrangement in question corresponding to any of those provisions,
applies to a court exercising its powers under section 342A.

(3) Where any sum is required by an order under section 342A to be paid to the trustee in bankruptcy, that sum shall be comprised in the bankrupt's estate.

(4) Regulations may, for the purposes of the recovery provisions, make provision about the calculation and verification of—
    (a) any such value as is mentioned in section 342B(4)(b);
    (b) any such amounts as are mentioned in section 342B(6)(a) and (b).

(5) The power conferred by subsection (4) includes power to provide for calculation or verification—
    (a) in such manner as may, in the particular case, be approved by a prescribed person; or
    (b) in accordance with guidance—
        (i) from time to time prepared by the prescribed person, and
        (ii) approved by the Secretary of State.

(6) References in the recovery provisions to the person responsible for a pension arrangement are to—
    (a) the trustees, managers or provider of the arrangement, or
    (b) the person having functions in relation to the arrangement corresponding to those of a trustee, manager or provider.

(7) In this section and sections 342A and 342B—
    'prescribed' means prescribed by regulations;
    'the recovery provisions' means this section and sections 342A and 342B;
    'regulations' means regulations made by the Secretary of State.

(8) Regulations under the recovery provisions may—

    (a) make different provision for different cases;

    (b) contain such incidental, supplemental and transitional provisions as appear to the Secretary of State necessary or expedient.

(9) Regulations under the recovery provisions shall be made by statutory instrument subject to annulment in pursuance of a resolution of either House of Parliament.

342D. Recovery of excessive contributions in pension-sharing cases

(1) For the purposes of sections 339, 341 and s342, a pension sharing transaction shall be taken—

    (a) to be a transaction, entered into by the transferor with the transferee, by which the appropriate amount is transferred by the transferor to the transferee; and

    (b) to be capable of being a transaction entered into at an undervalue only so far as it is a transfer of so much of the appropriate amount as is recoverable.

(2) For the purposes of sections 340 to 342, a pension-sharing transaction shall be taken —

    (a) to be something (namely a transfer of the appropriate amount to the transferee) done by the transferor; and

    (b) to be capable of being a preference given to the transferee only so far as it is a transfer of so much of the appropriate amount as is recoverable.

(3) If on an application under section 339 or 340 any question arises as to whether, or the extent to which, the appropriate amount in the case of a pension-sharing transaction is recoverable, the question shall be determined in accordance with subsections (4) to (8).

(4) The court shall first determine the extent (if any) to which the transferor's rights under the shared arrangement at the time of the transaction appear to have been (whether directly or indirectly) the fruits of contributions ('personal contributions')—

    (a) which the transferor has at any time made on his own behalf, or

    (b) which have at any time been made on the transferor's behalf,

  to the shared arrangement or any other pension arrangement.

(5) Where it appears that those rights were to any extent the fruits of personal contributions, the court shall then determine the extent (if any) to which those rights appear to have been the fruits of personal contributions whose making has unfairly prejudiced the transferor's creditors ('the unfair contributions').

(6) If it appears to the court that the extent to which those rights were the fruits of the unfair contributions is such that the transfer of the appropriate amount could have been made out of rights under the shared arrangement which were not the fruits of the unfair contributions, then the appropriate amount is not recoverable.

(7) If it appears to the court that the transfer could not have been wholly so made, then the appropriate amount is recoverable to the extent to which it appears to the court that the transfer could not have been so made.

(8) In making the determination mentioned in subsection (5) the court shall consider in particular—

    (a) whether any of the personal contributions were made for the purpose of putting assets beyond the reach of the transferor's creditors or any of them, and

    (b) whether the total amount of any personal contributions represented, at the time the pension-sharing transaction was made, by rights under pension arrangements is an amount which is excessive in view of the transferor's circumstances when those contributions were made.

(9) In this section and sections 342E and 342F—

'appropriate amount', in relation to a pension-sharing transaction, means the appropriate amount in relation to that transaction for the purposes of section 29(1) of the Welfare Reform and Pensions Act 1999 (creation of pension credits and debits);

'pension-sharing transaction' means an order or provision falling within section 28(1) of the Welfare Reform and Pensions Act 1999 (orders and agreements which activate pension-sharing);

'shared arrangement', in relation to a pension-sharing transaction, means the pension arrangement to which the transaction relates;

'transferee', in relation to a pension-sharing transaction, means the person for whose benefit the transaction is made;

'transferor', in relation to a pension-sharing transaction, means the person to whose rights the transaction relates.

342E. Orders under section 339 or 340 in respect of pension-sharing transactions

(1) This section and section 342F apply if the court is making an order under section 339 or 340 in a case where—

(a) the transaction or preference is, or is any part of, a pension-sharing transaction, and

(b) the transferee has rights under a pension arrangement ('the destination arrangement', which may be the shared arrangement or any other pension-arrangement) that are derived, directly or indirectly, from the pension-sharing transaction.

(2) Without prejudice to the generality of section 339(2) or 340(2), or of section 342, the order may include provision—

(a) requiring the person responsible for the destination arrangement to pay an amount to the transferor's trustee in bankruptcy,

(b) adjusting the liabilities of the destination arrangement in respect of the transferee,

(c) adjusting any liabilities of the destination arrangement in respect of any other person that derive, directly or indirectly, from rights of the transferee under the destination agreement,

(d) for the recovery by the person responsible for the destination arrangement (whether by deduction from any amount which that person is ordered to pay or otherwise) of costs incurred by that person in complying in the transferor's case with any requirement under section 342F(1) or in giving effect to the order,

(e) for the recovery, from the transferor's trustee in bankruptcy, by the person responsible for a pension arrangement, of costs incurred by that person in complying in the transferor's case with any requirement under section 342F(2) or (3).

(3) In subsection (2), references to adjusting the liabilities of the destination arrangement in respect of a person include (in particular) reducing the amount of any benefit or future benefit to which that person is entitled under the arrangement.

(4) The maximum amount which the person responsible for the destination arrangement may be required to pay by the order is the smallest of—

(a) so much of the appropriate amount as, in accordance with section 342D, is recoverable,

(b) so much (if any) of the amount of the unfair contributions (within the meaning given by section 342D(5)) as is not recoverable by way of an order under section 342A containing provision such as is mentioned in section 342B(1)(a), and

(c) the value of the transferee's rights under the destination arrangement so far as they are derived, directly or indirectly, from the pension-sharing transaction.

(5) If the order requires the person responsible for the destination arrangement to pay an amount ('the restoration amount') to the transferor's trustee in bankruptcy it must provide for the liabilities of the arrangement to be correspondingly reduced.

(6) For the purposes of subsection (5), liabilities are correspondingly reduced if the difference between—

(a) the amount of the liabilities immediately before the reduction, and

(b) the amount of the liabilities immediately after the reduction,

is equal to the restoration amount.

(7) The order—

(a) shall be binding on the person responsible for the destination arrangement, and

(b) overrides provisions of the destination arrangement to the extent that they conflict with the provisions of the order.

342F. Orders under section 339 or 340 in pension-sharing cases: supplementary

(1) On the transferor's trustee in bankruptcy making a written request to the person responsible for the destination arrangement, that person shall provide the trustee with such information about—

(a) the arrangement,

(b) the transferee's rights under it, and

(c) where the destination arrangement is the shared arrangement, the transferor's rights under it,

as the trustee may reasonably require for, or in connection with, the making of applications under section 339 and 340.

(2) Where the shared arrangement is not the destination arrangement, the person responsible for the shared arrangement shall, on the transferor's trustee in bankruptcy making a written request to that person, provide the trustee with such information about—

(a) the arrangement, and

(b) the transferor's rights under it,

as the trustee may reasonably require for, or in connection with, the making of applications under sections 339 and 340.

(3) On the transferor's trustee in bankruptcy making a written request to the person responsible for any intermediate arrangement, that person shall provide the trustee with such information about—

(a) the arrangement, and

(b) the transferee's rights under it,

as the trustee may reasonably require for, or in connection with, the making of applications under sections 339 and 340.

(4) In subsection (3) 'intermediate arrangement' means a pension arrangement, other than the shared arrangement or the destination arrangement, in relation to which the following conditions are fulfilled—

(a) there was a time when the transferee had rights under the arrangement that were derived (directly or indirectly) from the pension-sharing transaction, and

(b) the transferee's rights under the destination arrangement (so far as derived from the pension-sharing transaction) are to any extent derived (directly or indirectly) from the rights mentioned in paragraph (a).

(5) Nothing in—

(a) any provision of section 159 of the Pension Schemes Act 1993 or section 91 of the Pensions Act 1995 (which prevent assignment and the making of orders which restrain a person from receiving anything which he is prevented from assigning),

(b) any provision of any enactment (whether passed or made before or after the passing of the Welfare Reform and Pensions Act 1999) corresponding to any of the provisions mentioned in paragraph (a), or

(c) any provision of the destination arrangement corresponding to any of those provisions,

applies to a court exercising its powers under section 339 or 340.

(6) Regulations may, for the purposes of sections 339 to 342, sections 342D and 342E and this section, make provision about the calculation and verification of—

(a) any such value as is mentioned in section 342E(4)(c);

(b) any such amounts as are mentioned in section 342E(6)(a) and (b).

(7) The power conferred by subsection (6) includes power to provide for calculation or verification—

(a) in such manner as may, in the particular case, be approved by a prescribed person; or

(b) in accordance with guidance—

(i) from time to time prepared by a prescribed person, and

(ii) approved by the Secretary of State.

(8) In section 342E and this section, references to the person responsible for a pension arrangement are to—

(a) the trustees, managers or provider of the arrangement, or

(b) the person having functions in relation to the arrangement corresponding to those of a trustee, manager or provider.

(9) In this section—

'prescribed' means prescribed by regulations;

'regulations' means regulations made by the Secretary of State.

(10) Regulations under this section may—

(a) make different provision for different cases;

(b) contain such incidental, supplemental and transitional provisions as appear to the Secretary of State necessary or expedient.

(11) Regulations under this section shall be made by statutory instrument subject to annulment in pursuance of a resolution of either House of Parliament.

343. Extortionate credit transactions

(1) This section applies where a person is adjudged bankrupt who is or has been a party to a transaction for, or involving, the provision to him of credit.

(2) The court may, on the application of the trustee of the bankrupt's estate, make an order with respect to the transaction if the transaction is or was extortionate and was not entered into more than 3 years before the commencement of the bankruptcy.

(3) For the purposes of this section a transaction is extortionate if, having regard to the risk accepted by the person providing the credit—

    (a) the terms of it are or were such as to require grossly exorbitant payments to be made (whether unconditionally or in certain contingencies) in respect of the provision of the credit, or

    (b) it otherwise grossly contravened ordinary principles of fair dealing;

and it shall be presumed, unless the contrary is proved, that a transaction with respect to which an application is made under this section is or, as the case may be, was extortionate.

(4) An order under this section with respect to any transaction may contain such one or more of the following as the court thinks fit, that is to say—

    (a) provision setting aside the whole or part of any obligation created by the transaction;

    (b) provision otherwise varying the terms of the transaction or varying the terms on which any security for the purposes of the transaction is held;

    (c) provision requiring any person who is or was party to the transaction to pay to the trustee any sums paid to that person, by virtue of the transaction by the bankrupt;

    (d) provision requiring any person to surrender to the trustee any property held by him as security for the purposes of the transaction;

    (e) provision directing accounts to be taken between any persons.

(5) Any sums or property required to be paid or surrendered to the trustee in accordance with an order under this section shall be comprised in the bankrupt's estate.

(6) Neither the trustee of a bankrupt's estate nor an undischarged bankrupt is entitled to make an application under section 139(1)(a) of the Consumer Credit Act 1974 (re-opening of extortionate credit agreement) for any agreement by which credit is or has been provided to the bankrupt to be re-opened.

But the powers conferred by this section are exercisable in relation to any transaction concurrently with any powers exercisable under this Act in relation to that transaction as a transaction at an undervalue.

CHAPTER VI
BANKRUPTCY OFFENCES

Preliminary

350. Scheme of this Chapter

(1) Subject to section 360(3) below, this Chapter applies where the court has made a bankruptcy order on a bankruptcy petition.

(2) This Chapter applies whether or not the bankruptcy order is annulled, but proceedings for an offence under this Chapter shall not be instituted after the annulment.

(3) Without prejudice to his liability in respect of a subsequent bankruptcy, the bankrupt is not guilty of an offence under this Chapter in respect of anything done after his discharge; but nothing in this Group of Parts prevents the institution of

proceedings against a discharged bankrupt for an offence committed before his discharge.

(3A) Subsection (3) is without prejudice to any provision of this Chapter which applies to a person in respect of whom a bankruptcy restrictions order is in force.

(4) It is not a defence in proceedings for an offence under this Chapter that anything relied on, in whole or in part, as constituting that offence was done outside England and Wales.

(5) Proceedings for an offence under this Chapter or under the rules shall not be instituted except by the Secretary of State or by or with the consent of the Director of Public Prosecutions.

(6) A person guilty of an offence under this Chapter is liable to imprisonment or a fine, or both.

CHAPTER VII
POWERS OF COURT IN BANKRUPTCY

366. Inquiry into bankrupt's dealings and property

(1) At any time after a bankruptcy order has been made the court may, on the application of the official receiver or the trustee of the bankrupt's estate, summon to appear before it—

  (a) the bankrupt or the bankrupt's spouse or former spouse,

  (b) any person known or believed to have any property comprised in the bankrupt's estate in his possession or to be indebted to the bankrupt,

  (c) any person appearing to the court to be able to give information concerning the bankrupt or the bankrupt's dealings, affairs or property.

  The court may require any such person as is mentioned in paragraph (b) or (c) to submit an affidavit to the court containing an account of his dealings with the bankrupt or to produce any documents in his possession or under his control relating to the bankrupt or the bankrupt's dealings, affairs or property.

(2) Without prejudice to section 364, the following applies in a case where—

  (a) a person without reasonable excuse fails to appear before the court when he is summoned to do so under this section, or

  (b) there are reasonable grounds for believing that a person has absconded, or is about to abscond, with a view to avoiding his appearance before the court under this section.

(3) The court may, for the purpose of bringing that person and anything in his possession before the court, cause a warrant to be issued to a constable or prescribed officer of the court—

  (a) for the arrest of that person, and

  (b) for the seizure of any books, papers, records, money or goods in that person's possession.

(4) The court may authorise a person arrested under such a warrant to be kept in custody, and anything seized under such a warrant to be held, in accordance with the rules, until that person is brought before the court under the warrant or until such other time as the court may order.

PART X
INDIVIDUAL INSOLVENCY: GENERAL PROVISIONS

375. Appeals etc from courts exercising insolvency jurisdiction

(1) Every court having jurisdiction for the purposes of the Parts in this Group may review, rescind or vary any order made by it in the exercise of that jurisdiction.

(2) An appeal from a decision made in the exercise of jurisdiction for the purposes of those Parts by a county court or by a registrar in bankruptcy of the High Court lies to a single judge of the High Court; and an appeal from a decision of that judge on such an appeal lies to the Court of Appeal.

(3) A county court is not, in the exercise of its jurisdiction for the purposes of those Parts, to be subject to be restrained by the order of any other court, and no appeal lies from its decision in the exercise of that jurisdiction except as provided by this section.

PART XVI
PROVISIONS AGAINST DEBT AVOIDANCE
(ENGLAND AND WALES ONLY)

423. Transactions defrauding creditors

(1) This section relates to transactions entered into at an undervalue; and a person enters into such a transaction with another person if—

(a) he makes a gift to the other person or he otherwise enters into a transaction with the other on terms that provide for him to receive no consideration;

(b) he enters into a transaction with the other in consideration of marriage; or

(c) he enters into a transaction with the other for a consideration the value of which, in money or money's worth, is significantly less than the value, in money or money's worth, of the consideration provided by himself.

(2) Where a person has entered into such a transaction, the court may, if satisfied under the next subsection, make such order as it thinks fit for

(a) restoring the position to what it would have been if the transaction had not been entered into, and

(b) protecting the interests of persons who are victims of the transaction.

(3) In the case of a person entering into such a transaction, an order shall only be made if the court is satisfied that it was entered into by him for the purpose—

(a) of putting assets beyond the reach of a person who is making, or may at some time make, a claim against him, or

(b) of otherwise prejudicing the interests of such a person in relation to the claim which he is making or may make.

(4) In this section 'the court' means the High Court or—

(a) if the person entering into the transaction is an individual, any other court which would have jurisdiction in relation to a bankruptcy petition relating to him;

(b) if that person is a body capable of being wound up under Part IV or V of this Act, any other court having jurisdiction to wind it up.

(5) In relation to a transaction at an undervalue, references here and below to a victim of the transaction are to a person who is, or is capable of being, prejudiced by it; and in

the following two sections the person entering into the transaction is referred to as 'the debtor'.

424. Those who may apply for an order under s. 423

(1) An application for an order under section 423 shall not be made in relation to a transaction except—

   (a) in a case where the debtor has been adjudged bankrupt or is a body corporate which is being wound up or is in administration, by the official receiver, by the trustee of the bankrupt's estate or the liquidator or administrator of the body corporate or (with the leave of the court) by a victim of the transaction;

   (b) in a case where a victim of the transaction is bound by a voluntary arrangement approved under Part I or Part VIII of this Act, by the supervisor of the voluntary arrangement or by any person who (whether or not so bound) is such a victim; or

   (c) in any other case, by a victim of the transaction.

(2) An application made under any of the paragraphs of subsection (1) is to be treated as made on behalf of every victim of the transaction.

425. Provision which may be made by order under s. 423

(1) Without prejudice to the generality of section 423, an order made under that section with respect to a transaction may (subject as follows)—

   (a) require any property transferred as part of the transaction to be vested in any person, either absolutely or for the benefit of all the persons on whose behalf the application for the order is treated as made;

   (b) require any property to be so vested if it represents, in any person's hands, the application either of the proceeds of sale of property so transferred or of money so transferred;

   (c) release or discharge (in whole or in part) any security given by the debtor;

   (d) require any person to pay to any other person in respect of benefits received from the debtor such sums as the court may direct;

   (e) provide for any surety or guarantor whose obligations to any person were released or discharged (in whole or in part) under the transaction to be under such new or revived obligations as the court thinks appropriate;

   (f) provide for security to be provided for the discharge of any obligation imposed by or arising under the order, for such an obligation to be charged on any property and for such security or charge to have the same priority as a security or charge released or discharged (in whole or in part) under the transaction.

(2) An order under section 423 may affect the property of, or impose any obligation on, any person whether or not he is the person with whom the debtor entered into the transaction; but such an order—

   (a) shall not prejudice any interest in property which was acquired from a person other than the debtor and was acquired in good faith, for value and without notice of the relevant circumstances, or prejudice any interest deriving from such an interest, and

   (b) shall not require a person who received a benefit from the transaction in good faith, for value and without notice of the relevant circumstances to pay any sum unless he was a party to the transaction.

(3) For the purposes of this section the relevant circumstances in relation to a trans-action are the circumstances by virtue of which an order under section 423 may be made in respect of the transaction.

(4) In this section 'security' means any mortgage, charge, lien or other security.

PART XVII
MISCELLANEOUS AND GENERAL

[...]

429. Disabilities on revocation of administration order against an individual

(1) The following applies where a person fails to make any payment which he is required to make by virtue of an administration order under Part VI of the County Courts Act 1984.

(2) The court which is administering that person's estate under the order may, if it thinks fit—

   (a) revoke the administration order, and

   (b) make an order directing that this section and section 12 of the Company Directors Disqualification Act 1986 shall apply to the person for such period, not exceeding one year, as may be specified in the order.

(3) A person to whom this section so applies shall not—

   (a) either alone or jointly with another person, obtain credit to the extent of the amount prescribed for the purposes of section 360(1)(a) or more, or

   (b) enter into any transaction in the course of or for the purposes of any business in which he is directly or indirectly engaged,

   without disclosing to the person from whom he obtains the credit, or (as the case may be) with whom the transaction is entered into, the fact that this section applies to him.

(4) The reference in subsection (3) to a person obtaining credit includes—

   (a) a case where goods are bailed or hired to him under a hire-purchase agreement or agreed to be sold to him under a conditional sale agreement, and

   (b) a case where he is paid in advance (whether in money or otherwise) for the supply of goods or services.

(5) A person who contravenes this section is guilty of an offence and liable to impri-sonment or a fine, or both.

PART XVIII
INTERPRETATION

435. Meaning of 'associate'

(1) For the purposes of this Act any question whether a person is an associate of another person is to be determined in accordance with the following provisions of this section (any provision that a person is an associate of another person being taken to mean that they are associates of each other).

(2) A person is an associate of an individual if that person is the individual's husband or wife, or is a relative, or the husband or wife of a relative, of the individual or of the individual's husband or wife.

(3) A person is an associate of any person with whom he is in partnership, and of the husband or wife or a relative of any individual with whom he is in partnership; and a Scottish firm is an associate of any person who is a member of the firm.

(4) A person is an associate of any person whom he employs or by whom he is employed.

(5) A person in his capacity as trustee of a trust other than—

(a) a trust arising under any of the second Group of Parts or the Bankruptcy (Scotland) Act 1985, or

(b) a pension scheme or an employees' share scheme (within the meaning of the Companies Act),

is an associate of another person if the beneficiaries of the trust include, or the terms of the trust confer a power that may by exercised for the benefit of, that other person or an associate of that other person.

(6) A company is an associate of another company—

(a) if the same person has control of both, or a person has control of one and persons who are his associates, or he and persons who are his associates, have control of the other, or

(b) if a group of two or more persons has control of each company, and the groups either consists of the same persons or could be regarded as consisting of the same persons by treating (in one or more cases) a member of either group as replaced by a person of whom is an associate.

(7) A company is an associate of another person if that person has control of it or if that person and persons who are his associates together have control of it.

(8) For the purposes of this section a person is a relative of an individual if he is that individual's brother, sister, uncle, aunt, nephew, niece, lineal ancestor or lineal descendant, treating—

(a) any relationship of the half blood as a relationship of the whole blood and the stepchild or adopted child of any person as his child, and

(b) an illegitimate child as the legitimate child of his mother and reputed father;

and references in this section to a husband or wife include a former husband or wife and a reputed husband or wife.

(9) For the purposes of this section any director or other officer of a company is to be treated as employed by that company.

(10) For the purposes of this section a person is to be taken as having control of a company if—

(a) the directors of the company or of another company which has control of it (or any of them) are accustomed to act in accordance with his directions or instructions, or

(b) he is entitled to exercise, or control the exercise of, one third or more of the voting power at any general meeting of the company or of another company which has control of it;

and where two or more persons together satisfy either of the above conditions, they are to be taken as having control of the company.

(11) In this section 'company' includes any body corporate (whether incorporated in Great Britain or elsewhere); and references to directors and other officers of a company and to voting power at any general meeting of a company have effect with any necessary modifications.

436. Expressions used generally

In this Act, except in so far as the context otherwise requires (and subject to parts VII and XI)—

[...]

'associate' has the meaning given by section 435;

'business' includes a trade or profession;

'the EC Regulation' means Council Regulation (EC) No 1346/2000;

[...]

'property' includes money, goods, things in action, land and every description of property wherever situated and also obligations and every description of interest, whether present or future or vested or contingent, arising out of, or incidental to, property;

[...]

'transaction' includes a gift, agreement or arrangement, and references to entering into a transaction shall be construed accordingly.

INSOLVENCY RULES 1986

SI 1986/1925
(as amended)

THE SECOND GROUP OF PARTS
INDIVIDUAL INSOLVENCY; BANKRUPTCY
PART 5
INDIVIDUAL VOLUNTARY ARRANGEMENTS

CHAPTER 1
PRELIMINARY

5.1. Introductory

(1) The Rules in this Part apply in relation to a voluntary arrangement under Part VIII of the Act, except in relation to voluntary arrangements under section 263A, in relation to which only Chapters 7, 10, 11 and 12 of this Part shall apply.
(2) In this Part, in respect of voluntary arrangements other than voluntary arrangements under section 263A—
   (a) Chapter 2 applies in all cases;
   (b) Chapter 3 applies in cases where an application for an interim order is made;
   (c) Chapter 4 applies in cases where no application for an interim order is or is to be made;
   (d) except where otherwise stated, Chapters 5 and 6 apply in all cases;
   (e) Chapter 8 applies where a bankrupt makes an application under section 261(2)(a); and
   (f) Chapter 9 applies where the official receiver makes an application under section 261(2)(b).
(3) In this Part, in respect of voluntary arrangements under section 263A—
   (a) Chapter 7 applies in all cases; and
   (b) Chapter 10 applies where the official receiver makes an application under section 263D(3).
(4) In this Part, Chapters 11 and 12 apply in all cases

CHAPTER 2
PREPARATION OF DEBTOR'S PROPOSAL

5.2. Preparation of proposal

The debtor shall prepare for the intended nominee a proposal on which (with or without amendments to be made under Rule 5.3(3) below) to make his report to the court under section 256 or section 256A.

5.3. Contents of proposal

(1) The debtor's proposal shall provide a short explanation why, in his opinion, a voluntary arrangement under Part VIII is desirable, and give reasons why his creditors may be expected to concur with such an arrangement.

(2) The following matters shall be stated, or otherwise dealt with, in the proposal—

    (a) the following matters, so far as within the debtor's immediate knowledge—

        (i) his assets, with an estimate of their respective values,

        (ii) the extent (if any) to which the assets are charged in favour of creditors,

        (iii) the extent (if any) to which particular assets are to be excluded from the voluntary arrangement;

    (b) particulars of any property, other than assets of the debtor himself, which is proposed to be included in the arrangement, the source of such property and the terms on which it is to be made available for inclusion;

    (c) the nature and amount of the debtor's liabilities (so far as within his immediate knowledge), the manner in which they are proposed to be met, modified, postponed or otherwise dealt with by means of the arrangement and (in particular)—

        (i) how it is proposed to deal with preferential creditors (defined in section 258(7) and creditors who are, or claim to be, secured,

        (ii) how associates of the debtor (being creditors of his) are proposed to be treated under the arrangement, and

        (iii) in any case where the debtor is an undischarged bankrupt, whether, to the debtor's knowledge, claims have been made under section 339 (transactions at an undervalue), section 340 (preferences) or section 343 (extortionate credit transactions), or where the debtor is not an undischarged bankrupt, whether there are circumstances which would give rise to the possibility of such claims in the event that he should be adjudged bankrupt,

    and, where any such circumstances are present, whether, and if so how, it is proposed under the voluntary arrangement to make provision for wholly or partly indemnifying the insolvent estate in respect of such claims;

    (d) whether any, and if so what, guarantees have been given of the debtor's debts by other persons, specifying which (if any) of the guarantors are associates of his;

    (e) the proposed duration of the voluntary arrangement;

    (f) the proposed dates of distributions to creditors, with estimates of their amounts;

    (g) how it is proposed to deal with the claims of any person who is bound by the arrangement by virtue of section 260(2)(b)(ii);

    (h) the amount proposed to be paid to the nominee (as such) by way of remuneration and expenses;

    (j) the manner in which it is proposed that the supervisor of the arrangement should be remunerated, and his expenses defrayed;

    (k) whether, for the purposes of the arrangement, any guarantees are to be offered by any persons other than the debtor, and whether (if so) any security is to be given or sought;

    (l) the manner in which funds held for the purposes of the arrangement are to be banked, invested or otherwise dealt with pending distribution to creditors;

    (m) the manner in which funds held for the purpose of payment to creditors, and not so paid on the termination of the arrangement, are to be dealt with;

    (n) if the debtor has any business, the manner in which it is proposed to be conducted during the course of the arrangement;

   (o) details of any further credit facilities which it is intended to arrange for the debtor, and how the debts so arising are to be paid;

   (p) the functions which are to be undertaken by the supervisor of the arrangement;

   (q) the name, address and qualification of the person proposed as supervisor of the voluntary arrangement, and confirmation that he is, so far as the debtor is aware, qualified to act as an insolvency practitioner in relation to him or is an authorised person in relation to him; and

   (r) whether the EC Regulation will apply and, if so, whether the proceedings will be main proceedings or territorial proceedings.

(3) With the agreement in writing of the nominee, the debtor's proposal may be amended at any time up to the delivery of the former's report to the court under section 256 or section 256A.

5.4. Notice to the intended nominee

(1) The debtor shall give to the intended nominee written notice of his proposal.

(2) The notice, accompanied by a copy of the proposal, shall be delivered either to the nominee himself, or to a person authorised to take delivery of documents on his behalf.

(3) If the intended nominee agrees to act, he shall cause a copy of the notice to be endorsed to the effect that it has been received by him on a specified date.

(4) The copy of the notice so endorsed shall be returned by the nominee forthwith to the debtor at an address specified by him in the notice for that purpose.

(5) Where the debtor is an undischarged bankrupt and he gives notice of his proposal to the official receiver and (if any) the trustee, the notice must contain the name and address of the insolvency practitioner or (as the case may be) authorised person who has agreed to act as nominee.

5.5. Statement of Affairs

(1) Subject to paragraph (2), the debtor shall, within 7 days after his proposal is delivered to the nominee, or such longer time as the latter may allow, deliver to the nominee a statement of his (the debtor's) affairs.

(2) Paragraph (1) shall not apply where the debtor is an undischarged bankrupt and he has already delivered a statement of affairs under section 272 (debtor's petition) or 288 (creditor's petition) but the nominee may require the debtor to submit a further statement supplementing or amplifying the statement of affairs already submitted.

(3) The statement of affairs shall comprise the following particulars (supplementing or amplifying, so far as is necessary for clarifying the state of the debtor's affairs, those already given in his proposal)—

   (a) a list of his assets, divided into such categories as are appropriate for easy identification, with estimated values assigned to each category;

   (b) in the case of any property on which a claim against the debtor is wholly or partly secured, particulars of the claim and its amount, and of how and when the security was created;

   (c) the names and addresses of the debtor's preferential creditors (defined in section 258(7)), with the amounts of their respective claims;

   (d) the names and addresses of the debtor's unsecured creditors, with the amounts of their respective claims;

   (e) particulars of any debts owed by or to the debtor to or by persons who are associates of his;

(f) such other particulars (if any) as the nominee may in writing require to be furnished for the purposes of making his report to the court on the debtor's proposal.

(4) The statement of affairs shall be made up to a date not earlier than 2 weeks before the date of the notice to the nominee under Rule 5.4.

However, the nominee may allow an extension of that period to the nearest practicable date (not earlier than 2 months before the date of the notice under Rule 5.4); and if he does so, he shall give his reasons in his report to the court on the debtor's proposal.

(5) The statement shall be certified by the debtor as correct, to the best of his knowledge and belief.

5.6. Additional disclosure for assistance of nominee

(1) If it appears to the nominee that he cannot properly prepare his report on the basis of information in the debtor's proposal and statement of affairs, he may call on the debtor to provide him with—

(a) further and better particulars as to the circumstances in which, and the reasons why, he is insolvent or (as the case may be) threatened with insolvency;

(b) particulars of any previous proposals which have been made by him under Part VIII of the Act;

(c) any further information with respect to his affairs which the nominee thinks necessary for the purposes of his report.

(2) The nominee may call on the debtor to inform him whether and in what circumstances he has at any time—

(a) been concerned in the affairs of any company (whether or not incorporated in England and Wales) which has become insolvent, or

(b) been adjudged bankrupt, or entered into an arrangement with his creditors.

(3) For the purpose of enabling the nominee to consider the debtor's proposal and prepare his report on it, the latter must give him access to his accounts and records.

CHAPTER 3
CASES IN WHICH AN APPLICATION FOR
AN INTERIM ORDER IS MADE

5.7. Application for interim order

(1) An application to the court for an interim order under Part VIII of the Act shall be accompanied by an affidavit of the following matters—

(a) the reasons for making the application;

(b) particulars of any execution or other legal process or levying of any distress which, to the debtor's knowledge, has been commenced against him;

(c) that he is an undischarged bankrupt or (as the case may be) that he is able to petition for his own bankruptcy;

(d) that no previous application for an interim order has been made by or in respect of the debtor in the period of 12 months ending with the date of the affidavit; and

(e) that the nominee under the proposal (naming him) is willing to act in relation to the proposal and is a person who is either qualified to act as an insolvency practitioner in relation to the debtor or is authorised to act as nominee in relation to him; and

(f) that the debtor has not submitted to the official receiver either the document referred to at section 263B(1)(a) or the statement referred to at section 263B(1)(b).

(2) A copy of the notice to the intended nominee under Rule 5.4, endorsed to the effect that he agrees so to act, and a copy of the debtor's proposal given to the nominee under that Rule, shall be exhibited to the affidavit.

(3) On receiving the application and affidavit, the court shall fix a venue for the hearing of the application.

(4) The applicant shall give at least 2 days' notice of the hearing—

    (a) where the debtor is an undischarged bankrupt, to the bankrupt, the official receiver and the trustee (whichever of those three is not himself the applicant),

    (b) where the debtor is not an undischarged bankrupt, to any creditor who (to the debtor's knowledge) has presented a bankruptcy petition against him, and

    (c) in either case, to the nominee who has agreed to act in relation to the debtor's proposal.

5.8. Court in which application to be made

(1) Except in the case of an undischarged bankrupt, an application to the court under Part VIII of the Act shall be made to a court in which the debtor would be entitled to present his own petition in bankruptcy under Rule 6.40.

(2) The application shall contain sufficient information to establish that it is brought in the appropriate court.

(3) In the case of an undischarged bankrupt, such an application shall be made to the court having the conduct of his bankruptcy and shall be filed with the bankruptcy proceedings.

5.9. Hearing of the application

(1) Any of the persons who have been given notice under Rule 5.7(4) may appear or be represented at the hearing of the application.

(2) The court, in deciding whether to make an interim order on the application, shall take into account any representations made by or on behalf of any of those persons (in particular, whether an order should be made containing such provision as is referred to in section 255(3) and (4)).

(3) If the court makes an interim order, it shall fix a venue for consideration of the nominee's report. Subject to the following paragraph, the date for that consideration shall be not later than that on which the interim order ceases to have effect under section 255(6).

(4) If under section 256(4) an extension of time is granted for filing the nominee's report, the court shall, unless there appear to be good reasons against it, correspondingly extend the period for which the interim order has effect.

5.10. Action to follow making of order

(1) Where an interim order is made, at least 2 sealed copies of the order shall be sent by the court to the person who applied for it; and that person shall serve one of the copies on the nominee under the debtor's proposal.

(2) The applicant shall also forthwith give notice of the making of the order to any person who was given notice of the hearing pursuant to Rule 5.7(4) and was not present or represented at it.

5.11. Nominee's report on the proposal

(1) Where the nominee makes his report to the court under section 256, he shall deliver 2 copies of it to the court not less than 2 days before the interim order ceases to have effect.

(2) With his report the nominee shall deliver—

    (a) a copy of the debtor's proposal (with amendments, if any, authorised under Rules 5.3(3)); and

    (b) a copy or summary of any statement of affairs provided by the debtor.

(3) If the nominee makes known his opinion that the debtor's proposal has a reasonable prospect of being approved and implemented, and that a meeting of the debtor's creditors should be summoned under section 257, his report shall have annexed to it his comments on the debtor's proposal.

    If his opinion is otherwise, he shall give his reasons for that opinion.

(4) The court shall upon receipt of the report cause one copy of the report to be endorsed with the date of its filing in court and returned to the nominee.

(5) Any creditor of the debtor is entitled, at all reasonable times on any business day, to inspect the file.

(6) Where the debtor is an undischarged bankrupt, the nominee shall send to the official receiver and (if any) the trustee—

    (a) a copy of the debtor's proposal,

    (b) a copy of his (the nominee's) report and his comments accompanying it (if any), and

    (c) a copy or summary of the debtor's statement of affairs.

(7) Where the debtor is not an undischarged bankrupt, the nominee shall send a copy of each of the documents referred to in paragraph (6) to any person who has presented a bankruptcy petition against the debtor.

5.12. Replacement of nominee

(1) Where the debtor intends to apply to the court under section 256(3) for the nominee to be replaced, he shall give to the nominee at least 7 days notice of his application.

(2) No appointment of a replacement nominee shall be made by the court unless there is filed in court a statement by the replacement nominee indicating his consent to act.

5.13. Consideration of nominee's report

(1) At the hearing by the court to consider the nominee's report, any of the persons who have been given notice under Rule 5.7(4) may appear or be represented.

(2) Rule 5.10 applies to any order made by the court at the hearing.

CHAPTER 4
CASES WHERE NO INTERIM ORDER IS TO BE OBTAINED

5.14. Nominee's report to the court

(1) The nominee shall deliver 2 copies of his report to the court (as defined in Rule 5.15) under section 256A within 14 days (or such longer period as the court may allow) after receiving from the debtor the document and statement mentioned in

section 256A(2) but the court shall not consider the report unless an application is made under the Act or these Rules in relation to the debtor's proposal.

(2) With his report the nominee shall deliver—

(a) a copy of the debtor's proposal (with amendments, if any, authorised under Rule 5.3(3));

(b) a copy or summary of any statement of affairs provided by the debtor; and

(c) a copy of the notice referred to in Rule 5.4(3),

together with 2 copies of Form 5.5 listing the documents referred to in (a) to (c) above and containing a statement that no application for an interim order under section 252 is to be made.

(3) If the nominee makes known his opinion that the debtor's proposal has a reasonable prospect of being approved and implemented, and that a meeting of the debtor's creditors should be summoned under section 257, his report shall have annexed to it his comments on the debtor's proposal.

If his opinion is otherwise, he shall give his reasons for that opinion.

(4) The court shall upon receipt of the report and Form 5.5 cause one copy of the form to be endorsed with the date of its filing in court and returned to the nominee

(5) Any creditor of the debtor is entitled, at all reasonable times on any business day, to inspect the file.

(6) Where the debtor is an undischarged bankrupt, the nominee shall send to the official receiver and (if any) the trustee—

(a) a copy of the debtor's proposal,

(b) a copy of his (the nominee's) report and his comments accompanying it (if any), and

(c) a copy or summary of the debtor's statement of affairs.

(7) Where the debtor is not an undischarged bankrupt, the nominee shall send a copy of each of the documents referred to in paragraph (6) to any person who has presented a bankruptcy petition against the debtor.

(8) The filing in court of the report under section 256A shall constitute an insolvency proceeding for the purpose of Rule 7.27 and Rule 7.30.

5.15. Filing of reports made under section 256A—appropriate court

(1) Except where the debtor is an undischarged bankrupt, the court in which the nominee's report under section 256A is to be filed is the court in which the debtor would be entitled to present his own petition in bankruptcy under Rule 6.40.

(2) The report shall contain sufficient information to establish that it is filed in the appropriate court.

(3) Where the debtor is an undischarged bankrupt, such report shall be filed in the court having the conduct of his bankruptcy and shall be filed with the bankruptcy proceedings.

5.16. Applications to the court

(1) Any application to court in relation to any matter relating to a voluntary arrangement or a proposal for a voluntary arrangement shall be made in the court in which the nominee's report was filed.

(2) Where the debtor intends to apply to the court under section 256A(4)(a) or (b) for the nominee to be replaced, he shall give to the nominee at least 7 days' notice of the application.

(3) Where the nominee intends to apply to the court under section 256A(4)(b) for his replacement as nominee, he shall give to the debtor at least 7 days' notice of the application.

(4) No appointment of a replacement nominee shall be made by the court unless there is filed in court a statement by the replacement nominee indicating his consent to act.

CHAPTER 5
CREDITORS' MEETINGS

5.17. Summoning of creditors' meeting

(1) If in his report the nominee states that in his opinion a meeting of creditors should be summoned to consider the debtor's proposal, the date on which the meeting is to be held shall be—

(a) in a case where an interim order has not been obtained, not less than 14 days and not more than 28 days from that on which the nominee's report is filed in court under Rule 5.14; and

(b) in a case where an interim order is in force, not less than 14 days from the date on which the nominee's report is filed in court nor more than 28 days from that on which the report is considered by the court.

(2) Notices calling the meeting shall be sent by the nominee, at least 14 days before the day fixed for it to be held, to all the creditors specified in the debtor's statement of affairs, and any other creditors of whom the nominee is otherwise aware.

(3) Each notice sent under this Rule shall specify the court to which the nominee's report on the debtor's proposal has been delivered and shall state the effect of Rule 5.23(1), (3) and (4) (requisite majorities); and with it there shall be sent—

(a) a copy of the proposal,

(b) a copy of the statement of affairs or, if the nominee thinks fit, a summary of it (the summary to include a list of the creditors and the amounts of their debts), and

(c) the nominee's comments on the proposal.

5.18. Creditors' meeting: supplementary

(1) Subject as follows, in fixing the venue for the creditors' meeting, the nominee shall have regard to the convenience of creditors.

(2) The meeting shall be summoned for commencement between 10.00 and 16.00 hours on a business day.

(3) With every notice summoning the meeting there shall be sent out forms of proxy.

5.19. The chairman at the meeting

(1) Subject as follows, the nominee shall be chairman of the creditors' meeting.

(2) If for any reason the nominee is unable to attend, he may nominate another person to act as chairman in his place; but a person so nominated must be—

(a) a person qualified to act as an insolvency practitioner in relation to the debtor;

(b) an authorised person in relation to the debtor; or

(c) an employee of the nominee or his firm who is experienced in insolvency matters.

5.20. The chairman as proxy-holder

The chairman shall not by virtue of any proxy held by him vote to increase or reduce the amount of the remuneration or expenses of the nominee or the supervisor of the proposed arrangement, unless the proxy specifically directs him to vote in that way.

5.21. Entitlement to vote

(1) Subject as follows, every creditor who has notice of the creditors' meeting is entitled to vote at the meeting or any adjournment of it.

(2) A creditor's entitlement to vote is calculated as follows—

   (a) where the debtor is not an undischarged bankrupt and an interim order is in force, by reference to the amount of the debt owed to him as at the date of the interim order;

   (b) where the debtor is not an undischarged bankrupt and an interim order is not in force, by reference to the amount of the debt owed to him at the date of the meeting; and

   (c) where the debtor is an undischarged bankrupt, by reference to the amount of the debt owed to him as at the date of the bankruptcy order.

(3) A creditor may vote in respect of a debt for an unliquidated amount or any debt whose value is not ascertained, and for the purposes of voting (but not otherwise) his debt shall be valued at £1 unless the chairman agrees to put a higher value on it.

5.22. Procedure for admission of creditors' claims for voting purposes

(1) Subject as follows, at the creditors' meeting the chairman shall ascertain the entitlement of persons wishing to vote and shall admit or reject their claims accordingly.

(2) The chairman may admit or reject a claim in whole or in part.

(3) The chairman's decision on any matter under this Rule or under paragraph (3) of Rule 5.21 is subject to appeal to the court by any creditor or by the debtor.

(4) If the chairman is in doubt whether a claim should be admitted or rejected, he shall mark it as objected to and allow votes to be cast in respect of it, subject to such votes being subsequently declared invalid if the objection to the claim is sustained.

(5) If on an appeal the chairman's decision is reversed or varied, or votes are declared invalid, the court may order another meeting to be summoned, or make such order as it thinks just.

    The court's power to make an order under this paragraph is exercisable only if it considers that the circumstances giving rise to the appeal are such as give rise to unfair prejudice or material irregularity.

(6) An application to the court by way of appeal against the chairman's decision shall not be made after the end of the period of 28 days beginning with the first day on which the report required by section 259 is made to the court.

(7) The chairman is not personally liable for any costs incurred by any person in respect of an appeal under this Rule.

5.23. Requisite majorities

(1) Subject as follows, at the creditors' meeting for any resolution to pass approving any proposal or modification there must be a majority in excess of three-quarters in value of the creditors present in person or by proxy and voting on the resolution.

(2) The same applies in respect of any other resolution proposed at the meeting, but substituting one-half for three-quarters.

(3) In the following cases there is to be left out of account a creditor's vote in respect of any claim or part of a claim—

(a) where written notice of the claim was not given, either at the meeting or before it, to the chairman or the nominee;

(b) where the claim or part is secured;

(c) where the claim is in respect of a debt wholly or partly on, or secured by, a current bill of exchange or promissory note, unless the creditor is willing—

(i) to treat the liability to him on the bill or note of every person who is liable on it antecedently to the debtor, and against whom a bankruptcy order has not been made (or, in the case of a company, which has not gone into liquidation), as a security in his hands, and

(ii) to estimate the value of the security and (for the purpose of entitlement to vote, but not of any distribution under the arrangement) to deduct it from his claim.

(4) Any resolution is invalid if those voting against it include more than half in value of the creditors, counting in these latter only those—

(a) who have notice of the meeting;

(b) whose votes are not to be left out of account under paragraph (3); and

(c) who are not, to the best of the chairman's belief, associates of the debtor.

(5) It is for the chairman of the meeting to decide whether under this Rule—

(a) a vote is to be left out of account in accordance with the paragraph (3), or

(b) a person is an associate of the debtor for the purposes of paragraph (4)(c);

and in relation to the second of these cases the chairman is entitled to rely on the information provided by the debtor's statement of affairs or otherwise in accordance with this Part of the Rules.

(6) If the chairman uses a proxy contrary to Rule 5.20, his vote with that proxy does not count towards any majority under this Rule.

(7) The chairman's decision on any matter under this Rule is subject to appeal to the court by any creditor or by the debtor and paragraphs (5) to (7) of Rule 5.22 apply as regards such an appeal.

5.24. Proceedings to obtain agreement on the proposal

(1) On the day on which the creditors' meeting is held, it may from time to time be adjourned.

(2) If on that day the requisite majority for the approval of the voluntary arrangement (with or without modifications) has not been obtained, the chairman may, and shall if it is so resolved, adjourn the meeting for not more than 14 days.

(3) If there are subsequently further adjournments, the final adjournment shall not be to a day later than 14 days after that on which the meeting was originally held.

(4) If the meeting is adjourned under paragraph (2), notice of the fact shall be given by the chairman forthwith to the court.

(5) If following any final adjournment of the meeting the proposal (with or without modifications) is not agreed to, it is deemed rejected.

CHAPTER 6
IMPLEMENTATION OF THE ARRANGEMENT

5.25. Resolutions to follow approval

(1) If the voluntary arrangement is approved (with or without modifications), a resolution may be taken by the creditors, where two or more individuals are appointed to act as supervisor, on the question whether acts to be done in connection with the arrangement may be done by any one of them, or must be done by both or all.

(2) If at the creditors' meeting a resolution is moved for the appointment of some person other than the nominee to be supervisor of the arrangement, there must be produced to the chairman, at or before the meeting—

  (a) that person's written consent to act (unless he is present and then and there signifies his consent), and

  (b) his written confirmation that he is qualified to act as an insolvency practitioner in relation to the debtor or is an authorised person in relation to the debtor.

5.26. Hand-over of property, etc to supervisor

(1) Forthwith after the approval of the voluntary arrangement, the debtor or, where the debtor is an undischarged bankrupt, the official receiver or the debtor's trustee, shall do all that is required for putting the supervisor into possession of the assets included in the arrangement.

(2) On taking possession of the assets in any case where the debtor is an undischarged bankrupt, the supervisor shall discharge any balance due to the official receiver and (if other) the trustee by way of remuneration or on account of—

  (a) fees, costs, charges and expenses properly incurred and payable under the Act or the Rules, and

  (b) any advances made in respect of the insolvent estate, together with interest on such advances at the rate specified in section 17 of the Judgments Act 1838 at the date of the bankruptcy order.

(3) Alternatively where the debtor is an undischarged bankrupt, the supervisor must, before taking possession, give the official receiver or the trustee a written undertaking to discharge any such balance out of the first realisation of assets.

(4) Where the debtor is an undischarged bankrupt, the official receiver and (if other) the trustee has a charge on the assets included in the voluntary arrangement in respect of any sums due as above until they have been discharged, subject only to the deduction from realisations by the supervisor of the proper costs and expenses of realisation.

  Any sums due to the official receiver take priority over those due to a trustee.

(5) The supervisor shall from time to time out of the realisation of assets discharge all guarantees properly given by the official receiver or the trustee for the benefit of the estate, and shall pay all their expenses.

5.27. Report of creditors' meeting

(1) A report of the creditors' meeting shall be prepared by the chairman of the meeting.

(2) The report shall—

  (a) state whether the proposal for a voluntary arrangement was approved or rejected and, if approved, with what (if any) modifications;

(b) set out the resolutions which were taken at the meeting, and the decision on each one;

(c) list the creditors (with their respective values) who were present or represented at the meeting, and how they voted on each resolution;

(d) whether in the opinion of the supervisor,

    (i) the EC Regulation applies to the voluntary arrangement, and

    (ii) if so, whether the proceedings are main proceedings or territorial proceedings; and

(e) include such further information (if any) as the chairman thinks it appropriate to make known to the court.

(3) A copy of the chairman's report shall, within 4 days of the meeting being held, be filed in court; and the court shall cause that copy to be endorsed with the date of filing.

(4) The persons to whom notice of the result is to be given, under section 259(1), are all those who were sent notice of the meeting under this Part of the Rules and any other creditor of whom the chairman is aware, and where the debtor is an undischarged bankrupt, the official receiver and (if any) the trustee.

The notice shall be sent immediately after a copy of the chairman's report is filed in court under paragraph (3).

(5) In a case where no interim order has been obtained the court shall not consider the chairman's report unless an application is made to the court under the Act or the Rules in relation to it.

5.29. Reports to Secretary of State

(1) Immediately after the chairman of the creditors' meeting has filed in court a report that the meeting has approved the voluntary arrangement, he shall report to the Secretary of State the following details of the arrangement—

(a) the name and address of the debtor;

(b) the date on which the arrangement was approved by the creditors;

(c) the name and address of the supervisor; and

(d) the court in which the chairman's report has been filed.

(2) A person who is appointed to act as supervisor of an individual voluntary arrangement (whether in the first instance or by way of replacement of another person previously appointed) shall forthwith give written notice to the Secretary of State of his appointment.

If he vacates office as supervisor, he shall forthwith give written notice of that fact also to the Secretary of State.

5.30. Revocation or suspension of the arrangement

(1) This Rule applies where the court makes an order of revocation or suspension under section 262.

(2) The person who applied for the order shall serve sealed copies of it—

(a) in a case where the debtor is an undischarged bankrupt, on the debtor, the official receiver and the trustee;

(b) in any other case, on the debtor; and

(c) in either case, on the supervisor of the voluntary arrangement.

(3) If the order includes a direction by the court under section 262(4)(b) for any further creditors' meeting to be summoned, notice shall also be given (by the person who

applied for the order) to whoever is, in accordance with the direction, required to summon the meeting.

(4) The debtor or (where the debtor is an undischarged bankrupt) the trustee or (if there is no trustee) the official receiver shall—

    (a) forthwith after receiving a copy of the court's order, give notice of it to all persons who were sent notice of the creditors' meeting which approved the voluntary arrangement or who, not having been sent that notice, are affected by the order;

    (b) within 7 days of their receiving a copy of the order (or within such longer period as the court may allow), give notice to the court whether it is intended to make a revised proposal to creditors, or to invite reconsideration of the original proposal.

(5) The person on whose application the order of revocation or suspension was made shall, within 7 days after the making of the order, give written notice of it to the Secretary of State and shall, in the case of an order of suspension, within 7 days of the expiry of any suspension order, give written notice of such expiry to the Secretary of State.

5.31. Supervisor's accounts and reports

(1) Where the voluntary arrangement authorises or requires the supervisor—

    (a) to carry on the debtor's business or to trade on his behalf or in his name, or

    (b) to realise assets of the debtor or (in a case where the debtor is an undischarged bankrupt) belonging to the estate, or

    (c) otherwise to administer or dispose of any funds of the debtor or the estate,

he shall keep accounts and records of his acts and dealings in and in connection with the arrangement, including in particular records of all receipts and payments of money.

(2) The supervisor shall, not less often that once in every 12 months beginning with the date of his appointment, prepare an abstract of such receipts and payments, and send copies of it, accompanied by his comments on the progress and efficacy of the arrangement, to—

    (a) the court

    (b) the debtor, and

    (c) all those of the debtor's creditors who are bound by the arrangement.

If in any period of 12 months he has made no payments and had no receipts, he shall at the end of that period send a statement to that effect to all who are specified in subparagraphs (a) to (c) above.

(3) An abstract provided under paragraph (2) shall relate to a period beginning with the date of the supervisor's appointment or (as the case may be) the day following the end of the last period for which an abstract was prepared under this Rule; and copies of the abstract shall be sent out, as required by paragraph (2), within the 2 months following the end of the period to which the abstract relates.

(4) If the supervisor is not authorised as mentioned in paragraph (1), he shall, not less often than once in every 12 months beginning with the date of his appointment, send to all those specified in paragraph 2(a) to (c) a report on the progress and efficacy of the voluntary arrangement.

(5) The court may, on application by the supervisor, vary the dates on which the obligation to send abstracts or reports arises.

5.32. Production of accounts and records to Secretary of State

(1) The Secretary of State may at any time during the course of the voluntary arrangement or after its completion require the supervisor to produce for inspection—
   (a) his records and accounts in respect of the arrangement, and
   (b) copies of abstracts and reports prepared in compliance with Rule 5.31.
(2) The Secretary of State may require production either at the premises of the supervisor or elsewhere; and it is the duty of the supervisor to comply with any requirement imposed on him under this Rule.
(3) The Secretary of State may cause any accounts and records produced to him under this Rule to be audited; and the supervisor shall give to the Secretary of State such further information and assistance as he needs for the purposes of his audit.

5.34. Completion or termination of the arrangement

(1) Not more than 28 days after the final completion or termination of the voluntary arrangement, the supervisor shall send to all creditors of the debtor who are bound by the arrangement, and to the debtor, a notice that the arrangement has been fully implemented or (as the case may be) terminated.
(2) With the notice there shall be sent to each of those persons a copy of a report by the supervisor summarising all receipts and payments made by him in pursuance of the arrangement, and explaining any difference in the actual implementation of it as compared with the proposal as approved by the creditors' meeting or (in the case of termination of the arrangement) explaining the reasons why the arrangement has not been implemented in accordance with the proposal as approved by the creditors' meeting.
(3) The supervisor shall, within the 28 days mentioned above, send to the Secretary of State and to the court a copy of the notice under paragraph (1), together with a copy of the report under paragraph (2), and he shall not vacate office until after such copies have been sent.
(4) The court may, on application by the supervisor, extend the period of 28 days under paragraphs (1) and (3).

PART 6
BANKRUPTCY
CHAPTER 1
THE STATUTORY DEMAND

6.1. Form and content of statutory demand

(1) A statutory demand under section 268 must be dated, and be signed either by the creditor himself or by a person stating himself to be authorised to make the demand on the creditor's behalf.
(2) The statutory demand must specify whether it is made under section 268(1) (debt payable immediately) or section 268(2) (debt not so payable).
(3) The demand must state the amount of the debt, and the consideration for it (or, if there is no consideration, the way in which it arises) and—
   (a) if made under section 268(1) and founded on a judgment or order of a court, it must give details of the judgment or order, and

(b) if made under section 268(2), it must state the grounds on which it is alleged that the debtor appears to have no reasonable prospect of paying the debt.

(4) If the amount claimed in the demand includes—

(a) any charge by way of interest not previously notified to the debtor as a liability of his, or

(b) any other charge accruing from time to time,

the amount or rate of the charge must be separately identified, and the grounds on which payment of it is claimed must be stated.

In either case the amount claimed must be limited to that which has accrued due at the date of the demand.

(5) If the creditor holds any security in respect of the debt, the full amount of the debt shall be specified, but—

(a) there shall in the demand be specified the nature of the security, and the value which the creditor puts upon it as at the date of the demand, and

(b) the amount of which payment is claimed by the demand shall be the full amount of the debt, less the amount specified as the value of the security.

6.2. Information to be given in statutory demand

(1) The statutory demand must include an explanation to the debtor of the following matters—

(a) the purpose of the demand, and the fact that, if the debtor does not comply with the demand, bankruptcy proceedings may be commenced against him;

(b) the time within which the demand must be complied with, if that consequence is to be avoided;

(c) the methods of compliance which are open to the debtor; and

(d) his right to apply to the court for the statutory demand to be set aside.

(2) The demand must specify one or more named individuals with whom the debtor may, if he wishes, enter into communication with a view to securing or compounding for the debt to the satisfaction of the creditor or (as the case may be) establishing to the creditor's satisfaction that there is a reasonable prospect that the debt will be paid when it falls due.

In the case of any individual so named in the demand, his address and telephone number (if any) must be given.

6.3. Requirements as to service

(1) Rule 6.11 in Chapter 2 below has effect as regards service of the statutory demand, and proof of that service by affidavit to be filed with a bankruptcy petition.

(2) The creditor is, by virtue of the Rules, under an obligation to do all that is reasonable for the purpose of bringing the statutory demand to the debtor's attention and, if practicable in the particular circumstances, to cause personal service of the demand to be effected.

(3) Where the statutory demand is for payment of a sum due under a judgment or order of any court and the creditor knows, or believes with reasonable cause—

(a) that the debtor has absconded or is keeping out of the way with a view to avoiding service, and

(b) there is no real prospect of the sum due being recovered by execution or other process, the demand may be advertised in one or more newspapers; and the time limited for compliance with the demand runs from the date of the advertisement's appearance or (as the case may be) its first appearance.

6.4. Application to set aside statutory demand

(1) The debtor may, within the period allowed by this Rule, apply to the appropriate court for an order setting the statutory demand aside.

That period is 18 days from the date of the service on him of the statutory demand or, where the demand is advertised in a newspaper pursuant to Rule 6.3, from the date of the advertisement's appearance or (as the case may be) its first appearance.

(2) Where the creditor issuing the statutory demand is a Minister of the Crown or a Government Department, and—

   (a) the debt in respect of which the demand is made, or a part of it equal to or exceeding the bankruptcy level (within the meaning of section 267), is the subject of a judgment or order of any court, and

   (b) the statutory demand specifies the date of the judgment or order and the court in which it was obtained, but indicates the creditor's intention to present a bankruptcy petition against the debtor in the High Court,

   the appropriate court under this Rule is the High Court; and in any other case it is that to which the debtor would, in accordance with paragraphs (1) and (2) of Rule 6.40 in Chapter 3 below, present his own bankruptcy petition.

(3) As from (inclusive) the date on which the application is filed in court, the time limited for compliance with the statutory demand ceases to run, subject to any order of the court under Rule 6.5(6).

(4) The debtor's application shall be supported by an affidavit—

   (a) specifying the date on which the statutory demand came into his hands, and

   (b) stating the grounds on which he claims that it should be set aside.

   The affidavit shall have exhibited to it a copy of the statutory demand.

6.5. Hearing of application to set aside

(1) On receipt of an application under Rule 6.4, the court may, if satisfied that no sufficient cause is shown for it, dismiss it without giving notice to the creditor. As from (inclusive) the date on which the application is dismissed, the time limited for compliance with the statutory demand runs again.

(2) If the application is not dismissed under paragraph (1), the court shall fix a venue for it to be heard, and shall give at least 7 days' notice of it to—

   (a) the debtor or, if the debtor's application was made by a solicitor acting for him, to the solicitor,

   (b) the creditor, and

   (c) whoever is named in the statutory demand as the person with whom the debtor may enter into communication with reference to the demand (or, if more than one person is so named, the first of them).

(3) On the hearing of the application, the court shall consider the evidence then available to it, and may either summarily determine the application or adjourn it, giving such directions as it thinks appropriate.

(4) The court may grant the application if—

    (a) the debtor appears to have a counterclaim, set-off or cross demand which equals or exceeds the amount of the debt or debts specified in the statutory demand; or

    (b) the debt is disputed on grounds which appear to the court to be substantial; or

    (c) it appears that the creditor holds some security in respect of the debt claimed by the demand, and either Rule 6.1(5) is not complied with in respect of it, or the court is satisfied that the value of the security equals or exceeds the full amount of the debt; or

    (d) the court is satisfied, on other grounds, that the demand ought to be set aside.

(5) Where the creditor holds some security in respect of his debt, and Rule 6.1(5) is complied with in respect of it but the court is satisfied that the security is under-valued in the statutory demand, the creditor may be required to amend the demand accordingly (but without prejudice to his right to present a bankruptcy petition by reference to the original demand).

(6) If the court dismisses the application, it shall make an order authorising the creditor to present a bankruptcy petition either forthwith, or on or after a date specified in the order.

    A copy of the order shall be sent by the court forthwith to the creditor.

CHAPTER 2
BANKRUPTCY PETITION (CREDITOR'S)

6.6. Preliminary

The Rules in this Chapter relate to a creditor's petition, and the making of a bankruptcy order thereon; and in those Rules 'the debt' means, except where the context otherwise requires, the debt (or debts) in respect of which the petition is presented.

    Those Rules also apply to a petition under section 264(1)(c) (supervisor of, or a person bound by, voluntary arrangement), with any necessary modifications.

6.7. Identification of debtor

(1) The petition shall state the following matters with respect to the debtor, so far as they are within the petitioner's knowledge—

    (a) his name, place of residence and occupation (if any);

    (b) the name or names in which he carries on business, if other than his true name, and whether, in the case of any business of a specified nature, he carries it on alone or with others;

    (c) the nature of his business, and the address or addresses at which he carries it on;

    (d) any name or names, other than his true name, in which he has carried on business at or after the time when the debt was incurred, and whether he has done so alone or with others;

    (e) any address or addresses at which he has resided or carried on business at or after that time, and the nature of that business;

    (f) whether the debtor has his centre of main interests or an establishment in another member State.

(2) The particulars of the debtor given under this Rule determine the full title of the proceedings.

(3) If to the petitioner's personal knowledge the debtor has used any name other than the one specified under paragraph (1)(a), that fact shall be stated in the petition.

6.8. Identification of debt

(1) There shall be stated in the petition, with reference to every debt in respect of which it is presented—
  - (a) the amount of the debt, the consideration for it (or, if there is no consideration, the way in which it arises) and the fact that it is owed to the petitioner;
  - (b) when the debt was incurred or became due;
  - (c) if the amount of the debt includes—
    - (i) any charge by way of interest not previously notified to the debtor as a liability of his, or
    - (ii) any other charge accruing from time to time,
    the amount or rate of the charge (separately identified) and the grounds on which it is claimed to form part of the debt, provided that such amount or rate must, in the case of a petition based on a statutory demand, be limited to that claimed in that demand;
  - (d) either—
    - (i) that the debt is for a liquidated sum payable immediately, and the debtor appears to be unable to pay it, or
    - (ii) that the debt is for a liquidated sum payable at some certain, future time (that time to be specified), and the debtor appears to have no reasonable prospect of being able to pay it,
    and, in either case (subject to section 269) that the debt is unsecured.
(2) Where the debt is one for which, under section 268, a statutory demand must have been served on the debtor—
  - (a) there shall be specified the date and manner of service of the statutory demand, and
  - (b) it shall be stated that, to the best of the creditor's knowledge and belief—
    - (i) the demand has been neither complied with nor set aside in accordance with the Rules, and
    - (ii) no application to set it aside is outstanding.
(3) If the case is within section 268(1)(b) (debt arising under judgment or order of court; execution returned unsatisfied), the court from which the execution or other process issued shall be specified, and particulars shall be given relating to the return.

6.9. Court in which petition to be presented

(1) In the following cases, the petition shall be presented to the High Court—
  - (a) if the petition is presented by a Minister of the Crown or a Government Department, and either in any statutory demand on which the petition is based the creditor has indicated the intention to present a bankruptcy petition to that Court, or the petition is presented under section 268(1)(b), or
  - (b) if the debtor has resided or carried on business within the London insolvency district for the greater part of the 6 months immediately preceding the presentation of the petition, or for a longer period in those 6 months than in any other insolvency district, or
  - (c) if the debtor is not resident in England and Wales, or
  - (d) if the petitioner is unable to ascertain the residence of the debtor, or his place of business.

(2) In any other case the petition shall be presented to the county court for the insolvency district in which the debtor has resided or carried on business for the longest period during those 6 months.

(3) If the debtor has for the greater part of those 6 months carried on business in one insolvency district and resided in another, the petition shall be presented to the court for the insolvency district in which he has carried on business.

(4) If the debtor has during those 6 months carried on business in more than one insolvency district, the petition shall be presented to the court for the insolvency district in which is, or has been for the longest period in those 6 months, his principal place of business.

(4A) Notwithstanding any other provision of this Rule, where there is in force for the debtor a voluntary arrangement under Part VIII of the Act, the petition shall be presented to the court to which the nominee's report under section 256 or section 256A or 263C was submitted.

(5) The petition shall contain sufficient information to establish that it is brought in the appropriate court.

6.10. Procedure for presentation and filing

(1) The petition, verified by affidavit in accordance with Rule 6.12(1) below, shall be filed in court.

(2) No petition shall be filed unless there is produced with it the receipt for the deposit payable on presentation.

(3) The following copies of the petition shall also be delivered to the court with the petition—
   (a) one for service on the debtor,
   (b) one to be exhibited to the affidavit verifying that service, and
   (c) if there is in force for the debtor a voluntary arrangement under Part VIII of the Act, and the petitioner is not the supervisor of the arrangement, one copy for him.
Each of these copies shall have applied to it the seal of the court, and shall be issued to the petitioner.

(4) The date and time of filing the petition shall be endorsed on the petition and on any copy issued under paragraph (3).

(5) The court shall fix a venue for hearing the petition, and this also shall be endorsed on the petition and on any copy so issued.

(6) Where a petition contains a request for the appointment of a person as trustee in accordance with section 297(5) (appointment of former supervisor as trustee) the person whose appointment is sought shall, not less than 2 days before the day appointed for hearing the petition, file in court a report including particulars of—
   (a) a date on which he gave written notification to creditors bound by the arrangement of the intention to seek his appointment as trustee, such date to be at least 10 days before the day on which the report under this paragraph is filed, and
   (b) details of any response from creditors to that notice, including any objections to his appointment.

6.11. Proof of service of statutory demand

(1) Where under section 268 the petition must have been preceded by a statutory demand, there must be filed in court, with the petition, an affidavit or affidavits proving service of the demand.

(2) Every affidavit must have exhibited to it a copy of the demand as served.

(3) Subject to the next paragraph, if the demand has been served personally on the debtor, the affidavit must be made by the person who effected that service.

(4) If service of the demand (however effected) has been acknowledged in writing either by the debtor himself, or by some person stating himself in the acknowledgement to be authorised to accept service on the debtor's behalf, the affidavit must be made either by the creditor or by a person acting on his behalf, and the acknowledgement of service must be exhibited to the affidavit.

(5) If neither paragraph (3) nor paragraph (4) applies, the affidavit or affidavits must be made by a person or persons having direct personal knowledge of the means adopted for serving the statutory demand, and must—

    (a) give particulars of the steps which have been taken with a view to serving the demand personally, and

    (b) state the means whereby (those steps having been ineffective) it was sought to bring the demand to the debtor's attention, and

    (c) specify a date by which, to the best of the knowledge, information and belief of the person making the affidavit, the demand will have come to the debtor's attention.

(6) The steps of which particulars are given for the purposes of paragraph (5)(a) must be such as would have sufficed to justify an order for substituted service of a petition.

(7) If the affidavit specifies a date for the purposes of compliance with paragraph (5)(c), then unless the court otherwise orders, that date is deemed for the purposes of the Rules to have been the date on which the statutory demand was served on the debtor.

(8) Where the creditor has taken advantage of Rule 6.3(3) (newspaper advertisement), the affidavit must be made either by the creditor himself or by a person having direct personal knowledge of the circumstances; and there must be specified in the affidavit—

    (a) the means of the creditor's knowledge or (as the case may be) belief required for the purposes of that Rule, and

    (b) the date or dates on which, and the newspaper in which, the statutory demand was advertised under that Rule;

and there shall be exhibited to the affidavit a copy of any advertisement of the statutory demand.

(9) The court may decline to file the petition if not satisfied that the creditor has discharged the obligation imposed on him by Rule 6.3(2).

6.12. Verification of petition

(1) The petition shall be verified by an affidavit that the statements in the petition are true, or are true to the best of the deponent's knowledge, information and belief.

(2) If the petition is in respect of debts to different creditors, the debts to each creditor must be separately verified.

(3) The petition shall be exhibited to the affidavit verifying it.

(4) The affidavit shall be made—
  (a) by the petitioner (or if there are two or more petitioners, any one of them), or
  (b) by some person such as a director, company secretary or similar company officer, or a solicitor, who has been concerned in the matters giving rise to the presentation of the petition, or
  (c) by some responsible person who is duly authorised to make the affidavit and has the requisite knowledge of those matters.

(5) Where the maker of the affidavit is not the petitioner himself, or one of the petitioners, he must in the affidavit identify himself and state—
  (a) the capacity in which, and the authority by which, he makes it, and
  (b) the means of his knowledge of the matters sworn to in the affidavit.

(6) The affidavit is prima facie evidence of the truth of the statements in the petition to which it relates.

(7) If the petition is based upon a statutory demand, and more than 4 months have elapsed between the service of the demand and the presentation of the petition, the affidavit must also state the reasons for the delay.

6.13. Notice to the Chief Land Registrar

When the petition is filed, the court shall forthwith send to the Chief Land Registrar notice of the petition together with a request that it may be registered in the register of pending actions.

6.14. Service of petition

(1) Subject as follows, the petition shall be served personally on the debtor by an officer of the court, or by the petitioning creditor or his solicitor, or by a person instructed by the creditor or his solicitor for that purpose; and service shall be effected by delivering to him a sealed copy of the petition.

(2) If the court is satisfied by affidavit or other evidence on oath that prompt personal service cannot be effected because the debtor is keeping out of the way to avoid service of the petition or other legal process, or for any other cause, it may order substituted service to be effected in such manner as it thinks fit.

(3) Where an order for substituted service has been carried out, the petition is deemed duly served on the debtor.

(4) If to the petitioner's knowledge there is in force for the debtor a voluntary arrangement under Part VIII of the Act, and the petitioner is not himself the supervisor of the arrangement, a copy of the petition shall be sent by him to the supervisor.

(5) If to the petitioner's knowledge, there is a member State liquidator appointed in main proceedings in relation to the bankrupt, a copy of the petition shall be sent by him to the member State liquidator.

6.18. Hearing of petition

(1) Subject as follows, the petition shall not be heard until at least 14 days have elapsed since it was served on the debtor.

(2) The court may, on such terms as it thinks fit, hear the petition at an earlier date, if it appears that the debtor has absconded, or the court is satisfied that it is a proper case for an expedited hearing, or the debtor consents to a hearing within the 14 days.

(3) Any of the following may appear and be heard, that is to say, the petitioning creditor, the debtor, the supervisor of any voluntary arrangement under Part VIII of the Act in force for the debtor and any creditor who has given notice under Rule 6.23 below.

6.21. Petition opposed by debtor

Where the debtor intends to oppose the petition, he shall not later than 7 days before the day fixed for the hearing—
  (a) file in court a notice specifying the grounds on which he will object to the making of a bankruptcy order, and
  (b) send a copy of the notice to the petitioning creditor or his solicitor.

6.23. Notice by persons intending to appear

(1) Every creditor who intends to appear on the hearing of the petition shall give to the petitioning creditor notice of his intention in accordance with this Rule.
(2) The notice shall specify—
  (a) the name and address of the person giving it, and any telephone number and reference which may be required for communication with him or with any other person (to be also specified in the notice) authorised to speak or act on his behalf;
  (b) whether his intention is to support or oppose the petition; and
  (c) the amount and nature of his debt.
(3) The notice shall be sent so as to reach the addressee not later than 16.00 hours on the business day before that which is appointed for the hearing (or, where the hearing has been adjourned, for the adjourned hearing).
(4) A person failing to comply with this Rule may appear on the hearing of the petition only with the leave of the court.

6.24. List of appearances

(1) The petitioning creditor shall prepare for the court a list of the creditors (if any) who have given notice under Rule 6.23, specifying their names and addresses and (if known to him) their respective solicitors.
(2) Against the name of each creditor in the list it shall be stated whether his intention is to support the petition, or to oppose it.
(3) On the day appointed for the hearing of the petition, a copy of the list shall be handed to the court before the commencement of the hearing.
(4) If any leave is given under Rules 6.23(4), the petitioner shall add to the list the same particulars in respect of the person to whom leave has been given.

6.25. Decision on the hearing

(1) On the hearing of the petition, the court may make a bankruptcy order if satisfied that the statements in the petition are true, and that the debt on which it is founded has not been paid, or secured or compounded for.
(2) If the petition is brought in respect of a judgment debt, or a sum ordered by any court to be paid, the court may stay or dismiss the petition on the ground that an appeal is pending from the judgment or order, or that execution of the judgment has been stayed.

(3) A petition preceded by a statutory demand shall not be dismissed on the ground only that the amount of the debt was over-stated in the demand, unless the debtor, within the time allowed for complying with the demand, gave notice to the creditor disputing the validity of the demand on that ground; but, in the absence of such notice, the debtor is deemed to have complied with the demand if he has, within the time allowed, paid the correct amount.

6.26. Non-appearance of creditor

If the petitioning creditor fails to appear on the hearing of the petition, no subsequent petition against the same debtor, either alone or jointly with any other person, shall be presented by the same creditor in respect of the same debt, without the leave of the court to which the previous petition was presented.

6.32. Petitioner seeking dismissal or leave to withdraw

(1) Where the petitioner applies to the court for the petition to be dismissed, or for leave to withdraw it, he must, unless the court otherwise orders, file in court an affidavit specifying the grounds of the application and the circumstances in which it is made.
(2) If, since the petition was filed, any payment has been made to the petitioner by way of settlement (in whole or in part) of the debt or debts in respect of which the petition was brought, or any arrangement has been entered into for securing or compounding it or them, the affidavit must state—
    (a) what dispositions of property have been made for the purposes of the settlement or arrangement, and
    (b) whether, in the case of any disposition, it was property of the debtor himself, or of some other person, and
    (c) whether, if it was property of the debtor, the disposition was made with the approval of, or has been ratified by, the court (if so, specifying the relevant court order).
(3) No order giving leave to withdraw a petition shall be given before the petition is heard.

CHAPTER 3
BANKRUPTCY PETITION (DEBTOR'S)

6.37. Preliminary

The Rules in this Chapter relate to a debtor's petition, and the making of a bankruptcy order thereon.

6.38. Identification of debtor

(1) The petition shall state the following matters with respect to the debtor—
    (a) his name, place of residence and occupation (if any);
    (b) the name or names in which he carries on business, if other than his true name, and whether, in the case of any business of a specified nature, he carries it on alone or with others;
    (c) the nature of his business, and the address or addresses at which he carries it on;

(d) any name or names, other than his true name, in which he has carried on business in the period in which any of his bankruptcy debts were incurred and, in the case of any such business, whether he has carried it on alone or with others; and

(e) any address or addresses at which he has resided or carried on business during that period, and the nature of that business.

(2) The particulars of the debtor given under this Rule determine the full title of the proceedings.

(3) If the debtor has at any time used a name other than the one given under paragraph (1)(a), that fact shall be stated in the petition.

6.39. Admission of insolvency

(1) The petition shall contain the statement that the petitioner is unable to pay his debts, and a request that a bankruptcy order be made against him.

(2) If within the period of 5 years ending with the date of the petition the petitioner has been adjudged bankrupt, or has made a composition with his creditors in satisfaction of his debts or a scheme of arrangement of his affairs, or he has entered into any voluntary arrangement or been subject to an administration order under Part VI of the County Courts Act 1984, particulars of these matters shall be given in the petition.

(3) If there is at the date of the petition in force for the debtor a voluntary arrangement under Part VIII of the Act, the particulars required by paragraph (2) above shall contain a statement to that effect and the name and address of the supervisor of the arrangement.

6.40. Court in which petition to be filed

(1) In the following cases, the petition shall be presented to the High Court—

(a) if the debtor has resided or carried on business in the London insolvency district for the greater part of the 6 months immediately preceding the presentation of the petition, or for a longer period in those 6 months than in any other insolvency district, or

(b) if the debtor is not resident in England and Wales.

(2) In any other case, the petition shall (subject to paragraph (3) below), be presented to the debtor's own county court, which is—

(a) the county court for the insolvency district in which he has resided or carried on business for the longest period in those 6 months, or

(b) if he has for the greater part of those 6 months carried on business in one insolvency district and resided in another, the county court for that in which he has carried on business, or

(c) if he has during those 6 months carried on business in more than one insolvency district, the county court for that in which is, or has been for the longest period in those 6 months, his principal place of business.

(3) If, in a case not falling within paragraph (1), it is more expedient for the debtor with a view to expediting his petition—

(a) it may in any case be presented to whichever court is specified by Schedule 2 to the Rules as being, in relation to the debtor's own court, the nearest full-time court, and

(b) it may alternatively, in a case falling within paragraph (2)(b), be presented to the court for the insolvency district in which he has resided for the greater part of the 6 months there referred to.

(3A) Notwithstanding any other provision of this Rule, where there is in force for the debtor a voluntary arrangement under Part VIII of the Act the petition shall be presented to the court to which the nominee's report under section 256 or section 256A or 263C was submitted.

(4) The petition shall contain sufficient information to establish that it is brought in the appropriate court.

6.41. Statement of affairs

(1) The petition shall be accompanied by a statement of the debtor's affairs, verified by affidavit.

(2) Section B of Chapter 5 below applies with respect to the statement of affairs.

6.42. Procedure for presentation and filing

(1) The petition and the statement of affairs shall be filed in court, together with three copies of the petition, and two copies of the statement. No petition shall be filed unless there is produced with it the receipt for the deposit payable on presentation.

(2) Subject to paragraph (2A), the court may hear the petition forthwith. If it does not do so, it shall fix a venue for the hearing.

(2A) If the petition contains particulars of a voluntary arrangement under Part VIII of the Act in force for the debtor, the court shall fix a venue for the hearing and give at least 14 days' notice of it to the supervisor of the arrangement; the supervisor may appear and be heard on the petition.

(3) Of the three copies of the petition delivered—
    (a) one shall be returned to the petitioner, endorsed with any venue fixed;
    (b) another, so endorsed, shall be sent by the court to the official receiver; and
    (c) the remaining copy shall be retained by the court, to be sent to an insolvency practitioner (if appointed under section 273(2)).

(4) Of the two copies of the statement of affairs—
    (a) one shall be sent by the court to the official receiver; and
    (b) the other shall be retained by the court to be sent to the insolvency practitioner (if appointed).

(5) The affidavit verifying the debtor's statement of affairs may be sworn before an officer of the court duly authorised in that behalf.

(6) Where the court hears a petition forthwith, or it will in the opinion of the court otherwise expedite the delivery of any document to the official receiver, the court may, instead of sending that document to the official receiver, direct the bankrupt forthwith to deliver it to him.

(7) Where a petition contains a request for the appointment of a person as trustee in accordance with section 297(5) (appointment of former supervisor as trustee) the person whose appointment is sought shall, not less than 2 days before the day appointed for hearing the petition, file in court a report including particulars of—
    (a) a date on which he gave written notification to creditors bound by the arrangement of the intention to seek his appointment as trustee, such date to be at least 10 days before the day on which the report under this paragraph is filed, and
    (b) details of any response from creditors to that notice, including any objections to his appointment.

6.43. Notice to Chief Land Registrar

When the petition is filed, the court shall forthwith send to the Chief Land Registrar notice of the petition, for registration in the register of pending actions.

CHAPTER 8
PROOF OF BANKRUPTCY DEBTS

6.96. Meaning of 'prove'

(1) A person claiming to be a creditor of the bankrupt and wishing to recover his debt in whole or in part must (subject to any order of the court under Rule 6.93(2)) submit his claim in writing to the official receiver, where acting as receiver and manager, or to the trustee.

(2) The creditor is referred to as 'proving' for his debt; and the document by which he seeks to establish his claim is his 'proof'.

(3) Subject to the next two paragraphs, the proof must be in the form known as 'proof of debt' (whether the form prescribed by the Rules, or a substantially similar form), which shall be made out by or under the directions of the creditor, and signed by him or a person authorised in that behalf.

(4) Where a debt is due to a Minister of the Crown or a Government Department, the proof need not be in that form, provided that there are shown all such particulars of the debt as are required in the form used by other creditors, and as are relevant in the circumstances.

(5) Where an existing trustee proves in a later bankruptcy under section 335(5), the proof must be in Form 6.38.

(6) In certain circumstances, specified below in this Chapter, the proof must be in the form of an affidavit.

6.98. Contents of proof

(1) Subject to Rule 6.96(4), the following matters shall be stated in a creditor's proof of debt—

    (a) the creditor's name and address, and, if a company, its company registration number;

    (b) the total amount of his claim (including any Value Added Tax) as at the date of the bankruptcy order;

    (c) whether or not that amount includes outstanding uncapitalised interest;

    (d) particulars of how and when the debt was incurred by the debtor;

    (e) particulars of any security held, the date when it was given and the value which the creditor puts upon it;

    (f) details of any reservation of title in respect of goods to which the debt refers; and

    (g) the name, and address and authority of the person signing the proof (if other than the creditor himself).

(2) There shall be specified in the proof any documents by reference to which the debt can be substantiated; but (subject as follows) it is not essential that such documents be attached to the proof or submitted with it.

(3) The trustee, or the convener or chairman of any meeting, may call for any document or other evidence to be produced to him, where he thinks it necessary for the purpose of substantiating the whole or any part of the claim made in the proof.

6.109. Secured creditors

(1) If a secured creditor realises his security, he may prove for the balance of his debt, after deducting the amount realised.

(2) If a secured creditor voluntarily surrenders his security for the general benefit of creditors, he may prove for his whole debt, as if it were unsecured.

CHAPTER 9
SECURED CREDITORS

6.115. Value of security

(1) A secured creditor may, with the agreement of the trustee or the leave of the court, at any time alter the value which he has, in his proof of debt, put upon his security.

(2) However, if a secured creditor—

(a) being the petitioner, has in the petition put a value on his security, or

(b) has voted in respect of the unsecured balance of his debt,

he may re-value his security only with leave of the court.

CHAPTER 22
DISCHARGE

6.220. Certificate of discharge

(1) Where it appears to the court that a bankrupt is discharged, whether by expiration of time or otherwise, the court shall, on his application, issue to him a certificate of his discharge, and the date from which it is effective.

(2) The discharged bankrupt may require the Secretary of State to give notice of the discharge—

(a) in the Gazette, or

(b) in any newspaper in which the bankruptcy was advertised, or

(c) in both.

(3) Any requirement by the former bankrupt under paragraph (2) shall be addressed to the Secretary of State in writing. The Secretary of State shall notify him forthwith as to the cost of the advertisement, and is under no obligation to advertise until that sum is paid.

(4) Where the former bankrupt has died, or is a person incapable of managing his affairs (within the meaning of Chapter 7 in Part 7 of the Rules), the references to him in paragraphs (2) and (3) are to be read as referring to his personal representative or, as the case may be, a person appointed by the court to represent or act for him.

PART 12
MISCELLANEOUS AND GENERAL

12.3 Provable debts

(1) Subject as follows, in administration, winding up and bankruptcy, all claims by creditors are provable as debts against the company or, as the case may, the bankrupt, whether they are present or future, certain or contingent, ascertained or sounding only in damages.

(2)   The following are not provable—

    (a) in bankruptcy, any fine imposed for an offence, and any obligation arising under an order made in family proceedings or under a maintenance assessment made under the Child Support Act 1991;

    (b) in administration, winding up or bankruptcy, any obligation arising under a confiscation order made under section 1 of the Drug Trafficking Offences Act 1986 or section 1 of the Criminal Justice (Scotland) Act 1987 or section 71 of the Criminal Justice Act 1988 or under Parts 2, 3 or 4 of the Proceeds of Crime Act 2002.

    'Fine' … and 'family proceedings' have the meanings given by section 281(8) of the Act (which applies the Magistrates' Courts Act 1980 and the Matrimonial and Family Proceedings Act 1984.)

(2A) The following are not provable except at a time when all other claims of creditors in the insolvency proceedings (other than any of a kind mentioned in this paragraph) have been paid in full with interest under section 189(2), Rule 2.88 or, as the case may be, section 328(4)—

    (a) in an administration, a winding up or a bankruptcy, any claim arising by virtue of section 382(1)(a) of the Financial Services and Markets Act 2000, not being a claim also arising by virtue of section 382(1)(b) of that Act;

    (b) in an administration or a winding up, any claim which by virtue of the Act or any other enactment is a claim the payment of which in a bankruptcy, an administration or a winding up is to be postponed.

(3)   Nothing in this Rule prejudices any enactment or rule of law under which a particular kind of debt is not provable whether on grounds of public policy or otherwise.

Index